FICTION
INTERNATIONAL
22

Fiction International is a magazine of letters and arts published by San Diego State University Press. *Fiction International* magazine was founded, published, and edited by Joe David Bellamy at St. Lawrence University from 1973 to 1983. Business correspondence, including that related to subscriptions and advertising, should be directed to: **Harry Polkinhorn, San Diego State University Press, San Diego State University, San Diego, CA 92182.**

Unsolicited manuscripts will be considered for future issues only from September 1 through December 15 of each year. Contributors are asked not to submit from December 15 through August. All manuscripts, including those from agents, must be accompanied by SASE. Though we will exercise all due care in handling manuscripts, we cannot be responsible for loss. Please allow one to three months for reply or return of submissions. The freedom to opinions, views, and modes of expression in this periodical is supported by San Diego State University Press. The views expressed herein, however, are those of the authors, not the editors or sponsors. Editorial queries, books for review, and manuscripts should be directed to: **Editors:** *Fiction International,* **Department of English and Comparative Literature, San Diego State University, San Diego, CA 92182.**

Copyright © 1992 by San Diego State University Press. Authors of individual works retain copyright, with the restriction that any subsequent publication of any piece be accompanied by notice of prior publication in *Fiction International.*

Editors
Harold Jaffe
Larry McCaffery

Contributing Guest Editor, #22
Mel Freilicher

Managing Editors
James McMenamin
Harry Polkinhorn

Art Editor
Maggie Jaffe

Assistant Editors
Elizabeth Cook
Ken Jones
Andrew Koopmans
James Miller

Design
David Quattrociocchi

Contributing Editors
Kathy Acker
Robert Coover
Raymond Federman
Maggie Humm
James Scully

Editorial Assistants
Dennis Bennett
Lori Bettenga
Geoffrey Downes
Michael Filas
Geoffrey Holtz
Eric Madeen
Kelly Mayhew
David Otee

Contents

Inscribing the Body: An Introduction / 1

Jennifer Lane / "Girl Talk" / 7

Barbara O'Dair and Abby Tallmer / "Sex Premises" / 10

Dion Farquhar / "Pure Porn" / 19

Forum / 35

Edith Wharton / from "Beatrice Palmato" / 58

Marc Cholodenko / from "The Story of Vivant Lanon" (translated by John Satriano) / 65

Lisa Duggan, Nan D. Hunter, Carole S. Vance / "False Promises: Feminist Antipornography Legislation" / 71

Chris Martin / Transsexual Interview / "World's Greatest Cocksucker" / 101

Matias Viegener / "There's Trouble in That Body: Queer Fanzines, Sexual Identity and Censorship" / 123

Andrea Slane / "Unconventional Weapons" / 137

Ennio Flaiano / "1963" (translated by John Satriano) / 148

Marianne Hauser / "Scandal at the Bide-A-Wee Nursing Home for Mature Seniors" / 157

Mira-Lani Oglesby / "Henry and Ray and the Old Guy in the Wheelchair and Two Cops and Me and Sean Penn" / 161

Kathy Acker / from *The Fall of the United States*, "Murder" / 165

Mel Freilicher / "Fight the Power: *Diseased Pariah News*, etc." / 177

Samuel R. Delany / from *Citre et Trans* / 189

Raymond Federman / "Once Upon a Time in the Grass" / 200

Carole S. Vance / "The Pleasure of Looking: The Attorney General's Commission on Pornography versus Visual Images" / 205

John Greyson / from "The Making of Monsters: A Musical About Anti-Gay Violence" / 239

Barbara Henning / "Resumé" / 241

Karl Keller / "What It's Like to Grow Up in Manti, Utah" / 245

Cris Mazza / "Hesitation" / 247

Joyce Carol Oates / from "Martyrdom" / 251

Rob Hardin / "Still" / 269

Mark Wisniewski / "Full Circle" / 275

Kevin Ray / "Obvious Advertisement: Robert Duncan and *The Kenyon Review* / 286

Mel Freilicher / "Prolog" / 292

Edward Field / "Sex in Poetry, A Meditation On My Poem, 'Triad'" / 295

Greg Boyd / "Horny" / 298

Roy Schneider / "Pubic Skies" / 303

Richard Kostelanetz / "Flirting" / 306

Tom Jurek / from *Straight Fiction* / 313

Stephen-Paul Martin / "Double Bed" / 315

Lyn Butler Oaks / "Twins" / 321

Ronald Sukenick / "The Flood" / 327

Jean Mainil / "Pornography and Academe: Compulsory Introduction" / 335

Ben Marcus / "Urinating, A Forceful Endeavor" / 358

Michael Brodsky / from ✶ ✶ ✶ / 359

Rikki Ducornet / "Picotazo and Extravaganza," from *Birdland* / 365

Pasquale Verdicchio / "Censoring the Body of Ideology: The Films of Pier Paolo Pasolini" / 369

Stephen D. Gutierrez / "Wartime in Fresno" / 380

Robert Coover / from *The Adventures of Lucky Pierre,* "Man Walking at 24 Frames per Second" / 384

Harold Jaffe / "F2M" / 387

Art

Joel Lipman / "Jesse Helms' Body" / 30

Chris Martin / "World's Greatest Cocksucker" / 113

Tuli Kupferberg / "The Old Fucks at Home" / 166

M Rat / Three Polaroids / 186

Greg Boyd / Two Linocuts / 204

Gail Schneider / Acrylic on paper / 244

Tuli Kupferberg / "Some Kinda Asshole" / 268

Derek Pell / from "The Elements of Style" / 324

Contributors / 396

cover design by David Quattrociocchi

Inscribing the Body:
An Introduction

Question: Why this special issue on pornography/censorship now, Fall 1992?

Editors' Response: The body is in pain. The collective body is in agony. As much as the isolated inner cities, as much as U. S. foreign policy, as much as institutionalized voodoo economics, it is the flesh and blood body which is a site of oppression and potential rebellion in the United States.

Consider this image recalled by Dennis Barrie, director of the Contemporary Arts Center, Cincinatti. One day in 1990, while the Center was displaying Robert Mapplethorpe's "The Perfect Moment," about forty uniformed police officers walked into the Center and *forcibly* removed the patrons simply because they were looking at Mapplethorpe's photos. It is that image, Barrie says, "that's going to haunt me for the rest of my life. Because that isn't our country, or it shouldn't be our country."[1]

Well, it is our country, and has been since the Puritan fathers brutally "discovered" a virgin land that was already occupied, though by savages who evidently lacked the moral sagacity to employ the terms *pornography* or *censorship*.

Never mind that the United States was conceived on the principle of "life, liberty, and the pursuit of happiness." When happiness is construed as non-instrumental pleasure, especially sexual pleasure, it has always been subject to official intervention. The governing equation is: *Instrumental* sex equals commerce/leisure: good. *Non-instrumental* sex equals anti-commerce/pleasure: bad. Hence, during this time of AIDS and a baker's dozen of transmissible venereal diseases, consumerized sex is bigger and raunchier than ever on TV, on MTV, where it is equated with bought *leisure*; even as our official technocrats are sternly lecturing the same youthful consumers to practice celibacy, that is, to sidestep infectious *pleasure*.[2]

In a recent article in the first of two consecutive censorship issues of *Art Journal*, Robert Atkins cites a hundred or so well-publicized incidents of official censorship in the U. S. since the so-called Comstock crusade in the 1870s. Atkins pointedly notes that the decade of the 1870s also "featured the worst depression of the nation's first century, complete with bread riots and anti-strike violence."[3] The official employment of red herring issues to distract economically anxious citizens is a device that Jesse Helms and his allies know by heart. With communism no longer a factor, our defenders of virtuous capital have redoubled their energies and money on targeting pleasure in the forms of sexual desire and "substance abuse."

Though arts people are generally familiar with the history of consistent official U. S. censorship, it was the current repression's virulence which found many of us unprepared. Fairly recent instances of flagrant censorship, such as the Department of Labor's suspension of funding for the Neighborhood Art Programs National Organizing Committee (1979), or NEA's elimination of funding for art critics (1981), or the federal government's elimination of the Comprehensive Employment and Training Act (CETA), which put more than 10,000 artists who had been working on neighborhood arts projects out of their jobs (1981),[4] tended to be overlooked or viewed as isolated instances which did not portend any immediate threat. It could be that the "liberated" Sixties had lulled many arts people into a false sense of security.

The brief flame of the Sixties had been long spent when, in 1985, Attorney General Meese, in accord with the repressive ideology of the Reagan presidency, established a federal commission on pornography, which he staffed with professional sycophants, opportunists, and reactionaries. The commission was to be the crown jewel in the official "attack on sexual pleasure and desire. The chief targets of its campaign were sexually explicit images, [which were] dangerous, according to the logic of the commission, because they might encourage sexual desires or acts."[5]

The commission's nearly two-thousand-page report published in 1986, was, even by the degraded standards of that administration, an ungrammatical mishmash of patent illogic, lies, and repressive biases. Now, seven years later, Edwin Meese, tainted by his role in the Iran-Contra fiasco, has retired to some luxurious nook near some luxurious golf course. Yet the spectacle of the virtuous Right assaulting godless desire has actually gathered steam in what promises to be a delirious final decade of our second millenium, A.D.

Among the factors problematizing the body, in 1992, are the ongoing politicized debates on abortion and euthanasia, that is, on what constitutes actual birth and death. Within this vexed chronological frame are 1) AIDS and especially AIDS ideology, with its deliberate contradictions, misinformation, and innuendoes about transmission, risk, and affected groups; 2) the official suppression of desire, with its transformation of physical passion into criminal defiance or addiction, in line with the so-called moral majority and the sanctity of the nuclear family; 3) the irrepressible mania for more and more penal institutions ("*The U.S. prison population doubled between 1980 and 1988*"[6]), with their emphasis on privation and bodily torment rather than on rehabilitation; and 4) the feminist reinscription of inter-gender sexuality.

To cite "the feminist reinscription of inter-gender sexuality" is *not* to align it with the other calculated oppressions. Feminism is a liberating concept, obviously, but its popular representations are what the majority of people rely on. For many heterosexual males the burden of these representations—on TV, in tabloids, via word-of-mouth—is the toppling of male privilege and the preeminent phallus, which has amounted to a swift deconstruction of sexual desire in the only guise these males have ever known.

It is, then, in this current context of the body under extraordinary stress (and the country under extraordinary economic stress) that the perennial issue of pornography reared its Hydra head first in 1986 with the Meese Commission, then between 1988 and 1990 with the carefully orchestrated scandals which erupted in response to museums exhibiting, or planning to exhibit, Robert Mapplethorpe's "The Perfect Moment"; in response to a contemporary art museum in North Carolina for exhibiting Andres Serrano's "Piss Christ"; and in response to NEA awards to four performance artists who allegedly employed pornographic material in their acts. Deftly exploiting the Zeitgeist, Senator Jesse Helms and his collaborators exerted their considerable political influence to rescind the NEA awards, to introduce art-repressive legislation in the Congress, and to recharge the debate on pornography and censorship.

Not a *debate* so much as a *harangue*. Despite the principled protests of art celebrities like Leonard Bernstein and Joseph Papp, it was, predictably, the hypothetical Moral Majority-side which the mainstream media privileged. As a consequence, the censorship forces gathered even more steam, brazenly assaulting individual writers, visual artists, art institutions, granting agencies, libraries, schools. These assaults have come in several guises: denying grants and publication; demanding sanitized art for public display; pulling published books from library shelves and school curricula. Meanwhile the mainstream media sound their white noise of approval by marginalizing dissent and denigrating dissenters, functions they (the media) performed so uniformly and deplorably during the Persian Gulf War. Among other calculated omissions, they denied us images of the mutilations of war (the body in pain), even as they routinely deny us images of the body in pleasure.

Fiction International does not pretend to compete with *The Wall Street Journal, People, Vanity Fair,* or *The Atlantic Monthly.* Ours is a limited readership, obviously. On the other hand, if we were less limited, there would have been more pressure to sanitize our discourse and toe the line as we gathered material for this issue.

We haven't sanitized our discourse. In accord with what we view as our counter-ideological function, we have reinforced and elaborated on Barbara Kruger's pungent maxim to the dominant culture: "It is our pleasure to disgust you."

Regarding the form and contents of this expanded issue, we have deliberately desegregated fiction and art; that is, we have included fiction and art not as texture or marginalized "innovation," but as a crucial kind of social discourse, alongside the polemic, essay, review, and forum.

Our writings and visual art span the spectrum from the high precincts to the margins. The fact is that the most urgently anti-repressive passions emanate from those quarters which the official repression has most impacted and disenfranchised: gay people, trans-sexuals, transvestites, and gender-benders, who publish their writings and art in scores of marginal journals and "fanzines" throughout the country, in fierce, campy, passionate, persistent opposition to the dominant discourse. We feel privileged to count ourselves among their number.

Harold Jaffe
Mel Freilicher

Kelly Mayhew and Jim Miller also contributed to this essay.

Notes

[1] "The Scene of the Crime," *Art Journal,* "Censorship 1," (published by the College Art Association), Fall 1991, 30.

[2]"Against a society which employs sexuality as a means for a useful end, the perversions uphold sexuality as an end in itself; they thus place themselves outside the dominion of the performance principle and challenge its very foundation. They establish libidinal relationships which society must ostracize because they threaten to reverse the process of civilization which turned the organism into an instrument of work. They are a symbol of what had to be suppressed so that suppression could prevail and organize the ever-more efficient domination of man and nature." Herbert Marcuse, *Eros and Civilization* (Boston: Beacon Press, 1971), p. 50.

[3]"A Censorship Time Line," p. 33.

[4]*Art Journal*, 36.

[5]Carol Vance, "The Pleasures of Looking: The Attorney General's Commission on Pornography versus Visual Images," in *The Critical Image,* ed. by Carol Squiers (Bay Press, 1990), p. 38. Reprinted in this issue.

[6]*Art Journal*, 38.

Jennifer Lane

Girl Talk

Kay Lynn confided in me: "My boyfriend has this weird thing for coming all over my eyes. The first time he did it, he felt bad afterwards and acted all apologetic and everything. But then he just kept doing it until it became kind of a usual thing. . . I don't really MIND, I mean I'll admit that I'm a little kinky myself. . . it's really weird, though, how you find yourself doing these bizarre sexual things that you would never have even been able to dream up a year ago. . ."

"Everything changes when you turn sixteen," I say.

"Yeah, that's really true. For a while I was into being tied up, until the time he tried to throw a pillowcase over my head while he was fucking me. . . I got claustrophobic and completely FREAKED. I thought for a minute he wanted to kill me. Totally irrational, right?"

"Hell, that's happened to me during normal sex. Even with the sweetest, dumbest guy. . . sometimes after you fuck him you look at his face and your mind starts playing tricks on you. . . all of the sudden he looks different, you get the idea in your head this guy could be anybody, a KILLER, even if. . ."

We start giggling—

"Even if he's the most harmless thing in the world, you just start to think. . . shit, we must be crazy. I don't know—sex just does that to you."

"I know what you mean."

Trevor

Trevor Payne lived one street over. He killed himself when he was fifteen. Then it was revealed that he had been having an affair with his English teacher, a pretty twenty-five year old woman named Mary Ann. Trevor was a beautiful boy, with white blonde hair and blue eyes. Troubled. Who could resist a boy like that, fucked up and with smooth white skin?

J. D.

This is what the cheerleaders do at night: They make up their faces and put on their tight jeans and their halter tops and their high heeled sandals and they drive around. They smoke pot and snort cocaine and sometimes they don't care if any boys come along or not. Sometimes they just don't care. They run over mailboxes and smash them. They go into the 7-11 and steal cigarettes and beer and candy bars, and they throw rocks through the windows of their enemies. They're wild and so they drive fast down the highway and flash their tits out the window at passing cars. They start fires in the woods and let them burn, and every action they make is like a hot burst of light; it's not destruction, because they have real blonde hair and soft peach skin and because their limbs are perfectly compact, and they can jump high, and their bodies are light and horny and they never think. The world doesn't know it, but they can't be marred by the concepts of good and evil. Juvenile Delinquents.

She Told Me

Mrs. Kelly came to me in a dream and she told me all about the time that Laurie White let Skeeter Davis puke in her mouth and she swallowed it. She told me about the woman around the corner who pricked her daughter's ass with a thorn from a rose bush every time she misbehaved. She described to me the shape and the texture of Trevor Payne's erection, and how blonde he was; even his pubic hair was soft and fine and white blond (she called that kind of blond "towheaded"), only little boys ever have hair like that, like angels. . . can you imagine how it looked when he came, his pale teenage spunk surrounded by that angel hair. . . Mrs. Kelly was an enlightened woman; she could tell a girl who had someone's initials carved into her forearm by sight alone. She could sense it. . .

Mrs. Kelly

I'm having difficulty separating my sexual organs from the rest of the world. I feel as if they transcend my own brain, and I know that this is the result of making love to young boys. I feel that I possess all of that skin and it suits me, because I understand the life force is somehow contained within their testicles. In fact it's all through their blood stream in the form of semen and the more of it I receive, the better I feel. It doesn't matter if it's inside of my body or all over my skin. It's IN me and it's making me feel as if my body has no boundaries and that I have a perfect cunt. I still care about literature but this situation is simply becoming too volatile. Grammar no longer makes sense to me. I am involuntarily creating a totally new system for diagramming sentences. No one understands it. I have to go, I have to leave this job before I really get myself in trouble but I can't leave Trevor. He's my special baby and I'd die without him. I would not know what to do.

Barbara O'Dair
Abby Tallmer

Sex Premises

Within the domain of sexuality, hundreds of unanswered questions and untested ideas proliferate—about fantasy and its relationship to sex, about graphic imagery and its impact on experience, about power and sexual role-playing, and about what forms of behavior constitute "sexual violence." These ideas are often formed from and based on conjecture, and usually represent our fears about sex and the meaning it has, and can have, in our lives.

Some of these premises are false; others are certainly open to question. Many of these strings of ideas make up the framework for the current anti-pornography analysis, but they are not unique to this framework. In fact, they are also reflective of and inseparable from predominant ways we learn to think about gender and sexuality in our culture. We describe here the ways in which each premise can act as an integral component in a larger system of thought. Often this sort of thinking relies on gender stereotypes, and tends to emphasize the dangerous and negative in sex, rather than open up imaginative possibilities in sex and sexual thought for both women and men.

By presenting these interlocking assumptions and leaps of imagination, we hope to begin to unearth and deconstruct deeply entrenched views about sex, gender and pornography. In doing so, we wish to propose new ways for all of us to think about sex.

ONE
The male characters in pornography accurately portray male sexuality.

TWO
The female characters in pornography accurately portray female sexuality.

THREE
All men instinctively identify with male characters in pornography.

FOUR
All women instinctively identify with female characters in pornography.

FIVE
Pornography is male dominant/female submissive.

SIX
Pornography brings out dangerous tendencies in human behavior; self-denial is necessary in order to guard against this behavior.

SEVEN
Each one of us has a social responsibility to control the consumption of pornography. Women especially are responsible for upholding moral standards in our society.

EIGHT
Pornography is addictive and pornography users are addicts.

NINE
Because pornography users are sexual addicts, they are potential sex offenders.

TEN
Representation of degrading images is harmful to women.

ELEVEN
Pornographic images have clear, literal meanings.

TWELVE
Pornography and erotica are clearly distinguishable.

THIRTEEN
A pornographic image carries the same meaning to everyone who sees it.

FOURTEEN
There is a direct correlation between fantasy and behavior.

FIFTEEN
Explicit sexual imagery is violence against women.

SIXTEEN
Representations of violence against women carry the same social meaning as does violence. Pornographic acts, behavior, scenarios are indistinguishable from real sexual acts.

SEVENTEEN
The work of pornographic models and actors is never simulated.

EIGHTEEN
Female sex workers are too naive, brainwashed, or otherwise powerless to protect their own best interests.

NINETEEN
Feminists should protect and prevent other women from engaging in work in the sex industry.

TWENTY
Female sex workers can be easily identified by their dress, posture, and companions.

TWENTY ONE
Female sex workers are poor, uneducated, and nonwhite.

TWENTY TWO
No woman rationally chooses or consensually participates in sex work.

TWENTY THREE
No woman would ever work in the sex industry if she could get a decent, well-paying job anywhere else.

TWENTY FOUR
The sex industry should be abolished, not regulated.

TWENTY FIVE
Pornography that presents violence advocates violence against women.

TWENTY SIX
There is no distinction between consensual deviant behavior and assault.

TWENTY SEVEN
Sex should be a tranquil domain, a peaceful activity, where sadomasochistic behavior, dominance, submission, and violent fantasies do not belong.

TWENTY EIGHT
All people who oppose violence against women are also against pornography.

TWENTY NINE
All people who are anti-pornography also oppose violence against women.

THIRTY
No one who isn't against pornography truly opposes violence against women.

THIRTY ONE
There can be a single feminist standard for healthy sexual behavior.

THIRTY TWO
Women don't use, produce, or enjoy pornography.

THIRTY THREE
Because the pornography industry is controlled by men, all pornography subjugates women.

THIRTY FOUR
Sexual autonomy, pleasure, and liberation are not priorities for women and women's liberation.

THIRTY FIVE
The active pursuit of sex and pleasure is male-identified.

THIRTY SIX
Sexual experimentation for women which involves "violent" or "unequal" sex is never truly consensual.

THIRTY SEVEN
Male sexuality is inherently aggressive.

THIRTY EIGHT
Male sexuality is naturally promiscuous.

THIRTY NINE
Male sexuality is naturally objectifying and tends to link desire with impersonal physical gratification.

FORTY
Male sexuality needs to be contained.

FORTY ONE
Male sexuality is exclusively genitally oriented.

FORTY TWO
Male masturbation is dangerous and threatening to women.

FORTY THREE
Intercourse simulates and is often a paradigm for rape.

FORTY FOUR
Penetration is an act of dominance and submission.

FORTY FIVE
Sexuality is innate and gender-based.

FORTY SIX
There is an innate female sexuality.

FORTY SEVEN
Women whose sexuality does not fit this model are male-identified or perverse.

FORTY EIGHT
Female sexuality is inherently passive.

FORTY NINE
Female sexuality is naturally monogamous.

FIFTY
Female sexuality that is not monogamous is perverse, male-identified, or self-destructive.

FIFTY ONE
Women do not objectify their sexual partners; they naturally equate desire with romantic love.

FIFTY TWO
Female sexuality is naturally nurturing.

FIFTY THREE
Female sexuality is not genitally oriented.

FIFTY FOUR
It's permissible, or even advantageous, to work with the state in fighting pornography.

FIFTY FIVE
To effectively eliminate pornography women should work with any organized group regardless of its overall political/social agenda.

FIFTY SIX
Repressing the rampant expression of sexuality benefits women.

FIFTY SEVEN
Because sexual materials are, at best, trivial for women, censorship of them is a trivial concern.

FIFTY EIGHT
Containment and control of human sexual activity usually works for the social good.

FIFTY NINE
Pornography expresses and reflects a sick culture.

SIXTY
Pornography depicts unhealthy acts, and only unhealthy people enjoy it.

SIXTY ONE
Certain forms of sexual expression and fantasy are inherently less healthy than others.

SIXTY TWO
Least healthy sexual interests include s/m, homosexuality, transvestism, transsexualism, fetishism, cross-generational sex and sex for money. Pornography that attracts or includes these elements is especially dangerous.

SIXTY THREE
Male use of pornography signifies a "rape mentality."

SIXTY FOUR
Pornography should be abolished or regulated.

SIXTY FIVE
In an ideal feminist society, there would be no sex roles or preferences.

SIXTY SIX
Sex for fun or profit is immoral.

SIXTY SEVEN
Promiscuity is dangerous for women.

SIXTY EIGHT
Women who sell sex degrade all women.

SIXTY NINE
Gender is the strongest bond; sisterhood transcends racial identities, class identities, occupation and membership in specific sexual minorities or subcultures.

SEVENTY
Masturbation is dangerously antisocial.

SEVENTY ONE
Images trigger behavior.

SEVENTY TWO
Violence, and violent behavior, has its root in images of violence.

SEVENTY THREE
Women are more responsible and trustworthy censors than are men.

Originally published in *Caught Looking: Feminism, Pornography, & Censorship* (The Real Comet Press), 1988; reprinted with authors' permission.

Dion Farquhar

Pure Porn

> ... [the uncanny as it is depicted in literature] is a much more fertile province than the uncanny in real life, for it contains the whole of the latter and something more besides, something that cannot be found in real life.
> —Freud

On the el from the airport, they sat next to each other in a molded plastic seat designed to boundary two strangers via a slightly raised bump that travelled down the middle. Which they could feel as they sat very close to each other, bodies pressed left to right, leaning slightly against each other's side. He reached up and across her chest, grazing the front of her leather jacket with a prickly wool sleeve to grasp the raw silk scarf that lay around her neck. He slowly pulled on it until her face was very close to his, never breaking the gaze. She inadvertently fanned her fingers out to touch the side of his body as he pulled her toward him, feeling his chest through layers of wool and cotton as they sat on the rattling train, thighs warm and pressed against each other. They could only get together every other week, living as they did in different cities during the school term. But they were relatively mobile and able to arrange four- and five-day weekends.

They walked together, hip to hip, through the courtyard right up to the stairway of his building, where they separated to walk up the two squeaky flights to his apartment. She watched him walk ahead of her. In the apartment, she dropped her brown suede backpack into a Breuer chair by the door. They watched each other unzip and take off their jackets, flinging them onto the backs of chairs. Holding the gaze. Unwavering control. Unsure about what they were doing. In part. Playing with tropes. Mutual recognition. He lifted her bag from the floor to place it on a chair, saying, "You travel light. It's good." Then he walked away into the kitchen to pour them each an ice-cold seltzer. Coming back with two glasses, he handed one to her and then raised his glass in a gesture of acknowledgement. Which she responded to by leaning toward him, kissing his neck with a sweep of tongue and lips cooled by the liquid.

He walked slowly toward her. His hand reached over to her shoulder, gently pulling her body into contact with his. Her arms met his, embracing him back, pulling him toward her, feeling him along the length of their bodies. Noting her soft breasts against his hard chest, pubic bone to hardening cock, the firmness of their touching thighs. They began to kiss, slowly and gently at first. With a sweep of his tongue, he took her entire mouth in his, then resting his tongue at the entrance of her open mouth, poised, moving it only when he felt her tongue envelop his. Then, opening his mouth to contain hers, he sucked her in and released her, over and over, resting his lips against hers, for a moment resisting her tongue meeting his, then pushing against her with closed lips, now seeking out and trying to suck her tongue into his mouth.

They loved to kiss, she thought, running her tongue along his cheek all the way down to his chin. She licked the tiny ridge under his lower lip, feeling the pull of the rough texture of his nascent beard offer resistance. If she stayed more than a moment kissing or licking a cheek, or lip, or eyelid, he couldn't bear it. His tongue would then seek out her mouth, moving over her lips from side to side, savoring their moist pliancy. Their tongues darted around each other, slowing down and speeding up, drawing back, then hurrying on for more. He would moan and move to nibble her ear, to take the bird from her earlobe with his lips. In the same way he would kiss and lick her belly down to the top of her underpants, sometimes grasping the elastic band in his mouth and pulling them off with his mouth.

Their bodies pressed into one another, seeking out the radiant center of their genitals. They move against each other. She cannot stop herself from moaning slightly. Suddenly he grasped her, hands squeezing her shoulders, and pushed her away. "Not so fast," he says, reaching for her scarf. Which he placed over her eyes, winding it around her head and tying a knot with an emphatic tug. "Now, you will feel it more," he said, sucking and biting her lips before opening his mouth to kiss her deep and long and hard.

Then he stopped. Grasping her hand firmly by the wrist, he pulled her to walk with him, and led her around the apartment until she could feel her legs touch the side of the bed. He pushed her slightly so that she sat down, one hand caressing a breast with increasing firmness as he leaned into her until they were lying along side of, then under, and on top of each other for long intervals. Until one of them would indicate a desire to vary position. Slipping his hand underneath her blouse, he brushed her erect nipple with the side of his hand, running his fingers around the aureole. Then he pulled her shirt over her head, and nuzzled his head between her breasts, pillowing into her with a sweep of his head, then rising to take as much of a breast into his mouth as he could. He nibbled and sucked her breasts until she moaned, feeling some direct connection to her clitoris that pulsed in rhythm to the firm pressure of his tongue.

When he stopped, she would seek his mouth strongly, falling into him and opening herself to his eager lips. Their bodies pressed up hard against each other, moving their hips in sync with each other. She sighed to feel his hard cock through their clothes, delighted but almost alarmed by its hardness, her wetness, the power of their desire for each other. "Enough of this," she said suddenly, pulling the scarf-blindfold off her head and holding it as she looked at him, reaching over to stroke the outline of his erect cock through his jeans.

"Now, I will tie you up," she said to his moan, pushing against her hand. "Stand up," she said, grasping his belt and pulling him toward her. "Take your clothes off," she said, rubbing him through the thick jeans material. As he pulled off a cotton sweater and unbuttoned a flannel shirt, she unbuckled his belt and unzipped his fly. Then his hand met hers, cupping it and pressing it against him through his clothes for a moment before finally shedding his jeans. She sat down on the bed, savoring the sight of his body, naked now except for his shorts. She looked at his erection, tight up against the white cotton material, seeing a few drops of preejaculate, a circle of wet against the shorts. Lifting them over his cock in order to pull them off, she smiled, noticing a drop quivering on its glistening tip. Following her gaze, he smiled and said, "I'm very wet." Touching him lightly and smiling broadly, she said, "So I see." He moved closer to her, bringing his head close to hers. "Kiss me," he said, before wrapping her mouth in his.

Tying two long silk scarves together, she wrapped one scarf around his right wrist, running it like a chain under the mattress until it met his other wrist from the opposite side. Next, she attended to his legs, knotting old silk ties together to secure his feet. She made one loop gently but firmly around an ankle, proceeding under the mattress to the other. This way each wrist and ankle were held as widely spread as seemed comfortable. She looked at his legs spread far apart but held tightly in position, centering his outstretched body on his pelvis. She had tied him spreadeagle to the bed. She wanted to see him struggle, beg her to release him, entreat her to fuck him, to never let him loose.

He had watched her as she tied him up, a slight sweat bathing his forehead. "Kiss me," he said, "please." She watched him thrust his pelvis up as much as the bonds limiting his motion allowed, craning his neck up towards her. Coming over to the bed, she lay down next to him and began to kiss him, caressing his cock with her hand, as she rubbed herself against his leg, feeling her slippery wetness as she slid her hardening clitoris back and forth against the bone of his knee, noting that he moved slightly to meet her motion. "You're very hard," he said, with a deep sigh, head thrown back, as she moved to kiss him deeply in reply.

"What would you like to do?" she paused to ask, raising an eyebrow as she looked at him. She inclined her body towards his from her position stretched out next to him, resting her head on her hand, supported by an elbow. She had one leg slung over the "X" his body made on the middle of the double bed. Her knee slowly rubbed his penis lightly back and forth. With her free hand, she grazed his chest, stroking and pinching a nipple until it grew hard, bending over him to tongue it and suck it until he groaned. "So, are you going to tell me what you want to do?" she asked, moving her knee away from his hard penis and resting it on a thigh. "Well . . ." he said, casting a glance over his immobilized torso, the erection quivering slightly, delight and embarrassment mixing in his look.

She began to kiss him again, taking his lower lip between hers and sucking hard on it, then running her tongue over it from side to side, moving to his upper lip until his tongue came to meet hers. She opened her mouth to take him inside her, gulping him down with tiny sucking motions, their tongues finding each other and twisting around and around until one of them would alter the motion.

She moved over to lie on top of him, holding herself up with her arms so that their bodies were touching only at the groin. He thrust his hips up, pushing his cock hard up against her belly, and she leaned into him, savoring his hardness. "Fuck me," he said, "please. I can't stand it any more." "We'll see what you can stand," she said, moving herself over him so that his penis slid effortlessly against her totally slippery wet vulva, rippling against her hard clit with each stroke. "Oh. Fuck me," he moaned, straining to push his cock against her as far as his bonds would allow. "Take me inside you," he said, looking hard at her. "Stop torturing me."

"Not so fast," she said, as she rolled off of him and lay next to him. She reached for the seltzer bottle on the night table and filled her glass again, greedily sipping it because she was parched. "Do you want some," she offered. He nodded, so she refilled a glass and held it to his lips until he had drunk his fill. Then she slowly began to kiss his face, making her way down from his lips to his ears, then biting and sucking his neck until she rested at a nipple. "Oh, I love it when you do that," he said of her hardening a nipple with her tongue. She loved the absurdity of mouths on breasts.

Moving herself slowly over him, she changed directions on the bed to suck his toes, tickle and rub his feet, making her way to the center of his body, to nibble the inside of his thighs, alternately licking, sucking, kissing, and biting him there with her mouth while her hand kneaded and softly caressed his other thigh and leg.

Taking his balls into her mouth made her dizzy with his smell, anchored by their rougher texture. He moaned continuously now, moving his hips and straining against the scarves that spread him open, setting a rhythm to her sucking and biting, which had not yet reached his penis. "Oh, God. Suck me. I can't stand it. Not another minute." She nipped at the many tiny folds of skin around its base, then licked him from base to tip, first hard, then softly, alternating the top and then the underside of her tongue, back and forth. He lifted his pelvis to meet her mouth, emitting cries and tossing his head from side to side. His body shuddered in waves of desire.

She ran her tongue around and around the top of his penis, taking his head between her lips and making shallow thrusting motions with her mouth and tongue. With one hand, she grasped his penis, encircling it and taking special care to press hard against the ridged area just below its lip that connected the sides. She sucked him, especially forcefully down the backside of its shaft, which he had told her was particularly sensitive. With each thrust she would rest her half-closed mouth firmly around the lip of its head and pressing her lips against him for intervals that she varied, until his groans urged her on. "Oh, more. More, more," he said. Then she swept her tongue around the head of his penis, sucking him deeply into her mouth and moving her tongue over its length, while her hand ringed him at the same time, attentive to his most sensitive spot.

Sliding her hands under his ass on one of his lifting motions, she grasped his cheeks, rubbing and working them along with the motion of her mouth on his cock. "Put your fingers inside me," he moaned, "fuck me." In answer, she moved her fingers back and forth along the crack of his ass until she felt the tiny wrinkled opening, warm and moist, throb against her gently circling finger. Pausing to lubricate her fingers thoroughly with the bottle of almond massage oil they kept on the night table, her hand followed the line from the base of his balls right up to the crack of his ass.

He opened to meet her like a flower, and she eased her middle finger into him, hearing him cry out in pleasure, feeling his sphincter tighten around her finger, release, then tighten again. She worked it to his rhythms, never going further until invited, but stopping only when her finger could easily enter him no further. She moved her finger inside him, slowly back and forth, pressing up against the front of his rectum, allowing his thrusting to work her hand, setting the pace. "Now try two fingers," he said in between gasps. All the while her mouth and other hand never left his cock, moving over him, in rhythm to her fingers fucking him easily as he pressed his ass against her fingers with each inward motion, allowing her more deeply inside him.

They fucked each other like this for a long delicious while. She had no idea. Her awareness contracted almost completely to the sensate liquid cosmos of her mouth and fingers and the sounds of their pleasure. Her world the feel and heat of him between her lips, reaching deep into her throat, the rhythm of his cock back and forth at the same time her fingers slid deeply in and out of his ass, feeling his thrusts meet her fingers. Then, his cock reached all the way down into the curve of her throat at the same time his ass took her fingers all the way in. His body pushed against her hard, stilling into a strong thrusted orgasm that she felt go on for what seemed to be minutes. Her mouth registered the spurts of semen, warm and briny like seawater, flowing into her mouth in several short spasms at the same time she felt his anus contract in little pulses of ringing afterpleasure. After a moment, she swallowed the ejaculate, and slowly leaned over him to kiss him. "Taste," she said.

"Oh, God. Oh, God," he spat out, rolling his head from side to side, still breathing in gasps, "it's too much." "Untie me, so I can torture you." She kissed him on the lips. "Twist my arm," she said, fiddling with the silk knots around his wrist.

They took a break to pee, wash a little, and refill seltzers. "We forgot to smoke," he said, returning to the bedroom with a joint and an ashtray. "And here's an extra bathrobe in case you get chilled," he said, draping a terry robe over her shoulders, and pausing to kiss her neck. "It's a smooth strong green," he said, sitting down next to her and lighting the joint, taking a long, slow puff. He held it out to her. "Hmm," she said, reaching for the joint, "smells great." "What shall we do now?" he said, looking playfully at her. "That depends on what you want to know," she said, as she coughed, laughing and exhaling a mouthful of smoke. Leaning back into a cluster of pillows, she passed the joint back to him. "I can't smoke too much. I want to do some work later," she said. "Good, I have tons to do myself. You can have the computer if you want. I have stuff to read." "Great. And let's get some takeout, then we'll work." "Thai, all right?" "Fine." He put the joint out, moved the ashtray, and began to kiss her until they were rolling around again on the bed. It was so easy when they weren't cripples or psychos, she thought, her arms around him, tongues intertwined, completely happy being with him.

Never predictable, he chose to replicate for her the spreadeagle position from which he had recently been released. "It had a lot going for it," he thought, as he looked at her body extended in a classic "X". He loved the way she looked tied up—helpless and completely open to him, her hipbones prominent and breasts flatter and rounder because of her raised and out-stretched arms, her pubic hair wet with surplus secretions. Maybe they liked the trust and the hypothetical risk. Though they had each never felt safer.

After he had tied her up in the same spreadeagle position, he sat up next to her, leaning down to kiss her, tonguing her deeply. Pulling away slightly, he bent over her and kissed her belly, continuing down to her pubic triangle. Moving his hand over her body to cup her vulva, he rocked her with his hand. "Let's see how turned on you are," he said, feeling her wetness even on the longer pubic hair that he grasped and pulled at, twirling a small clump around his fingers, absorbing its wetness.

Then he skillfully parted her inner lips with two fingers, sliding his middle finger far inside her, feeling her wetness and the ever-changing texture of her vagina. "Oh," he said, "very nice," working a second finger into her and moving in and out with harder and faster thrusts until she moaned and strained against the scarves, meeting his hand. Suddenly, he took his fingers out of her and began to work the area just a tiny bit above her clitoris with gentle firm rhythmic caresses that made her scream in pleasure. Moving down to cover its length and circle the small knob of hard flesh, he moved his middle finger higher up to grasp its hood. Then he opened her inner lips with a separating sweep of his second and fourth fingers, holding them apart as he slid his middle finger firmly over her clit, a gesture he knew she loved because she would always moan more. He worked his middle finger rhythmically back and forth over her clit, rubbing it ever so slightly harder in time to her increasing pelvic movement against his hand. With his other hand, he thrust two, then three, fingers all the way up inside her, faster and faster until her body tensed into immobility, lifting her into a high-pitched moan of an orgasm that rippled through her, rising and falling for a long time.

He immediately arranged himself on top of her in order to enter her while her orgasm went on in wave after wave, which his fucking now skimmed and rode, taking his cues from her thrusting. After slowing to meet her subsiding motion, instead of stopping altogether, he slowly began to increase the rhythm knowing that she could often be brought back into another pitch of pleasure following immediately upon a first. She opened further to this quick thrust fucking, raising her hips to meet his cock, burning with such exquisite feeling she felt almost faint. "Oh, God. Oh, God," she moaned, "it's so good."

    He leaned over her, kissing and biting her breasts, sucking hard on one and then another as he thrust high into her, or licking her neck as he withdrew to the entrance of her vagina, then plunging all the way into her until she screamed with pleasure, rocking with him, tightening her vaginal muscles to grip him when he was deepest inside her, making him gasp, squeeze his eyes shut, and whisper, "Oh, God. It's so good."

    He stopped for a moment to bend over and untie her legs so she would move more. They both reached for pillows to slide under her hips, and she lifted her legs high, wrapping them tightly around his neck, and guiding him back into her. Each thrust pleasured her differently. After a while, she lost the ability to know which one of them initiated a stroke or set of strokes. She couldn't feel their borders. Who was who. What was what. Sometimes it felt as if they moved in and out of each other fast, fast, fast, with strokes that were close together. Other times their fucking was long and slow, it reaching so deeply into her that she would cry out. Sometimes there was anger in the force of their fucking, and they fucked as much from need as from desire, hate as much as love. She never knew in advance of their bodies joining who or what would move the other or how. Loving invention.

    They fucked for a long time until he pulled out of her in order to move to her mouth. "I love being inside all of you," he said as he straddled her, bringing his cock very near her mouth. Opening to him with a sucking kiss, she could taste the mixture of their secretions, licking and moving her mouth over him, taking him all the way into her, then pulling back on him. Just as she was falling into a smooth rhythm of taking him in and wrapping her mouth around him as he rocked back on each thrust, he pulled out of her mouth, saying, "It's getting very sensitive."

    He began to kiss her mouth, running his hands over her entire body, pausing to slide his fingers over her vulva, again seeking her inner labia and finally, as she moaned more and more, her clitoris. He opened her slowly, separating the inner lips carefully with his fingers, and pulling the hood firmly back until her clit lay completely exposed to his tongue. He knelt over her, his erect cock resting against her belly, and began to lick her there with wide gulps, wrapping his mouth around her. Her entire body shuddered with pleasure. Then he held her lips apart with the fingers of one hand as he slowly worked the tip of his tongue back and forth over the length of her clit, returning to the spot just above its most sensitive area for a more intense tonguing.

With each motion, she moved to meet his tongue and lips, breathing herself into his mouth, and pushing her pelvis against him when she wanted him to suck her harder and stronger, and moving ever so slightly up or down in the bed to guide his tongue. His other hand reached into her, thrusting hard and slipping partly out of her, then thrusting into her again with gathering force while his tongue worked her clit steadily. He sensed her lifting herself up to him and pressed his tongue harder onto her, moving back and forth faster until her moaning looped itself into an orgasmic cry that seemed to go on for minutes. Her arms strained hard against the scarves that held her taut, his tongue blanketing her vulva hard and safe, and his fingers pressing up hard against her as far into her as he could go, evoking strong sensation inside her as well.

Again, he entered her, though this time their pleasure was even more strong, pushing himself all the way into her, thrusting up, over and over, coming partly out only to come hard back into her, sighing and moaning more with each motion. She could feel his sweat mix with hers as he nuzzled his face against her neck. They smelled of sex. Yum. When he finally came, crying out, she felt, not orgasm, but a series of tiny but pleasurable ripples in her vagina reverberating from the cessation of motion, that she could intensify by contracting her muscles against his ejaculating penis.

Their weekend continued much in the same vein, their being talking sex, *pace* Foucault.

Joel Lipman

The working premise of the series is that "upon death the body of Jesse Helms is donated to art." The pieces are overprintings done on selected pages from standard medical textbooks; the materials are lead, wood, and rubber type.

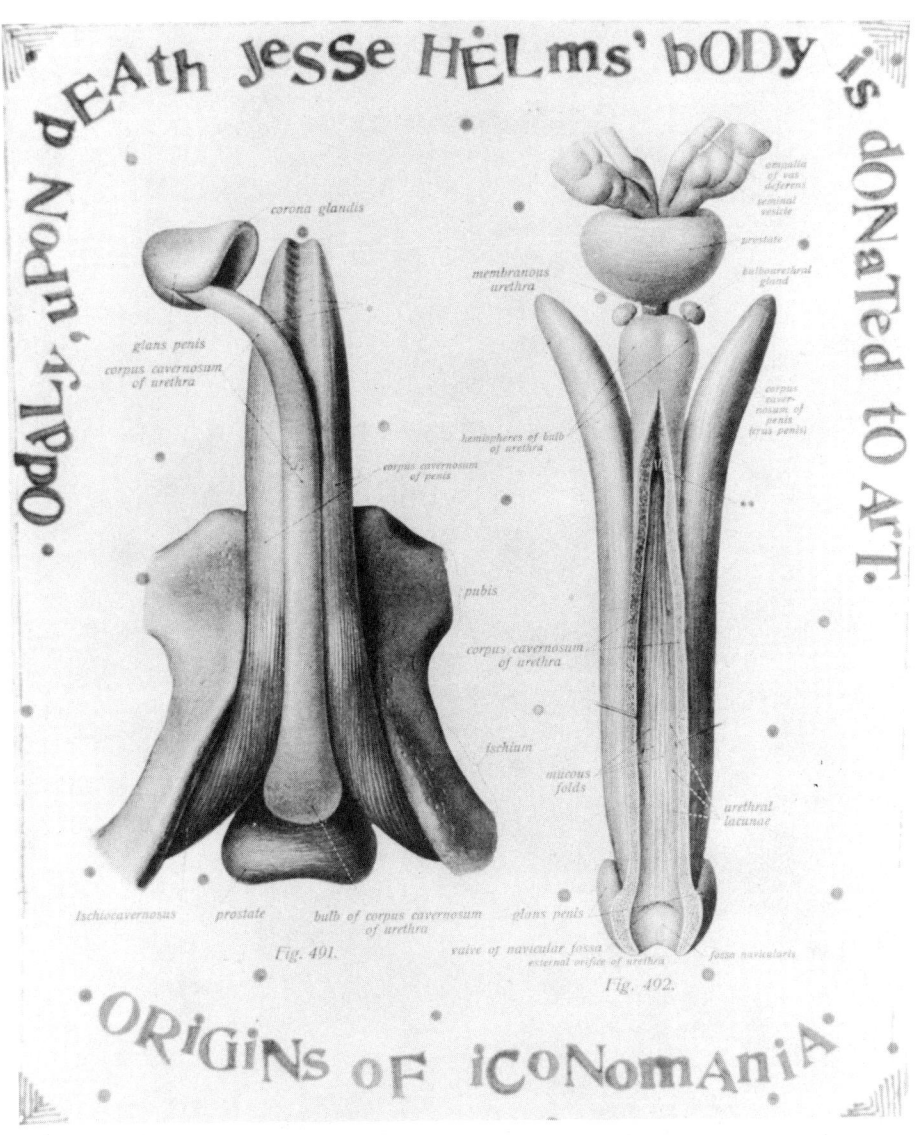

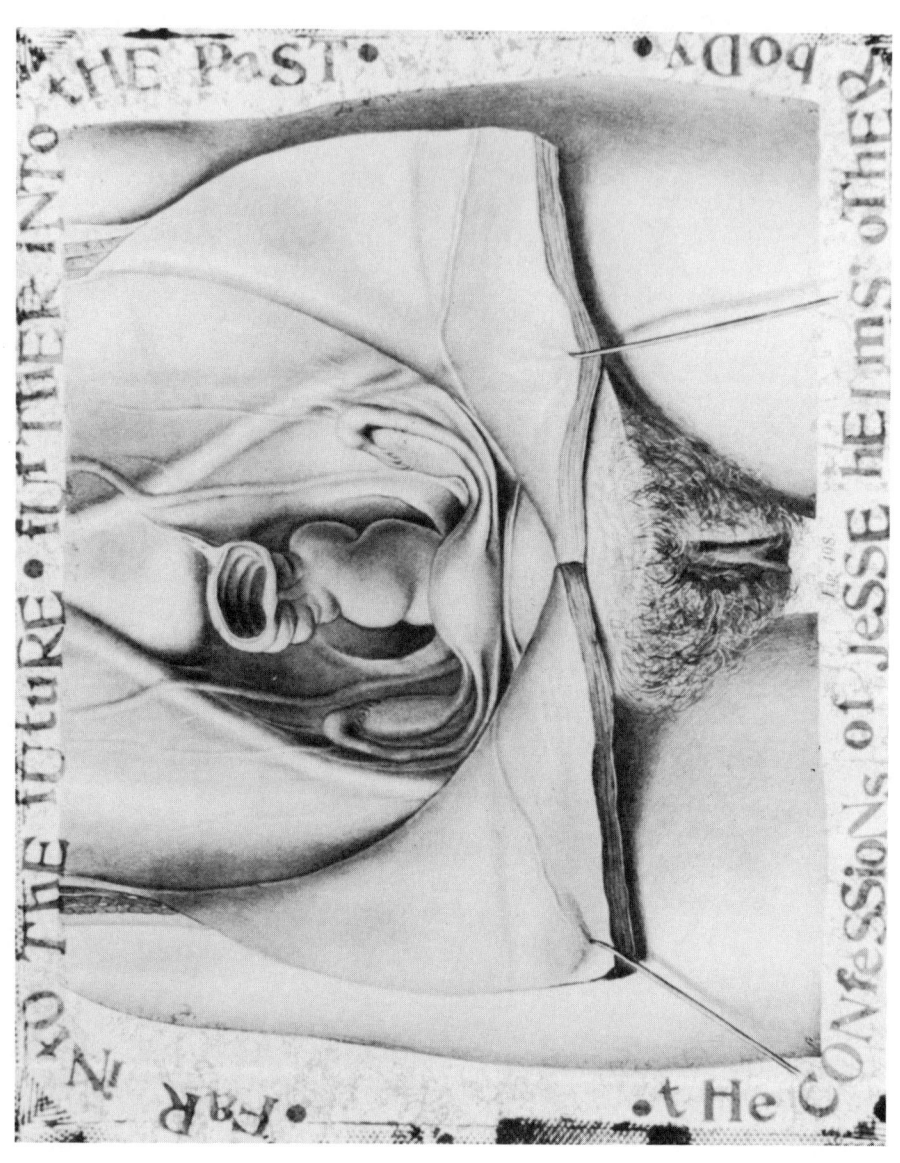

Jesse Helms' Body   32   Joel Lipman

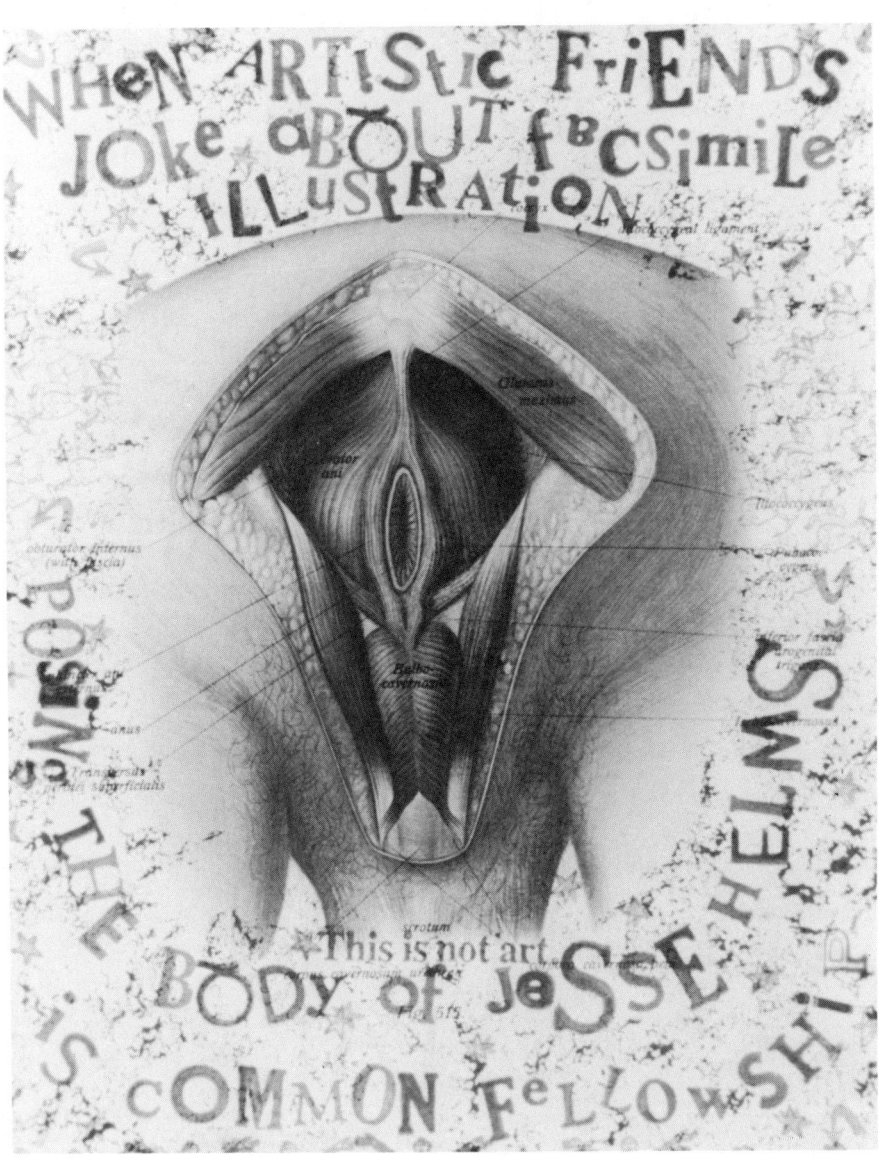

Jesse Helms' Body — Joel Lipman

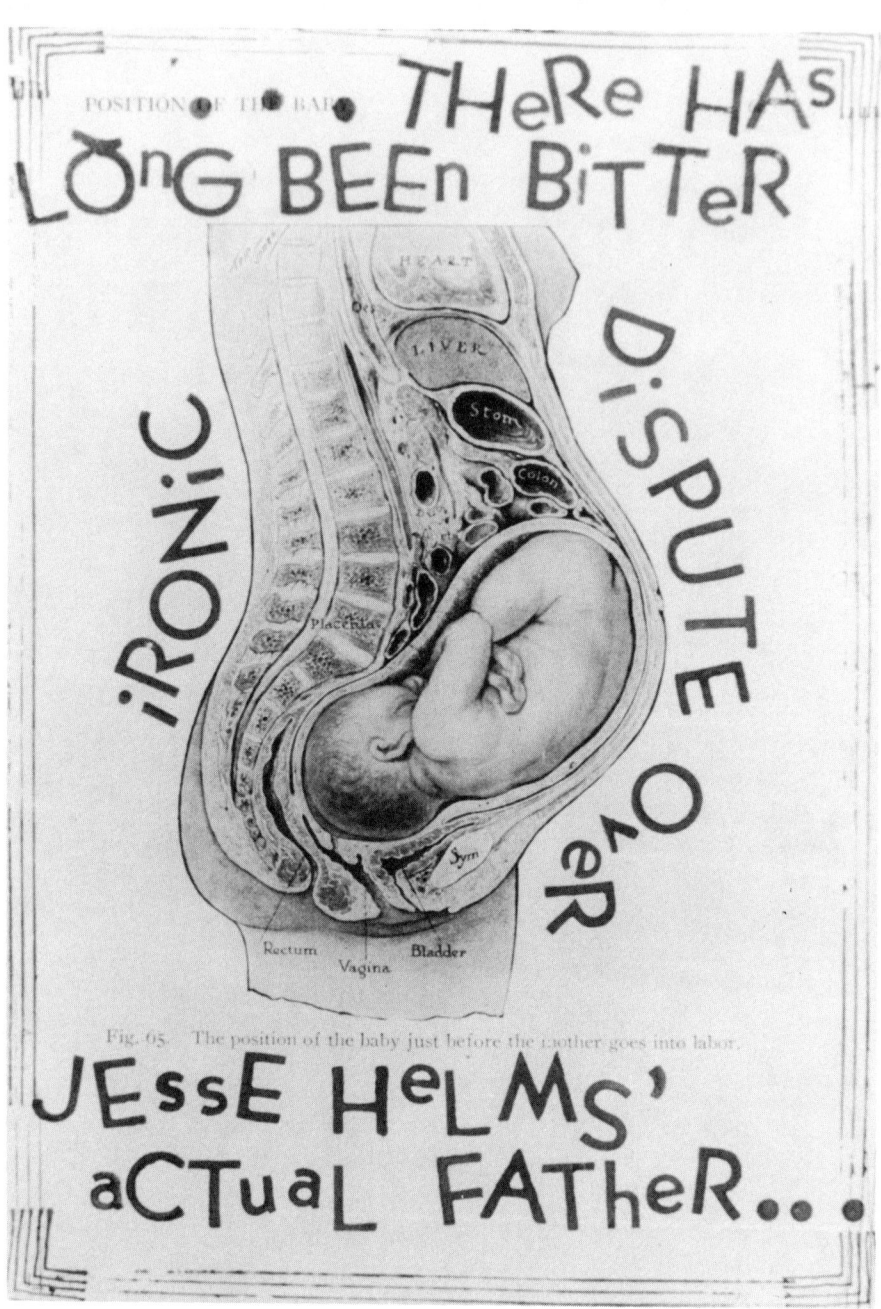

Forum

Ours is a time of sanctimony and repression. In *Civilization And Its Discontents*, Freud conceded that a degree of sublimated repression was necessary to erect social structures. But as Marcuse put it twenty-five years later, in *Eros and Civilization*: social structures had long been erected and re-erected and yet the repression intensified. "Surplus repression," he termed it, imposed in order to imprison the populace in simulated satisfactions, to turn the populace into mindless consumers of counterfeit passions.

Censorship is the social application of repression. But equally crucial to the repressive strategy is the manipulation of language and images, including the re-routing of signifiers such as *pornography*.

For our special issue on pornography/censorship we are asking selected writers, artists, and critics to address the following two-part question which we will publish in a forum format. Your response may be as brief or lengthy as you wish.

Forum Question

What constitutes pornography, in your opinion?

Can you point to a (or more than one) contemporary text, image, event, sound-bite, personage, etc., which you would call pornographic?

Carol Becker

In the last few years of art scandals the term pornographic has often been inappropriately used to condemn work which presents an explicit version of sexuality unknown and unacknowledged by many Americans and therefore thought to be unnatural. In this sense that which makes people uncomfortable and forces them to question the assumptions of their daily lives has too often been termed pornographic. But pornography is much more specific. It can be found in sexuality only when the motivation for the sexual act, or its representation in art work and erotic display, is ill-willed, hate driven, or predicated on the abuse of power, subjugation, and humiliation. Such pornographic manifestations can also occur intrasubjectively: One could have a pornographic relationship to the self—as in substance abuse and anorexia. Or a nation could become pornographic to its constituency—as in racism, or Bush's war against the poor. There could also be global pornography: A group of nations banned together to decimate another, citing as their justification, crimes of aggression they themselves have committed many times before with impunity.

Whenever pornography is suspected it should be analyzed contextually. Nancy Reagan's dresses could be considered pornographic, for example, not in themselves, but when positioned against images of homelessness, the degenerating public school system, or the burning oil fields of Kuwait. These surreal juxtapositions could easily demonstrate the pornographic contradictions upon which our political reality is constructed.

Edmund White

Pornography is a communication designed to excite sexually and is used to enhance ordinary sexual acts or to replace them. Artistically it is necessarily banal and confined to a few key situations and words; any attempt to make it more "artistic" will defeat its purpose and throw off the rhythms of the masturbator. Like polite verse in *The Tale of Genji*, pornography admits of only the subtlest variations on classic themes. Those themes are well-defined for each perversion.

Pornography is useful in helping young or inexperienced people to identify or cultivate their erotic tastes and skills. It is an essential adjunct to the art of loving, one of life's most refined (and least natural) pleasures.

Marjorie Agosin

Pornography consists of the obsessive manipulation of inauthentic images with the sole purpose of distorting truth and, therefore, the gesture of the imagined body. In repressive societies like my own in Chile, pornography was used as a form of torture where the beauty of the body that had a soul and luminosity was mutilated, cut, exposed in its fragility and vulnerability with the specific purpose of censoring and transforming truth. Confession became a form of torture.

Kingsley Widmer

While an apologist for obscenity—sexual explicitness, open and mixed language and images, libidinal freedoms, and defiance of the repressive gentilities of power and authority—I object to much pornography. The writings and images of prostitutes (to emphasize the primal condition of pornography), servicing the manipulation of the obscene for profit, control, revenge, and ideologies of domination and destruction, screws us all. Advertisers, popular publishers, and other media manipulators, commercial writers and artists, and similar whores exploiting and falsifying sexuality, provide many of the lubricities of control so pervasive in our technocracy. It is also not very adequate sensuality. Desire as product is itself considerably pernicious.

However, that is no argument for the recurrent demands for censorship, or covert controls and "standards" doing its work. Some contemporary feminists have better censuring cases against some pornography than other fundamentalists, such as the Christian and Islamic, but not for official censoring and control. As one involved for decades for the defense in censorship cases (on modernist literary works, a student arts magazine, an alternative newspaper, "adult movies," self-help advocacy, public obscenity as political speech, etc.), I know too well how institutional proceedings work. Whether run by a state prosecutor, a TV producer/interviewer, an administrator/professor, a mass media editor, a corporate arbitrator, or a law court judge, they are almost always intellectually as well as sexually falsifying. Social reality and artistic quality are never decently dealt with. The authorities rest on the crasser bigotries, socioeconomic advantage taking, and statist and other institutional coercions. Any official censorship at all comes out repressively arbitrary. (In the U.S., obscenity as such is not constitutionally protected; the tortuous exemptions for "redeeming social significance," and "recognized community standards," including official "literary merit," mostly rationalize control.) "Liberalized rules" remain falsified standards imposed on others. All hierarchies are out to fuck over someone lesser. They also usually subserve those out to impose an agenda of correctness. In practice as well as on enlightenment principle, those favoring any kind of institutional censorship are shitheads.

When sex is not exploited, people may not be so inclined to misuse "cunts," and "pricks," in several senses. Much of the manipulation of sexuality that I object to can be drastically reduced only by radically eliminating the rewards and other advantages for the repressive falsifications of pornography, which are mirrored in its censoring control. Good obscenity, including the encouragement of sensual responsiveness, variousness, and polymorphous sensibility, deserves to be defended. And so, of course, does blasphemy, that most contemporary as well as ancient role of obscenity, in everlasting resistance to the pornography of the pieties of power.

Even defend it when good obscenity is mixed with Sadean fantasies of female abuse, or pedophilia, or commercial exploitation, or disguises for domination? Probably so, for in a highly syncretistic and corrupt culture such as ours, the separation of true obscenity from pornographic manipulation, which always tends to repress sexuality into other purposes, other aggrandizements, may often not be easy. No institutional authorities are up to it. They will just impose some old domination in whatever fashionable guise. We should double their brains by farting in their ears.

Still, much of the issue seems clear enough. Encourage true obscenity, in word, image, gesture, and purpose, while resisting the pornographic *and* the censoring manipulations of techno-bureaucracies. To paraphrase Spinoza on happiness: Obscenity is its own reward. We always fucking-well need it.

Judith Halberstam

Fundamentalists and liberals alike have insisted upon definitions of pornography that link obscenity to minority sexual practices, to the making visible of non-reproductive, non-heterosexual, anti-romantic sex. But sex is in fact not really the realm in which bodily acts are obscene, disgusting, unwatchable. For example, the uproar last year about Madonna's "Justify My Love" video created discussion about that thin line dividing eroticism from pornography; what Madonna's video revealed, with its slick production and its aestheticized images, was that the representation of sexuality itself has little if anything to do with pornography.

What is pornographic then? Watching President Bush vomit into the lap of a Japanese dignitary on television recently, I realized that I was witnessing a pornographic act, an act that made visible what should never have been seen, a kind of reverse fellatio that left both actors drained and disgusted. Like the pictures of Reagan's colon that filled prime-time news during his last term, the pictures of Bush's pale face with his jaw slack from nausea opened up a new space in which to consider pornography. Reagan's bowels and the contents of Bush's stomach represent for me the body as obscene, the body as grotesque spectacle, the body turned inside out.

Reagan and Bush, the guardians of morality themselves, are protected from the pornographic gaze by the machinery of mass media which in both cases produced clinical and professionalized information on colon and vomit in order to sanitize the breach in good taste produced by the scenes of a body in crisis. Bush's vomiting episode, rather than eliciting a general outcry of disgust, produced stories in the news on winter flu, on the gag reflex, and in general on the vulnerability of the human body to the banality of infection. And yet, the news cameras thrilled to the spontaneity of Bush's act, the sheer "liveness" of his collapse, the abjection of his nausea. Somewhere between the puking scene and the sanitized rhetorical clean-up lies the pornographic like so much vomit in the lap of luxury.

Stephen-Paul Martin

Pornography means, literally, "writing about prostitutes." The term is generally used in our society to refer to verbal or graphic modes of expression designed to seduce their audience into an erotically charged condition, to induce masturbatory cravings and obsessions. In the United States, a line is generally drawn between "X-rated" films, videos, magazines, and books and those that are somehow more "legitimate" or "respectable." It seems to me that this distinction is artificial and serves no intelligent function.

A more useful way to think about published erotic expression is to see it in terms of the economic logic of our culture. From this perspective, the important distinction to be made is between statements designed to stimulate erotic self-awareness and statements designed to seduce the reader/viewer into buying a product. It's been said many times that the United States is a culture of addictions and compulsions, a vast network of enticing simulations in which desires are generally aroused for materialistic purposes. Without going into a lengthy discussion of this condition, I think it's safe to say that without this constant hormonal manipulation our economic structure would have collapsed long ago, and we would have been forced to confront the predatory realities of "advanced" capitalism without the cosmetic barrage of images that has always made it seem that our country's sociopolitical initiatives were in some way noble and humane.

The debate about pornography strikes me as being a pseudo-issue. The real question is how to distance ourselves from the psycho-sexual enticements that mainstream information systems depend on. Over the past thirty years or so, much has been written about the seduction techniques that allow our media system to control or at least influence the way we perceive. Yet the seduction continues because in our "free" market economy the ideological manipulation of public space is an absolute necessity. Neil Postman once wrote that we are in a headlong "race between education and disaster," suggesting that if high schools, colleges, and universities were really doing their jobs, people would be given interpretive skills that would help them respond with intelligence to the eroticized images and messages that surround them. But is education enough?

Recently, in all the trains of the New York City subway system, an ad appeared that made me question the power of interpretive consciousness when faced with a seductive message. The ad focused on the inviting gaze of a woman dressed in a red skin-tight gown. Her hands were reaching back behind her long black hair, and her breasts were thrown forward. Beside her was a bottle of beer, and above it, in red, was the phrase: "SET YOUR SIGHTS ON BALLANTINE ALE."

At first glance, the ad seemed to be relying on one of the crudest, most easily recognized Madison Avenue seduction techniques, the conflation of sexual desire and physical thirst. But on closer examination, the message became more subtle. The woman's pose was so blatantly inviting as to seem ironic, as if to announce its own effect, as if the ad were a joke about the process of erotic seduction in advertising. It seemed to be openly thumbing its nose at feminist objections about using women as sex objects, and yet at the same time making this sexist process seem ridiculous. In taking an ironic stance toward various well-known Madison Avenue strategies, the ad was similar in its approach to some of Madonna's videos, which parody the gestures, facial expressions, and verbal rhetoric of Cold War media attitudes about female sexuality. And like Madonna's videos, the ad was able to include an element of self-deflation without losing any of its power to entice. Although my analysis had given me a certain amount of critical distance from the ad's seductive machinations, and although I had previously done a good amount of research and writing on the subject of media politics, I looked forward to setting my sights on Ballantine Ale every time I rode the subway. Although I don't usually think of myself as one of Marcuse's "mindless consumers," I was only too eager to imprison myself in a "counterfeit satisfaction."

It seems to me that the kind of "pornography" practiced in this ad, and by the mass media in general, is of a far more dangerous and insidious variety than that which appears in X-rated magazines and videos. At least in the latter the images and messages are fairly straightforward, and people know what to expect when they make use of them. The more significant struggle is with images that have not been consigned to the demi-monde of 42nd Street, but instead are presented with a veneer of respectability and are even widely celebrated and honored—images that appear not just in advertisements, rock videos, and Hollywood movies, but in newspapers and history textbooks, in the White House, in televised wars in the Middle East, and (closer to home) in the celebrity systems that operate in various intellectual disciplines—in short, in the "counterfeit satisfactions" that sustain the economic and psychological motions of our culture.

John Greyson

1. "What constitutes pornography, in your opinion?"

Any aspect of culture which produces sexual arousal.

2. "Can you point to a contemporary text image event etc. which you would call pornographic?"

The answer to the first question.

Gerald J. Butler

Last year, I often spent lonely days and nights in train stations and shabby hotels in the heart of France, *la France profond*. A couple of times, I resorted to pornography. In buying it, I had the strong feeling that the pornography on the newsstands was the only thing that conveyed any *truth* that was for sale there. I mean it was the only stuff for sale there that required any moment of truth to buy. No one I saw ever seemed embarrassed to buy the Communist newspaper, even while the USSR was falling apart. But to buy a magazine of "a hundred pages of domination" or "teenage bourgeois bitches turned on by sodomy" made for what I saw was a moment of self-admission for every poor bastard who had to bring the magazine up to the vendor and lay out the exorbitant price. The porn, I came to see, was the only thing there that told us—if we could have faced it—of the sad condition we were in.

But, after all, pornography is only a *genre* the way sci-fi, westerns, romances, murder-mysteries, even a certain kind of "highbrow" fiction are *genres*, with its own rules and restrictions, its own tight formulas like the others. It often resembles the now defunct *genre* of the saint's life, but a saint of a gnostic, anti-conventional "religion." As Susan Sontag pointed out in her brilliant essay "The Pornographic Imagination," its "celebrated intention of sexually stimulating readers is really a species of proselytizing."

Harmful effects of any *genre* material can be easily demonstrated because all of it must inevitably flatter the narcissism of its consumer. Even the *genre* of "ideological" writing provides its consumer with reassurance about who the "enemy" is, about the correctness of simple political or moral principles, and so on. *Genre* material in some ways always allows us to go on doing what we are already doing or already want to do. Its fundamental rule is to initiate no profound change in us. Otherwise it would be too upsetting.

Pornography seems to help produce what our society wants, i.e., masturbators. As I understand it from experience and reading, and speaking from a male point of view, masturbation, either by hand or by means of the vagina of a woman you don't really love or desire, does not result in even the same *physiological* consequences to you as does loving, warm-hearted fucking. My own experience agrees with the old psychoanalyst Sandor Ferenczi's explanation that there is an important difference between genital excitement fed by perception from your eyes, touch, mouth, your whole body warmed by contact with someone tenderly loved and eagerly desired, and genital excitement fed only by a fantasy held with hallucinatory vividness in conscious attentiveness, a strained wakefulness. Ferenczi points out there is also a difference when you come. In the first case, the "wave of lust" explodes in a body whose senses are already warm and active; in the second, in a body whose senses are *cold*. And you feel different afterwards. Instead, after a little sleep, of feeling fresh and alert and ready for life, you feel fatigued, irritable, not able to fix your attention very well, futile, drained—what Ferenczi calls "One-Day-Neuresthenia." I think this neuresthenia is just the state that helps would-be rebels submit to the reality provided by our so-called "society."

But writing, pictures, movies, can do more than help us to stay in our various emotional ruts by using the *genre* to undercut itself or break out of its limits. *The Brothers Karamazov* breaks out of murder-mystery, *Wuthering Heights* breaks out of romance, Kafka's tales break out of routine fantasy. Why can't something break out of pornography as well? Essentially this is the question that Sontag poses. But I don't agree that the examples she gives of pornography becoming what she calls "literature" really prove that it can. I don't see, for instance, that the novellas of Bataille take us anywhere very new. His conception of the erotic as the *result* of "interdiction" essentially reinforces the value of Puritanical attitudes. No interdiction, no shock, and no shock, no excitement. Evil, the forbidden—all old hat, isn't it?

The difficulty seems to be that as soon as we try to make pornography into "art" it just seems to turn into what Ugo Volli called "pornokitsch." It just becomes *weak* pornography, if not just sugary and sentimental then intellectual and cold like Bataille: something for kitsch people who can't face the truth of their own morbidity which that reaction to the crude *genre* stuff just might happen to reveal to them. The arty, pretentious, "erotic" literature—disdainful of any association with pornography—that is published by the relatively new magazine *Yellow Silk* seems to me pornokitsch of the worst sort. *Yellow*

Silk doesn't break out of the *genre*; it merely dilutes it with arty respectability.

The French writer Boris Vian offered a suggestion at a conference given on erotic literature quite a long time ago. He claimed that what were really erotic were great works of fiction. I take it what he meant was that great fiction helps us to break out of the confines of the moralistic, sadistic, morbid, essentially anti-flesh images and ideas that we acquire from our "society" and that all our *genre* stuff, not just pornography, invariably reinforces in us endlessly. Again, we can disagree with his examples: *A Farewell To Arms, le Blé en Herbe.* But even if we accept such examples as "great literature," they do not break out of the *specifically* pornographic, whose matter for proselytizing is, after all, what we used to call *perversion.*

I think what I was looking for on those newsstands wasn't there. I was looking for something that hasn't yet come into existence, something that would break out of the *genre* and so be not only a true *sign*, but be able to give us the mind, the feelings, the soul we need to be able to face and understand the truth.

Jeff Weinstein

Pornography is to sex what art is to life; pornography is the art of sex. Like art it perpetuates whatever cage of values it finds itself in. Also, like art, it dangles the keys to that cage.

William T. Vollmann

1. Pornography has two components. The first is the aim of the pornographer, which may or may not be realized: to give pleasure. The second is the effect which it inevitably has on some people (who may or may not be distinct from the pornographer's intended group); it offends. Both these elements must exist for a work to be pornography, just as both sex and compensation must be present to constitute prostitution. A work which sets out only to offend cannot titillate, and so is not pornography. A work which titillates everybody cannot aspire to pornography's underdog status.

2. Pornography need not be sexual in content. The vicious mendacity of President Bush and his managers on the subject of the

Gulf War is a good example of political pornography. These statements gave many Americans pleasure and disgusted me. By my standards they were obscene.

3. Because pornography as I define it must produce opposing feelings in people, it's clear that any definition of pornography must be relative. (Examples of the problem: certain Inuit folktales which even ethnographers have bowdlerized: the painting *Dejeuner sur l'herbe*: *Mein Kampf*: the *Kama Sutra*.) Since the term is pejorative, it is those who are repelled by the work who will apply it, not those who are pleased. But since there must also be people who are pleased and since, being pleased, they will prefer the word "art" or "sexiness" or "patriotism" or "Holy Writ," it becomes clear that nothing is inherently pornographic.

4. What this means is that each of us has the right to define pornography as we see it. No one has the right to regulate it.

5. When I look at a human body, I make aesthetic judgments. I think most of us do. I see nothing wrong with looking at a cunt (on a real woman or in a photograph) and deciding whether it's pretty or not. I've never seen a girlie magazine or a self-styled dirty book that I thought shouldn't exist. I've seen plenty of "pornographic" products that don't interest me, and in general I prefer to get my sexual gratification from sexual acts, but live and let live.

6. When a "feminist" tells me that I have to say "woman" instead of "girl," I immediately say "girl." I think "girl" is a prettier word, and sometimes it's a more appropriate word, too. No one word can substitute for another word. The "feminists" seek to impoverish our language, and I won't stand for it. They are free to be offended or insulted by what I say, but I'm free to say it. Forbidden words are like guns. No one should be denied the possession of them a priori, and no one should use them carelessly or viciously. If they do happen to be abused (for instance, to yell at a passing woman, "Hey, cunt!" instead of using the word "cunt" in an innocuous context as I did in #5 above), the abuse can be condemned, but the word itself shouldn't be prohibited.

7. Well, what SHOULD the reaction be to "Hey, cunt!"? I don't know if there could ever be a general rule. It depends on how much you think you can do. (I've written about this in my "Epitaph for a Coward's Heart" in *Thirteen Stories and Thirteen Epitaphs*.) In any event, that's not pornography, that's hate speech. It almost certainly doesn't titillate anybody, even the man who yells.

8. And what should the reaction be to pornography as you define it? I'd say, if it doesn't appeal to you, leave it be; don't censor it. If you can admit that there might be another side to the issue, leave it be. If it's a work of words or images or plaster or whatever, not a real-life situation, not a "Hey, cunt!", then leave it be.

9. Are you a censor? Do you tell people not to say "girl"? Shame on you! If nothing offends you, you're a saint or you're psychotic. If a few things offend you, deal with them—fairly. If you're often offended by things, you're probably a self-righteous asshole and it's too bad you weren't censored yourself—by your mother in an abortion clinic.

10. A friend of mine who used to be a Nazi gave me his authentic swastika armband. I was touched that he would give me something with meaning to him, but embarrassed by my ownership of that particular object. I still have it, locked up where it can't hurt people. Many people wouldn't want a swastika armband in their house. But I'd have to say that it's no one else's business whether or not I have one in my house.

Raymond Federman

Pornographic: Anything (including of course sexual acts, images, texts, photos, cartoons, gestures, etc.) that insults, aggresses, exploits, manipulates human (*and even animal*) intelligence and sensitivity.

All television commercials are pornographic—especially beer commercials. Why can't a guy enjoy a good beer without having a lovely pair of thighs and a gorgeous ass (squeezed in a pair of short shorts) being paraded before his beer can?

All television commericals are obscene therefore pornographic because they take us for idiots in their efforts to peddle their shit on us. In other words, television commercials (but that's also true of all forms of advertising) insult, aggress, exploit, manipulate our intelligence.

Rikki Ducornet

The cosmologist V. S. Krishnamurti informs me that in the archipelago of Zim the *erotic* is defined as *im-ki-zaka*: any passionate, affectionate, stimulating and *transcendent* encounter with an equally ravenous member of one's own species (or an equivalent species) who is both autonomous and *of age*, and any images, word-games, *quapüti* (literally oral-tale-webbing) which inspire affection and tumescence.

Pornography extends *im-ki-zaka* into the bestial, comical, or grotesque (i.e., Paul Zam-Waba's notorious speaking banana-leaf codpieces). *Obscenity*—a thing they have little understanding of—brings *zargh* to mind (i.e., the Cosmic Abyss). *Zargh* (literally: bug shit) refers to the droppings of the quapütl beetle which are toxic, contain murderous thorns, and have the capacity to remind anyone who steps in them that he is mortal and that his days are therefore numbered.

Ronald Sukenick

Pornography is a subject about which I have nothing to say. I don't like it. What I like is erotic what you like is pornographic. That's the best definition I've heard.

Pornography is the shadows cast by our daytime identities. The shadows are distorted and often grotesque, depending probably on the degree of horniness generated by mounting hormonal pressure. In this shadow land odd metamorphoses occur. Staunch democrats become stern authoritarians or revel in enslavement. Addicts of freedom yearn for bondage. Chief executive officers beg to be spanked. Macho types don skirts and tutus. Feminists demand rape. Victims love their executioners. Masturbation usurps conjugation. And besides, it's naive to talk about daytime identities. These shadows are with us all the time, day or night, awaiting their cues. You might as well try to outlaw dreams. So what's the story?

Well, you can't censor shadows. The harder you try the more distortion you get in the shadows. Unless you plunge everything into total darkness, in which case we stop knowing anything about anything and ignorance reigns. And there's nothing more dangerous than ignorance, ignoring what's there until you crash into it. So in whose interest is it to ignore the erotic? Whoever is interested in cultivating ignorance. Ignorance of what? Ignorance of whatever illicit thing they are doing that won't bear the scrutiny of daylight. Whatever illicit thing they happen to get off on, whether it's hot money or cold manipulation or slipping into seedy motels with sleazy hookers. Or whatever they happen to find pornie when they're horny.

I'll tell you frankly, pornography disgusts me. Especially when I'm eating. Although I've known people who prefer it when they're eating. What I like is esthetically priapic stimulation shared by a sensually consensual partner or partners leading to heightened delight and loving pleasure, i.e., better fucking. But I put it in its most reputable light to make a point. It's dumb to keep talking about whether pornography is good or bad. It's there, it's always been there, it will always be there. It seems to be part of the human condition. For those of you who don't like the human condition, well, try some other condition, but don't impose it on me. Whether pornography represents childish regression or surplus repression or erotic delicatessen is beside any useful point. Pornography is power. Power that comes out of the mouth of a vagina or the head of a penis. How it's used depends strictly on the user. Hey, but let's not us good guys cede the territory and turn over the weapons. No, let's use them to the hilt. Here's to more pornography, better pornography, sexier pornography, wholesomer pornography, more constructive pornography, more loving pornography, more ecological pornography, more intelligent pornography, more learned pornography, pornography for peace, pornography for sex education, pornography against AIDS, pornography to save the dolphins, pornography against Jesse Helms, pornography against sexual harassment, pornography for bag ladies, pornography for decent housing, pornography for fair distribution of income, pornography for universal health care, pornography against racism, pornography against oppression, pornography against death. Come on all you fuckers out there. Let's get it on!

R. U. Sirius

The term pornography originally meant writing about prostitutes and their customers. So you have artifice (writing) and the commodification of sex. Proceed with all of your favorite postmodern leftist intellectual fascinations/demons: commodity culture, transference/advertising, representation, simulacra, ad infinitum.

Commodity culture is the original sin of pomo left intellectuals. Like original sin, opposition is pointless. All one can do is stand outside of it and feel superior, taking refuge in Bible or intellect.

I'd rather be a whore.

I hate to be banal, but I'm happy with the common usage. Film: *The Brat*. Magazines: *Hustler, Personages; Ebony Age*. Etcetera. I'm 101% pro porn!

John A. Williams

I am not sure what constitutes pornography these days. It seems to be everywhere, especially on television, and I mean, not MTV, but the commercials. I suppose by that statement I mean sexually suggestive. I know, however, that pornography isn't limited to that.

If this seems muddled, it is because I do believe that sexual practices should be private, and not imposed on those who have no predisposition toward witnessing or participating in pornographic acts. And that is my sense: that much of it is being imposed. I admit to the probability of being a reluctant witness to displays of porn, live or still, because I grew up at a time when the "hottest" thing going were the "dirty books" featuring comic strip characters. They bored me to tears.

Soft porn has been used to hustle products on television for a couple of decades. Cars, Coke, clothes, etc., etc. It will not go away. Few movies are made without the obligatory sex scene. These will not go away either. As to censorship, I favor it on the community, certainly not the Federal level, just as I would exclude certain groups now active in this country from coverage under the First Amendment, since their activities historically have violated laws that seemed cut in stone, but turned out instead to have been drawn in sand.

Camille Paglia

Michelangelo was a pornographer. Everything he did, including the great *Pieta*, the Virgin with the nude Christ in her lap, was pornography. If you don't respond to the sexuality in his work, you're not appreciating what he was doing. The only time people recognize something as porn is when it's bad art.

If you're a feminist theorist who says she can't deal with porn, then you're incompetent—get out. Because it is sexual reality, pornography is lust. At the same time, I feel that pornography should not push itself into all public areas. When someone comes out of a subway, they should not have to see ten naked women's bodies in full display at the newsstand.

The Madonna video ["Justify My Love"] was fabulous. I loved it. But I still felt it was bad for children to see, not because it would corrupt them but because it would jade them. Children should have difficulty getting their hands on something like that. It should be like, "Oh, Mommy and Daddy are gone: let's get it out of their closet!" Then if they see it, it's hot.

Nothing should ever be censored, not even violent porn. If you are for porn, you are for it all the way. How about snuff films, that big bugaboo of feminism? I'm dying to see one: where are they? Obviously, when we go to a mystery movie, we don't want to see an actual murder on the screen. The same thing with snuff films—we don't want to see a woman really being killed. But when I hear these feminists carrying on against snuff films, that makes me want to see one. If there's a taboo, I want to break it. Whenever I see a taboo arising, I think that the artist and the intellectual have the absolute obligation to shatter it. A truly avant-garde filmmaker today would make use of these films. (*San Francisco Examiner Image Magazine*)

Samuel R. Delany

Arguments over pornography—whether pro or con—seem most intelligent when the critic him- or herself admits to having been aroused (Auden; Jane Gallup on Sade). Those arguments become their most lunatic when the critic, unaroused by a given text, starts speculating on the results of possible arousal in other people—the "general community," "ordinary men and women," "children," etc.—and inveighs against the dangers that might result should someone from one of these groups—to whom clearly the critic does not belong—stumble over an arousing text on bookstore rack or library shelf. . . .

In a population which basically feels Sex is Bad—or at best a necessary evil—often sex will occur, whether within the bounds of marriage or outside it, only at those moments of extreme need, and then in a paroxysm of guilt, so that the sexual incident itself is likely to be infrequent, desperate, brutal, and brief—and satisfactory, if such a word can even be used for an act which, in their different ways, both "perpetrator" and "victim" probably come to dread—for only the most basal needs of the more aggressive partner.

Within such a populace, where this is the basic sexual model and where this is the sort of act arousal leads to, it's small wonder that situations of arousal in general—which include the pornographic—are thought by all concerned to be basically Bad Things.

Straight or gay, most men don't "approve" of this sort of sex any more than straight or gay women—even those among all four groups who are sure that this is the only sort of sex there really is. And though probably not the majority any more, sadly there are still many of those. . . .

This brings us to the other topic in this discussion: censorship. At various times I've experienced the political niggling and pussyfooting in the name of the commercial that is how a good deal of real censorship is exercised in this country (the editor who rejected a 1967 novel of mine not because he was bothered by the fact that my main character was black but because he was sure his readers would be—

readers who, incidentally, once the book was published a year on, kept the book in print for the next twenty-five years; the print run on a 1985 book, third in a series, slashed in half because the topic was AIDS; and the manuscript of the fourth book in the series returned to me by the same publisher, unread). But I would not think to use a term like "censorship" for the treatment of, say, *Hogg*—a "serious" pornographic novel I finished in 1973 and which has been to a number of publishers, legitimate and pornographic, all of whom have refused it. An editor's rejecting a book because he or she didn't like it—whether the dislike was aesthetic, political, or sexual—doesn't, in a free economy, fulfill my criteria for censorship. Censorship—for me—requires that someone become deeply involved in deciding whether *other* people will be offended, or dislike it, or be outraged by a work—usually to the point of wholly suppressing his or her own response. (The editor who slashed my print run had gone out of his way, three months before, to tell me that the book was among the most powerful he had ever read in his life, and had left him, in his own words, dazed—however hyperbolic the praise may have been.) It's that repression of the self which creates the dangerous and deleterious field of projections, out of control and wholly away from any possibility of pursuing real profit or even common sense. In this country, the commercial terror of the experimental and the controversial has the same psychologcal structure—and finally much the same effect—as the hardcore censorship we are so ready to condemn when it happens abroad.

  Having said that, I think that in sexual terms, those people who share my basic context for arousal are precisely those who are inclined to say: let other people do with they want, whether it involves pornography or perversion or whatever—as long as no one is hurt or made miserable. We feel this way because we are under the impression that such a context is pretty much what characterizes the context of pleasure for everyone. Similarly, I suspect that those people for whom a significant proportion of situations of arousal have lead them to pain, distress, guilt, and unhappiness are the people who are likely to question seriously the advisability of such a liberal attitude toward the arousal of others. But that—as I said—is a question of context, and it may never be resolved until the context itself is interrogated, articulated, and understood in its own right.

By such lights, the two sections of "*Citre et Trans*" published in this issue do not seem to me pornographic at all. Their writing did not arouse me. Nor did I intend them to arouse anyone else. If, however, out of context they turn someone else on, and he or she wishes to do the revisionary work of the sort described at the end of the piece to put them to masturbatory use, I have no objection. (Rarely does anyone else's narrative match your own sexual fantasy; even with works intended as pornographic, to put them to your own use always requires readerly input and imaginary revison!) Some people may even be aroused by them because they appear here in the context of a Special Issue devoted to Pornography and Censorship: the pornographic is as much an "aura"—and is as contagious—as Walter Benjamin's notion of the aesthetic.

For many years, in matters of art (literary and paraliterary), I've called myself a First Amendment Fundamentalist. But I have no illusions that the often stated notion, "Freedom of Speech is the Bedrock on which Our Country is Founded," is more than a wildly inaccurate metaphor. Freedom of Speech exists primarily as a healthy *symptom*—specifically a symptom of a healthy and stable societal infrastructure. That is why, as soon as society becomes infrastructurally unstable, Freedom of Speech is, so tragically, one of the first freedoms abridged or snatched away. That is why, as a positive symptom for a society's health, Freedom of Speech is to be so jealously guarded and so carefully watched over and nurtured, even in its most extreme cases. The places where one cannot sustain it, despite great efforts, are precisely the places where the society has become radically and dangerously infrastructurally weak.

I think it is terribly important to have a genre—or genre-set—in which it is possible to say *anything*: true, untrue, or at any level of fantasy, metaphor, violence, or simple outrageousness. And I would rather such a genre-set be the genre-set of art than that it be the associated texts of religion, say (consider the hell-fire Sermon in Chapter III of *A Portrait of the Artist as a Young Man* as an example of a religious genre repeatedly presented to young children from the 19th century on, if you want an example of what I consider immoral religious license), or those that comprise journalism (consider the allegations of supernatural happenings and the like that are the hallmark of the "popular" tabloid press, *The National Enquirer, The Sun, The Star*). But there are social forces a-plenty—and often the same forces that would take away the Freedom of Speech we vouchsafe for the arts—that, as they would deny that freedom *to* the arts, would redistribute it to religion and reportage—genres whose relation to that troublesome concept "truth" I, at any rate, am fairly glad to see a bit more heavily scrutinized at the more respected levels than, certainly, they are on the lowest and least sophisticated planes. It is not only the freedom to suppress what others say that is wanted, but the freedom to lie as well when necessary—because such lies are assumed somehow to be for "everyone's good."

But we cannot forget those planes. They are always there to grow, to take over, and to swamp what I am perfectly content to call more responsible attitudes in religious and reportorial practices.

Art seems the best genre-set in which to allow total freedom of expression (the full range, as Kenneth Koch put it, of "wishes, lies, and dreams") *because* that genre-set is the symbol making engine for the culture.

If artists who wish majorly to criticize or even shame the country for national acts they consider immoral are not allowed to set up installations in which American flags are burnt or otherwise desecrated, then it is precisely the resonance, significance, and luminescence to the flag waving high for the country's palpable accomplishment which is reduced by the proscription. (A symbol that is only allowed to function in one context and that restricted to an uplifting one invariably becomes trite—if not kitsch.) And necessary limitations on the esthetic presentation of what the body may undergo, either in pleasure or in suffering, immediately and *a priori* restricts what the mind is allowed to contemplate: for nothing encourages the practice of political torture and sabotages the pursuit of happiness more than blanket restrictions on speaking in precise, articulate, and graphic terms about either.

Fanny Howe

The Discreet Porn of the Bourgeoisie. Pornography is a substitute for political consciousness when it is used in commercial films to both stimulate and pacify the audience. Erotic footage between two privileged people whom the audience has only just met is extra footage. It is "beautified" as a class action against "trash" porn. It is elitist sex. After all, is it aesthetically necessary to include erotic film footage in most movies? Intercourse generally contributes nothing to the unfolding of narrative. A glance, a quick kiss, a pinch—these would indicate more in the way of intention than the sounds of pleasure do. Why therefore is erotic film footage necessary to so many Western filmmakers? It keeps teenagers—the ultimate rabble—out of the theaters, and it makes each member of the audience feel vaguely disturbed, empty, and impotent. . . . all those things you're supposed to feel after "trash" porn, masturbation, and Presidential addresses.

Tuli Kupferberg

1. I would prefer to glide by the pornography questions and, because "pornography" (almost by definition) implies the right to censor, to jump immediately to the question of censorship itself.

2. We *all* censor (or edit) including self-censor. Every act of editing is an act of censorship. The only questions are who or what and why and how much? I discovered this amazingly (after considering myself a 100% free speecher) one fall afternoon when I found myself in a rage tearing down cigarette advertising posters on the hoarding of an empty lot on the street where I walked my pre-teen kids to school. I considered these an immediate death threat to my children.

3. Concealment, camouflage, and "lies" *are* an individual and species life preserving strategy (behavior). Would you 100% truth advocates refuse to lie (or tell the truth you knew) when Nazis asked you if there were Jews hiding in your neighborhood, and where were

they hiding? And Blake said: "The truth that's told with ill intent beats all lies man can invent." This is not an argument for deceit or repression. We should stretch our tolerance and open-mindedness as far as possible because these of course *are* life enhancing, but absolutism here is *absolutely* wrong! and my rough (and pacifist) measure is: what immediate (and future) physical or mental harm will the offending material do, and likewise what will be the negative effect of its repression?

4. I find myself finding little or no excuse for repression of 99.9999% of political and sexual material. The only things I hate that come to mind are immediate invitations to violence (including armed services, CIA etc. ads), and in the marketplace, the advertising of physically harmful and/or deceitful products.

5. As disgusting or stupid as many (in America *most*) displays of politics, "sex," and product advertising may be, I would prefer to answer with counter-displays (ideally side by side): Equal time, equal money, equal access. After all, isn't this the "Land of Opportunity"?!

Kathy Acker

I think that the word *pornography* is pornographic. If we all recognized that all is holy. . .

Edith Wharton

from Beatrice Palmato

The outline and the brief fragment of the story "Beatrice Palmato," here presented, are in the Beinecke Library of Yale University, along with a mass of other unfinished stories and novels. They seem to have been written some time in 1935. The name "Beatrice Palmato" appears in a notebook as early as about 1920, but it stands alone on an otherwise blank page, between fairly detailed outlines of novels (including *The Age of Innocence*) that Edith Wharton did in fact write and stories she did not go on to compose. It may well be that the ingredients of "Beatrice Palmato"—including those that went into that choice of name, as I have suggested in Chapter Twenty-seven,—were in Edith Wharton's mind by 1920. But it remains probable that she was not ready to write it for another fifteen years. The manuscripts show that she revised as meticulously and felicitously in these cases as in all others.

She could not conceivably have intended the fragment to be part of "Beatrice Palmato," had the story ever been sent to press. It does not really accord with the outline (which planned to *conceal* the incest until the last page), and in any event, no respectable magazine in the world would have published it. This makes it only the more intriguing that the fragment got written. Cynthia Griffin Wolff—a psychologist and a professor of literature who is well launched on a psychologically oriented study of Edith Wharton's fiction—has speculated persuasively, in conversation, about the matter. She suggests that Edith Wharton wrote the fragment in order to articulate fully to herself the precise nature, feeling, and history of the incestuous experience which was to lie behind and to color the actual narrative. Mrs. Wolff remarks that it was as though Joseph Conrad had written out a private account, for his own imaginative purposes, of "the horror," that unspecified phenomenon that overwhelms Kurtz in *The Heart of Darkness*.

One possible literary source of the fragment is Alfred de Musset's classic work of pornography, *Gamiani*, written in the early nineteenth century. There is a likelihood that Edith Wharton knew this novel, which was circulated in a private edition in 1926. Its central figure was based at a certain remove upon her lifelong favorite, Musset's mistress George Sand. Morton Fullerton, it may be recalled, meant it as a high compliment when he said that Edith Wharton in love displayed the reckless ardor of a George Sand.

Outline of "Beatrice Palmato"

Beatrice Palmato is the daughter of a rich half-Levantine, half-Portuguese banker living in London, and of his English wife. Palmato, who is very handsome, cultivated and accomplished, has inherited his father's banking and brokering business, but, while leaving his fortune in the business, leads the life of a rich and cultivated man of leisure. He has an agreeable artistic-literary house in London, and a place near Brighton. The wife is handsome, shy, silent, but agreeable. There are two daughters and a son, the youngest. The eldest, Isa, who looks like her mother, commits suicide in mysterious circumstances at seventeen, a few months after returning from the French convent in which she has been educated. The mother has a bad nervous break-down, and is ordered away by the doctors, who forbid her to take little Beatrice (aged 12) with her. After a vain struggle, she leaves the child in the country with an old governess who has brought her up, and whom she can completely trust. The governess is ill, and is obliged to leave, and Beatrice remains in the country with her father. He looks for another governess, but cannot find one to suit him, and during a whole winter takes charge of Beatrice's education. She is a musical and artistic child, full of intellectual curiosity, and at the same time very tender and emotional: a combination of both parents. The boy, whom Mrs. Palmato adores, and whom her husband has never cared for, is a sturdy sensitive English lad. He is at school, and spends his holidays with his tutor. Mrs. Palmato is still abroad, in a sanitorium. The following autumn (after a year's absence) she comes home. At first she seems better, and they return to London, and see a few friends. Beatrice remains with them, as neither parent can bear to be separated from her. They find a charming young governess, and all seems well.

Then suddenly Mrs. Palmato has another nervous breakdown, and grows quite mad. She tries to kill her husband, has to be shut up, and dies in an insane asylum a few months later. The boy is left at school, and Mr. Palmato, utterly shattered, leaves on a long journey with Beatrice and a new maid, whom he engages for her in Paris. After six months he returns, and re-engages the same governess. Eighteen months after his wife's death he marries the governess, who is a young girl of a good family, good-looking and agreeable, and to whom Beatrice is devoted.

The intimacy between father and daughter continues to be very close, but at 18 Beatrice meets a young man of good family, a good-looking rather simple-minded country squire with a large property and no artistic or intellectual tastes, who falls deeply in love with her.

She marries him, to every one's surprise, and they live entirely in the country. For some time she does not see her father or the latter's wife; then she and her husband go up to town to stay for a fortnight with the Palmatos, and after that they see each other, though at rather long intervals. Beatrice seems to her friends changed, depressed, overclouded. Her animation and brilliancy have vanished, and she gives up all her artistic interests, and appears to absorb herself in her husband's country tastes. The Palmato group of friends all deplore her having married such a dull man, but admit that he is very kind to her and that she seems happy. Once her father takes her with him on a short trip to Paris, where he goes to buy a picture or some tapestries for his collection, and she comes back brilliant, febrile and restless; but soon settles down again. After 2 1/2 years of marriage she has a boy, and the year after a little girl; and with the birth of her children her attachment to her husband increases, and she seems to her friends perfectly happy. About the time of the birth of the second child, Palmato dies suddenly.

The boy is like his father, the little girl exquisite, gay, original, brilliant, like her mother. The father loves both children, but adores the little girl; and as the latter grows to be five or six years old Beatrice begins to manifest a morbid jealousy of her husband's affection for this child. The household has been so harmonious hitherto that the husband himself cannot understand this state of mind; but he humours his wife, tries to conceal his fondness for his little daughter, and wonders whether his wife is growing "queer" like her mother.

One day the husband has been away for a week. He returns sooner than was expected, comes in and finds the little girl alone in the drawing-room. She utters a cry of joy, and he clasps her in his arms and kisses her. She has put her little arms around his neck, and is hugging him tightly when Beatrice comes in. She stops on the threshold, screams out: "Don't kiss my child. Put her down! How dare you kiss her?" and snatches the little girl from his arms.

Husband and wife stand staring at each other. As the husband looks at her, many mysterious things in their married life—the sense of some hidden power controlling her, and perpetually coming between them, and of some strange initiation, some profound moral perversion of which he had always been afraid to face the thought—all these things become suddenly clear to him, lit up in a glare of horror.

He looks at her with his honest eyes, and says: "Why shouldn't I kiss my child?" and she gives him back a look in which terror, humiliation, remorseful tenderness, and the awful realization of what she has unwittingly betrayed, mingle in one supreme appeal and avowal.

She puts the little girl down, flies from the room, and hurries upstairs. When he follows her, he hears a pistol-shot and finds her lying dead on the floor of her bedroom.

People say: "Her mother was insane, her sister tried to kill herself; it was a very unfortunate marriage."

But the brother, Jack Palmato, who has become a wise, level-headed young man, a great friend of Beatrice's husband, comes down on hearing of his sister's death, and he and the husband have a long talk together—about Mr. Palmato.

The End.

Fragment of "Beatrice Palmato"

"I have been, you see," he added, "so perfectly patient—"

The room was warm, and softly lit by one or two pink-shaded lamps. A little fire sparkled on the hearth, and a lustrous black bear-skin rug, on which a few purple velvet cushions had been flung, was spread out before it.

"And now, darling," Mr. Palmato said, drawing her to the deep divan, "let me show you what only you and I have the right to show each other." He caught her wrists as he spoke, and looking straight into her eyes, repeated in a penetrating whisper: "Only you and I." But his touch had never been tenderer. Already she felt every fibre vibrating under it, as of old, only now with the more passionate eagerness bred of privation, and of the dull misery of her marriage. She let herself sink backward among the pillows, and already Mr. Palmato was on his knees at her side, his face close to hers. Again her burning lips were parted by his tongue, and she felt it insinuate itself between her teeth, and plunge into the depths of her mouth in a long searching caress, while at the same moment his hands softly parted the thin folds of her wrapper.

One by one they gained her bosom, and she felt her two breasts pointing up to them, the nipples hard as coral, but sensitive as lips to his approaching touch. And now his warm palms were holding each breast as in a cup, clasping it, modelling it, softly kneading it, as he whispered to her, "like the bread of the angels."

An instant more, and his tongue had left her fainting mouth, and was twisting like a soft pink snake about each breast in turn, passing from one to the other till his lips closed hard on the nipples, sucking them with a tender gluttony.

Then suddenly he drew back her wrapper entirely, whispered: "I want you all, so that my eyes can see all that my lips can't cover," and in a moment she was free, lying before him in her fresh young nakedness, and feeling that indeed his eyes were covering it with fiery kisses. But Mr. Palmato was never idle, and while this sensation flashed through her one of his arms had slipped under her back and wound itself around her so that his hand again enclosed her left breast. At the same moment the other hand softly separated her legs, and began to slip up the old path it had so often travelled in darkness. But now it was light, she was uncovered, and looking downward, beyond his dark silver-sprinkled head, she could see her own parted knees and out-stretched ankles and feet. Suddenly she remembered Austin's rough advances, and shuddered.

The mounting hand paused, the dark head was instantly raised. "What is it, my own?"

"I was—remembering—last week—" she faltered, below her breath.

"Yes, darling. That experience is a cruel one—but it has to come once in all women's lives. Now we shall reap its fruit."

But she hardly heard him, for the old swooning sweetness was creeping over her. As his hand stole higher she felt the secret bud of her body swelling, yearning, quivering hotly to burst into bloom. Ah, here was his subtle fore-finger pressing it, forcing its tight petals softly apart, and laying on their sensitive edges a circular touch so soft and yet so fiery that already lightnings of heat shot from that palpitating centre all over her surrendered body, to the tips of her fingers, and the ends of her loosened hair.

The sensation was so exquisite that she could have asked to have it indefinitely prolonged; but suddenly his head bent lower, and with a deeper thrill she felt his lips pressed upon that quivering invisible bud, and then the delicate firm thrust of his tongue, so full and yet so infinitely subtle, pressing apart the close petals, and forcing itself in deeper and deeper through the passage that glowed and seemed to become illuminated at its approach . . .

"Ah—"she gasped, pressing her hands against her sharp nipples, and flinging her legs apart.

Instantly one of her hands was caught, and while Mr. Palmato, rising, bent over her, his lips on hers again, she felt his firm fingers pressing into her hand that strong fiery muscle that they used, in their old joke, to call his third hand.

"My little girl," he breathed, sinking down beside her, his muscular trunk bare, and the third hand quivering and thrusting upward between them, a drop of moisture pearling at its tip.

She instantly understood the reminder that his words conveyed, letting herself downwards along the divan till her head was in a line with his middle she flung herself upon the swelling member, and began to caress it insinuatingly with her tongue. It was the first time she had ever seen it actually exposed to her eyes, and her heart swelled excitedly: to have her touch confirmed by sight enriched the sensation that was communicating itself through her ardent twisting tongue. With panting breath she wound her caress deeper and deeper into the thick firm folds, till at length the member, thrusting her lips open, held her gasping, as if at its mercy; then, in a trice, it was withdrawn, her knees were pressed apart, and she saw it before her, above her, like a crimson flash, and at last, sinking backward into new abysses of bliss, felt it descend on her, press upon the secret gates, and plunge into the deepest depths of her thirsting body . . .

"Was it . . . like this . . . last week?" he whispered.

Special thanks to Yale Collection of American Literature, Beinecke Rare Book and Manuscript Library, Yale University

Marc Cholodenko

from The Story of Vivant Lanon

The next day, when Frederic was taking his nap, I was dozing in a chaise-longue on the balcony underneath the awning when she came looking for me. She sat down at the end of the chair next to my feet and put her hands between her closed knees. She bent towards me and said, practically in a whisper: "Well, Vivant, it seems you didn't give complete satisfaction yesterday?"

I responded, in a fairly brutal manner: "I'm not a toy, or a tool either."

What I wanted to tell her next, I would never have had the courage to say at any length, I only managed to find these few words, which I was barely able to get out, with a lump in my throat: "I belong to you."

She knew exactly what they meant, but she pretended to pass them off frivolously, when she immediately replied: "You belong to me? How sweet that is, my little Vivant."

She was tapping my foot.

"Well then, if you belong to me, I can lend you out, can't I? Quick, quick, go put our little friend in and meet me in the rotunda."

Despite my excitement, getting it in hurt me horribly. The pain subsided though once it was all the way up. I buttoned my pants again. I was forced to walk with my legs spread, bent forward. It came down a little with each step, making a bulge at the bottom of my pants, so I had to keep tucking it in behind my balls.

When I came in sight of the rotunda, I forced myself to walk as normally as I could. It was a kind of little clearing in a clump of laurel trees which bordered the grass in front of the house. Since there was only one armchair, the two girls were sitting on the grass. I noticed that Elizabeth was holding a laurel branch with the leaves stripped off. I stayed at the edge of the clearing. She made a gesture towards me.

"Come here, Vivant. Get on your knees, in front of me."

I knelt down as close as possible to her, my knees practically between her feet. I was afraid she would move further back, but she didn't do any such thing. In fact, she actually bent towards me, to whisper to me, feigning an exaggerated terror: "Did you see what's in store for you?" Then she added, out loud, in a quick, jaunty voice: "Come on, come on, get your pants down and put your little hands here." As she said it, she lightly tapped her thighs. My happiness was as violent as it was unexpected. Meanwhile, the girls had gotten up and were probably standing behind me. I heard their exclamations of surprise—"Oh!"—when I uncovered myself, and then giggles.

Finally I felt her firmness, her softness, her heat underneath the fabric of her pants. She took me by the wrists and said, with mock severity: "Let us proceed, Mesdemoiselles, this is a serious business."

Which did, at least, have the effect of calming down their laughter.

"But before we begin," she added, "I would like Vivant to say why he is here."

"Because you ordered me to be here," I answered.

"No, no. You are here to be punished. Punished because. . ."

". . ."

"Because. . . you didn't. . ."

"Get an erection," I replied.

"Obey, would be a better way of putting it, I think. And so you're going to have to make an act of contrition and vow that you will not disobey again."

The whole time I was there in front of her, my eyes hadn't once left hers, which were going back and forth between the girls and me.

"I will never disobey you again," I said. "Never again."

"There's some good news. Did you hear him, girls? Well, we'll certainly know how to take advantage of it. Begin, Elizabeth."

They were still giggling and whispering, in their own language. I felt the dildo very gently sliding out and I supposed that that was what they found amusing. They fell quiet, when Elizabeth began to strike.

The blows were very soft, but I immediately made a show of pain, which allowed me to press against her thighs. She continued to hold my wrists, without squeezing them. Her eyes kept going from the girls to me.

"Does that turn you on, Elizabeth?" she said, before long.

After a certain silence, I heard a feeble: "*Oui.*"

"Well then, take advantage of it and give him a *real* whipping. And what about you, Harriet, does that turn you on?"

The "oui" was immediate and a lot clearer.

"Well then, show me that it does, that it really does."

The blows began to fall harder, scattered and irregular, they landed on my buttocks, on the small of my back, on the dildo, which then lurched up into my belly. I heard Elizabeth's panting, Harriet's sighs. The pain increased, but I was kneading her legs, I had the warmth of her hands on mine and, more than anything else, her eyes, which took my breath away a lot more than the whip did. That I continued to feel pleasure under the lashes must have annoyed Elizabeth, or just astonished her, because she stopped hitting me to say:

"Madame, he's still. . . still hard!"

"I know," she replied, looking at her. "That's why you have to keep at it. Continue."

I don't know what she meant by that, whether it was that they had to increase my pleasure or put an end to it, but the fact that she saw my desire gave me a courage I would never have had otherwise. I asked: "Does that mean. . . does that mean I can. . . ?"

I didn't have to say any more. She nodded in the affirmative and let go of my right hand.

She didn't take her eyes off mine. I was weeping, I was groaning, I even cried out a few times. I gave vent to my pleasure with so little constraint that the outward signs of it could have passed for signs of pain. Finally she said: "Enough." And the blows stopped at the same moment I gushed forth, with a howl.

That evening she and the two girls went out and came back with another car. They went to the tower. I stayed in my bed. I had promised never to disobey her again. Besides, I didn't feel any need to go there.

The next evening, we all dined together. Afterwards, she and I went up to put Frederic to bed. As we were leaving his room, she said to me: "Come with me." Passing into the parlor, she said to the girls: "We're on our way." I entered her bedroom behind her. Her perfume was everywhere. We went into the bathroom.

"Sit down there," she said, rapping the edge of the bathtub. "I'm going to make you up."

She painted me for a long while, carefully, my eyelids, my lashes, my cheeks, my cheekbones, my lips. Never had her face been so close to mine. She put out her tongue a little, absorbed in her work. Her breath caressed my face. In the meantime, she explained that she wanted to take advantage of the presence of the girls—who had to leave the next day—to put together a photo-novel, of which I would be the hero—or heroine, rather. She put the finishing touch on her work by making me a sort of little pony-tail. My hair was just long enough to hold the rubber-band, which she wrapped with a ribbon of pink silk. When she finished, she brought me to the mirror.

"Look how beautiful you are."

And it was true, I really was beautiful.

She opened the door of the parlor a crack to say: "Get ready, girls, we're coming." And then we went down to their room.

The series of photos that she took that night was entitled: *Guests of Honor* or, alternatively, *Mischievous Guests*.

I was entering the room, dressed only in a white, pleated apron which covered me from my navel to the middle of my thighs. I was carrying a tray.

I was dropping the tray, putting my hands on my cheeks, my mouth opened in an expression of terrified amazement.

The girls, lying naked on the bed, side by side, were throwing the sheet back, to reveal the enormous dildos attached to their waists and extending from their crotches to just under their breasts.

I had one hand on the door-knob, Elizabeth was holding me by the other.

I was on my knees, my hands joined in front of them, while they were darting their dildos out at my face and threatening me, their fists raised over their heads.

Still on my knees, I was taking Harriet's cock in my right hand, covering my eyes with my left.

I was holding Harriet's cock with both hands. I was sticking my tongue out as far as it would go, the tip grazing the end of the dildo, my eyes closed.

I was lying on the bed, Elizabeth and Harriet were kneeling on each side of my head. I was sucking Elizabeth's cock and stroking Harriet's. With an arm under each of my knees, they were holding up my thighs. Their hands met between my legs at the spot where a woman has her sex, fingers interlaced. Their bent-in knuckles gave the impression that they were penetrating me.

I was on my knees on the floor. While I was sucking Elizabeth, who was standing in front of me, Harriet was taking me from the rear.

They had changed places. So I wouldn't have to go through two separate penetrations, Harriet had left the dildo she was wearing in my rear-end and strapped on Elizabeth's.

Sitting on the floor between the two of them—who were standing up—I was putting the tips of the two cocks in my mouth.

For the last photo, since they were supposed to come on my face at the same time, they had need of my sperm. She hit on the idea of having me come in the mouth of whichever one I preferred, which was Elizabeth, who immediately spit it back on my face, so that as little saliva as possible would mix in with it.

I was lying on the floor. I had a cock in each hand, right next to my face. My eyes half-open in mock ecstasy, I was licking off my lips the sperm that had dripped down my forehead and cheeks, taking part of the make-up with it.

She especially wanted to end the series with a big close-up of my face alone, with this same expression on it. She kneeled on my chest to take it, and my cock, which had gotten hard again, caught the edge of her skirt as she got into position.

We had to take the photo twice because, the first time, just as she was snapping the shutter, I had opened my eyes to look at her.

translated by John Satriano

*Lisa Duggan, Nan D. Hunter,
Carole S. Vance*

False Promises: Feminist Antipornography Legislation

On February 24, 1986, the U. S. Supreme Court ruled that the Indianapolis version of the anti-pornography ordinance was unconstitutional. Although this ruling settles the legal question of the ordinance's validity, the political debate on the wisdom of invoking state power to suppress sexual materials continues. That debate, which will be with us for many years to come, encompasses many of the same points of disagreement—over the social meanings of language and imagery and the political risks to women of protectionist strategy—which we analyze in this article.

In the United States, after two decades of increasing community tolerance for dissenting or disturbing sexual or political materials, there is now growing momentum for retrenchment. In an atmosphere of increased conservatism, evidenced by a wave of book banning and anti-gay harassment, support for new repressive legislation of various kinds—from an Oklahoma law forbidding schoolteachers from advocating homosexuality to new antipornography laws passed in Minneapolis and Indianapolis—is growing.

The antipornography laws have mixed roots of support, however. Though they are popular with the conservative constituencies that traditionally favor legal restrictions on sexual expression of all kinds, they were drafted and are endorsed by antipornography feminists who oppose traditional obscenity and censorship laws. The model law of this type, which is now being widely copied, was drawn up in the politically progressive city of Minneapolis by two radical feminists, author Andrea Dworkin and attorney Catharine MacKinnon. It was passed by the city council there, but vetoed by the mayor. A similar law was passed in Indianapolis, but later declared unconstitutional in federal court. The city is appealing that ruling to the Supreme Court. Other versions of the legislation have been considered, and either discarded or defeated, in several other cities including Suffolk County, New York, Madison, Wisconsin, Los Angeles County, California, and Cambridge, Massachusetts. Pennsylvania Senator Arlen Specter has introduced legislation modeled on parts of the Dworkin-MacKinnon bill in Congress, and the Reagan-initiated Attorney General's Commission on Pornography is weighing its merits as a censorship strategy.

Dworkin, MacKinnon, and their feminist supporters believe that the new antipornography laws are not censorship laws. They also claim that the legislative effort behind them is based on feminist support. Both of these claims are dubious at best. Though the new laws are civil laws that allow individuals to sue the makers, sellers, distributors, or exhibitors of pornography, and not criminal laws leading to arrest and imprisonment, their censoring impact would be substantially as severe as criminal obscenity laws. Materials could be removed from public availability by court injunction, and publishers and booksellers could be subject to potentially endless legal harassment. Passage of the laws was therefore achieved with the support of right-wing elements who expect the new laws to accomplish what censorship efforts are meant to accomplish. Ironically, many antifeminist conservatives backed these laws, while many feminists opposed them. In Indianapolis, the law was supported by extreme right-wing religious fundamentalists, including members of the Moral Majority, while there was *no* local feminist support. In other cities, traditional procensorship forces have expressed interest in the new approach to banning sexually explicit materials. Meanwhile, anticensorship feminists have become alarmed at these new developments and are seeking to galvanize feminist opposition to the new antipornography legislative strategy pioneered in Minneapolis.

One is tempted to ask in astonishment, how can this be happening? How can feminists be entrusting the patriarchal state with the task of legally distinguishing between permissible and impermissible sexual images? But in fact this new development is not as surprising as it at first seems. Pornography has come to be seen as a central cause of women's oppression by a significant number of feminists. Some even argue that pornography is the root of virtually all forms of exploitation and discrimination against women. It is a short step from such a belief to the conviction that laws against pornography can end the inequality of the sexes. But this analysis takes feminists very close—indeed far too close—to measures that will ultimately support conservative, anti-sex, procensorship forces in American society, for it is with these forces that women have forged alliances in passing such legislation.

The first feminist-inspired antipornography law was passed in Minneapolis in 1983. Local legislators had been frustrated when their zoning restrictions on porn shops were struck down in the courts. Public hearings were held to discuss a new zoning ordinance. The Neighborhood Pornography Task Force of South and South Central Minneapolis invited Andrea Dworkin and Catharine MacKinnon, who were teaching a course on pornography at the University of Minnesota, to testify. They proposed an alternative that, they claimed, would completely eliminate, rather than merely regulate, pornography. They suggested that pornography be defined as a form of sex discrimination, and that an amendment to the city's civil rights law be passed to proscribe it. City officials hired Dworkin and MacKinnon to develop their new approach and to organize another series of public hearings.

The initial debate over the legislation in Minneapolis was intense, and opinion was divided within nearly every political grouping. In contrast, the public hearings held before the city council were tightly controlled and carefully orchestrated; speakers invited by Dworkin and MacKinnon—sexual abuse victims, counselors, educators, and social scientists—testified about the harm pornography does women. (Dworkin and MacKinnon's agenda was the compilation of a legislative record that would help the law stand up to its inevitable court challenges.) The legislation passed, supported by antipornography feminists, neighborhood groups concerned about the effects of porn shops on residential areas, and conservatives opposed to the availability of sexually explicit materials for "moral" reasons.

In Indianapolis, the alignment of forces was different. For the previous two years, conservative antipornography groups had grown in strength and public visibility, but they had been frustrated in their efforts. The police department could not convert its obscenity arrests into convictions; the city's zoning law was also tied up in court challenges. Then Mayor William Hudnut III, a Republican and a Presbyterian minister, learned of the Minneapolis law. Mayor Hudnut thought Minneapolis's approach to restricting pornography might be the solution to the Indianapolis problems. Beulah Coughenour, a conservative Republican stop-ERA activist, was recruited to sponsor the legislation in the city-county council.

Coughenour engaged MacKinnon as consultant to the city—Dworkin was not hired, but then, Dworkin's passionate radical feminist rhetoric would not have gone over well in Indianapolis. MacKinnon worked with the Indianapolis city prosecutor (a well-known anti-vice zealot), the city's legal department, and Coughenour on the legislation.

The law received the support of neighborhood groups, the Citizens for Decency, and the Coalition for a Clean Community. There were no crowds of feminist supporters—in fact, there were no feminist supporters at all. The only feminists to make public statements opposed the legislation, which was nevertheless passed in a council meeting packed with 300 religious fundamentalists. All 24 Republicans voted for its passage; all five Democrats opposed it to no avail.

A group of publishers and booksellers challenged the law in Federal District Court, where they won the first round. This initial decision was then upheld by the Federal Appeals Court. The city is appealing again to the Supreme Court, though it may take a year or two for a final decision to be reached.

In the meantime, other versions of the Dworkin-MacKinnon bill have appeared. A version of the law introduced in Suffolk County on Long Island in New York emphasized its conservative potential—pornography was said to cause "sodomy" and "disruption" of the family unit, in addition to rape, incest, exploitation, and other acts "inimical to the public good." In Suffolk, the law was put forward by a conservative, anti-ERA male legislator who wishes to "restore ladies to what they used to be." The Suffolk County bill clearly illustrates the repressive anti-feminist potential of the new antipornography legislation.

Versions of the bill, nearer to the original intent of the authors, have been considered in Madison, Los Angeles, and Cambridge. In these cities, feminist opposition to antipornography ordinances was organized, and Feminist Anti-Censorship Taskforce groups helped to defeat the idea. In Madison, the measure was not introduced after a FACT press conference wiped out support for an ordinance on the Dane County Board of Supervisors. In Los Angeles, FACT efforts helped defeat a measure before the County Board of Supervisors, though the vote was close and individual supervisors responded little to feminist opinion on either side. In Cambridge, voters defeated the measure after a heated referendum campaign in which feminists dominated both sides of the debate.

At present, Edwin Meese's Commission on Pornography is preparing a report on new ways to control pornography. The Commission is controlled by moral conservatives, and it is expected to issue repressive recommendations designed to help legislators and courts suppress sexual images. The Commission is considering the "feminist" antipornography arguments and legislation. It is likely to try to use what it can, while discarding those aspects of the feminist approach which conflict with a conservative outlook. The Meese Commission's report may very well show how far the right-wing will go in coopting feminist language and laws in the service of its own repressive agenda.

Yet it is true that some of the laws hve been proposed and supported by antipornography feminists. This is therefore a critical moment in the feminist debate over sexual politics. As anticensorship feminists work to develop alternatives to antipornography campaigns, we also need to examine carefully the new laws and expose their underlying assumptions. We need to know why these laws, for all their apparent feminist rhetoric, actually appeal to conservative antifeminist forces, and why feminists should be preparing to move in a different direction.

Definitions: The Central Flaw

The antipornography ordinances passed in Minneapolis and Indianapolis were framed as amendments to municipal civil rights laws. They provide for complaints to be filed against pornography in the same manner that complaints are filed against employment discrimination. If enforced, the laws would make illegal public or private availability (except in libraries) of any materials deemed pornographic.

Such material could be the object of a lawsuit on several grounds. The ordinance would penalize four kinds of behavior associated with pornography: its production, sale, exhibition, or distribution ("trafficking"); coercion into pornographic performance; forcing pornography on a person; and assault or physical attack due to pornography.

Under this law, a woman "acting as a woman against the subordination of women" could file a complaint; men could also file complaints if they could "prove injury in the same way that a woman is injured." The procedural steps in the various versions differ, but they generally allow the complainant either to file an administrative complaint with the city's equal opportunity commission, or to file a lawsuit directly in court. If the local commission found the law had been violated, it would file a lawsuit. By either procedure, the court—not "women"—would have the final say on whether the materials fit the definition of pornography, and would have the authority to award monetary damages and issue an injunction (or court order) preventing further distribution of the material in question.

The Minneapolis ordinance defines pornography as "the sexually explicit subordination of women, graphically depicted, whether in pictures or words." To be actionable, materials would also have to fall within one of a number of categories: nine in the Minneapolis ordinance, six in the Indianapolis version. (See p. 97 for text of the original Minneapolis ordinance, from which the excerpts of the legislation quoted in this article are taken.)

Although proponents claim that these ordinances represent a new way to regulate pornography, the strategy is still laden with our culture's old, repressive approach to sexuality. The implementation of such laws hinges on the definition of pornography as interpreted by the court. The definition provided in the Minneapolis legislation is vague, leaving critical phrases such as "the explicit subordination of women," "postures of sexual submission" and "whores by nature" to the interpretation of the citizen who files a complaint and to the civil court judge who hears the case. The legislation does not prohibit just the images of gross sexual violence that most supporters claim to be its target, but instead drifts toward covering an increasingly wide range of sexually explicit material.

The most problematic feature of this approach, then, is a conceptual flaw embedded in the law itself. Supporters of this type of legislation say that the target of their efforts is misogynist, sexually explicit and violent representation, whether in pictures or words. Indeed, the feminist antipornography movement is fueled by women's anger at the most repugnant examples of pornography. But a close examination of the wording of the model legislative text, and examples of purportedly actionable material offered by proponents of the legislation in court briefs, suggests that the law is actually aimed at a range of material considerably broader than what proponents claim is their target. The discrepancies between the law's explicit and implicit aims have been almost invisible to us, because these distortions are very similar to distortions about sexuality in the culture as a whole. The legislation and supporting texts deserve close reading. Hidden beneath illogical transformations, non-sequiturs, and highly permeable definitions are familiar sexual scripts drawn from mainstream, sexist culture that potentially could have very negative consequences for women.

The Venn diagram illustrates the three areas targeted by the law, and represents a scheme that classifies words or images that have any of three characteristics: violence, sexual explicitness, or sexism.

Clearly, a text or image might have only one characteristic. Material can be violent but not sexually explicit or sexist: for example, a war movie in which both men and women suffer injury or death without regard to or because of their gender. Material can be sexist but not sexually explicit and violent. A vast number of materials from mainstream media—television, popular novels, magazines, newspapers—come to mind, all of which depict either distraught housewives or the "happy sexism" of the idealized family, with mom self-sacrificing, other-directed, and content. Finally, material can be sexually explicit but not violent or sexist: for example, the freely chosen sexual behavior depicted in sex education films or women's own explicit writing about sexuality.

As the diagram illustrates, areas can also intersect, reflecting a range of combinations of the three characteristics. Images can be violent and sexually explicit without being sexist—for example, a narrative about a rape in a men's prison, or a documentary about the effect of a rape on a woman. The latter example illustrates the importance of context in evaluating whether material that is sexually explicit and violent is also sexist. The intent of the maker, the context of the film, and the perception of the viewer together render a depiction of a rape sympathetic, harrowing, even educational, rather than sensational, victim-blaming, and laudatory.

Another possible overlap is between material that is violent and sexist but not sexually explicit. Films or books that describe violence directed against women by men in a way that clearly shows gender antagonism and inequality, and sometimes strong sexual tension, but no sexual explicitness fall into this category—for example, the popular genre of slasher films in which women are stalked, terrified, and killed by men, or accounts of mass murder of women, fueled by male rage. Finally, a third point of overlap arises when material is sexually explicit and sexist without being violent—that is, when sex is consensual but still reflects themes of male superiority and female abjectness. Some sex education materials could be included in this category, as well as a great deal of regular pornography.

The remaining domain, the inner core, is one in which the material is simultaneously violent, sexually explicit, and sexist—for example, an image of a naked woman being slashed by a knife-wielding rapist. The Minneapolis law, however, does not by any means confine itself to this material.

To be actionable under the law as pornography, material must be judged by the courts to be "the sexually explicit subordination of women, graphically depicted whether in pictures or in words that also includes at least one or more" of nine criteria. Of these, only four involve the intersection of violence, sexual explicitness, and sexism, and then only arguably. Even in these cases, many questions remain about whether images with all three characteristics do in fact cause violence against women. And the task of evaluating material that is ostensibly the target of these criteria becomes complicated—indeed, hopeless—because most of the clauses that contain these criteria mix actions or qualities of violence with those that are not particularly associated with violence.

The section that comes closest to the stated purpose of the legislation is clause (iii): "women are presented as sexual objects who experience sexual pleasure in being raped." This clause is intended to cover depictions of rape that are sexually explicit and sexist; the act of rape itself signifies violence. But other clauses are not so clearcut, because the list of characteristics often mixes signs or byproducts of violence with phenomena that are unrelated or irrelevant to judging violence.

For example, clause (iv) presents: "women are presented as sexual objects tied up or cut up or mutilated or bruised or physically hurt." All these except the first, "tied up," generally occur as a result of violence. "Tied up," if part of consensual sex, is not violent and, for some practitioners, not particularly sexist. Women who are tied up may be participants in nonviolent sex play involving bondage, a theme in both heterosexual and lesbian pornography. (See, for example, *The Joy of Sex* and *Coming to Power*.) Clause (ix) contains another mixed list, in which "injury," "torture," "bleeding," "bruised," and "hurt" are combined with words such as "degradation" and "shown as filthy and inferior," neither of which is violent. Depending on the presentation, "filthy" and "inferior" may constitute sexually explicit sexism, although not violence. "Degradation" is a sufficiently inclusive term to cover most acts of which a viewer disapproves.

Several other clauses have little to do with violence at all; they refer to material that is sexually explicit and sexist, thus falling outside the triad of characteristics at which the legislation is supposedly aimed. For example, movies in which "women are presented as dehumanized sexual objects, things, or commodities" may be infuriating and offensive to feminists, but they are not violent.

Finally, some clauses describe material that is neither violent nor necessarily sexist. Clause (v), "women . . . in postures of sexual submission or sexual servility, including by inviting penetration," and clause (viii), "women . . . being penetrated by objects or animals," are sexually explicit, but not violent and not obviously sexist unless one believes that penetration—whether heterosexual, lesbian, or autoerotic masturbation—is indicative of gender inequality and female oppression. Similarly problematic are clauses that invoke representations of "women . . . as whores by nature" and "women's body parts . . . such that women are reduced to those parts."

Briefs filed in support of the Indianapolis law show how broadly it could be applied. In the amicus brief filed on behalf of Linda Marchiano ("Linda Lovelace," the female lead in *Deep Throat*) in Indianapolis, Catharine MacKinnon offered *Deep Throat* as an example of the kind of pornography covered by the law. *Deep Throat* served a complicated function in this brief, because the movie, supporters of the ordinance argue, would be actionable on two counts: coercion into pornographic performance, because Marchiano alleges that she was coerced into making the movie; and trafficking in pornography, because the content of the film falls within one of the categories in the Indianapolis ordinance's definition—that which prohibits presenting women as sexual objects "through postures or positions of servility or submission or display." Proponents of the law have counted on women's repugnance at allegations of coerced sexual acts to spill over and discredit the sexual acts themselves in the movie.

The aspects of *Deep Throat* that MacKinnon considered to be indicative of "sexual subordination" are of particular interest, since any movie that depicted similar acts could be banned under the law. MacKinnon explained in her brief that the film "subordinates women by using women . . . sexually, specifically as eager servicing receptacles for male genitalia and ejaculate. The majority of the film represents 'Linda Lovelace' in, minimally, postures of sexual submission and/or servility." In its brief, the City of Indianapolis concurred: "In the film *Deep Throat* a woman is being shown as being ever eager for oral penetration by a series of men's penises, often on her hands and knees. There are repeated scenes in which her genitalia are graphically displayed and she is shown as enjoying men ejaculating on her face."

These descriptions are very revealing, since they suggest that multiple partners, group sex, and oral sex subordinate women and hence are sexist. The notion that the female character is "used" by men suggests that it is improbable that a woman would engage in fellatio of her own accord. *Deep Throat* does draw on several sexist conventions common in the entire visual culture—the woman as object of the male gaze, and the assumption of heterosexuality, for example. But it is hardly an unending paean to male dominance, since the movie contains many contrary themes. In it, the main female character is shown as both actively seeking her own pleasure and as trying to please men; a secondary female character is shown as actually directing encounters with multiple male partners. Both briefs described a movie quite different from the one viewers see.

At its heart, this analysis implies that heterosexual sex itself is sexist; that women do not engage in it of their own volition; and that behavior pleasurable to men is necessarily repugnant to women. In some contexts, for example, the representation of fellatio and multiple partners can be sexist, but are we willing to concede that they always are? If not, then what is proposed as actionable under the Indianapolis law includes merely sexually explicit representation (the traditional target of obscenity laws), which proponents of the legislation vociferously insist they are not interested in attacking.

Some other examples offered through exhibits submitted with the City of Indianapolis brief and also introduced in the public hearing further illustrate this point. Many of the exhibits are depictions of sadomasochism. The court briefs treat SM material as depicting violence and aggression, not consensual sex, in spite of avowals to the contrary by many SM practitioners. With this legislation, then, a major question for feminists that has only begun to develop would be closed for discussion. Instead, a simplistic reduction has been advanced as the definitive feminist position. The description of the material in the briefs focused on submissive women and implied male domination, highlighting the similarity proponents would like to find between all SM narratives and male/female inequality. The actual exhibits, however, illustrated plots and power relations far more diverse than the descriptions provided by MacKinnon and the City of Indianapolis would suggest, including SM between women and female dominant/male submissive SM. For example, the Indianapolis brief stated that in the magazine *The Bitch Goddesses*, "women are shown in torture chambers with their nude body parts being tortured by their 'master' for 'even the slightest offense' . . . . The magazine shows a woman in a scenario of torture." But the brief failed to mention that the dominants in this magazine are all female, with one exception. This kind of discrepancy characterized many examples offered in the briefs.

This is not to say that such representations do not raise questions for feminists. The current lively discussion about lesbian SM clearly demonstrates that this issue is still unresolved. But in the Indianapolis briefs all SM material was assumed to be male dominant/female submissive, thereby squeezing a nonconforming reality into prepackaged, inadequate—and therefore dangerous—categories. This legislation would virtually eliminate all SM pornography by recasting it as violent, thereby attacking a sexual minority while masquerading as an attempt to end violence against women.

Analysis of clauses in the Minneapolis ordinance and several examples offered in court briefs filed in connection with the Indianapolis ordinance show that the law targets material that is sexually explicit and sexist, but ignores material that is violent and sexist, violent and sexually explicit, only violent, or only sexist.

Certain troubling questions arise here, for if one claims, as some antipornography activists do, that there is a direct relationship between images and behavior, why should images of violence against women or scenarios of sexism in general not be similarly proscribed? Why is sexual explicitness singled out as the cause of women's oppression? For proponents to exempt violent and sexist images, or even sexist images, from regulation is inconsistent, especially since they are so pervasive.

Even more difficulties arise from the vagueness of certain terms crucial in interpreting the ordinances. The term "subordination" is especially important, since pornography is defined as the "sexually explicit subordination of women." The authors of this legislation intend it to modify each of the clauses, and they appear to believe that it provides a defintion of sexism that each example must meet. The term is never defined in the legislation, yet the Indianapolis brief, for example, suggests that the average viewer, on the basis of "his or her common understanding of what it means for one person to subordinate another" should be able to decide what is pornographic. But what kind of sexually explicit acts place a woman in an inferior status? To some, *any* graphic sexual act violates women's dignity and therefore subordinates them. To others, consensual heterosexual lovemaking within the boundaries of procreation and marriage is acceptable, but heterosexual sexual acts that do not have reproduction as their aim lower women's status and hence subordinate them. Still others accept a wide range of nonprocreative, perhaps even nonmarital, heterosexuality but draw the line at lesbian sex, which they view as degrading.

The term "sex object" is also problematic. The City of Indianapolis's brief maintains that "the term sexual object, often shortened to sex object, has enjoyed a wide popularity in mainstream American culture in the past fifteen years, and is used to denote the objectification of a person on the basis of their sex or sex appeal. . . . People know what it means to disregard all aspects of personhood but sex, to reduce a person to a thing used for sex." But, indeed, people do not agree on this point. The definiton of "sex object" is far from clear or uniform. For example, some feminist and liberal cutlural critics have used the term to mean sex that occurs without strong emotional ties and experience. More conservative critics maintain that any detachment of women's sexuality from procreation, marriage, and family objectifies it, removing it from its "natural" web of associations and context. Unredeemed and unprotected by domesticity and family, women—and their sexuality—become things used by men. In both these views, women are never sexually autonomous agents who direct and enjoy their sexuality for their own purposes, but rather are victims.

In the same vein, other problematic terms include "inviting penetration," "whores by nature," and "positions of display."

Through close analysis of the proposed legislation one sees how vague the boundaries of the definitions that contain the inner core of the Venn diagram really are. Their dissolution does not happen equally at all points, but only at some: the inner core begins to include sexually explicit and sexist material, and finally expands to include purely sexually explicit material. Thus "sexually explicit" becomes identified and equated with "violent" with no further definition or explanation.

It is also striking that so many feminists have failed to notice that the laws (as well as examples of actionable material) cover so much diverse work, not just that small and symbolic epicenter where many forms of opposition to women converge. It suggests that for us, as well as for others, sexuality remains a difficult area. We have no clearly developed framework in which to think about sex equivalent to the frameworks that are available for thinking about race, gender, and class issues. Consequently, in sex, as in few other areas of human behavior, unexamined and unjustifiable prejudice passes itself off as considered opinion about what is desirable and normal. And finally, sex arouses considerable anxiety, stemming from both the meeting with individual difference and from the prospect—suggested by feminists themselves—that sexual behavior is constructed socially and is not simply natural.

The law takes advantage of everyone's relative ignorance and anxious ambivalence about sex, distorting and oversimplifying what confronts us in building a sexual politic. For example, antipornography feminists draw on several feminist theories about the role of violent, aggressive, or sexist representations. The first is relatively straightforward: that these images trigger men into action. The second suggests that violent images act more subtly, to socialize men to act in sexist or violent ways by making this behavior seem commonplace and more acceptable, if not expected. The third assumption is that violent, sexually explicit, or even sexist images are offensive to women, assaulting their sensibilities and sense of self. Although we have all used metaphor to exhort women to action or illustrate a point, antipornography proponents have frequently used these conventions of speech as if they were literal statements of fact. But these metaphors have gotten out of hand, as Julie Abraham has noted, for they fail to recognize that the assault committed by a wife beater is quite different from the visual "assault" of a sexist ad on TV. The nature of that difference is still being clarified in a complex debate within feminism that must continue; this law cuts off speculation, settling on a causal relationship between image and action that is starkly simple, if unpersuasive.

This metaphor also paves the way for reclassifying images that are merely sexist as also violent and aggressive. Thus, it is no accident that the briefs supporting the legislation first invoke violent images and rapidly move to include sexist and sexually explicit images without noting that they are different. The equation is made more easy by the constant shifts back to examples of depictions of real violence, almost to draw attention away from the sexually explicit or sexist material that in fact would be affected by the laws.

Most important, what underlies this legislation and the success of its analysis in blurring and exceeding boundaries is an appeal to a very traditional view of sex: sex is degrading to women. By this logic, any illustrations or descriptions of sexually explicit acts that involve women are in themselves affronts to women's dignity. In its brief, the City of Indianapolis was quite specific about this point: "The harms caused by pornography are by no means limited to acts of physical aggression. The mere existence of pornography in society degrades and demeans all women." Embedded in this view are several other familiar themes: that sex is degrading to women, but not to men; that men are raving beasts; that sex is dangerous for women; that sexuality is male, not female; that women are victims, not sexual actors; that men inflict "it" on women; that penetration is submission; that heterosexual sexuality, rather than the institution of heterosexuality, is sexist.

These assumptions, in part intended, in part unintended, lead us back to the traditional target of obscenity law; sexually explicit material. What initially appeared novel, then, is really the reappearance of a traditional theme. It's ironic that a feminist position on pornography incorporates most of the myths about sexuality that feminism has struggled to displace.

The Dangers of Application

The Minneapolis-style ordinances embody a political view that holds pornography to be a central force in "creating and maintaining" the oppression of women. This view appears in summary form in the legislative findings section at the beginning of the Minneapolis bill, which describes a chain reaction of misogynistic acts generated by pornography. The legislation is based on the interweaving of several themes: that pornography constructs the meaning of sexuality for women and, as well, leads to discrete acts of violence against women; that sexuality is the primary cause of women's oppression; that explicitly sexual images, even if not violent or coerced, have the power to subordinate women; and that women's own accounts of force have been silenced because, as a universal and timeless rule, society credits pornographic constructions rather than women's experiences. Taking the silencing contention a step further, advocates of the ordinance effectively assume that women have been so conditioned by the pornographic world view that if their own experiences of the sexual acts identified in the definition are not subordinating, then they must simply be victims of false consciousness.

The heart of the ordinance is the "trafficking" section, which would allow almost anyone to seek the removal of any materials falling within the law's definition of pornography. Ordinance defenders strenuously protest that the issue is not censorship because the state, as such, is not authorized to initiate criminal prosecutions. But the prospect of having to defend a potentially infinite number of privately filed complaints creates at least as much of a chilling effect against sexual speech as does a criminal law. And as long as representatives of the state—in this case, judges—have ultimate say over the interpretation, the distinction between this ordinance and "real" censorship will not hold.

In addition, three major problems should dissuade feminists from supporting this kind of law: first, the sexual images in question do not cause more harm than other aspects of misogynist culture; second, sexually explicit speech, even in male-dominated society, serves positive functions for women; and third, the passage and enforcement of antipornography laws such as those supported in Minneapolis and Indianapolis are more likely to impede, rather than advance, feminist goals.

Ordinance proponents contend that pornography does cause violence because it conditions male sexual response to images of violence and thus provokes violence against women. The strongest research they offer is based on psychology experiments that employ films depicting a rape scene, toward the end of which the woman is shown to be enjoying the attack. The ordinances, by contrast, cover a much broader range of materials than this one specific heterosexual rape scenario. Further, the studies ordinance supporters cite do not support the theory that pornography causes violence against women. Taken at their strongest, some studies indicate that exposure to some pornography promotes sexist attitudes and beliefs in some subjects. Interestingly, researchers have found that subjects exposed to "debriefing" sessions at the end of the experiments, in which rape myths are identified and dispelled, are found to have fewer sexist attitudes when tested months later than the "controls" who were not exposed to any pornography. This indicates that education efforts can indeed be effective in countering the sexist messages of pornography.

In addition, the argument that pornography itself plays a major role in the general oppression of women contradicts the evidence of history. It need hardly be said that pornography did not lead to the burning of witches or the English common law treatment of women as chattel property. If anything functioned then as the prime communication medium for woman-hating, it was probably religion. Nor can pornography be blamed for the enactment of laws from at least the eighteenth century that allowed a husband to rape or beat his wife with impunity. In any period, the causes of women's oppression have been many and complex, drawing on the fundamental social and economic structures of society. Ordinance proponents offer little evidence to explain how the mass production of pornography—a relatively recent phenomenon—could have become so potent a causative agent so quickly.

The silencing of women is another example of the harm attributed to pornography. Yet if this argument were correct, one would expect that as the social visibility of pornography has increased, the tendency to credit women's accounts of rape would have decreased. In fact, although the treatment of women complainants in rape cases is far from perfect, the last 25 years of work by the women's movement has resulted in marked improvements. In many places, the corroboration requirement has now been abolished; cross-examination of victims as to past sexual experiences has been prohibited; and a number of police forces have developed specially trained units and procedures to improve the handling of sexual assault cases. The presence of rape fantasies in pornography may in part reflect a backlash against these women's movement advances, but to argue that most people routinely disbelieve women who file charges of rape belittles the real improvements made in social consciousness and law.

The third type of harm suggested by the ordinance backers is a kind of libel: the maliciously false characterization of women as a group of sexual masochists. The City of Indianapolis brief argues that pornography, like libel, is "a lie [which] once loosed" cannot be effectively rebutted by debate and further speech.

To claim that all pornography as defined by the ordinance is a lie is a false analogy. If truth is a defence to charges of libel, then surely depictions of consensual sex cannot be thought of as equivalents to a falsehood. For example, some women (and men) do enjoy bondage or display. The declaration by fiat that sadomasochism is a "lie" about sexuality reflects an arrogance and moralism that feminists should combat, not engage in. When mutually desired sexual experiences are depicted, pornography is not "libelous."

Not only does pornography not cause the kind and degree of harm that can justify the restraint of speech, but its existence serves some social functions which benefit women. Pornographic speech has many, often anomalous, characteristics. One is certainly that it magnifies the misogyny present in the culture and exaggerates the fantasy of male power. Another, however, is that the existence of pornography has served to flout conventional sexual mores, to ridicule sexual hypocrisy, and to underscore the importance of sexual needs. Pornography carries many messages other than woman-hating: it advocates sexual adventure, sex outside of marriage, sex for no reason other than pleasure, casual sex, anonymous sex, group sex, voyeuristic sex, illegal sex, public sex. Some of these ideas appeal to women reading or seeing pornography, who may interpret some images as legitimating their own sense of sexual urgency or desire to be sexually aggressive. Women's experience of pornography is not as universally victimizing as the ordinance would have it.

The new antipornography laws, as restrictions on sexual speech, in many ways echo and expand upon the traditional legal analysis of sexually explicit speech under the rubric of obscenity. The U. S. Supreme Court has consistently ruled that sexual speech defined as "obscenity" does not belong in the system of public discourse and is therefore an exception to the First Amendment and hence not entitled to protection under the free speech guarantee. (The definition of obscenity has shifted over the years and remains imprecise.) In 1957 the Supreme Court ruled that obscenity could be suppressed regardless of whether it presented an imminent threat of illegal activity. In the opinion of the Supreme Court, graphic sexual images do not communicate "real" ideas. These, it would seem, are only found in the traditionally defined public arena. Sexual themes can qualify as ideas if they use sexuality for argument's sake, but not if they speak in the words and images of "private life"—that is, if they graphically depict sex itself. At least theoretically, and insofar as the law functions as a pronouncement of moral judgment, sex is consigned to remain unexpressed and in the private realm.

The fallacies in this distinction are obvious. Under the U. S. Constitution, for example, it is acceptable to write "I am a sadomasochist" or even "Everyone should experiment with sadomasochism in order to increase sexual pleasure." But to write a graphic fantasy about sadomasochism that arouses and excites readers is not protected unless a court finds it to have serious literary, artistic, or political value, despite the expressive nature of the content. Indeed, the fantasy depiction may communicate identity in a more compelling way than the "I am" statement. For sexual minorities, sexual acts can be self-identifying and affirming statements in a hostile world. Images of those acts should be protected for that reason, for they do have political content. Just as the personal can be political, so can the specifically and graphically sexual.

Supporters of the antipornography ordinances both endorse the concept that pornographic speech contains no ideas or expressive interest, and at the same time attribute to pornography the capacity to trigger violent acts by the power of its misogyny. The city's brief in defence of the Indianapolis ordinance expanded this point by arguing that all sexually explicit speech is entitled to less constitutional protection than other speech. The antipornography groups have cleverly capitalized on this approach—a product of a totally nonfeminist legal system—and are now attempting, through the mechanism of the ordinances, to legitimate a new crusade for protectionism and sexual conservatism.

The consequences of enforcing such a law, however, are much more likely to obstruct than advance feminist political goals. On the level of ideas, further narrowing of the public realm of sexual speech coincides all too well with the privatization of sexual, reproductive, and family issues sought by the far right—an agenda described very well, for example, by Rosalind Petchesky in "The Rise of the New Right," in *Abortion and Woman's Choice*. Practically speaking, the ordinance could result in attempts to eliminate the images associated with homosexuality. Doubtless there are heterosexual women who believe that lesbianism is a "degrading" form of "subordination." Since the ordinances allow for suits against materials in which men appear "in place of women," far-right antipornography crusaders could use these laws to suppress gay male pornography. Imagine a Jerry Falwell-style conservative filing a complaint against a gay bookstore for selling sexually explicit materials showing men with other men in "degrading" or "submissive" or "objectified" postures—all in the name of protecting women.

And most ironically, while the ordinances would do nothing to improve the material conditions of most women's lives, their high visibility might well divert energy from the drive to enact other, less popular laws that would genuinely empower women—comparable worth legislation, for example, or affirmative action requirements, or fairer property and support principles in divorce laws.

Other provisions of the ordinances concern coercive behavior: physical assault which is imitative of pornographic images, coercion into pornographic performance, and forcing pornography on others. On close examination, however, even most of these provisions are problematic.

Existing law already penalizes physical assault, including when it is associated with pornography. Defenders of the laws often cite the example of models who have been raped or otherwise harmed while in the process of making pornographic images. But victims of this type of attack can already sue or prosecute those responsible. (Linda Marchiano, the actress who appeared in the film *Deep Throat*, has not recovered damages for the physical assaults she describes in her book *Ordeal* because the events happened several years before she decided to try to file a suit. A lawsuit was thus precluded by the statute of limitations.) Indeed, the ordinances do not cover assault or other harm incurred while producing pornography, presumably because other laws already achieve that end.

The ordinances do penalize coercing, intimidating, or fraudulently inducing anyone into performing for pornography. Although existing U. S. law already provides remedies for fraud or contracts of duress, this section of the ordinance seeks to facilitate recovery of damages by, for example, pornography models who might otherwise encounter substantial prejudice against their claims. Supporters of this section have suggested that it is comparable to the Supreme Court's ban on child pornography. The analogy has been stretched to the point where the City of Indianapolis brief argued that women, like children, need "special protection." "Children are incapable of consenting to engage in pornographic conduct, even absent physical coercion and therefore require special protection," the brief stated. "By the same token, the physical and psychological well-being of women ought to be afforded comparable protection, for the coercive environment in which most pornographic models work vitiates any notion that they consent or 'choose' to perform in pornography."

The reality of women's lives is far more complicated. Women do not become pornography models because society is egalitarian and they exercise a "free choice," but neither do they "choose" this work because they have lost all power for deliberate, volitional behavior. Modeling or acting for pornography, like prostitution, can be a means of survival for those with limited options. For some women, at some points in their lives, it is a rational economic decision. Not every woman regrets having made it, although no woman should have to settle for it. The fight should be to expand the options and to insure job safety for women who do become porn models. By contrast, the impact of the ordinance as a whole would be either to eliminate jobs or drive the pornography industry further underground.

One of the vaguest provisions in the ordinance prohibits "forcing" pornography on a person. "Forcing" is not defined in the law, and one is left to speculate whether it means forced to respond to pornography, forced to read it, or forced to glance at it before turning away. Also unclear is whether the perpetrator must in fact have some superior power over the person being forced—that is, is there a meaningful threat that makes the concept of force real.

Again, widely varying situations are muddled, and a consideration of context is absent. "Forcing" pornography on a person "in any public space" is treated identically to using it as a method of sexual harassment in the workplace. The scope of "forcing" could include walking past a newsstand or browsing in a bookstore that had pornography on display. The force involved in such a situation seems mild when compared, for example, to the incessant sexist advertising on television.

The concept behind the "forcing" provision is appropriate, however, in the case of workplace harassment. A worker should not have to endure, especially on pain of losing her job, harassment based on sex, race, religion, nationality, or any other factor. But this general policy was established by the U. S. courts as part of the guarantees of Title VII of the 1964 Civil Rights Act. Pornography used as a means of harassing women workers is already legally actionable, just as harassment by racial slurs is actionable. Any literature endorsing the oppression of women—whether pornography or the Bible—could be employed as an harassment device to impede a woman's access to a job, or to education, public accommodations, or other social benefits. It is the usage of pornography in this situation, not the image itself, that is discriminatory. Appropriately, this section of the ordinances provides that only perpetrators of the forcing, not makers and distributors of the images, could be held liable.

Forcing of pornography on a person is also specifically forbidden "in the home." In her testimony before the Indianapolis City Council, Catharine MacKinnon referred to the problem of pornography being "forced on wives in preparation for later sexual scenes." Since only the person who forces the pornography on another can be sued, this provision becomes a kind of protection against domestic harassment. It would allow wives to sue husbands for court orders or damages for some usages of pornography. Although a fascinating attempt to subvert male power in the domestic realm, it nonetheless has problems. "Forcing" is not an easy concept to define in this context. It is hard to know what degree of intrusion would amount to forcing images onto a person who shares the same private space.

More important, the focus on pornography seems a displacement of the more fundamental issues involved in the conflicts that occur between husbands and wives or lovers over sex. Some men may invoke images that reflect their greater power to pressure women into performing the supposedly traditional role of acceding to male desires. Pornography may facilitate or enhance this dynamic of male dominance, but it is hardly the causative agent. Nor would removing the pornography do much to solve the problem. If the man invokes instead his friends' stories about sexual encounters or his experiences with other women, is the resulting interaction with his wife substantially different? Focusing on the pornography rather than on the relationship and its social context may serve only to channel heterosexual women's recognition of their own intimate oppression toward a movement hailed by the far right as being antiperversion rather than toward a feminist analysis of sexual politics.

The last of the sections that deals with actual coercive conduct is one that attempts to deal with the assault, physical injury or attack of any person in a way that is directly caused by specific pornography. The ordinances would allow a lawsuit against the makers or distributors of pornographic materials that were imitated by an attacker—the only provision of the ordinance that requires proof of causation. Presenting such proof would be extremely difficult. If the viewer's willful decision to imitate the image were found to be an intervening, superceding cause of the harm, the plaintiff would not recover damages.

The policy issues here are no different from those concerning violent media images that are nonsexual: Is showing an image sufficient to cause an act of violence? Even if an image could be found to cause a viewer's behavior, was that behavior reasonably foreseeable? So far, those who have produced violent films have not been found blameworthy when third persons acted out the violence depicted. If this were to change, it would mean, for example, that the producer of the TV movie *The Burning Bed*, which told the true story of a battered wife who set fire to her sleeping husband, could be sued if a woman who saw the film killed her husband in a similar way. The result, of course, would be the end of films depicting real violence in the lives of women.

The ordinances' supporters offer no justification for singling out sexual assault from other kinds of violence. Certainly the experience of sexual assault is not always worse than that of being shot or stabbed or suffering other kinds of nonsexual assault. Nor is sexual assault the only form of violence that is fueled by sexism. If there were evidence that sexual images are more likely to be imitated, there might be some justification for treating them differently. But there is no support for this contention.

These laws, which would increase the state's regulation of sexual images, present many dangers for women. Although the ordinances draw much of their feminist support from women's anger at the market for images of sexual violence, they are aimed not at violence, but at sexual explicitness. Far-right elements recognize the possibility of using the full potential of the ordinances to enforce their sexually conservative world view, and have supported them for that reason. Feminists should therefore look carefully at the text of these "model" laws in order to understand why many believe them to be a useful tool in *anti*feminst moral crusades.

The proposed ordinances are also dangerous because they seek to embody in law an analysis of the role of sexuality and sexual images in the oppression of women with which all feminists do not agree. Underlying virtually every section of the proposed laws there is an assumption that sexuality is a realm of unremitting, unequaled victimization for women. Pornography appears as the monster that made this so. The ordinances' authors seek to impose their analysis by putting state power behind it. But this analysis is not the only feminist perspective on sexuality. Feminist theorists have also argued that the sexual terrain, however power-laden, is actively contested. Women are agents, and not merely victims, who make decisions and act on them, and who desire, seek out, and enjoy sexuality.

The key provisions of the original Minneapolis ordinance are reprinted below:

(1) *Special Findings on Pornography:* The council finds that pornography is central in creating and maintaining the civil inequality of the sexes. Pornography is a systematic practice of exploitation and subordination based on sex which differentially harms women. The bigotry and contempt it promotes, with the acts of aggression it fosters, harm women's opportunities for equality of rights, in employment, education, property rights, public accommodations, and public services; create public harassment and private denigration; promote injury and degradation such as rape, battery, and prostitution and inhibit just enforcement of laws against these acts; contribute significantly to restricting women from full exercise of citizenship and participation in public life, including in neighborhoods; damage relations between the sexes; and undermine women's equal exercise of rights to speech and action guaranteed to all citizens under the constitutions and laws of the United States and the State of Minnesota.

(gg) *Pornography.* Pornography is a form of discrimination on the basis of sex.
(1) Pornography is the sexually explicit subordination of women, graphically depicted, whether in pictures or in words, that also includes one or more of the following:

(i) women are presented as dehumanized sexual objects, things, or commodities; or
(ii) women are presented as sexual objects who enjoy pain or humiliation; or
(iii) women are presented as sexual objects who experience sexual pleasure in being raped; or
(iv) women are presented as sexual objects tied up or cut up or mutilated or bruised or physically hurt; or

(v) women are presented in postures of sexual submission; [or sexual servility, including by inviting penetration;]* or

(vi) women's body parts—including but not limited to vaginas, breasts, and buttocks—are exhibited, such that women are reduced to those parts; or

(vii) women are presented as whores by nature; or

(viii) women are presented being penetrated by objects or animals; or

(ix) women are presented in scenarios of degradation, injury, abasement, torture, shown as filthy or inferior, bleeding, bruised, or hurt in a context that makes these conditions sexual.

(2) The use of men, children, or transsexuals in the place of women . . . is pornography for purposes of . . . this statute.

(1) *Discrimination by trafficking in pornography:* The production, sale, exhibition, or distribution of pornography is discrimination against women by means of trafficking in pornography;

(1) City, state, and federally funded public libraries or private and public university and college libraries in which pornography is available for study, including on open shelves, shall not be construed to be trafficking in pornography, but special display presentations of pornography in said places is sex discrimination.

(2) The formation of private clubs or associations for purposes of trafficking in pornography is illegal and shall be considered a conspiracy to violate the civil rights of women.

(3) Any woman has a cause of action hereunder as a woman acting against the subordination of women. Any man or transsexual who alleges injury by pornography in the way women are injured by it shall also have a cause of action.

(m) *Coercion into pornographic performances.* Any person, including a transsexual, who is coerced, intimidated, or fraudulently induced (hereafter, "coerced") into performing for pornography shall have a cause of action against the maker(s), seller(s), exhibitor(s), or distributor(s) of said pornography for damages and for the elimination of the products of the performance(s) from the public view.

(1) *Limitation of action.* This claim shall not expire before five years have elapsed from the date of the coerced performance(s) or from the last appearance or sale of any product of the performance(s); whichever date is later;
(2) Proof of one or more of the following facts or conditions shall not, without more, negate a finding of coercion:

(aa) that the person is a woman; or
(bb) that the person is or has been a prostitute; or
(cc) that the person has attained the age of majority; or
(dd) that the person is connected by blood or marriage to anyone involved in or related to the making of pornography; or
(ee) that the person has previously had, or been thought to have had, sexual relations with anyone including anyone involved in or related to the making of the pornography; or
(ff) that the person has previously posed for sexually explicit pictures for or with anyone, including anyone involved in or related to the making of the pornography at issue; or
(gg) that anyone else, including a spouse or other relative, has given permission on the person's behalf; or
(hh) that the person actually consented to a use of the performance that is changed into pornography; or
(ii) that the person knew that the purpose of the acts or events in question was to make pornography; or
(jj) that the person showed no resistance or appeared to cooperate actively in the photographic sessions or in the sexual events that produced the pornography; or
(kk) that the person signed a contract, or made statements affirming a willingness to cooperate; or
(ll) that no physical force, threats, or weapons were used in the making of the pornography; or
(mm) that the person was paid or otherwise compensated.
(n) *Forcing pornography on a person.* Any woman, man, child, or transsexual who has pornography forced on them in any place of

employment, in education, in a home, or in any public place has a cause of action against the perpetrator and/or institution.

(o) *Assault or physical attack due to pornography.* Any woman, man, child, or transsexual who is assaulted, physically attacked, or injured in a way that is directly casued by specific pornography has a claim for damages against the perpetrator, the maker(s), distributor(s), seller(s), and/or exhibitor(s), and for an injunction against the specific pornography's further exhibition, distribution, or sale. No damages shall be assessed (A) against maker(s) for pornography made, (B) against distributor(s) for pornography distributed, (C) against seller(s) for pornography sold, or (D) against exhibitor(s) for pornography exhibited prior to the effective date of this act.

(p) *Defense.* Where the materials which are the subject matter of a cause of action under subsections (1), (m), (n), or (o) of this section are pornography, it shall not be a defense that the defendant did not know or intend that the materials are pornography or sex discrimination.

★The bracketed phrase appears in an early version of the Minneapolis ordinance but may have been removed before the bill was formally introduced in the city council. It has reappeared, however, in subsequent defenses of the ordinance by its supporters. See J. Miller, "Civil Rights, Not Censorhip," *Village Voice*, Nov. 6, 1984, p. 6.

Chris Martin

World's Greatest Cocksucker: Transsexual Interviews

My intention in researching the gender community (transvestites, crossdressers, transgenderists, and transsexuals) is not to make sense of it, but rather to disturb current models and categories of sexuality: gay and straight. One fundamental lesson of these two interviews with female to male (F2M) transsexuals is that genetic gender does not guarantee sexual relations as either homosexual or heterosexual. Transsexuals shake up these categories, opening up new spaces for identity. The F/M Fraternity International Support Network lists 20 categories of gender and 6 categories of sexual preference, and when we examine how these categories intersect with race and class the question of identity becomes increasingly complex, and the possibilities multiply.

Another motivation behind this work is to discuss the problems of conservatives, Queers, and activism. While a Queer alliance is imperative, it is important not to ignore the tensions which the political alliance of sexual minorities struggle with. Any political alliance will be wrought with tensions of "incommensurable" differences such as gender, race, class, and sexuality. In the first interview Vern explains that there is genderphobia in the gay community and homophobia in the gender community, outlining some of the tensions of a Queer political alliance and warning us against conservative tendencies in the gay movement.

I would like to present these interviews as evidence of a research practice. A lot has been said recently in the critical theory world about ethnography and "ethnomethodology." One of the things this discussion has shown us is that there is a politics to research. I am not a transsexual. Fundamentally I like being a G.G. (genetic girl). My motivations are in part theoretical but also in part erotic. F2Ms and gay sex turn me on. I am not conducting surveys, or trying to quantify measurements of behavior. My manner of working is sort of a "hanging out" for anecdotes. Everyone loves the autobiographical. Through the telling of everyday stories and sexual narratives we see the production of a subject and subjectivity. The second interview, with Danny, provides us with frank and intimate talk about alternative ways of operating. These interviews are an important witness to the practice of different social and sexual knowledges.

I would like to thank Danny and Vern for their generosity in conducting these interviews. They are truly pioneers and have my full admiration and respect, and I will continue to advocate their positions and politics.

Taped March 29, 1991

Chris: *What did you mean when you said that there is genderphobia in the gay community and homophobia in the gender community?*

Vern: "Genderphobia" is my term. I made it up because there is a clone movement in the non-heterosexual community to make everybody look just like heterosexuals who sleep with each other. The fact is that there is a whole large section of the gay community or the sexual minority community who is never going to vote republican. There are drag queens, there are transsexuals, there are transgenderists, and there is a real ground swell in the "gay community" to try and pretend that these people don't exist and it drives me crazy.

Chris: *Sounds like an attempt to "clean up" the gay community.*

Vern: Yeah, and to make the gay community look like the straight community. If you want to just be straight and sleep with other straight people of the same gender, well, that's your own business, and I'm not going to tell you not to do it, but what Stonewall and all this other shit is about is the freedom to be who you are, and if you are a crossdresser or a transsexual, or if you are a three-eyed monster from Mars, it's nobody else's business to tell you not to be that.

Chris: *Is there prejudice in the gay community against transvestites, either in the bars or in the bedrooms?*

Vern: There is one real asshole bar owner here in Buffalo—he's a real scumbag. His name is John Little—please feel free to publish his name. All of his bars restrict entrance to crossdressers. Most of the gay community's transvestites don't have any lack of sleeping partners, but they do lack the respect they should get. These are people who deserve the same rights and privileges as everybody else. Human rights should be equally applied to everybody. You can't just point fingers at people who are not just like you, and say, "You aren't as good as me so you don't get the same rights that I do."

Chris: *I heard that 40% of male-to-female transsexuals are lesbians, and I was wondering about the percentage of female-to-males who were practicing gay men.*

Vern: There was a show taped for Geraldo, on transsexual gays, but they cut it; they never showed it. It was too controversial. Nobody wants to talk about it, especially the gay community. People want to be able to say, "You're a transsexual so you must do this," and straight people especially think that transsexualism is just an extreme form of homosexuality. It makes everyone much more comfortable to believe this. It's a nice and tidy way to understand the world.

Chris: *Have you gained male privilege as female to male?*

Vern: In that video by Johnny Armstrong, "Linda Les and Annie," Les Nichols says he feels like a spy, and that's true. It is amazing the amount of respect you get as a man. In my tenth-grade auto shop class the mechanics would pull the men out onto the floor to show them the parts and explain what they were doing, whereas if you were a woman they would assume you were a complete twit. I'm 26. This time last year I was "Miss." Now it's "Sir." It didn't go from "Miss" to "Son" or "Ma'am" to "Sir." It went from "Miss" to "Sir."

Chris: *That is a step up in terms of respect. All the F2Ms I have met have been very attractive, very virile guys, and I wonder how that masculinity is being invented. I see gay male codes influencing their style.*

Vern: Last night I was at an overdressed activity, which was crawling with crossdressers, and there was this meta-crossdressing there: genetic males who were transvestites who were dressing like women in men's clothing. Some people analyze it too much. People want there to be neatness and tidiness, and there isn't. Transsexuals make a big scrap heap out of everybody's tidy life. If they can file us some place they are happy, but when they can't they are tormented.

Chris: *You sleep with both men and women. How does it happen?*

Vern: Actually, I'm not sleeping with anybody lately because I don't do relationships very well.

Chris: *Neither do I.*

Vern: I just broke up with somebody really badly and have felt like a swine for weeks.

Chris: *I wanted to talk about F2Ms who sleep with men (even if their preference may be for women), and how man-to-man sexual experiences differ from other sexual experiences for you. What's the difference?*

Vern: One of the big differences is the power relationship. Between men there is more of a power parity than there can ever be in any heterosexual relationship. As a woman I dated men whom I was perfectly capable of beating to a pulp, but there was no power parity, and this goes for even the most egalitarian "fluff ball" of guys. There are women who are my friends who recognize this and are even bothered by me now, and I'm still the same "fluff ball" I always was. In this society, just being perceived as male increases your power relative to your partner. The difference with lesbian relationships is that you are two of the disaffected. Two white males in this society are almost like the "aristocracy" because you have the trappings of the power structure.

Chris: *Are you a top or a bottom, and does that change if you are with men or women?*

Vern: I'm sort of fluid, and it varies with who I'm with. People want to stick me and everyone into a little pigeon-hole, and I, more so than most, don't have one. Most people don't, but there are a lot of people who will try to fit into one anyway. There is so much less struggle that way. It's good to be shaken up. If nothing else, transsexuals in this society shake things up a little.

Chris: *The gay and lesbian community needs to be shaken up, too. For example, the separatism that lesbians have been practicing just doesn't make sense any more, especially now when there are no guarantees regarding gender.*

Vern: I tend bar at a lesbian bar one day a week. A few weeks ago there were these two women there who were real men-haters. They were upset at the fact that I was tending bar there. They were making anti-man comments all night, and what was I going to say? It wasn't worth the effort to get into it all. After they left, I was alone in the bar, and these three men came in. They had come from the strip bar up the street. They were real assholes. They were everything the women before had believed all men to be. What it is that those women hated about men does exist out there. It's easy to generalize. Those men had perceived me as a guy and didn't get heavy with me, but the power play was interesting because if they had perceived me as a woman things would have been very different.

Chris: *Are you ever concerned with the threat of violence?*

Vern: No, not really, because I pass very well.

Chris: *Even though you have now gained a certain amount of male privilege, couldn't you be subjected to the homophobic violence which threatens gay men?*

Vern: I don't really worry about that too much. I really live on the fringe.

Chris: *Are you out as a transsexual?*

Vern: I'm really out. Buffalo is a small town. There isn't a bar I can go to where I don't know someone. Heterosexuals usually have no clue because they don't read the gay papers.

Chris: *Most of my political associations have been with gay men (specifically through ACT UP and the AIDS crisis), my roommates are always gay men, and I think my sexual identity, desire, and fantasies are as much a production of the gay male community as the lesbian community. For example, my relationships are short, and my sexual partners are frequent. These practices and tastes are typically associated with gay men.*

Vern: In Buffalo there is no gay community separate from a lesbian community. There are some "women-only dances," but mostly it's a very integrated gay *and* lesbian community. There isn't enough volume of either group on its own to support the social services that we need, so we really need to keep it together.

Chris: *How do you tell someone that you are sleeping with that you are not a genetic man?*

Vern: That hasn't really come up. People usually know me. There have been a few sort of frenetic things where it wasn't a genital thing. But so far there hasn't been a problem.

Chris: *What is more essential to masculinity: testosterone or a penis? What are some of the different priorities F2M transsexuals have when choosing the different phalloplasty procedures available, for example, urination, erection, orgasm, or ability to penetrate?*

Vern: I will probably never have phalloplasty. Maybe if I was really rich and had a long vacation. . .

Chris: *I guess it's pretty expensive equipment.*

Vern: I have fully functioning equipment now. I know men who have equipment that doesn't work or don't have equipment, and it doesn't make them any less men. I have a lot of connections with the handicapped community, or the differently abled community (I hate that term). I know a lot of people who through car accidents or meningitis or whatever don't have functional equipment. It doesn't make them less of a man. No one says to my friend Steve, "You're not a man anymore."

Chris: *A lot of people want to deny that there is a sexuality to anyone who is handicapped.*

Vern: Both of my parents were disabled. My mother had acute arthritis. She had two artificial knuckles, two artificial knees, and an artificial ankle. I have dated people who were handicapped. You don't stop being sexual because certain equipment doesn't work. You don't stop being sexual because you stop looking like a GQ ad. We are sexual beings from cradle to grave. To deny that is to delude oneself. There is more to sex than orgasm. I hope people realize this, and maybe some of them don't. There's human interaction. There's a whole wealth of physical manifestations of personhood (I can't believe I said that). There is physical stuff that doesn't involve genital contact of a specific sort. Where is it written that "This is the activity you should engage in"?

Chris: *I agree.*

Vern: I read an article in an anarchist 'zine. They were talking about how we treat our children and youths, as if they should be insulated from all sex or sexuality. Then, suddenly at some specified age we expect them to be conversant and competent. Then we are surprised when they are not, and we are surprised at the mental insecurities that most of us have regarding sex.

Chris: *There are sexual accidents going on all the time. That is why we have to talk, write, and make pictures about sex, to avoid these accidents. Sex is too important to keep "behind closed doors."*

Vern: Sex is about life, and everybody wants to make it unrelated to the everyday. As if our genital life, our sexual life, our late-night activities are somehow unrelated to the person who walks around on the street. As long as we keep this mythical dichotomy, we are going to doom ourselves.

Chris: *I often attempt to talk about sex in my classes. I often get ridiculed for having a "one-track mind." If people think sex is "one-track," they* *are thinking a singular orgasm-oriented, penis-vagina "track." Well, that is NOT the only thing to talk about. That's so limiting. No wonder they want to change the subject.*

Vern: You can describe almost anything for hours, and people won't think anything of it, but if you describe any kind of sexual pleasure, people think you're a pervert, for example, if you like such and such a person for oral sex because of the musky smell of their genitals.

Chris: *I don't mind if people think I'm a pervert.*

Vern: Fitting in is less work than dealing with the fallout from not fitting in. No one has been beat up in a subway for being an accountant.

Chris: *When did you decide you were a transsexual?*

Vern: I told my family when I was 6. But I didn't do anything about it until a few years ago. It's not that uncommon that people in their 30s and 40s find out that their parents had guessed wrong about their genders. Changing gender doesn't change who people are for the most part. You just remove certain parts, and everything can go on happily.

Chris: *What did you do first?*

Vern: First you have to go to counseling, so I went to counseling, and after the minimum 90 days I got a blood test but couldn't go on hormones because I had elevated testosterone levels. It explains a lot because I'm relatively muscular (underneath the fat), and I have a lot of unexplained body hair.

Chris: *So you don't do any hormone treatment at all?*

Vern: I do now, but at first I had this condition that was confusing them. I've been on hormones for about a year most of the time.

Chris: *I've heard that testosterone increases your sex drive.*

Vern: It does, but I already had a pretty active libido.

Chris: *Are you considering any surgery?*

Vern: Well, I'll probably get a hysterectomy pretty soon for unrelated reasons, and I think my insurance will cover it. If nothing else that will allow me to reduce the level of hormones that I'm taking.

Chris: *What about long-term health effects. A few men in the group (especially the young ones) were complaining about hair loss and the possibilities of liver damage.*

Vern: I come from a fuzzy family, so that's not a problem for me. It's difficult to say whether cardiovascular risk in transsexuals is due to hormone treatment or eating hamburgers. The sample size is still too small to make decisions. I am concerned with other health worries, but suddenly being on the male side of the risk pool is not something I worry about.

Chris: *I want to go back to this notion of genderphobia.*

Vern: OK.

Chris: *There is a big movement in the gender community (transvestites, transgenderists, crossdressers, and transsexuals), the ones who aren't gay, to cut themselves off from the gay community. Many crossdressers are heterosexual, probably most. If there was ever a natural coalition it's among the gender community and the gay community. If you're a straight genetic male* *wearing a dress in the subway you are going to get beaten up by the same punks, and the phrase they will use is faggot. The people who aren't us don't differentiate so it's silly for us to. There was only one person from the gender community on the New York State pride agenda committee.*

Vern: We are all Queers.

Chris: *As far as the straight world is concerned, we are all Queers. If we don't work together, it's stupid.*

Vern: You have the gays saying, "Sure, we want domestic partnership and anti-violence rights, but just leave us alone, we're not like those queer ones, we're just regular folk, we want to be left alone in our condo." You have the transsexuals saying, "We're not queer, we have our own thing, and we just want to be left alone." It's a war zone out there. "Always vigilant" should be the slogan for the gay community. You have to always be watching out. A gay man was killed in Buffalo recently, and the killer got away with it. The jury brought up the excuse that the killer was acting in self-defense. A big strapping 19-year-old beats up and kills a 40-year-old fat guy who was drunk. Self-defense? The jury bought it. We have to be aware these things are happening, and we have to stick together.

Chris: *We can't believe that by becoming conservative we may integrate into straight society.*

Vern: No, you can't, because some day you will let your guard down, or someone will see through your windows. Do you want to live the lie: "We're good neighbors; we're just like you"? We're *not* just like you. This is about being who you are and not being ashamed or afraid of who you are. Brenda from Brenda and Glenda said to me, "It would be great if tomorrow every gay person woke up with lavender skin because then people would have to confront it." The teacher who is teaching your second-grader whom you really like and trust, your pediatrician, your next-door neighbor with the nice roses, your cousin Kathy. Holy mackerel! This would be great, but it isn't going to happen.

Taped April 19, 1991

Chris: *What percentage of F2Ms sleep with men after the change?*

Danny: It's really hard to say exactly, because until about 3 years ago it was totally unacceptable to present a gay male identity, so people didn't really present it (outwardly).

Chris: *Do you mean people weren't "out" about it?*

Danny: Yes, and I think the numbers are going to end up being a lot higher than people would even think. It makes sense to me. It's the same as males to females wanting to be lesbians. I really understand why females to males would want to be gay, to reject femininity totally.

Chris: *You've told me that while you prefer to sleep with women you do occasionally sleep with men.*

Danny: I don't know about *sleeping*.

Chris: *I think the readers would be interested in the details. . . where you pick your potential partners up and what you do.*

Danny: Well, I write my name on men's room walls, and I distribute these little cards.

Chris: *Can I see one?!*

Danny: *Sure!* Here's a good one. Each one is a little different.

...ow me to be in control.

"THAT'S A GOOD BOY! SUCK DADDY'S BIG HARD DICK!!"

"YES SIR! THANK-YOU, SIR! I LOVE TO SERVICE HOT MAN-MEAT!!"

World's Greatest Cocksucker   Chris Martin

Chris: *"World's greatest cocksucker 353-3810." These are great! I love them!*

Danny: I leave them in various places—bathroom stalls, and phone booths. If I went to bars I would hand them out, but I don't go to bars because I don't drink.

Chris: *So mostly people phone you or you meet them anonymously?*

Danny: I also cruise. Wherever you are, you can seek out the cruise spots, porno houses and parks. All parks are fair game. This is funny because this is just the standard gay shit.

Chris: *So the methods so far are standard, but when you've picked the person up, is it also standard from then on?*

Danny: Well, no. That's when things change. Well, actually on *one* side it's exactly the same. On the other side it's not the same at all. I *only* have "one-*sided* sex," and it's actually very easy, because most guys don't give a shit; it's fine with them.

Chris: *They just want to get off?*

Danny: Look, I don't want to make a generalization. There are *lots* of guys who are into more than just getting off. There are guys that want more. There are guys that try to do more than that. They may want to see and do stuff to me, but that's the key. I am always totally in control of the situation. It's funny because sexually I am submissive, but nonetheless I am completely in control of what's going on.

Chris: *I was going to ask if you are a top or bottom and if it changes with men and with women.*

Danny: Absolutely. With women I am dominant, with men I am submissive. There you go. That's the difference. It's probably terribly sexist and awful.

Chris: *Not at all. I think I am the same way.*

Danny: From my point of view, though, it's pretty sexist because I'm the *man* so I am dominant over the woman. But with men they are the man (I mean I am the man, too), but they can dominate *over* me. I respond submissively to older men. It's like they can dominate me because they're "above" me.

Chris: *What's so different about man-to-man sex?*

Danny: This may not be true for everyone, but for me it's really a good affirmation of masculinity. It helps me to affirm my masculinity, to be accepted as a gay male in the gay male community. I really like that. When I used to hang out with women I really liked the feeling of community with just one gender, you know what I mean, even though I felt like an imposter. But I could appreciate that sense of community which was there. It was really nice. Sisterhood *is* powerful. So is brotherhood.

Chris: *Are there prejudices in the gay male community against F2M gays?*

Danny: In terms of being gay I am not out about being a transsexual. Forget it. No way! In fact, there is this transsexual group meeting at the gay center, and I was considering going but then I thought, I don't want to be known in the gay community as a transsexual. It's difficult. Well, I shouldn't say that, because it's not difficult. It's actually quite easy, and that's the way I like it.

Chris: *You don't want to blow your cover?*

Danny: I don't want them to know. I worked really hard to attain my manhood, and I don't want the integrity of my masculinity in any way compromised. There was a support group a while back called "Group Integrity." That's really important to most transsexuals, the integrity of their chosen gender identity. There are some transsexuals who want to be out, about their gender situation. I think that's really great, and I support them wholeheartedly.

Chris: *I guess that's a different sense of identity, if someone wants to identify themselves as one chosen gender or as a transsexual.*

Danny: People who want to identify as transsexuals. . . but most of us want to be just the one gender. The support group is great because those who aren't out can get together one day every few months and accept the past, and I think that's very healthy. But I can understand why people don't want to be recognized as transsexuals.

Chris: *You've told me before that the final test of "passing" was to be able to go into a gay male bar where men scrutinize each other much more closely.*

Danny: Yes. You see, they have a more refined sense of gender. They are so much more sensitive to the nuances, the variations, and the differences that are within the male gender. They know through experience that there are transsexuals, crossdressers, and variations of gender. Gays and lesbians know that a woman can look like a man just as easily as a man can look like a woman. So they look to the core when they see you.

Chris: *They are more sophisticated in gender.*

Danny: They've seen a lot of butch women. So if you can go into that community and pass, that's a really good test.

Chris: *Why is transsexual sexual desire so unintelligible to heterosexuals?*

Danny: If you haven't ever experienced gender confusion, you can't imagine what it's like. Gender is immutable. No matter how feminine a man is inside, he knows he's a man. Even transvestites know their core identity is male. They *feel* male, and know they are male in their hearts. If your core identity is female, you *feel* female. You can take hormones and grow a beard, but that's not going to make you a man. In fact, many women are androgynized by natural hormone imbalance, and yet they remain female-identified. No one can change your core gender identity. People think that transsexuals change their gender, but they don't. If you're a true transsexual, your gender identity is unchanging. Any transsexual would say that if they could be "normal" they would. No one *wants* to go through this, but if your core gender identity is at odds with your body, then you *have* to change your body because you cannot change your core identity. No one can. That's the way it is, in general. All the gender experts agree with that, too, for what it's worth.

Chris: *At one of the meetings it seemed that the lovers of F2Ms were mostly bisexual women. Why is that?*

Danny: Many are also straight women but they'd be having "one-sided sex." Most transsexuals do not involve their genitals in sex because it's too incongruous.

Chris: *You talked about a man who had been castrated in a car accident. He's still a sexual being.*

Danny: Which is what we are. We really are castrated men—castrated by God, if you will. Of course, we unfortunately have some *other* parts which have to be dealt with here. We are not *just* castrated.

Chris: *What's the most important thing to a sexually functional masculinity, penis or hormones?*

Danny: Well, a bottom line is that *hormones* make you male, physically. As far as *surgery*, it's different for different people. There are a lot of surgical alternatives for reconstructing the genitals. People have different choices, and what you choose must reflect your own personal priorities. It really varies. For some men it's important to have a penis that can urinate. For others it depends. Many female-to-male transsexuals feel that the only way they they can be men is to have a full-sized penis, functioning to some degree, whatever that may mean— ability to achieve intromission or orgasm with the penis.

Chris: *When it gets down to the possibility of genital interaction, when do you tell them that you are not a genetic male?*

Danny: It depends. As I said before, I try to be in control of the situation, and if I *am* totally in control of the situation, then they will never know. I'm talking to *whatever* degree, even anal sex.

Chris: *You're the bottom?*

Danny: I'm the bottom. It just requires that I don't get totally undressed, and that's why I have to be totally in control of the action. I have to have at least a jockstrap on. That's as naked as I can get, but that's easy to achieve. I've had hundreds of sexual encounters, and most of the time no one finds out what's in my jock. Most of them are not that overly curious. Even though I'm sexually submissive, they respect my limits and allow me to be in control. But if someone really wanted to get nosey, they *would* find something out. I mean, *I have a sexual response, too!*

Chris: *What's the difference in having sex with men now and having sex with men before?*

Danny: I didn't really... if I did it was oral sex... it was already gay sex... umm... that's a grey area. It depends on your partner's perception. If a man thought that I was a woman... we didn't do it. *Now* I know that it doesn't *matter* what my *partner* thinks. *My* perception is the true one, but it took me a really long time to get to that point. Most transsexuals are totally hung up on their partners' perceptions of them.

Chris: *You've talked about having a virtually bionic cock, and I think that is such a powerful image.*

Danny: Yes, that's one of the *positive* aspects. But that is not really a factor in gay sex. I wouldn't use the bionic cock except with women.

Chris: *Well, I'm really interested in both those things.*

Danny: You, like most women, are different from men in that way. In general, women are more flexible in terms of what they will accept. Most men feel that biology is destiny.

Chris: *Whatever is between the legs.*

Danny: Right. The average jerk thinks that, but the average woman is more flexible. Maybe this is just in my own experience, because I know more feminists and lesbians. But I think on the whole, *enlightened* women are more flexible than enlightened *men*.

Chris: *All the F2Ms I have met have been very attractive, very virile guys. I perceive a style of masculinity which is not unlike gay male codes of masculinity. You know, leather and denim, well built, and macho!*

Danny: You've seen a lot of F2Ms who are great examples (there *are* those who aren't so well balanced). You're talking about some pretty self-confident people.

Chris: *What is that swaggering style?*

Danny: I guess it's self-confidence and a little over-compensation for the fact that you are a castrated man; maybe we have to be more "cocky." Also if you show that you're not confident, that's when people start to question you.

Chris: *Why these gay male codes?*

Danny: Well, maybe *they* are over-compensating, too, you know, proving they're a man, and all.

Chris: *Well, I guess everything's a construction.*

Danny: That's true.

Chris: *Do you think the gay male community has its own prejudices about masculinity? It seems that everyone loves a drag queen at the bar, but they all only sleep with the butch boys and macho men.*

Danny: Yes, and that type of limited acceptance is exactly what we would get if we were out. But I want to go back for a minute because we didn't talk about the part of my gay male sexual encounters when they find out, when I'm *not* in control of the situation.

Chris: *Has that happened?*

Danny: It's really interesting. I've gotten different reactions . . . Well, I don't go to bars (except The Spike). Usually I cruise the parking lots of bars (in the suburbs). On this one evening, nothing was happening, so I figured I'd leave. Then this other guy came in a car and made some signal. He was a really big guy (I mean fat), but I'm not prejudiced. So we both drove down this dead-end street, and I pulled up beside him to talk. You know, the usual horny remarks and, "Hi, how are ya doin?" So we decided to go to this motel. I don't remember how it happened, but something happened. Somehow he grabbed me the wrong way and knew something was up. I said my standard rap for when this sort of thing happens. Usually I can anticipate things and say this *before* anything happens, but this time was different, and I think that is why I got the bad response. So I say, "I'm not *like* other guys. Do you know what a hermaphrodite is?" They usually say no, and I say, "That's what I am. A hermaphrodite is someone with both genders, part male and part female." Well, this guy could not deal with it. He kept giggling (he was pretty young). I said, "Don't worry about it." I tried to make light of the situation instead of making it a really heavy thing. Anyway I think I ended up giving him a blowjob or something just to get it over with, but that was the only time I got a negative reaction. In general, people are pretty accepting. I think I've been found out maybe ten times out of a thousand (I've had a lot of sexual encounters). A couple of times there were gay guys who had never been with a woman who wanted to penetrate me vaginally. I'm not into that at all, but I let this one guy do it because it was such a revelation to him. It was what he had been looking for all of his life, only he hadn't realized it. When he saw me all of a sudden it was like, "Wow, I want a man with a vagina." The same way that some guys want a "she-male" (a woman who has a penis), but I was what he wanted. This has happened twice. They were both totally gay guys, and neither of them had ever had sex with a woman. The first time was in the park at 3 in the morning. It was incredible. It was so risky, so scary, but that really adds to the whole thing, too. This totally gay guy was really turned on. He had never even allowed himself to think that *this* was what he wanted. I hope that some guys reading this article might recognize something there. Maybe one or two guys will say, "Oh shit!" It's just like the guys who are attracted to she-males. Unfortunately, I'm not really into it.

Chris: *Are there many gay men who seek pre-op F2Ms as lovers?*

Danny: I've spoken to three other gay guys (genetic males) through the network who are totally homosexually identified but are attracted to this concept of a man with a vagina. One, I remember, told me that he and his F2M lover would go to gay male bars, and this guy would get off on putting his hands down his lover's pants and getting them *wet*, and then deliberately getting his hands near someone's face, or rubbing it on someone's beard, so they would smell it, just to see their reaction. He was somewhat of a rebel.

Matias Viegener

There's Trouble in That Body: Queer Fanzines, Sexual Identity and Censorship

The national flowering of "underground" gay punk fanzines offers us signposts for a new map through alternative gay identities, recolonizing areas such as punk, drag, hardcore, camp, and SM. Mounting a challenge against "assimilationist" gays, they are a product of a generation of gay people *born after* Stonewall, who have hardly known gay life without the specter of AIDS. In a play of nasty photo montages and true confessions, these magazines raise dual sets of problems in regard to oppositional politics—the kinds of gay identities that have been made available—and to the questions of censorship. Both oppositional "identity" politics (what we call gay liberation) and the refusal of censorship are products of Enlightenment thought; the gay fanzine calls the relationship between these two "liberal" positions into question Rejecting bourgeois gay culture as embodied in *The Advocate*, for example, gay punk subcultures develop out of the hardcore rock community and often pirate straight culture for their material.[1]

Blending star lore, anarchy, camp sex, punk rock, and gender dysphoria in homemade packages which range in tone from harsh to arch, gay fanzines alter and appropriate images (publicity photos of actors, models, and politicians), fictionalize (and usually sexualize) histories of the stars, and subvert all the codes of "pure" desire, breaking down the distance between spectator and performer, reader and text, or audience and star. Some of their antecedents are pulp novels, photo-novellas, and slasher novels, such as those around *Star Trek*, which involve sadomasochistic scenes between Captain Kirk and Dr. Spock.[2] However, unlike movie fan magazines or music magazines like *Cream* or *Rolling Stone*, these fanzines do not serve any kind of publicity function.

These "underground" magazines are usually self-published and badly distributed; they are cheap, a dollar or two, and must usually be ordered by mail, one issue at a time, arriving in plain brown envelopes, "to accommodate your potentially oppressive environment."[3] Like straight fanzines, they are how gay punks speak "for themselves to themselves," a defense against misrepresentation in the established media; they are the main forum, not only for the communication about gay punk, but for its construction, the "means by which punk writes itself."[4] *Sin Bros.* and *J.D.s* are xeroxed, folded, and stapled; many are unpaginated, typewritten, or hand-written instead of laser-printed. This is low-tech, desk-top publishing with a nasty twist, street aesthetics in combat against corporate ones. *My Comrade* is a gay men's magazine that flips upside down to *Sister*, a lesbian magazine; both ends display many of the same models dressed in drag or leather (or both—musclemen in bras, for example)—and often playing out multi-page spreads styled like photo-novellas.[5]

The work in these fanzines is either blatantly pseudonymous (one assumes the editors generate the writing) or, most often, from readers—making them unusually participatory. *Homocore* in particular has a frenzied section of letter exchanges, a kind of reader-response network; the editors and readers of all these magazines are highly conscious of the whole sub-genre and refer to each other with regularity. There are frequent first-person narratives: "Tails from the Pit," "My Life as a Celebutante," or "I Had Gay Sex with Bigfoot." The fascination with celebrities and the media, and in this case (from *Sin Bros.* #3) the homophobia and racism of Guns n' Roses lead singer

Axl Rose, generate work that plays both on high ("poetic") and low culture:

> You finally achieved your MTV fame,
> but I remember when you'd squeal my name.
> I first saw your zit-filled face
> in quite a different place.
> Fake I.D., The Rage, 1983.
> "Would you like to come home with me?"
> Bad hairdo from '75, fine-boned and petite,
> you really did like my big black meat.
> Now you play to the fears of this Reaganite nation,
> when Blueboy and Mandate turn your thoughts to masturbation.
> Thirteen year old girls may believe your rock star poses,
> But you'll always prefer my gun to their roses.

Rising stylistically from the hardcore movement and expressing its most reactionary (homophobic and racist) tendencies, Axl Rose's dress and manner are identifiable derivatives of gay leather style. This signals the re-appropriative power of youth subcultures, from the time gay punks first copied the juvenile-delinquent stylizations of straight punk, with its subliminal vampire-like homoeroticism. Likewise "straight" punks were attracted to gay leather and bondage accoutrements (especially piercing and tattooing), imitating "tactics pioneered by the sexual outlaws on the fringes of gay life."[6] The revenge enacted in the "outing" of the poem is ironically intensified through reference to these shifts in style and sexual identification.

The style of these fanzines is graphically reminiscent of the mid-seventies, while the content often echoes the rancor and pessimism of gay pulp novels from the 50s. As in straight fanzines, the two typographic models are graffiti—seen in "magic marker" script—and the ransom note, found typefaces taped together to form an anonymous note; the ransom note suggests a connection to terrorism and crime as well as a "documentary" intervention; graffiti functions as a kind of signature attached to a fictive creation, ironically grounded in the "real." Fanzine images, primarily photographs, are almost always cannibalized from other publications and often altered by graphics or collaged together. Aesthetically, gay fanzines link up to punk subculture more than any other; yet they work through different alliances and allegiances: *Sin Bros.* leans more to the mod or pop/camp aesthetic, while *J.D.s* devotes itself to a more skinhead punk; *Homocore* combines hardcore rock and punk with radical fairies, while *Pansy Beat* and *My Comrade/Sister* invokes a more New York underground club or glam rock aesthetic. What all of them share is a fusing of punk with drag and camp sensibility and a revisionist articulation of the social construction of gender, race, and sexuality.

A spectrum of political activism, from anarchist to libertarian, is often clothed in costumes unfamiliar to a mainstream gay or straight audience. There are articles on ACT-UP, on the Anarchist's Convention, on beauty pageant protests, and on Pro Choice rallies. The logic to these articles operates quite differently from what one sees in the *Advocate*; it isn't just good, correct, and reasonable to be an activist for these causes: it is also pleasurable. It's cool. In a certain sense this merely rehearses what already exists within ACT-UP, which has its singular manner of fusing fashion with function. These fanzines share ACT-UP's penchant for turning political issues into spectacles; for every direct or declarative challenge made against social hegemony, homophobia, and AIDS discrimination, another indirect one is lodged in terms of style. Homophobe Axl Rose becomes a closet cocksucker, not just an ordinary one, but a tacky cocksucker with a bad haircut; conservative senator Jesse Helms is transformed into a carnival stick figure, a lecherous Colonel Sanders. The contradictions in the political situation of gay people are formulated and "magically" resolved at the superficial level of style. The rigidity of compulsory heterosexuality, as Adrienne Rich terms it, is inverted through outraged accounts of the horrors of child-bearing heterosexuals in "Underground in the Land of the Breeders."

Clad in uniforms of leather, torn jeans, safety pins, and nasty haircuts (uniforms elaborated in local dialects of skateboards, pink triangles, lingerie, and false breasts), these new gay magazines impose a sharp break between those inside the subculture and those outside it. The eclecticism itself is hard to figure: junkie narratives, drag-queen exposes, Jacobean revenge fantasies, photos of punks with their pants down, high school locker fetishism, photo montages, "kinky escapades, bedroom techniques, unbridled passion, and secret sex codes."[7] The work that these publications foster is a kind of festive combat: they employ style to decenter a totalizing cultural hegemony. Style in this formulation involves a reterritorialization, a vocabulary stolen from the master, much in the way Jamaican patois developed as the basis for reggae, in which suppressed issues of race and colonialism could be articulated in popular form.

Style in these works functions to rehearse and sarcastically resolve cultural contradictions. On the one hand, style generates a mark of difference, a code visible only to the initiated. On the other it signals a certain refusal—a classic example would be Jean Genet's adaptation of the tube of vaseline, which moves from being the dirty object that proclaims Genet's homosexuality to the world to being a kind of fetish for him; the fetish function of style in this underworld is to subvert the codes of the master.[8] It is, as Dick Hebdige says, a kind of guarantee: of absolute visibility and absolute hatred, projecting the abstraction of homophobia into a concrete, if provisional symbolic structure.

This codification of oppositional identities is a central enterprise in gay fanzines:

> J.D.s like all girl gangs, had a code, for even among kids like these, there is a code. She denies her girlhood and flaunts her sex. . . . It's not easy to love a delinquent girl. She's vulgar, she's coarse. She despises the world.[9]

Within the context of refusal and negation, these kinds of subcultures generate "noise" as opposed to sound, as Hebdige puts it, "an actual mechanism for semantic disorder: a kind of temporary blockage in the system of representation."[10] They are perceived by the gay mainstream as reactionary, trashy, unreadable. The texts themselves are unreasonable, badly printed, often xeroxes of xeroxes, and filled with aggressive, raw graphics. In both style and content, they are opposed to the sense and sensibility of such mainstream gay publications as *Christopher Street*, *The Advocate*, or *Gay Sunshine*. Clarity and universality are objects of contempt. The enemy is less heterosexuals than gay yuppies, or as the editor of *Bimbox* puts it, "crypto-fascist clones and dykes... telling us how to think."[11] They celebrate the useless fetish, the bad seed, the ugly adolescent; *Homocore*'s Tom Jennings states that "One thing everyone here has in common is that we're all *social mutants*; we've outgrown or never were part of any 'socially acceptable' categories. You don't have to be gay . . . any decision that makes you an outcast is enough."

That these magazines have more than just an oppositional (or civil-libertarian) relation to censorship is born out in the difficulty they have had in getting distributed; most issues have letters from readers that complain about the difficulty of finding the magazine at conventional *or alternative* outlets. *J.D.s* received a scathing indictment from Toronto's leftist art magazine *Fuse*, and was refused distribution at the Montreal Anarchist Bookstore and Glad Day Bookstore, a world-famous gay bookstore in Toronto.[12] *On Our Backs*, the punkish lesbian porno magazine out of San Francisco, has been locked in a long-standing battle with the feminist Sisterhood bookstore.

These are the moments when the issues of censorship are at their thorniest. The flimsiness of the left's civil libertarian arguments around censorship are difficult to separate from the whole project of oppositional politics. Both of these are products of the Enlightenment, which proclaimed the right of individual citizens to band together (to identify themselves and claim rights, much as the gay movement itself did with Stonewall) and overthrow the absolutism of the monarch and the state censor: the state office became a private one, left for every individual to determine.[13] Under free-market liberalism, one was free to sell whatever was desired by the consumer, which invoked a more modern form of censorship, that of the marketplace.[14] What could and could not be circulated becomes more implicit, controlled by its own invisible hand.

Censors, as we all know, worry only about the corruption of others: they construct vulnerable others (usually women and children) and invulnerable selves. Enlightened thought always holds censors to be someone else, a foreigner, or at worst, when caught in the role of censoring, to attribute it to a need to keep us free from foreign (communist, homosexual, etc.) contamination. This is sustained by the claims of the Enlightenment to have separated theory (knowledge) from practice (power) to create a kind of objectivity—and a kind of science. There are those who know (philosophers, anthropologists, doctors) and those who are known (women, natives, and homosexuals). Once this relation is recognized by the disenfranchised as one of power tied with knowledge, the known begin to claim to know themselves and thereby deserve to master themselves; this constitutes the basis of most modern movements of liberation.

Philosophically, the role of the censor was replaced by the rule of reason; reason displaced the "divine" power of the monarch and has fueled most oppositional movements, including gay liberation. The gay identity embroidered by the magazine *Gay Sunshine,* by Rita Mae Brown or David Leavit—or even historically by Walt Whitman—is a kind of Enlightenment project: homosexuality is both natural and reasonable, different from but the same as heterosexuality.[15] Some books can be judged by their covers—or by their titles. *Homocore* and the slew of new fanzines are informed by quite a different sensibility: queerness is both natural and unnatural, good and bad, reasonable and irrational.

While generating the basis for modern liberal culture, the Enlightenment also saw the growth of the first large-scale pornographers and the first obscenity trials. The writings of the Marquis de Sade typify the Manichean underside of the Enlightenment project, one that has always been troubling for good liberals. Enormous social resources are devoted to policing the line between acceptable representations of sexuality (heterosexual married couples) and the unacceptable ones (anal sex, rape, incest).[16] One has merely to look at the gay movement's troubled relation to transvestism and pederasty to see these distinctions at work within an oppositional microcosm. One reaction to this appears in *Homocore* #4, an interview with the boyish co-founder of NAMBLA, the North American Boy Lover's Association; what it reproaches is the ruthless habit of the oppositional movements to divest themselves of their extremities, to sever the troubling parts of homosexuality or sexuality in general.

The Sadean scenario has always been disturbing for enlightened culture, and it is seen as a kind of medieval throwback to feudal relations in place of "positive" or reasonable sexual relations based on equality or the "reasonable" hierarchy between citizens of the first and citizens of the second order, between men and women.[17] What these readings always depend upon is ignoring both the reversals and the ritual functions involved in the scenario. Nothing in Sade is merely symbolic. Power relations are played out and turned around, ritualized so as to manifest all the contradictions which are normally carefully hidden in the clarity and reason of Enlightenment thought. When the Society of the Friends of Crime asks Juliette what she thinks of whipping, she answers: "I like to whip and be whipped." One can hardly fail to notice that the clinical coolness of *100 Days of Sodom* is infused with a resistance to optimistic reason; like Voltaire, Sade opposes optimistic rationality, and his texts always empty the sound center of a system based on reason. Setting cultural oppositions such as sadism and masochism into play against normative rules (of behavior and logic) is a recurrent strategy for unmooring fixed social hegemonies.

The kinds of contradictions which are enacted by this generation of gay magazines are those of post-war, Western urban culture: grow up/stay young, sex is good/sex is bad, be nice/be cool, upward mobility/downward, be private/be public. Even the relation to authority and authorized codes—defer to/rebel from—is one we've seen before. What is different is a questioning of gay-identity politics and the articulation and engagement of style, which one sees on the simplest level by the fusion of punk and camp, two once-antithetical aesthetics.

Much of issue #6 of *J.D.s* is devoted to Kristy McNichol, the child actress who starred as the androgynous "Buddy" in the 70s TV series *Family*. One page has "live" photos (taken off the TV screen) with the sidebar "Tomboy Buddy uses her gnarly board as a weapon against the evil child molester/rapist in a special two-part episode of *Family* that had a chilling one-word title which I can't remember." The two sequential photographs show the man's plaid-clad back and Buddy's face as she swings the stick. They constitute a classic moment of 70s gritty "realism," showing the enlightened viewer how by facing evil one can control it. The documentary quality of the photographs reflects the documentary spirit of the show: cool rationality was the baggage it required of its audience to generate understanding.

On the page opposite the "live" photo there is an untitled and uncaptioned sketch, much like an unpolished Tom of Finland. It shows a short-haired girl hitching a ride as she stands on her skateboard, her breasts thrust forward, looking for trouble. Positioned in the same place as the attacker in the two Buddy photos is an androgynous skinhead "male," also in a plaid shirt. He has his hands on his crotch, and as the girl dominates the frame, it is unclear if he will threaten her or just urinate; looking further at his hips, it is very likely that he is a woman. He/she embodies a rewriting of *Family*—a post-feminist, post-liberal paradigm in which it is conceivable that one might want to court danger or be the object of a "male" gaze. While hardly advocating rape or acquiesence to rapists, this sketch highlights two versions of possibly compatible desire, displacing the model of aggressive perverse sexuality versus victimized normal sexuality. While the "live" photos demonstrate the tendency to re-appropriate found material, the sketch underscores the main axiom of punk anarchism, which is *do it yourself*, whether to take up a guitar or a pen.[18] The dialogue of these two pages sets up a paradigm of gay identity around the poles of pleasure and danger, between enlightened understanding and guilty delight. It also wrestles with the distinctions of inside and outside, of defining the subculture by the terms of liberalism (moderating the social repression of "natural" desires) or by the terms of the subculture: the negation of cultural hegemony, sexual mores, and commodity culture through deliberate strategies of anti-grammaticality.

The contradictions between liberal gay culture and queer subculture come up later in the tragicomic Kristy McNichol centerfold spread. "'Everyone thinks Kris is so innocent,' said her ex-housemate Ina Liberace. 'Deep down, there's trouble in that body.'" We are treated to Kristy trivia, such as the fact that *Family* lived in Pasadena, "the birthplace of Dennis Cooper." As she neared her 18th birthday, "she started acting less like a little adult and more like an adolescent." The final blurbs are about the palimony suit filed by her lover, Ina Liberace (Liberace's niece), which is the moment in which McNichol's sexuality became a tabloid scandal and a public issue. But the focus here is less on the "outing" (no surprise to anyone. . .) than on the scandal; while they all play with the closet, few of these fanzines make *coming out* the determinant of gay identity. This corresponds to the argument John D'Emilio has made against gay liberation's "overreliance on a strategy of coming out" which has "allowed us to ignore the institutionalized ways in which homophobia and heterosexism are reproduced."[19]

The McNichol saga offers us an anatomy of the de-sexualized "lesbian" identity built by the post-Stonewall movement of the 70s. The actress's mute face is covered by xerox lines and copier dirt, almost effacing her; the kind of gay identity constructed by *Gay Sunshine* is rendered particularly untenable: the "naturalness" of being gay, of celebrating ("good") gay sex. McNichol's surprised, melancholy face shines through the xerox dirt, a metempsychosis of her (pure onscreen) life with her troubled afterlife: once the archetype of the adult child, she becomes the emblem of the childish adult who won't behave. By describing McNichol through her confusion, both text and graphics reject the concept of monologic sexual identity. As Holly Hughes has described the imagery of lesbianism, "So much of lesbian experience has been represented in this really *precious*, sentimental, gooey way—like a lesbian Disneyland.[20] In response to the use of conventional but problematic values, gay fanzines construct displays such as the McNichol piece. They give voice to a gay constituency that proclaims the value of being bad, of being unnatural and perverse, and chooses to remain in a dysphoric underworld rather than submit to the normalizing eye of mass culture and be absorbed within it. This kind of negation preserves a space for social alterity that works against the Disneyfication of queers.

The proliferation of gay fanzines signals a resistance to rationalization. In the context of current cultural politics, arguments around "nature" and the status of "the natural" dominate any kind of social or activist reasoning. But the rhetoric of nature spurs wildly various political agendas.[21] Anchoring gay identity to the shifting sands of "the natural" is a perilous strategy at a time when the logic of reasonable nature is being used to clean the air but also to prevent abortions, to question the authority of the American Medical Association over knowledge of the human body but also to make provisions for quarantining gay men. In most appeals to the unity of nature and reason the line between utopianism and authoritarianism is perilously thin. Through their combination of images and texts, the gay fanzines speak to the current crisis in identity formation—in knowledge of oneself and one's sexuality—and to the recognition that knowledge aligned with power can cease to liberate and become a mode of surveillance and repression.[22]

Notes

[1]See David James' "Hardcore: Cultural Resistance in the Postmodern," *Film Quarterly*, 42:2, Winter 1988-89, pp. 31-9. Straight hardcore music mounted "a deliberately anachronistic attempt to sustain early punk's negativity against its diffusion and assimilation by the music industry as various forms of new wave. The entirely recalcitrant music provided a besieged subculture with the basis for

defensive rituals in which the sonic (and other forms of) violence and the obstinate anti-professionalism that signalled rejection of overproduced corporate rock also informed strategies of negation and antigrammaticality for everyday self-presentation. . ." p. 35.

[2]An excellent survey of Star Trek slasher novels can be found in Constance Penley's "Brownian Motion: Women, Tactics, and Technology," in *Technoculture*, ed. Constance Penley and Andrew Ross (Minneapolis: University of Minnesota Press, 1991).

[3]*Homocore* masthead.

[4]Virginia Boston, *Punk Rock* (New York: Penguin, 1978), p. 14. David James, "Poetry/Punk/Production: Some Recent Writing in LA," *Postmodernism and Its Discontents*, ed. E. Anne Kaplan (London: Verso, 1988), p. 178.

[5]For descriptive surveys of queer fanzines, see Dennis Cooper's "Homocore Rules," *The Village Voice*, 4 Sep. 1990, 92; Bill Van Pary's "Fag Rags Come of Age," *The Advocate*, 6 Nov. 1990, 70-2; Wickie Stamps' "Queer Girls With an Attitude," *The Advocate*, 20 Nov. 1990, 56-7; and Adam Block's "The Queen of 'Zine," *The Advocate*, 20 Nov. 1990, 75.

[6]Craig Lee, "Getting Down With the Third Sex: Gay post-kids build a scene of their own," *L.A. Weekly*, 20 July 1990, 56.

[7]*My Comrade/Sister*, Summer 1989, n.p.

[8]Dick Hebdige, *Subculture: The Meaning of Style*, (London: Methuen, 1979), pp. 1-19.

[9]G. B. Jones, "Gang Girl," *J.D.s*, #5, n.p.

[10] Hebdige, p. 90.

[11] Quoted in Dennis Cooper, "Homocore Rules," *The Village Voice*, 4 Sep. 1990, 92.

[12] See *Homocore*, #1, 4.

[13] This transformation has a cognate in the creation of Bentham's Panopticon, which Michel Foucault identifies as symptomatic of the shift in social paradigms in the 18th century. See *Discipline & Punish* (New York: Vintage, 1979), p. 197.

[14] Much of my argument here is indebted to Sue Curry Jansen's *Censorship: The Knot That Binds Power and Knowledge* (Oxford: Oxford University Press, 1988).

[15] The earliest American gay magazines, *ONE* and *Mattachine Review*, stressed how "homosexuals were just like anyone else except for their sexual orientation"; the *Advocate* added "pride in difference" to this same "longing to be a part of the mainstream." Michael Bronski, *Culture Clash: The Making of Gay Sensibility* (Boston: South End Press, 1984), pp. 146-47. See Dennis Altman's *The Homosexualization of America* (Boston: Beacon, 1982) for an analysis of post-Stonewall gay "identity politics" on the model of ethnic minority communities.

[16] See Gayle Rubin's "Thinking Sex," in Carole S. Vance, ed., *Pleasure and Danger: Exploring Female Sexuality* (Boston: Routledge & Kegan Paul, 1984), pp. 267-319.

[17] A determining factor in this de/cision is the replacement of the unacceptable categories of master and slave (or king and subject) with the bourgeois ethos of employer and employee.

[18]"The self-consciously amateurish style . . . is a trademark of fanzine literature, as it is of punk in general. The fanzines clearly project the ambivalent attitude with which punks approached their work, both in writing and in music. The punk mindset presents us with a paradox. It combines the hatred of apathy and a sense of urgency concerning everything related to punk culture, with an acute awareness of sociopolitical impotence, a belief that actions were inconsequential, that an improvement of self or society was at best elusive and at worst utterly futile. . . . Self-effacement is a constant theme in the fanzines." Tricia Henry, *Break All Rules: Punk Rock and the Meaning of a Style* (Ann Arbor: UMI Research Press, 1989), p. 97.

[19]John D'Emilio, "Capitalism and Gay Identity," in Snitow, et al., *Powers of Desire: The Politics of Sexuality* (New York: Monthly Review Press, 1983), p. 111.

[20]"An Interview with Holly Hughes," *My Comrade/Sister*, Winter 1990, n.p.

[21]In terms of sexuality, Rubin's "Thinking Sex" is still invaluable here: a widespread refusal to see how sexuality is cultural, not natural, or to think of sexuality in terms of "natural" drives and cultural limits, still exists. See also, of course, Michel Foucault, *The History of Sexuality*, trans. Alan Sheridan (New York: Vintage, 1978).

[22]Addresses for the fanzines discussed in this article are: *Homocore*, c/o World Power Systems, P. O. Box 77731, San Francisco, CA 94107; *MyComrade/Sister*, 326 E. 13th St., #15, New York, NY 10003; *Sin Bros.*, P. O. Box 618, North Hollywood, CA 91630; *J.D.s*, P. O. Box 1110, Toronto, Ontario, Canada M5C 2K5

Andrea Slane

Unconventional Weapons

Tape recorder strapped to my thigh, I wander, looking hard for trouble in a woman. Suffering for a mental joy ride, moral inertia, I lash out wildly in the direction of my own most resistance. Soul search and destroy, I rip at thin membranes against fear, an act which strengthens muscle fiber, heart and stomach, and threatens to spew me splayed out tumbling on the other side of a callous situation. A masochist by craft, I engineer displays of my own helplessness: given over to a violent scene, a momentary cure or gospel, the trick to pressing gently someone's gun, my gun, into my quivering anticipation. The tape plays endless loops of brutal nightly news, ample source material for my wayward plans. The stories feed me, let me reclaim abandon.

    I squirm in self-imposed arousal, basking in the disapproving frowns of women who excite me for the acts I make them do in my mind's dungeon as I pass. . . This one's tongue stays firmly in her mouth; she does not gasp with us or speak her want to have a hand, an arm inside her open cunt. Her set mouth pulls me as her image quivers in my viewfinder. She glances scorn in my direction. Pushed to the verge of under-exposure, mitigated only by her lighter skin, I imagine she imagines herself against, above, aside from me. She is acting in a different story, one that glorifies her. And I have not asked her permission.

Another woman passes and distracts me, causing brilliant flashes in my eyes as the iris opens in compensation for her darker hue. I've been warned to keep my mind's hands off her. She complicates my aims and I defile her by association. I am not so sure. But I am drawn by her purposeful indifference as she does not notice me.

I picture myself, unclothed in chains and leather, draped in wires, cables, cords, regalia which belies my vulnerability. I expose myself strategically, between the cuts on movement, forcing each again to tell more my distorted narrative than hers. Incorporated in a larger frame and played out in a space nearly imagined, I promise to bring them to the brink of something live.

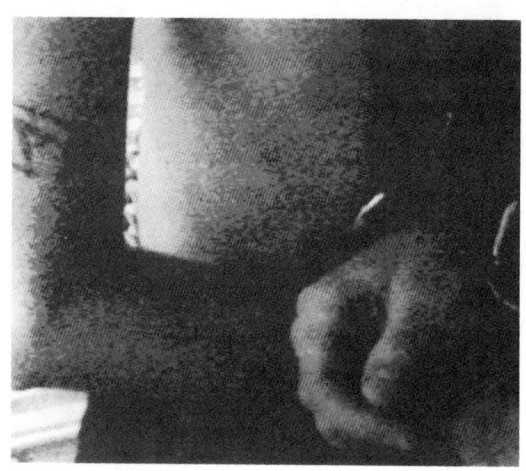

Sucked in from the street to this place where signals cross and messages mix, we stand together loosely as at a party not going well. I tell the story of a friend of mine, long lost, as the flickers from the TV sets cast different shades of blue across their somber faces. I tell them of my wish to see her, a survivor of random abuses, who metes out retribution randomly as well. They walk, nearly parallel, along opposite walls of monitors, fascinated but as yet unmoved. My thigh-strapped recorder begins playing subliminally the soundtrack of the Senate Judiciary Committee in session set to muzak. I stop my telling and try to convince them that we form a community, women in a violent context. They do not respond. I push a red button insistently and begin to tell another story, while the video rewinds.

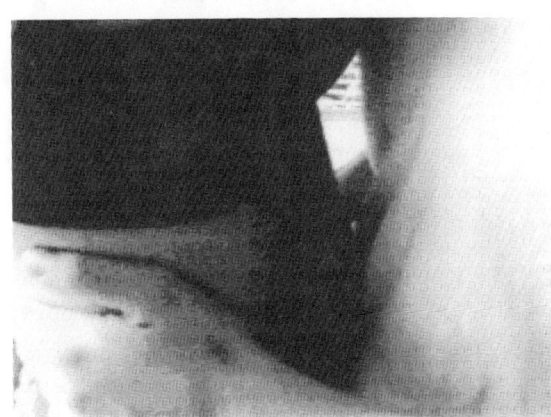

"She is one of my favorites, Wanda, the cheerleader hit-mom. I like to stare at pictures of her red blush much too heavily applied against her too pale skin," I say. "Wanda and her daughter Shanna, 13 at the time, resided in a middle class abode amid the tumble down. The neighbors found her suspect, as they'd watched her three-times marry always to a richer man, and so cast Wanda as a woman willing to stop at nothing." The taller woman doesn't get it I can tell. She hasn't read the papers in a year, or maybe that the story in itself is true does not attract her. She has gained my attention by her lack thereof. "Pretty and intelligent," I continue, "Shanna still could not make the pompom squad at school. Her mother, risking a second disqualification, aimed her frustration at a one-time friend and now arch-rival, Amber." As I approach her she can hear for the first time the thigh-strapped recorder under my skirt, droning on the words of a black executive fantasizing the infatuation and sequential rejection suffered by a law professor, black as well. I have touched a taut strung cord, I can tell, as she has tensed in recognition.

The other one is already caught, ready to take me on in argument, filtering her arousal through elaborate attempts to interrupt my telling. They both watch me now as I stop the tape, and brush my varied skins as I remove it. "I believe in friendship," I say, "and I believe in its danger for us." I pull from my pocket and insert the one I want. I finger the volume, increasing the pitch. "I hate this girl, I want to get rid of her and her mother too. I want to get rid of these people forever. You know what I'm saying?" Wanda's voice booms forth to corroborate my own.

The paler woman comes closer, thrown off guard and attracted by the smallness of the machine. She has forgotten who I'm talking for, she confesses, and I laugh out loud at having gotten her to speak so frankly. She looks annoyed, perhaps that I would interrupt seduction with a mockery that forces her to self-reflection. She pouts and claims she will not watch or listen anymore, and this at last intrigues me. As I respect her need to keep apart from that which I entice her with, I tie her down, her legs clamped shut the way she likes them, face so close to the TV I can watch it in her eyes. I've cared for her, and now she can enjoy unfettered.

Interrupting my own presumption, I push play and caress the knobs a second longer than was bearable for either, adjusting the volume so it mixes with the voice of Wanda, now subdued and matter of fact. The sudden appearance of color-bars in uniform across the walls has startled the loose one, so studiedly ignoring us before as we were wrestling. She turns her head, against her will, in my direction. I smile and catch her eye before she can turn back unnoticed. A point.

A 57-second home video, court evidence, shows Diedre, 21, in the act of shooting a man three times in the chest. "This man believed himself to be an initiate into an assassin's club," I fill them in, this story more obscure than those I've 'til now used. "Her boss is at the camera." My bound and unbound lovers are transfixed. "They too were lovers. But she was utterly dependent on him, through and through." I emphasize this last with motions one to each with concentrated gaze. They both stare, mesmerized, as Diedre grabs him by the hair, delivering a final shot, a shot to the head. "Shot instead because he knew of a counterfeiting scheme her lover-boss involved her in," I say over the soundtrack. The loop begins again. The woman strolls on long legs along the wall, pretending not to be as fascinated as my current favorite looks, her face positioned so close and fixed to a screen. "I feel I do not wholly understand her photo-tears," I say, so close to her pretended strolling that her jump reveals she was indeed not paying mind to anything except the woman on the many screens.

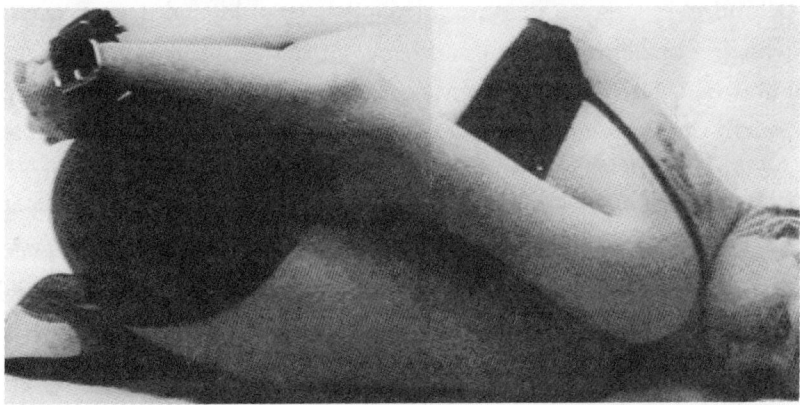

I hold before her the newsprint picture. She reads, and asks me, breaking from her role, if I could please replay the Senate hearing tape again. She wants to hear the strong Anita stand alone before a giant while the ashen Diedre deals a blow of death which masks her inability to stand alone. She is intrigued, like me, with the duplicity of the strength of victims.

But the tape has ended, 5 loops gone, and though she still looks hopeful at the static, thinking it might loop again, I do

not permit her this indulgence. She tries not to betray her want, her need to see the woman's face once more, then serving six concurrent terms of life. I tell her she has been sentenced to death. I match her former gestures of indifference, make sacrifices of a different kind, and let her keep the article and treasured picture, tuck it in her purse unnoticed. "Perpetrators become victims, victims perpetrators, and nobody moves," I say, as if they hung on my words.

As I draw a breath to continue I feel the impact of an engine from behind. My captive is loose, clawing in a sudden flurry of wildly whirring blades from front and back, an onslaught from her tongue unleashed. She speaks and shrieks as though a chorus of wise sisters barked out with her voices clear and loud, as she hurls herself against me and we fall. She pins me in an instant, and I grin beneath her, let her recognize the charge of violence in her lust for retributions. Edges of a shadow sweep like razors over the surface of her unblinking eyes, one layer at a time as each car passes, removed again, again, a funeral procession seven times until the meat of the matter, flesh, truth is exposed to the stinging splash of impact. I think she notices with the shock that I am with her, crossing elements that do not mix for me acknowledged, and for her disguised. She looks paler still as a metaphor she clung to falls open and apart, rising before us.

With the spectacle of my self-orchestrated surrender, I mimic her gestures of empowerment now that I have set her free. She's startled long enough to let me change the tape. The screens spring back to life the further testimony of our white-skinned culture, heavy metal, black leather and lace attitude. She scowls. The standing woman also does not hide her disappointment, but for her it's at the loss of Diedre, not my substitution. She does not glance but once, and frustrates me with temperance, as I before did her with my temerity, I am convinced. I let the other blindfold me, which she believes to be a sign of my capitulation. I smile beneath the leather strip, knowing better, pulling it down when I adjust the camera. My image dominates my dominatrix which she unwittingly becomes behind her. I do not need to see the image I have made. I hunger for the spectacle itself. The darker woman protests, I can hear, involving herself finally again. She does not want me to be gagged. She wants to hear my stories.

I imagine my opponent has been duped to still believe in the efficacy of an image, not yet given over to video atheism. The tapes play on behind her, split screen she and I now live transmitted next to me before with others. I implicate her in the jealousies of three women of dubious association. The other woman watches now, despite herself afraid that 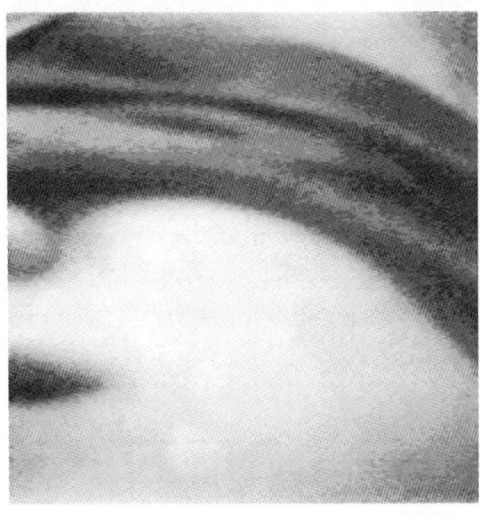 I am challenging her claims to subjectivity by forcefully exerting mine. She says as much to the whiter one who does not miss a beat in binding me still further as she talks. They watch me pornographically displayed, handled, fondled, tasting myself through the relay of another woman's hand, twitching at the touch of both a drop of wax and a caress. These images disturb them both, they say, ignoring that they're juxtaposed beside now standing thus above me. As they complain, I am amused they do not think to turn the power off the sets. Apparently they can only complicate the seductions I have staged, and I have surpassed myself.

But I still depend on them for my arousal. I need them each to want to live without me. I need to have it documented. In order to distract them from the images, I return to telling stories. The taller, smarter woman perks and instantly concurs that counterfeit intentions and conspiracy aside, Diedre was, for instance, an emotionally damaged person, threatened and controlled by him, the man who put her up to it. "I remember that the words around her story end abruptly at a sordid summary," I say. ""I looked in vain back then for the continuation. You have the article," I gesture with my head towards where the darker woman stands. "Why don't you read it for us, Honey?" I take her pause as an embarrassed thank-you as the lighter woman moves her knee off of my chest, all details of expression abandoned, and rummages around in the purse of the other still standing stoic and unmoving, not more than several inches from my head. "Diedre's mother, several aunts, uncles, and cousins testified that she was raped at 11 by a neighbor, and was rejected by her father." Her voice carries with it a throaty texture between self-righteousness and fascination.

A small silence lets us think before my long forgotten tape clicks into auto-reverse and Wanda, would-be author of the Last Hurrah, proceeds to never really speak the overt violent deaths of Amber and her mom in conversations coming from my thigh-strapped recorder. "Maybe a car wreck, impact or explosion. Then it wouldn't be so obvious." Wanda's raucous laughter almost always punctuates the conversations. "Terry, her former brother-in-law, angry at his inability to score a fuck, 'hated the bitch' and tried to set her up. Exploiting Wanda's fantasy, he plots and schemes to trap her, have her punished, then to sell her story he concocted big, to movie rights, already now before the case is tried in full," I explain, driven to eloquence by the slow caress of my ankles by each of my distracted captors.

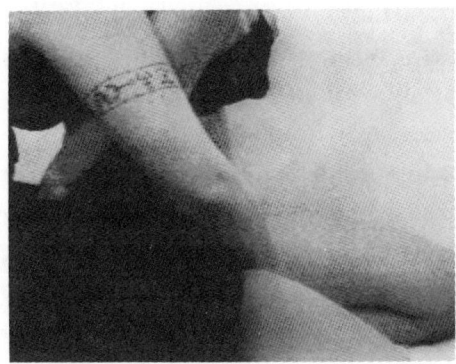

Despite its success I feel as though this story has played itself out. I have them choose another audio tape from the collection lining the baseboards in custom-made cabinets. The lighter woman bends on all fours to see the titles, calling out one after the other a sordid list of cases, alphabetically arranged by perpetrator, cross-referenced by victim. She hands her partner one on which they both agree. The darker one is charged to change the tape itself, brushing maddeningly as she does my clit so close as it is to the play button.

They've chosen the story of a local girl, La Jolla socialite sensation, battered ex-wife of a fortune, my second-favorite tape. I realize that they love me still. We listen now to Betty's psychologist, defender of the double-murderess. "A woman whose husband cheats on her is a victim who, driven by the infidel-man's lies, typically sinks into stages of rage and can erupt in a sudden and explosive reality." With that I ask my mistresses, pleading as I do, "What woman now will be allowed to author her own violence?"

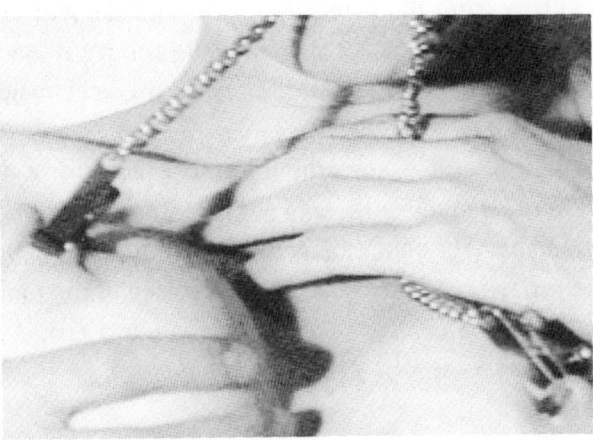

The question saddens them and they untie me, ritually slow, all but my hands. They move together, casting off their clothing piece by piece, draping them randomly across what little furniture there is. They want to sit near naked in armchairs across from each other and sleep—I've seen this one before. Just as I've resigned myself to watching their coziness still partially immobilized from afar, I catch a glimpse of your buttocks and smile. As I struggle to my feet, I think about the last time, when I watched a sliver off my knuckle as it drifted so soundlessly towards the carpet. It took a long time to heal. Forgotten then already as I ran my fingers slowly over the ridges of your teeth where just before I tasted the resistance of the impact of my hand, balled up too small to give you much but pleasure as I plunged deep within the darkness that I don't imagine. I follow you down the hallway and back towards the entrance. Newspaper photographs are strewn, yellowed, across the floor. I notice a cute girl's face lodged among a cluster of 4 more. I bend to look more closely again at her face. I have a crush, a secret to no one, and read aloud as usual accounts of her, one girl's body stabbed for 50 more, to draw you nearer.

"Stand-in again, again, for maniac's commotion. Exposed bare-breasted, she was first in the series. Brown hair and clean-cut looks, they dragged her un-all-American across the driveway gravel, suburbs of a road's shoulder to shoulder." My voice gets louder with each word, caught up in the story and your lack of response. "Nude dancing Tiffany from the front page, it took three good girls more before she was absolved of dancing. . ." With this last shout you catch my eye, pull, drag, lift and push me back in the passion I imagine before her death.

A sigh resembles something lost as I reach for a nipple that comes off in my bound hands, held fast by a strand of stubborn tissue, soft and resilient. Our coming together depends upon embracing the depths of the purest victim. We hold her between us and mourn in our glow, waiting for a love to take shape in an anti-erotic so vast it includes us, eludes us.

I startle awake and land feet first from a forty-story fall. You've left. I wander to the foyer, tired myself, thinking of the two girls sleeping in the other room and of that long lost friend somewhere beyond the limits of the current scene. Without much ceremony, outside on the sidewalk, I recall again her story: that she was one of two baby girls, Silver and Kristina, 6 and 3, abandoned in the desert, who lived despite the scorching heat; that they grew up to have 21 personalities each; that the younger one was raped, and that the defense claimed the consent of at least one of 42. That I'd lost track of her.

We meet again now. Right after she has thrown an unknown caustic chemical into a cabbie's face when asked to pay, trying then to strangle him. She drove off in his cab and picks me up unexpectedly in the pink haze of dawn. She holds the gleaming handcuff key beneath her tongue and so I do not wonder why at first she doesn't speak. A sparkling drop of blood escapes my trembling bitten lip as I climb in, awkward still by virtue of the cuffs. I grin again in thanks for the sureness of the presence of blood, its discipline. I do not even think of moving and am told, "You are where you do not think," as she spits the key out on her lap. She kisses me. "Car wreck, impact, or explosion. . ." plays from my cunt recorder. We leave no trace.

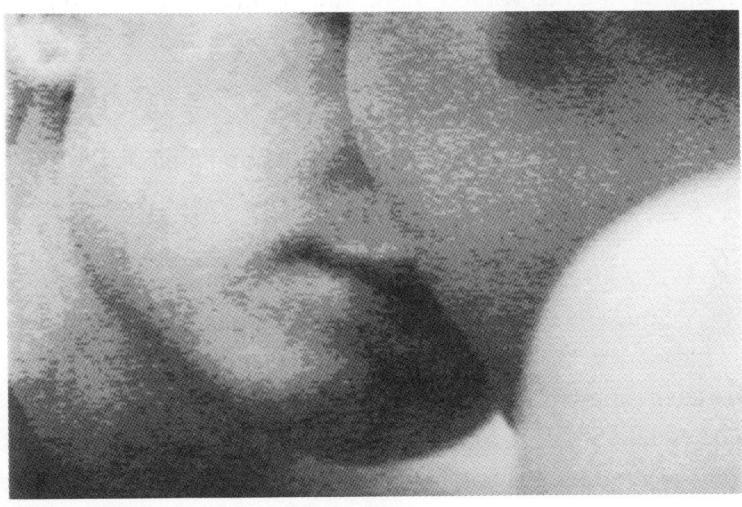

Ennio Flaiano

1963

"This is what I think hell is like," R. was telling me. "A place where sinners continuously and forever repeat the things that they were particularly fond of on earth and which were the cause of their damnation. Example: the lustful will experience all the horrors and disgusts of eternal copulation, the violent sinner will repeat his violent acts, incessantly, but without result, the glutton will have to devour repugnant mountains of food all by himself, along with his own vomit, the traitor will keep on betraying, forever, even himself, the wrathful . . ."

"Enough," I tell him, "you're describing life itself."

★   ★   ★   ★   ★

End of interview. "Do you believe that television has lowered the cultural level of the public?" "No, I believe that television has lowered the cultural level of the intellectuals." "If you had to define the drama of modern life in a few words . . . ?" "The drama of modern life is this: everyone is looking for peace and solitude. And for the very reason that they're looking for these two things, they chase them away from the very places where they can be found." "And now an indiscreet question: why is it that you write so little?" "My dear sir, I don't have a vocation for narrative. I write, which is something a great deal different ."

*   *   *   *   *

Italians don't love nature because they themselves *are* in nature. This was the starting point of a conversation with L., in a trattoria of fishermen near the mouth of the Arrone. We were lamenting the fact that those same fishermen who frequented the trattoria had transformed the beach into a flattened wasteland, burnt to a crisp and blown away, destroying all forty-seven species of plant-life which make up the Mediterranean bush and which are interdependent (that is, each one helps the others to live). We remembered together a landscape that was once Arcadian and solemn, suited in every way for a landing by Aeneas, thick with tamarisks, with cardoons, with wild cherry trees, junipers . . . shaggy and green thickets that protected the young holm oaks from the salt and which, in their turn, protected the old pines of the forest. The woodlands that made their way out towards the shore with their needles, their violet flowers, their stout branchings-out, and which molded sand dunes together making them every year more imposing and impassable, upon which neither the southwesterlies nor the northwesterlies could make an impression, have now all disappeared. Whenever a car passes by nowadays it raises up a cloud of dust. We asked ourselves then how it could be that the fishermen (who certainly know the sea and the winds) hadn't understood the necessity of saving that vegetable hierarchy established by nature, which defended their houses and tempered their climate. Well, the answer is the one we've already given. The "poor" Italian isn't moved in front of a landscape, that is, he doesn't see it as a harmonious and intangible thing (an inspiration of various emotions and the keeper of memory, if you will) but he takes it apart for its singular utilitarian elements. Whatever is of use to him, he takes, the rest he destroys. He acts, in other words, like a being inserted so very much into nature as not to have the capacity to admire it, but only to make it serve his needs. In certain respects, the poor Italian is a rodent. But the "rich" Italian is perhaps something even worse. The "rich man" understands the landscape as an ornament of the things he possesses and he even succeeds in dividing it into two categories: representative landscape and serviceable landscape. In order to obtain these two landscapes, which are indispensable to his prestige, the rich man acts the part of a commando, he demolishes the sand dunes that hide his view of the sea (which, according to Flaubert, "inspire in him profound thoughts"), he excavates, he fills in, levels, squares, he tears out thickets and plants trees which don't take root, he erects little walls and fences, adorns them, he tosses his house down next to a palm tree by the shoreline or thrusts it into the middle of a forest, and there has a tree-trunk to admire that goes through his living room from top to bottom; in short, he also modifies the original landscape, which seems un-elegant to him, un-ordered and, above all, un-modern. And wherever he can, he spreads a handful of asphalt.

As a conclusion then—and the entire coast of Lazio is the proof of this drama—whether it's the "poor man" or the "rich man" they both destroy nature: the one because he is a part of it, the other because he wants to make it into his own image and likeness. Can the desolation of certain places continue without becoming unendurable? The thought of living in a country that is crumbling into ugliness often disheartens us.

*　　*　　*　　*　　*

The little Swedish girl who saw the flocks of weary quail coming from the sea and alighting in the underbrush to catch their breath knows that an army of hunters is already out looking for them. So she tries to save the lives of those poor migratory birds by rummaging through the bushes with a pole and shouting: "Go away, go away, they're going to kill you!" She demands that her friend get up at night and go with her to warn the quail of the danger that awaits them with the coming of the dawn. She doesn't know that the hunters serve to indiscriminately eliminate the weak species. She runs into a hunter and explains to him that he isn't being fair, above all he isn't being sporting, shooting an animal worn out with tiredness. The hunter smiles at her, looking at her legs and breasts. Returning towards home the girl sees a man, a solid, likeable man whom she knows, rummaging through the cabbages in his garden and plucking out two quail. "I'm going to eat them right away," the man says festively. "No, no, no!" shouts the distraught girl. The man looks at her without understanding, makes the timid offer of a gift, thinks better of it, puts the quail into his pouch. Which doesn't at all take away from the fact that the inhabitants of this seaside village are full of virtue, of gentleness, of human kindness, unshakeable in their stubbornness and often the bearers of ancient melancholies.

*   *   *   *   *

Little short story. Giacomo got out of his car and dug the key out of his pocket to open the gate to the courtyard, where the garage was located. There he dug another key out of his pocket. After he rolled down the shutter, he went back towards the entrance hall: he had to use violence to get it open, with another key, and the glass on the storm door trembled. The elevator was also opened with a key, to keep children from writing dirty words on the wood panelling. The door to his house had to be opened with two keys, this ever since Giacomo had received a visit from thieves. The second lock clicked four times. Giacomo went into his study, opened a drawer in his writing desk with another key and took out a box. It was full, of course, with keys: the remnants of other places he had lived, of old trunks in the attic, of doors long forgotten, of faraway elevators. They all had opened something once upon a time and Giacomo had never dared to throw them away for the fear—which keys always inspire in us—of their still being of some possible use or other. Here, exhausted, Giacomo set himself to thinking about his future. He proposed two hypotheses. The first of them was full of more keys. Three of these keys were for the villa he wanted to have at the sea; actually, on second thought (gate, front door, service door, garage), there were four: without counting the cellar. Then there was the key to his motorboat (or were there two?) and the key to the bath-house. Then he saw another key . . . which would be indispensable . . . the family chapel. However, there was time to think about all that. Another bunch of keys, these more genteel, were dangling before his eyes, in the void, tinkling. They were the keys to a garconniere that a friend wanted to leave him. He didn't know what he was going to decide yet.

The second hypothesis was without keys. The little hut where he would end his days didn't have any keys. Over there, not only did they not lock doors, but very often they didn't even have doors. Thieves didn't go into houses over there because there was nothing to take. Even he, Giacomo, was poor. In the pockets of his pants, just as when he was a boy, he would only have a dirty handkerchief, a rubber band and a seashell. Sometimes, to amuse himself, he would go to the city near-by and loiter about the ruins.

Cheered up by this second hypothesis, Giacomo opened the liquor cupboard up with a gilded little key and poured himself out two fingers of cognac.

*   *   *   *   *

Yesterday evening, there I was in a movie-house. In the disagreeable wait before the movie started, the hall was poorly lit. And in addition: just the opposite of spectators at a theater, the spectators at a movie-house always have the air of being ashamed of something, they spread out among the empty rows and sit where they're at sunk into their armchairs, without turning or getting up. They seem to be brooding upon sinister resolutions. Many of them look at the ceiling.

Meanwhile, slides were passing across the screen, advertising beauty salons, furniture stores, dry cleaners' shops, breeding houses for chickens. The film shorts that followed treated the following subjects with petulant seriousness: what to put on your hair to make it shine, why it's necessary to prefer certain pots and pans, why the lady of the house is happy washing dishes, why pure breath enhances romantic activity. Finally a young family, which I seemed to be personally acquainted with (or are they all the same?) was sitting at table and eating mayonnaise. Then came other young men and girls pursuing one another on a beach, diving into the waves, protected by a cream for their skin. Other young men, in evening dress, were drinking liqueurs. All these idylls came to an end. The young man was looking at the girl and smiling, the girl responded with a smile of acceptance. Probably they were happy.

When the actual film itself started I felt not only tired but disturbed by the idea of not being in my time, of not loving society, of "not understanding the young." Were these young people who were enunciating axioms on the screen all my neighbor then? Possible that they didn't have anything else to say? I took on the same air of guilt and expectation that the other spectators already had and meanwhile I was ruminating upon this misgiving, that the mass-man cannot hope to separate his own entertainment from the sin that is at the origin of it and therefore determines it: the dissatisfaction with his own state, the desire to escape it through complacent dreams . . . which advertising makes its allies.

* * * * *

At home, I start to read a novel of erotic experiences and a great sadness comes over me, like a toothache. It seems as though the author wanted to allude to something that was the sum total of our existence, but that he didn't know how to go about it. The messenger has forgotten the message and, dismayed, is searching to evoke the most boorish sense of it, which has remained impressed upon his memory, but the true message won't come out, it refuses to compose itself into a single simple word. I throw the book away and take up a little anthology of Greek poets. The feeling of dismay, of impotence, of prison is now mine, the reader's. A thick crystal interposes itself between those representations of love over there and "our" love over here. I can see "their" love, but as an object which no longer belongs to me. I would like to be on the other side of the crystal... but it takes something else! The possession of the object loved gives happiness then, in the same way that today it gves a certain pleasure, certain anxieties, a certain boredom? What has love become? For the young today, an experience: a way of acceding to a certain level of experience. But the collectivity doesn't counsel them to carry this experience all the way through to its heart, it needs to know that the only true love each person experiences is for it alone. It proposes a pleasurable derivative: eroticism, which agrees with everybody. For the majority of the young does love, instead of being the recognition of one's own existence in another being, become an exercise, a technique of systemization, which inserts them each one by one into the collectivity? Something which, by being acquired patiently, like a job, the esteem of one's superiors, becomes part of the list that includes the other machines and accoutrements of our imprisonment? Thus it happens that the young recognize "their" love in the books that they read and in the films that they go to see, where love "is made," where love is not a mystery but a study of gymnastics and, like all exercises, can lead to boredom and to loneliness.

At certain times, it also leads to innocence. On account of this perhaps we lean towards forms of art that are far away from us, primitive or barbaric, which can still suggest, with the frankness of erotic representation, ideas of a lost purity, of a recoverable (in its strictest sense) innocence in man's connections to nature and to the mysteries that are tightly bound up to life. What no longer manages to move us in contemporary representations, moves us in those that precede or deny our civilization. The representation of pleasure in the Indian temples of the XII century carries us back to a lost paradise where love didn't make a mystery out of its bodily expressions but forthrightly consecrated them in a ritual which the man and the woman were the priests of: it is a representation without reins and without caste, and I wouldn't be surprised if it has saved the souls of some few tourists.

Then there is the professional artist, who sees eroticism as a fault from which he can liberate himself by confessing it. Like that sinner of Stendhal's, he experiences the pleasure of the sin twice, doing it and telling it to his confessor in every detail. Immersed in life the artist asserts that he is looking for an explanation of existence: which are two different things. He makes me think of the geologist who, having fallen into quicksand, tries to figure out what the magma that is swallowing him up is made out of. For the geologist the conclusion is so foregone and so irrepressible that he derives a certain gloomy satisfaction from it.

*   *   *   *   *

The movie producer wants to make a film out of an eighteenth century comedy. The public seems disoriented and needs to be given something that's reliable, that's stable, that's well-constructed, something that won't make waves, but . . . naturally . . . in such a way that the end result is a little, even a great deal, sufficiently, in any case, sexy. The director and the actors will take care of the rest, but first it's necessary to come up with a large number of risque situations, to shift a few scenes from the dining room to the bedroom . . . do we understand each other? A long silence, then F., shaking his head: "It's not possible," he says, "unless you shift the action over to our own times, it seems like a mere waste of time to me. Sex . . . yes, *sexiness,*" and he smiles, "is a commemorative exercise that calls for a strip-tease, but of our own clothes, of those that we ourselves wear, not of those that our ancestors wore." The producer looks at him with a thoughtful look on his face. "Yes," adds F., "the costumes of another epoch act upon the movie-goer as an inhibiting memory, as a brake, as a block . . ." The producer bats his eyelashes. "Yes," insists F., "these costumes make us think about our dead, about our grandparents, and we don't like to see our grandparents in prurient situations. We preserve a certain respect for..." Another silence. "Okay," concludes F., rising, "we can telephone somebody, I know who, a psychoanalyst, and ask him for major studies that have been done in this area, have him explain them to us, but I believe that every sexy thing you attempt outside of our own time will have results that are, at best, historical, that is, not instinctive and natural, but cultural."

At this word the producer shuddered a little and opened up his arms, desolately. F. took advantage of it to turn quickly towards the sea.

Marianne Hauser

Scandal at the Bide-A-Wee Nursing Home for Mature Seniors

(an excerpt from a story in the making)

Breathless whispers in the dining hall and corridors. Giggles and shocked outcries as ears are bent to catch the scandal. Miss Nobody? My stars! Did I hear right? But she was such a meek little thing. . .

She was. That's why the nickname stuck to the pint-sized nonagenarian. Her death has brought the Bide-a-Wee to life—a frequent reaction upon the passing of another inmate, my mom observes from her wheelchair in the remotest corner. As to the ado over this latest casualty, she considers it absurd and childish. And having stated her opinion, she shrugs and returns to her crossword puzzle.

My mom has no sense of humor. She won't see the comical side of Miss Nobody's death.

The body was discovered at lunch time by a young nurse's aide who found her curled up in bed, tinier than ever in a bulky flannel robe, and with the granny glasses still on her nose as if she had just dozed off for a short nap. The night lamp was burning, and a pink dildo was buzzing atop a well-thumbed copy of *Playboy* dating back to the sixties.

The doctor signs the death certificate and delivers it to the inner office where an all-male all-white directorship of three receives the report from the black nurse's aide. She gives them the facts, unresponsive to their winks, innuendos, and righteous indignation as they grill her for intimate details. How much flesh was bared on the centerfold—which region of the human form exactly? Pornography, the gentlemen agree, leads to drugs, rape, murder, or worse and should be banned in every state of this great nation. By the way, how did she know that the object she saw was a dildo?

The cool young nurse plays dumb, whereupon she is dismissed with a final smirk and a wink. And now the padded door opens to admit selected members of the staff for an in-depth briefing.

At the Bide-a-Wee, a "fatality" is routinely minimized. No gain in reminding "our guests" of what's looming ahead for them. However, in this present case, circumstantial evidence implies such undesirable conclusions, it must be handled with the utmost care. Top secret. Classified material—agreed? Frankly, the scenario is revolting and so bad for our public image, we wish it would just go away.

Here the doctor steps from the shadows to meddle. He has no vote. But he loves to confound the establishment. Why the hush hush? The Bide-a-Wee image hasn't been tarnished. On the contrary, it has been vastly enhanced. Sexual activity among the aged is a sign of health and should be advertised as such, not covered up. Granted, the old like the young and the restless—forgive the pun—have died during coitus or masturbation. But very, very rarely have they died because of it. Indeed, masturbation is easiest on the heart and thus provides an extra margin of safety for graying America.

The directors are shuffling their feet. The doctor is smiling.

Speaking of safe sex, he proceeds, fondling his stethoscope, the old are far more safe than are the young. In our society, with teenage pregnancies, AIDS, and illiteracy raging, I strongly advocate a mandatory course in onanism for every first-grader.

The directors are leaving and the doctor sits down on top of the shiny desk.

Our main concern is the safety of our residents, of course, he remembers as he thoughtfully strokes his gray beard. Their welfare is our business, their longevity our mission. Ladies and gentlemen, may I suggest that we distribute so-called skin magazines together with autoerotic gadgets to those who want them regardless of sexual preference or gender. Japanese high tech has developed a dazzling variety of finely honed tools to stimulate the oft neglected private parts of the elderly and afford them orgiastic adventures which far surpass those produced by the old-fashioned dildo, not to mention primitive manipulation by hand. . .

But just as doc is warming up to his topic, the PR person, former beauty queen from Platzburg, cuts him short.

The Bide-a-Wee has no plans to convert into a sex shop, she snaps.

The doctor smiles. He slides off the desk and leaves. And as the padded door falls softly shut behind him, he reaches under his overcoat and turns off the tape recorder.

Of course the lid blew off Miss Nobody's secret well before the management got wind of it. Bide-a-Weeans who yesterday didn't know a dildo from a doodle, toss the word around at dinner over the soup.

>dilly dally
>dill de dollar
>doll do die

Miss Nobody has become somebody, a shot in the arm, and in the lingo of one social worker "a therapeutic experience for our girls."

The male wards are less impressed. Who looks at *Playboy* anymore 'cept little boys and old biddies?

And from a fat, always sleepy saloon keeper to a clientele of ghosts: I used to finger fuck my old lady. . .

My mom in the window corner remains impervious to it all. Down on the sidewalk a child is skipping the rope. A boy? A girl? These days you can't be certain. She knocks on the pane. The child looks up at her, then swings the rope above its head like a lasso and runs off like the wind.

Has mom read *Playboy*?

Oh, many years ago. I skimmed through it, at the dentist's. I can't recall anything in it that I would consider risqué. If the publishers were out to sell erotica, why would they print an interview with Jimmy Carter?

Mom, who is Jimmy Carter?

Mira-Lani Oglesby

Henry and Ray and the Old Guy in the Wheelchair and Two Cops and Me and Sean Penn

Henry, a guy in my class at L.A.C.C., wrote a paper about mandatory, random drug testing. Henry has no problem with mandatory, random drug testing. Henry thinks that all of the students at L.A.C.C. should be subject to mandatory, random drug testing. Henry thinks that if any student's test comes up dirty, then that student's picture should be put on display in the school cafeteria. Henry believes that this humiliation will lead to the culprit's rehabilitation.

Henry's next paper was about how he wants to be a cop.

I think he'll be a good one. Henry has no problem with authority.

I have problems with authority. This is what makes me a lousy student and an okay teacher.

A little over a year ago, before I quit being an art model and started being a teacher, I was driving on the freeway from Pasadena back to L.A. It was a little after three in the morning.

I'd been at Ray's house watching a Sean Penn movie on his VCR. I could imagine having sex with Sean Penn. I couldn't imagine having sex with Ray.

Ray wanted to have sex with me for a few different reasons. One of the reasons was that he thought I thought he was a good artist.

Ray wasn't a good artist. His drawings were boring. Ray was into drawing pictures of geometric shapes. These pictures of geometric shapes were supposed to be interesting because they looked three-dimensional even though they were two-dimensional. They were supposed to be interesting, but they weren't interesting. They were boring.

Ray's pictures were boring the same way golf is boring. Ray was also into golf. Before Ray decided to be a professional artist, he was a professional golfer and an amateur artist. Now Ray was a professional artist and an amateur golfer.

Ray was like his pictures and golf. Boring.

I felt bad that I didn't want to have sex with Ray. Guilty and resentful—the way I always feel when I don't want to have sex with someone who wants to have sex with me.

I told Ray that the reason I had to go home was because of what happened at the modelling job I had been at before I came over to his house.

The job was at a house in Silverlake. It was for this old guy in a wheelchair who was a member of a retired art teacher's drawing group I sometimes posed for in Glassell Park.

I didn't like taking private modelling jobs, but this was right after Keith left with all the money, and I was desperate. Also, I thought nothing weird would happen because the guy was an old guy in a wheelchair.

I was wrong. When I got there, the old guy had chilled champagne and a present waiting for me. He wanted me to unwrap the present and I did and it was a bottle of cheap perfume, the kind you get at Thrifty. The bottle of perfume had a fifty dollar bill wrapped around it.

The old guy wasn't interested in drawing me. He pretended to be interested in drawing me for a while, but then he admitted that what he really wanted to do was play with my vagina.

I said no. Felt guilty. Felt resentful. And ended up letting him take two polaroid pictures of it. My face wasn't in them. I checked.

Then the old guy showed me his photo albums. The pictures in his photo albums weren't of vaginas. They were of the vacations he took with his ex-girlfriend.

She was a young Mexican woman with a hard, pretty face who the old guy had met through an ad he put in the personals after his wife left him. The young Mexican woman lived with the old guy for a while and they took lots of vacations together. Then she left to get married to someone her own age who wasn't in a wheelchair.

After we finished looking at the photo albums, the old guy gave me another fifty dollars and I took it and drove to Ray's house in Pasadena and watched the Sean Penn movie.

Ray didn't understand exactly how what had happened before, with the old guy, fit in with what was happening at the moment, with him, but he accepted it without question.

Ray didn't know me well enough to ask me questions. If Ray had known me well enough to ask me questions, he would've known that I thought his pictures were boring even though I said they weren't.

Anyway, while I was driving back to L.A. on the Pasadena Freeway at a little after three in the morning, I saw a red light flashing in my rear view mirror.

The freeway was deserted except for me and the police car. I pulled over to the side. The voice on the loudspeaker said, GET OFF AT THE NEXT EXIT. TAKE THE NEXT OFF RAMP.

I didn't understand. There was no traffic to disrupt by pulling over to the side and I wasn't doing anything wrong. I thought about the Hillside Strangler thing. I thought about driving away fast. The Hillside Strangler guys posed as policemen to get their victims. But the Hillside Strangler guys had been caught a long time ago. And my car couldn't drive away fast anyway.

I got off at the next exit, took the next off ramp.

Have you been drinking?
No. Why?
You were swerving.
No I wasn't.
Where are you going?
Home.
So early?

Big smile. Wink. They'd pulled me off the Pasadena Freeway on my way back to Los Angeles at a little after three in the morning. To flirt.

I drove away and they were following me so instead of driving home, I drove back to Ray's.

It's a little after three in the morning and Ray is asleep. He sleeps like his pictures.

I don't think Henry would ever do a thing like that. I mean, he might be into a girl liking him because he's a cop. And I'm sure he'll enjoy his power. But I don't think he'd ever do a thing like that. I hope not.

The Old Fucks at Home — Tuli Kupferberg

Kathy Acker

Murder, *from* The Fall of the United States

I had found the school for which I had been looking.

    Found in that pouring rain.

    To the taxi-driver, I said, "Wait for me."

    The blue and red rain soaked me.

    When one of the red double doors opened, a gray head appeared and asked,

    "Do you want something?"

    I replied that they were expecting me.

    In no uncertain terms she told me to go away.

    No matter how long I knocked, the door wouldn't open again.

    The rain fell down more heavily than it had before. According to my memory.

    Inside the taxi where it was warm, though I couldn't see through the rain, I watched the other red door open and a girl who looked like me race past it. I couldn't see clearly.

    When I tried to see more definitively, I saw only rain and the colors of gunmetal.

I have always wanted my dream to be like that of childhood or of Radley Metzger's film of the book *Therese and Isabelle*.

A women returns to her school.

A private school like mine.

I had wandered away from the others to the lavatories. The sound of Baudelaire still in my ears. An odor hung inside the cubicle . . . A tenderness defined my hairs. I leaned over the bowl.

My best friend came into the toilet.

"Kiss me on the mouth."

"No. It's too soon."

I hadn't wanted to go to school in the first place. My mother made me.

Memory: I can't go to sleep so I walk to the library. The real or interesting library lies in a room which is like large drawers above this library. But I descend series of spiraling stairs until I reach bottom. Here is the magic room, a library, which the witch inhabits.

In the next memory, I see girls sobbing. It's night and Isabelle tells me that she wishes we could be alone together. It was usual for us to spend the night in our best girlfriend's bed in that dorm full of single cots because, for us, there was no difference between sex and no sex.

The next morning there was no Isabelle. She had gone to her mother's for the weekend. I had nothing to do so I went into town. There the man whom Isabelle and I had seen in the car asked me for a date.

I stayed there with him. The closer sexually I let him get to me, though I was scared, the more bored I became. Between sex and friendship there seemed to be an impassable gulf that was increasing.

We lay on the dirt in a graveyard. He said that now I had to fuck with him and I wanted to and I didn't want to so I ran away from him.

Returned to my miasma of indecisions.

I didn't understand why all the girls (except for Isabelle) talked about their boyfriends or superstars with whom they were in love, but I couldn't.

All the schoolgirls passed me by.

My mother's new husband was saying, "You know what they say about finishing school for girls?"

No one said anything.

"When they come out, they're finished as girls."

"But that happens everywhere." My mother was in her dressing-room.

I had come home for the weekend. I ignored the pervert. I wanted to tell my mother I loved her so I informed her I now had a best friend named Isabelle. For the moment the creep shut up. My mother replied by informing me that she and *her husband* were rejecting me again by taking their summer in Algeria, like all the rich Parisians, and I would remain in school so that my presence wouldn't ever bother them.

Back in school, I masturbated in my cot while I thought about my parents.

Being able to come, I decided while touching myself, necessitates being able to relax and enter another world. To come is to dream. I don't know how it is for males. But I just can't come when I need to protect myself from my parents and this is the time when I need to most.

Must.

Another memory: I had now become one of the top students in the school, not because I was scared of the teachers, but because the world of learning had nothing to do with my parents. I. (Isabelle) returned from one of her mother's weekends to the school. Her waist had become tiny and her breasts were as huge as pillows.

All of us used to ask her how she could sleep on those fluffy things. She tried to explain that they don't hurt.

Miss St. Pierre, the literature teacher, was a lesbian because she stuffed her bra with pads and their tips stuck upwards like WASPS' noses.

After she had come back, Isabelle and I arranged to meet alone in the church.

"I missed you."

"I missed you."

I dug her neck into my teeth. Then I nailed her hands against the floor. Her pincers tore at me. I followed everything inside me. From now on her legs would always be spread open. I stormed her openings as if she was a beleaguered fortress.

"Tell me."

"I love you."

"Again."

"I love you."

"Again."

"I love you."

Another memory: Night after night when it was dark I crawled into I's bed. We held hands and told each other our stories of childhood.

"The school," she said, "was burning down."

No, Our Cunts.

I don't remember. Don't describe what can't be remembered. What will never be seen. What's between the legs, I and I. She's discovering the little organ that the cock imitates. My limitations are too painful. I transformed into the sex of a dog, red and unbearable to my own eyes.

It has come.

(For this reason women don't need Christ.)

Our comings can't end.

Then I peered out from beneath the sheets at the overflow of nipples.

I began once more where I had left off. A kitten rubbing and rubbing its own fur which reeks overflows into total sex. I know that night will soon be leaving us. I want to run away because this sex cannot stop but we can't run away because we have to be at school.

We both knew that soon it would be morning and that morning, not the orgasm, was our end.

We both knew that soon it would end and that the end would be, not orgasm, but morning.

I told me to go and to be careful, for one of the other students might be awake.

The next day the girls mocked us because they knew what we had been doing in the chapel.

Girls'll do anything, especially something nasty, in order to destroy what they think isn't normal. I remember that Wendy Janover became the class creep when she announced that the United States was a racist society. We began our torture by ostracizing her for a week.

All my childhood I thought about running away.

Sex goes on and on. One day, desperate to be alone, I and I went to a brothel we had heard about, but we didn't like it there. Everyone was laughing at us so we couldn't have sex.

I did learn that anyone will do anything for money and that man-eating plants die from food poisoning.

That night, both of us horny as hell, we fucked inside the forest that was right outside the school. In our fantasies, the murderers were hiding. I made my way inside as I climbed outside. Our corpses decayed. Now the night, no humans, watched us. My clit turned into a crawling sea-monster, hers likewise, until we were nothing but sea-monsters leaving trails of slime.

Whoever was 'I' became traces of dust.

As her fingers withdrew, pleasure turned into something else, for nothing in this world can disappear.

"We'll never reject and abandon each other."

"Never."

A few mornings later, when I looked for I., she was no longer there. Her drawers had been emptied of all their belongings. I's mother had taken her away to foreign, unknown lands.

And I learned that absence which is the same as death.

I sob. I stand over myself and watch myself sob. My lips are very thick.

The guard told the woman that it was time to close up the school. Her visit was over.

The guards closed the gates.

Memory isn't able to return the rememberer to reality.

The girl whom I had watched dart past the red door ran down lightless streets until she reached the apartment building in which the most popular (bitchy) student in the school resided.

The bathroom of this apartment was the pink that a young girl's dress should be.

One of its window panes, blowing open, showed the blackness that lay beyond. The student, Thais, whose hair was as black as the outside, closed the window as quickly as possible because she was scared. The pane slammed against her finger.

She felt safe.

Being Catholic, she crossed herself.

When, to test her safety, Thais looked through the glass a second time, she saw gigantic cat's eyes looking at her and touched the bottom of the cross, her cunt.

Then a man's arm moved through the open window so that she could be strangled. Another hand, cased in a black leather glove, sliced her neck with a knife.

Perhaps in response to the lack of sight, the heart poured out its blood.

There's no memory of the words "I love you", but there is of the hymen being broken.

Thais' body hung from a long tampax string, attached to the bathroom ceiling, all the way down to the luxurious tiled vestibule below. Her blood streamed out of every part of her and made all of the apartment smell like bleeding cunt.

A jagged piece of glass had cut her hymen or identity into two parts.

A DREAM OF YOUNG GIRLS

That night I didn't know that a girl's murder was taking place. I dreamt that I had been invited to a party. Even in dream, going to a party is a rarity for me. I protested to the inviter that I didn't have the proper clothes. The inviters, my friends, told me that I could wear whatever I liked to this party, that no one cares what anyone wears anymore.

The next morning when I woke up, I felt lost so I decided to go to the party. In the bathroom or in one of the bathrooms in the house in which the party was being held, a heavy-set man in his forties or fifties who was with his wife in this bathroom clearly indicated that he wanted to fuck me in the bathtub.

"I don't know whether it's right because you're not my husband." But I really wanted to. (In the dream, I remembered that B has a wife.) "And this isn't my house."

Both of us were on fire for each other.

After we had fucked, paint lay splashed over bathtub, walls, and floor tiles.

No matter how hard I cleaned, I couldn't make the paint go away.

I kept trying because this wasn't my house.

The bed in the room outside this bathroom, which must be a bedroom because a bed occupies most of its space, was covered with make-up. Each bit of make-up—mascara, eyeliner, lipstick, etc.—came in a tiny paint tube. Fucking always erases my eyeliner. But every time I put on some makeup, as soon as I laid it down, that paint tube began squishing out its contents. I decided that either the room or I was too hot.

Paint was covering everything. That must mean that I destroy either myself or the world whenever I fuck. Especially, destruct rich peoples' houses.

Lots of mazes lay outside this bedroom.

The beginning of the actual party was taking place in the largest room I had as yet seen. Dark wood-panelled ceilings and walls striped by olive velvet curtains that swept to the floor. For several minutes I watched a living still-life of soberly-dressed old people sitting like dolls in armchairs so huge they made these people into children.

I strolled past the portraits of American death to the room's end, then past the party's hostess whom I recognized as the editor of Poseidon Press.

An almost-as-large long room lay perpendicularly off the first room. As I entered this room, I first saw a long table laid out with delicate, expensive appetizers. Right behind me, my hostess shrilled, "Why's she here?" because she recognized me as an enemy-of-the-literary-world-according-to-the-literati.

I ran out of the joining rooms because I was being condemned as an outcast and, perhaps, because I am.

I was caught in the maze or in a maze.

Tried to escape by figuring out where I was, by finding out who I was, but I couldn't because I was in a maze. (Amazed.)

Then I saw an exit. Walked through the door. Once I was in that room, I realized it was a closet. It was all gray and the doors were locked. I knew that finally they had captured me.

Even in dream, my deepest fear is being enclosed, trapped, or lobotomized.

The next day, the sun was clearly shining and in an oversized, elegant doorman's suit and cap, I stood in front of the house in which the party had taken place. I was the doorman and my will was gone.

The house plus winding street in front of it covered in snow was a scene out of Paris.

The confusions and terrifying dream of the night had passed. I trotted up the four steps to the red doors and knocked.

"Where have you been? We expected you last night," another nag said.

I was introduced to Mrs. Selby, a handsome women in her late thirties or early forties. A bun imprisoned black hair. She was the acting directress of the school, I was informed, for the actual directress was absent.

Police were walking everywhere over gleaming black and white tiles. Mrs. Selby explained them to me: last night when I should have been at the school, a student who had just been expelled had been murdered.

Then she began talking to a cop.

The athletic gym teacher informed me that since the room in the school which I had reserved was not yet ready for me, I would be staying in the apartment where the ex-student had been killed.

I didn't want to live in the room of a murder victim.

She assured me that the arrangement was temporary. She herself would introduce me to the student who owned this apartment, the wealthiest and most popular girl in the school.

"You should consider yourself very lucky."

Since this was one of the finest women's universities in the world, there were almost no men on its premises.

The teeth of one of the few remaining men, the janitor, formed the most visible part of his face. Deep rot had turned each one a different color. Besides that, dog hairs were jutting out of every other inch of facial flesh.

Besides the janitor, a few other deviants lay in the cracks.

Before going to my new apartment, I visited the locker room. Some of my classmates, sprawling all over the benches and floor, were discussing the one they had recently ostracized. Her insecurity and vulnerability were exciting their derision. If she wanted to ever be spoken to again, one girl said, she would have to learn how to fight.

My new landlady, a natural blonde, didn't give a shit. The little jailbird wasn't worth her attention. She deigned to talk to very few girls and only to ones with intelligence.

Here and there a few boys' names cropped up. They weren't worth much—boys—and they were always handsome and rich.

All of the girls, I learned, arrogant or not, overworked at their studies and their bodies.

I asked why the murdered girl had been expelled. Later, when I lay in her bed, I wondered whether she had been the one whom I had seen in the pouring rain.

Then I tried to imagine murder. The more I tried to understand, the closer I came to the place where murder is that which isn't conceivable.

Only emotion conceives in sensual forms that which isn't conceivable.

I remembered that the girl at the red door had uttered certain words. Verbal forms. Whenever I want to remember definite names or verbal forms, my memory fails.

I was dreaming about sexuality or, more precisely, about something just prior to sexuality. Later I would realize that I am dreaming about young girls . . .

Mel Freilicher

Fight the Power:
Diseased Pariah News, etc.

My involvement with this issue of *FI* began, appropriately, on an antiwar march. Bumping into Hal Jaffe, we talked about his plans for the upcoming censorship and pornography issue. Circling the lily pond in San Diego's luscious Balboa Park, I mentioned some of the *Village Voice* and *Gay Community News*' excellent coverage of the nefarious Jesse Helms. Third time around the pond or so, again bumping into Hal, he asked me to co-edit the issue with him and Larry McCaffery.

The Gulf War provided the dire frame of mind for my thinking about and soliciting material for *FI*. The world had recently become a nightmare in a chillingly technical sense: Everyday life—known rather accurately in San Diego as somewhat hedonistic—seemed suddenly ominous. Not only were the nation's "leaders" capable of literally anything, but more surprising, so was the grocer, the student sitting next to you on the campus shuttle, the guy next door. This last being, in my case, a 60ish ex-drag queen, who used to chatter to me about his poor health, and who'd admirably volunteered for years at the AIDS Assistance Fund; overnight he turned into a rabid patriot, heartily vying for Largest Yellow Ribbon in town. He did comply when I asked him to move the gigantic flag to his side of our shared balcony, but that was also when he suggested that I should go back to Russia.

My neighbor was, unfortunately, typical of the enthusiastic gay response to the war. One of the few publicly dissenting voices, a woman columnist for a local paper, was viciously attacked in, and out of, print. The San Diego lesbian and gay community had been primed: honored speakers at the last few annual gay pride marches included an ex-FBI agent and several policemen who'd recently come out, also a gay man and a lesbian litigating to get reinstated into the military.

So these weekly Sunday afternoon marches quickly became crucial to our sanity: the one time you could rely on being in the company of like-minded souls—friends and colleagues, but also several thousand strangers, carrying signs like "Bring My Brother Home" or "Military Family Support Group." A type of instant community, cutting across a variety of lines, and the more necessary because of that.

I started looking for publications to review for *FI* that seemed to make a vital difference to the sanity of the people who created and sustain them, as the anti-war marches did. Friends and colleagues pointed me to excellent resources like *DISEASED PARIAH NEWS*, that exist precariously outside the mainstream, with minimal funding—also like the marches (which got virtually no media coverage). Magazines, periodicals, fanzines advocating the pursuit of consensual pleasure. Taking for granted that desire will assume many varied and complex forms, particularly in this society with such highly defined and dominant power hierarchies.

DISEASED PARIAH NEWS is a sharply designed desk-top quarterly, billing itself as "a publication of, by, and for people with HIV disease... a forum for infected people to share their thoughts, feelings, art, writing and brownie recipes in an atmosphere free of teddy bears, magic rocks and seronegative guilt." In the first issue, the editors discuss the need for levity in their own lives, but warn that this does not include "the concept that AIDS is a Wonderful Learning Opportunity and

Spiritual Gift from Above. Or a punishment for our Previous Badness."

DISEASED PARIAH NEWS lives up to its wonderful name, and then some. The cover of issue #1 is a close-up of two hands: the female's (presumably Madge from the detergent commercials) is dipping the other hand into a bowl of liquid, while her bubble says: "The blood of over 100,000 Americans who have died of AIDS, Mr. President? You're soaking in it!" Many delightfully campy pieces in *DPN*'s first three issues—take "My Mother is a Channel for John Sununu," "Zen and the Art of Teddy Bear Burning", and "I Fisted Jesse Helms." *DPN*'s ongoing pornographic cartoon, "FURTHER ADVENTURES OF CAPTAIN CONDOM," stars "lowly Clay Carpenter, disease-ridden hulk transformed into Captain Condom, the world's premier safer sex superhero." Captain C's adventures in *DPN* #3 take him to "the city's most infamous" bathhouse where, in an exciting cliff hanger, he meets a hunk in black leather, sporting a huge erection sheathed in a black condom. Hunk invites our hero back to his room, with the caption announcing, "The end of the beginning." For further regular erotic titillation, *DPN* also features "Porn Potato" with graphic and funny reviews of the latest male videos.

DPN also offers plenty of informative pieces: "AIDS Testing in Prison"; lists of AIDS resources; the safest condoms and lubes ("A Lube for All Reasons," playfully illustrated by a single highly articulated splash over the "L"). "Get Fat, Don't Die" or "High Calorie Cooking with Biffy Mae," a regular column, contains recipes for high-fat, high protein diets ("Maggie Mae's Sleazy Wine Cake," "Randy Mae's Comforting Onion Soup") along with witty advice on how to make food palatable when you have thrush, or "taste perversions" (which, they tell us, is not a sudden urge to redecorate wlth Sears "mock opulent") from medicines like AZT.

Probably *DPN*'s most amazing quality is its revelations into the mind-set of people living and coping daily with HIV, in communities where AIDS has already taken such a devastating toll. "Cranky Words" by Beowulf Thorne (Your Cranky Editor) is about the death of one of the editors, and redefines black humor. A crooked contact sheet of images of a sad and tender, emaciated man in hospital garb is laid out across from a page with a large photo of the author, a thoughtful and handsome blond guy. The subheads proclaim: "Darn!/ One of our editors is dead!/ Can *DPN* withstand the test of fire?" And the text opens: "First of all, know your Toms: Tom S., the dead guy, Tom E, his erstwhile boyfriend; Tom R., Tommy's friend, patient advocate, and all-around swell guy."

The narrator relates spending the night with his dying friend, "where we shared the bonding experience of cleaning yoghurt from his oxygen hose." Next day, he's called back to the hospital, to find Tom had become terribly jaundiced overnight. Tom didn't realize his friend was dead. "But Tom R. mercifully prevented me from committing a horrible *faux pas* in front of the family by apologizing for not telling me on the phone that Tom had just croaked. (He would have wanted me to use that word honest!)" The rest of this sardonic tale describes a surreal trip to the Neptune Society, "the bargain basement cremation place," and discussion of how many parts Tom's ashes could be divided into, and what kinds of containers. Tom's piece ends with: "What a strange day, I felt as though I were trapped on the set of *Longtime Companion*. Goodbye, Tommy, we'll miss you a lot."

An angry coda, though, asks, "So, humor magazine, what's so funny about this?" The answer: "the reality of Tommy's death isn't funny. But then, neither is it funny that the first President to preside over the age of AIDS couldn't make himself say the name of the syndrome. Or that a septuagenarian senator would obstruct prevention programs because he would rather see his nation's children die than 'promote deviant sexual behavior' (all the while forcing us to endure tobacco subsidies and its retinue of smoking related deaths)." Tom's conclusion? "You can either laugh or cry, but crying gives you crow's feet."

Incidentally, a bold sidebar announces THE GOLDEN PARIAH AWARD, "bestowed by editorial whim to Mr. X, the now infamous truck driver who contracted HIV by fagbashing. According to a letter written to *The Lancet* by a physician, Mr. X reported getting 'large quantities of blood' on his hands while practicing this favorite sport. Presumably, the HIV got into his system through cuts in his skin caused by repeatedly punching suspected homosexuals in the face." Of this "seropoetic justice," *DPN* proclaims, "Serves you right! We hope that you receive the same lack of compassion that you no doubt would have shown any person with HIV. In fact, why don't you save all a lot of misery and just do the honorable thing, shoot yourself in the head."

SCREAM BOX announces itself as "an L.A. dyke zine committed to experimentation, confrontation and titillation." Funkier than *DPN*, as befits an official xeroxed and stapled 'zine, *SB*'s strength is its diversity of graphic and literary materials (poems, fiction, interviews, mock confessionals), and particularly its offbeat and striking layout. Each page is rife with graphics: cartoons, photocollages, ornate borders. Many outstanding pages appear in the first two issues unsigned—contributors are all listed together in the front. There's the photo of a butch dyke, black leather jacket, hands thrust in pockets, posing squarely centered at the foot of a crumbling stone stairway. Her challenging and well-lit stare is framed by hazy ivy in the foreground, and overtopping dark vigorous bushes behind. Above this romanticized image is, in crooked script: "Your parents/ should be happy" and below: "that you have such a man/ for a girlfriend." The back inside covers of *SB* #1 and #2 feature "Apt. 3-D", a sharp and funny appropriation of the strip as a lesbian soap about a gynecologist whose girlfriend likes to call her at work ("I was eating a too ripe nectarine, and you came to mind"), to make raunchy jokes about women with their legs spread.

Although many individual pieces concern serious issues, particularly interracial desire, more often than not the tone is poking good, sometimes raucous, fun at the politically correct. But *SCREAM BOX* can be brilliant on the attack too, as witnessed by its account of an LAPD raid of an *SB* party, "for running a dance hall and selling alcohol wlthout permits."

"Vice cops are sewer-slime-eating boils who don't deserve the air they breathe," begins "Dyke Defense," vividly describing their bust. "A couple of women were handcuffed and tormented by a sinister male voice coming over the police radio saying 'We are the silence of the lambs.'" Calling them "the self-acknowledged cream of the psychopathic police mentality crop," our "editrexes analogize the LAPD to worldwide U.S. military genocide, devastating Iraq, and using hundreds of thousands of people of color and poor people as cannon fodder."

"Dyke Defense" has a very effective two-page spread. The written text is on the upper half. Photos mirror each other: the LAPD lined up (labelled "Combat Ready"), the sole female in the foreground, and a suggestive photocollage of third world military women. Like bookplates, on the outside corners of each page, are rubber-stamped piles of skeleton heads, with the words NEW WORLD ODOR. A banner head running along the bottom of both pages announces: TIMELINE OF *SCREAM BOX* VS. THE LAPD. Turning the mag on its side, small print reveals the blow by blow account, ending on 4/30 with: "Knowing that *SCREAM BOX* is on the docket, police chief Darryl Gates interrupts his regular regimen of insensitivity training of rookies to defend himself. *SCREAM BOX* stages impromptu court and delivers retribution upon Gates' revolving head until he dissolves in a festering pool of pure evil, which within minutes implodes into an alternate universe of eternal purgatory. Justice has been served."

MOVEMENT RESEARCH PERFORMANCE JOURNAL #3 is about Gender Performance. Guest editor Tom Kalin comments that the works collected here represent a "sampling of 'navigational options'" for a world of "gender disarray," which should "expand consideration of both 'gender' and 'performance,' spotlighting, among other things, the artifice of 'normality' and the seriousness of affectation."

Performing artists like Cheryl Clarke and John Kelly (pictured as Dagmar Onassis), and dance critic Jill Johnston, use a variety of formats to delve into the evolution and political contexts of their own work. *MPRJ* #3 also features a number of compelling interviews, including one with the performance group, LESBIANS WHO KILL. "The World's Greatest Cocksucker" is a graphic and intimate interview with male to female transsexuals, focussing on their polymorphic desires. Interviewer Chris Martin's introduction boldly suggests that "The Female to Male Fraternity International Support Network lists 20 categories of gender and 6 categories of sexual preference: when we examine how these categories intersect with race and class, the question of identity becomes increasingly complex, and the possibilities multiply."

This newspaper format journal is laid out in deliberate provocation. A series of Annie Sprinkle's stunning and memorable photo portraits runs across the bottom of most of the issue, 2 or 4 to a page, interweaving and contextualizing different works. Only the first shots are identified: SURGICALLY MADE HERMAPHRODITE IN WOMAN'S DRAG, then IN WOMAN'S DRAG SANS WIG. The rest, with names underneath, include nude hermaphrodites, and crossdressers appearing in many poses. The back cover of *MPRJ* #3 is another of its decidedly un-journal like aspects—an almost full page orange photo of a blond, leering as one of her enormously long nails fingers a nipple through her tee shirt.

But most provocative is a full-page quasi ad, dominated by a close-up of a vagina. Under it, bold letters say: READ MY LIPS/ BEFORE THEY'RE SEALED. The text protests the Supreme Court's ban on dispensing abortion information in 4,500 federally funded clinics. A short and eloquent plea for personal and artistic freedom reads, in part: "We come out as gay men and lesbians, rejecting a sexuality we don't feel. We put on tits and strap on dicks, slipping out of genders that restrain us. Our heroism is daring to imagine our bodies not as the machinery of reproduction, but as our theaters of pleasure. Our bodies should be playgrounds, not just battlefields."

Ostensibly this piece is designed to incite readers to call Senators Moynihan and D'Amato to "reverse" the Supreme Court decision—rather unlikely. Clearly, there is a more profound and pragmatic agenda here, which struck pay dirt unexpectedly rapidly, even in this dire age. The *Nation* recently reports that the NEA has charged Movement Research wlth improper lobbying, and wants its money back—the $1,400 they gave *PERFORMANCE JOURNAL* to publish such filth! Movement Research has refused.

Tom Kalin anticipated this struggle in his editorial intro: "Rigid cultural assumptions about sexuality and gender are under attack in both dominant and emergent culture, reflecting the war that continues to be waged over control and surveillance of the individual and collective body." *MOVEMENT RESEARCH JOURNAL* succeeds admirably in laying bare the issue, hopefully to generate lots of publicity: Who controls images?—particularly of the body.

These three publications, and similar others, are critical forums of, and for, historically mute, or recently coalesced communities. Particularly recommended is the sensational *CAUGHT LOOKING: Feminism, Pornography and Censorship* from Seattle's Bay Press, and *FRAME-WORK: The Journal of Images and Culture* double issue on censorship (vol. 3 #2&3) from the Los Angeles Center for Photographic Studies—also see Matias Viegener's piece here on *HOMOCORE*, and other gay fanzines.

Networking is crucial: all three journals call for reader involvement. *MPRJ* by providing extensive information about the calendar of events and classes at Movement Research's New York space at 179 Varick Street, and at the Judson Street Church, which has hosted a significant dance and Intermedia scene since the 60s, where Movement Research performs regularly. *DPN* "encourages people with HIV to submit." *SCREAM BOX* also solicits submissions, and sponsors contests, like THE DILDO OF MY DREAMS—winning entries vividly displayed.

That these forums are urgently needed is testified to by their terrifically interesting conceptions and formal strategies. Partly what's so impressive, and heartening, are the sophisticated and playful approaches to genre questions. But more to the point are bold methods of framing the discourse, in their conceptions and design, also in individual works like READ MY LIPS/ BEFORE THEY'RE SEALED. The importance of sustaining a strong offensive can't be overestimated, as we've learned from ACT UP's considerable victories (in which graphics have played no small part) in calling media and public attention to the FDA's criminal sloth. And in ACT UP's herculean challenge of the medical establishment at worldwide AIDS conferences, raising crucial ethical questions about the double blind placebo protocol of drug testing.

These publications are alternative media in the truest sense, keeping the spirit alive.

Three Polaroids M Rat

Three Polaroids　　　　　　　　　　　　　　　　M Rat

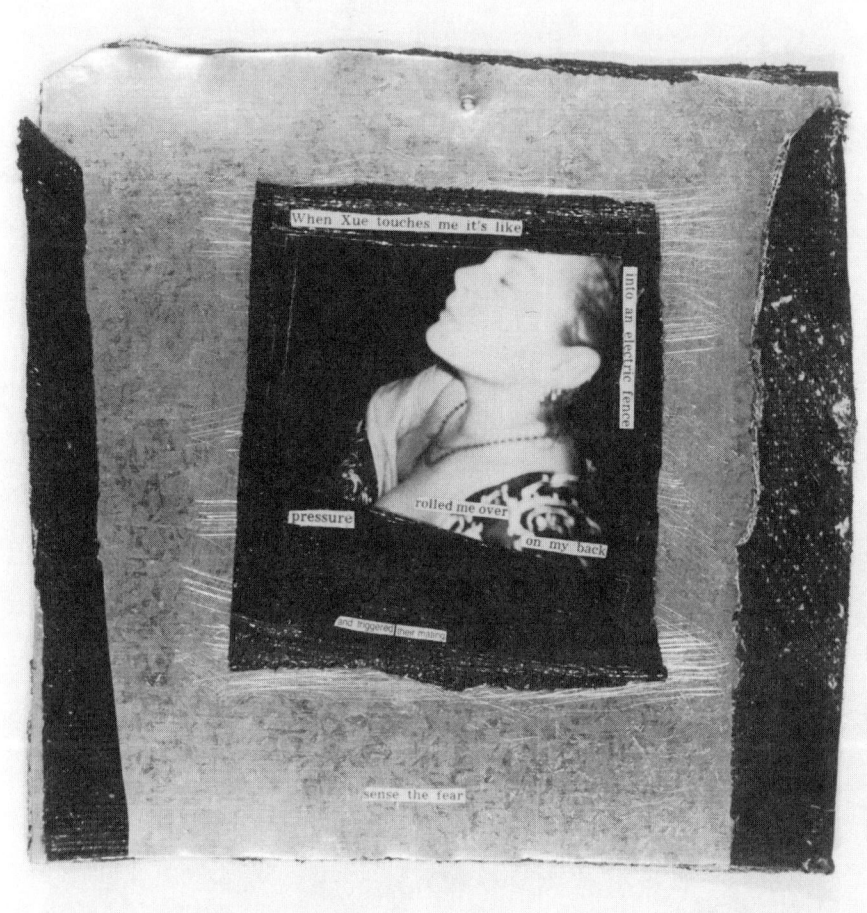

Three Polaroids　　　　　　　　　　　M Rat

Samuel R. Delany

from Citre et Trans

"I may be bringing someone home with me," [Turkish] John said. "A man, I mean." John had a long nose. "You won't mind, will you? We'll use the bed in the kitchen; I promise we won't bother you. But . . ." John's blond hair was half gray; his skin was faintly wrinkled and very dry—"it probably isn't a good idea to mention it to DeLys."

"I won't," I said. "I promise. By the time she's back, I'll be gone anyway."

"I meant in a letter, or something. But believe me," he said, "I only pick up nice men. Or boys. There won't be any trouble."

And later, on the cot bed in the front room of the tiny, two-room Anaphiotika house, set into the mountain behind the Acropolis, I went to sleep.

In 'Stamboul, just off Istiqlal, John had had a sumptuous third-floor apartment, full of copper coffee tables, towering plants, rich rugs and hangings. When I'd been staying at the Youth Hostel, one afternoon he'd fed me a wonderful high tea at his place that had kept me going for two days. A pocket full of the leftovers, in a cloth napkin, had—an hour later—even made lunch for towering, timid Jerry.

I woke to whispered Greek, the lock, and two more Greek voices. One laughed as though he were coughing. *Shhhh*ing them, John herded two sailors, in their whites, through the room. The squat one halted in the door to the kitchen (in which was DeLys's bed that John used), to paw the hanging back. He had a beer bottle in one hand. He laughed horsely once more. Then the tall one, towering him by almost two heads, shoved past, with John right after.

I turned over—then turned back. Frowning, I reached down and pulled my wallet out of the pocket of my jeans where I'd dropped them over the neck of my guitar case sticking from under the bed; it was also my suitcase. I sat, slipped the wallet behind the books on the shelf beside me. Then I lay back down.

John came back through the hanging. All he wore now was a blue shirt with yellow flowers. He squatted beside me, knees jackknifed up, to whisper: "There're two of them, I'm afraid. So if you wanted to entertain one—just to keep him busy, while I did the other one—really, I wouldn't mind. Actually, it would be a sort of favor."

"I'm sorry, John," I said. "Thanks. But I'm awfully tired."

"All right." He patted my forearm, where it was bent under my cheek. He smelled drunk. "But you can't say I didn't ask. And I certainly don't mind sharing—if you change your mind." Then he said: "I haven't spoken Demotiki with anyone in more than a year. I'm surprised I'm doing as well as I am." Chuckling, he was up and back into the kitchen, thin buttocks grinding below blue and yellow shirt tails. He disappeared around the hanging, into the lighted kitchen, Greek, and laughter.

I drifted off—despite the noise . . .

Something bumped my arm. I opened my eyes. The little lamp in the corner was on. The squat sailer stood by my bed, leg pressed against my arm. Looking down at me, with one hand he joggled his crotch. Then he said, questioningly: "*Poosty-poosty* . . . ?"

I looked up. "Huh . . . ?"

"*Poosty-poosty!*" He rubbed with broad, Gypsy dark fingers. A gold ring hugged deep into the middle one's flesh. Pointing at my face with his other hand, he began to thumb open the buttons around his lap-flap. Once he reached over to squeeze my backside. Hard, too.

"Aw, *hey* . . . !" I pushed up. "No . . . No . . . !" I made dismissive gestures. "I don't want to. *Dthen thello. Phevge! Phevge!*" (I don't want to! Go away! Go away!)

"*Ne!*" Then he repeated, "*Poosty-poosty*," emphatically.

The flap fell from black groin hair, that, I swear, went halfway up his belly. His penis swung up, two-thirds the length of mine, half-again as thick. His nails were worn short from labor, and you could tell his palms and the insides of his fingers were rock rough.

"Hey, come on!" I pulled back and tried to sit up. "Cut it out, will you? *Dthen thello na kanome parea!*" (I don't want to mess around with you!)

But he grabbed the back of my head to pull my face at his groin—hard enough to hurt my neck. For a moment, I figured maybe I should go along, so he wouldn't hurt me more. I opened my mouth to take him—and he pushed in, hard. I tasted the bitter sharpness of the cologne he'd doused himself with—and cologne on a dick is my least favorite taste in the world. Under it was the sweat of someone who'd been drinking steadily at least two days. While he clawed into the back of my neck, I thought: This is stupid. I tried to pry my head from under his hand and push him out with my tongue. And thought I'd done it; but he'd just moved, fast—across the bed, on one knee.

It was a hot night. I hadn't been sleeping with any covers.

He grabbed my underpants and, when I tried to dodge away, ripped them down my legs.

"Hey—!" I squirmed around, trying to pull them back up.

But he pushed me, hard, down on the bed. With one knee on my buttock and leaning full on my shoulders, he shouted into the other room—while I managed to lift myself (and him) up first on one elbow, then on the other.

I was about to try and twist him off, so I didn't see the tall one come through; but suddenly he loomed, to grab my arms and yank both, by my wrists, forward. I went off my elbows and down. The sailor on top began to finger between my buttocks. "Ow!" I said. "Ow—stop! . . . *Pauete!*" That made the sailor holding my arms laugh—because it was both formal and plural; and it probably struck him as a funny time for me to be asking him formally to stop.

The tall one let go one wrist and made as if to sock me in the face. He had immense hands. And when he did it, his knuckles looked like they were coming at me hard. I jerked my head aside, squeezed my eyes, and said: "*Ahhh . . . !*"

But nothing connected—it was only a feint. Still, I hit my jaw on the bed's iron rim.

When I opened my eyes, the tall one grinned, and said: "Ha-Ha!"—then shook one finger, in a slow warning. Still holding my wrist with one hand, he moved to the right, grabbed my leg just above the knee, and yanked it aside.

The one on top got himself in, then. Holding both my shoulders, he pushed, mumbling in Greek. The tall one moved back to take my free wrist again and squatted there, his face very close. He kind of smiled, curious. His breath smelled like Sen-sen; or maybe chewing gum. He had very black hair (his white cap was still on), hazel eyes, and dark skin. (By his knee, the other's cap had fallen on the rug.) Cajolingly, he began to say, now in Greek, now in English: "You like . . . ! You like . . . ! *Su aresi* . . . ! Good boy . . . ! *Su aresi* . . . ! You like . . . !"

I grunted. "I *don't* like! It *hurts*, you asshole . . . !"

This pharmacologist, who'd first fucked me, told me that if I pushed out as if I was taking a shit, it wouldn't sting.

But not this time.

The one on me bit my shoulder and, panting, came. The one kneeling glanced up at him, then sighed too, let go, stood, and grunted down at me, as if to say, "See, it wasn't that bad. . . ?"

The one behind got off the bed and stood, pushing himself back into his uniform. Once he said to me, in English: "Good! See? You like!" like the tall one had. He picked up his cap from the floor—and (he'd missed two buttons on his lap) pulled it carefully over his head, then pushed one side back up to get the right angle.

I sucked my teeth at him and tried to look disgusted. Frankly, though, I was scared to death.

In Greek the squat one said: *You want him now? I'll hold him for you—*

The tall one said: *You jerk-off! Let's just get out of here!*

The squat one bent down again, picked up my jeans, and began to finger through my pockets. Then the tall one drew back his hand with the same faint he'd used on me: *Come on! Forget that, jerk-off! Let's get out of here, I told you!*

The squat one threw my jeans back down, and they went through the kitchen hanging. There was a back door, but I don't remember if I heard it or not.

I lay on the bed a minute, without moving, propped up on one elbow. Then I reached back between my buttocks. When I looked at my fingers, there were little pads of blood on two fingertips. I got up and went to the stall toilet in the corner—

Urine puddled the stone floor. On DeLys's blue rug, it had darkened an area three times the size of someone's head. John must have sent one of them in to use the toilet while I was still sleeping— before the first guy woke me.

I reached inside, holding the jamb with one hand, and got some paper from the almost empty roll. Still standing, I wiped myself, but with a blotting motion. It hurt too much to rub. When I looked at the yellow paper, there were a red smear, with some drops running from it, and slimy stuff on one side. My rectum stung like hell.

I felt like I had to take a crap in the worst way; but the other thing the pharmacologist had said was to wait at least half an hour before you did that.

When I went back to the bed, I saw the light in the kitchen had been turned out. As I sat down, gingerly, on the edge, on one cheek more than the other, from the dark behind the hanging, John asked: "Are you all right in there?" He sounded plaintive. For a moment I wondered if he was tied up or something.

I called back: "I think so." Then: "Yeah, I'm okay."

A moment later: "Did they take anything from you?"

I pulled my jeans back across the floor toward the bed with my foot. Then I looked at the book shelf. Between fat volumes by Mann and Michener was a much read Dell paperback of Vonnegut's *Cat's Cradle*, a quarto hardcover of Daisy Ashford's *The Young Visitors*, a chapbook of poems by Joyce Johnson, and Heidi's copy of *L'Ecume de jour*, which every few hours I'd taken out to struggle through another paragraph of Vian's playful French.

"No," I said. "My wallet's safe."

At the very end were the paperbacks of my own few novels—and the typewritten sheaf of my wife's poems, sticking up between two of them. Wherever I stayed, I'd always put them on a shelf so I could see them. To make me feel better. They were the books I'd stuck my wallet behind.

"Good," John said. Twenty seconds later, he said: "I don't think they'll come back." And, a few seconds on: "Good-night."

After a minute, I got up again, went to the kitchen door, and switched off the little lamp. I didn't even look behind the hanging. (The big light, still out, you had to stand in the middle of the room to reach up and turn on.) But John wasn't asking for help. So I went back and lay down.

I tried to think of all the reasons I hadn't called for help. They might have beat me up, or hurt me more than they had. What would neighbors—or the police—have thought, coming in and finding me like that? Or thought of John? I might have gotten DeLys in trouble with Costas, from whom she rented the house. Or I might have gotten Costas in trouble with the Police: he was a nice guy—a Greek law student at Harvard, home for spring break, who probably wasn't supposed to be renting his house out to foreigners anyway. But, lying there, I couldn't really be sure if any of those thoughts had been in my mind while it had been happening.

Again, I pushed out like I was trying to shit.

The stinging was just as painful. Then a muscle in back of my left thigh cramped sharply enough to make me cry out.

* * *

A good number of people were on the platform when I got there. I had my guitar case—and a shopping bag. At the bottom of the bag was Heidi's Vian. Then my underwear and my balled up suit. On the top were my novels. Two had actually been published while I was here—though I'd written them before. My wife had sent me a single copy of each, as they came out. I'd figured to reread the newest one on the train—for more typographical mistakes; or for stylistic changes I might want to make. And maybe the typescript of her poems. It was as sunny as it had been on the Piraeus docks when I'd seen Heid off to Aegina. Shabby-coated lottery vendors ambled about. Ticket streamers tentacled their sticks. A cart rolled by, selling milk-pudding and spinach pie and warm Orangata, big wheels grumbling and squeaking. Sailors and soldiers stood in groups, talking together, among the civilian passengers.

When I saw him—the tall one—with four others in their whites, my heart thudded hard enough to hurt my throat, from the surprise. The back of my neck grew wet. I swallowed a few times—and tried to get my breath back. But—no!—I wasn't going to go up to the other end of the platform. I wasn't going to let the son of a bitch run me all around the train station. I took a deep breath, turned, and looked toward the empty tracks.

But I hoped the train would hurry up.

Not that he could do anything here, with all these people.

The third time I glanced at him, he was looking at me—smiling. He was smiling!

Another surge of fear; but it wasn't as big as the terror at my initial recognition.

Next time I caught him looking, I didn't look away.

So he raised his hand—and waved: that little "go away" gesture that, in Greek, means "come over here."

When I frowned, he broke from his group to lope toward me.

He came up with a burst of Greek: "*Kalimera, sas! Ti kanis? Kalla?*" (Hello, you! How you doing? All right?)

"*Kalimera*," I said, dry as a phrase book.

But with his big (nervous? Probably, but I didn't catch it then) smile, he rattled on. In front of me, the creaseless white of his uniform was as near-blinding as a tombstone at noon; he towered over me by a head and a half. Now, with a scowl, he explained: "... *Dthen eine philos mou* ... *Dthen eini kalos, to peidi* ..." He's isn't a friend of mine ... he's no good, that fellow ... Where're you going? It's beautiful today ... Yes? ("*Orea, simera* ... *Ne?*") You all right? He's crazy, that guy. He just gets everybody in trouble. Me, I don't do things like that. I don't like him. I go out with him, I always get in trouble—like with you and your friend, up there, that night. That wasn't any good. You're taking the train today? Where're you going? You're Negro, aren't you? ("*Mavros, esis?*") You like it here, in Greece? It's a beautiful country, isn't it? You had a good time? How long have you been here?

I didn't want to tell him where I was going; so I mimed ignorance at half his questions, wondering just what part he thought *he'd* played in the night before last.

I was surprised, though, I wasn't scared any more. At all. Or, really, even that angry. Suddenly, for a demonic joke, I began to ask *him* lots of questions, fast: What was his name? ("*Petros, ego.*" Peter, that's me.) Where was he going? ("*Sto 'Saloniki.*" To Thessalonika.) Where was he from? (Some little mountain town I'd never heard of before.) Did he like the Navy? (With wavering hand, "*Etsi-getsi.*" So-so.) He answered them all quite seriously, the grin gone and—I guess—a slightly bewildered look, hanging above me, in its place.

Finally, though, he dropped a hand on my shoulder and bent to me. He'd come over to me, he explained, because he had something to show me. *No, no—it's all right. Let me show it to you. Here.* He went digging in his back pocket—for a moment I thought he was going to pull out his wallet to show me pictures. But when his hand came back around, he was holding a knife. *No, don't be afraid. Don't be afraid—I just want to show you something.* I pulled back, but, by the shoulder, he forced me forward—still smiling. *Here,* he said. *Here—go on. You take it. Go ahead. Take it. Hold it.* While he held the knife in his amazingly large hand, I saw the nails on his big fingers were clean, evenly clipped, and with ivory scimeters about the crowns—under clear polish.

Like many Greek men, he wore his little nail half an inch or more long.

I hadn't noticed any of that, the night at DeLys's.

I took the closed knife from him and thought: Greek sailors don't usually have manicures. Briefly I wondered if he was queer himself.

He said: "*Orea, eine* . . . ?" (Beautiful, isn't it . . . ?) He didn't make any other gesture to touch it but, with motions of two fingers together and the odd word, told me to open it up. *It isn't very expensive. It's cheap—but it's a pretty knife. Good. Strong. You like it? It's nice, yes? Come on, open it up. A good knife. That button there—you push it up. To open it. Yes. Come on.*

I pushed the button up, and the blade jumped out, a sliver of light, of metal, of sky. *Here!* He laughed. *It's a good knife, yes?*

I nodded—that is, moved my head to the side, the Greek gesture for Yes. "*Ne,*" I said. "*Kallos, to eine.*" (Yes. It's a good one.)

He said in Greek: *You want this knife? You like it? Go on, take it. For you. You keep it. You like it, yes? I give it to you. For a present. Maybe you need it, sometimes. It's a good knife.*

"*Yati* . . . ?" I asked. (Why are you giving this to me?)

You want to kill me now, he said, with sideways nod, then added a chuckle. *Cut something of mine off, I bet. I wouldn't blame you.*

No, I said. I shook my head (or rather, raised it in negation). "*Ochi.*" I told him, "*You take it.*" I pressed the button. But it didn't close.

He took it from me now. There was another pressure point you had to thumb to make the blade slip in. With his big, manicured fingers, he thumbed it. *Like that.* The metal flicked into the silver and tortoise shell handle. *You sure? You don't want it?*

I said: "*Ochi—efharisto. Ochi.*" (No—Thank you. No.)

He put it in his back pocket again, and regarded me a little strangely, blinking his green-gray eyes in the sun. Then he said: *"Philli, akomi—emis?"* (We're friends, now—us?)

"Okay," I said, in English. "Just forget it."

"*Esis. Ego.* O-kay!" he repeated. *You. Me.* "O-kay. You like . . . I like . . ." With a flipped finger, he indicated him and me. "Okay. Friend: me, you." He laughed once more, clapped me on the shoulder, then turned to go back to the others. As he walked away, knife and wallet-square were outlined on one white buttock.

I didn't feel like his friend at all.

The other sailors were laughing again—I'm sure about something else.

I watched them, wondering if I could see some effeminacy in any of their movements—queer sailors, camping it up on the station platform. Him . . . maybe. But not the others.

Just once more he caught me looking and grinned again—before the train came.

When we pulled from the station, his group was still talking out on the platform—so he wasn't on my train. I was glad about that.

That night, in my couchette, while we hurtled between Switzerland and Italy, in the dark compartment I thought about the two sailors; and when my body told me what I was about to do, I had some troubled minutes, when it was too easy to imagine the armchair psychiatrists, over their morning yogurt and rolls at the white metal tables in front of American Express, explaining to me (in three languages) how, on some level, I had liked it, that—somehow—I must have wanted it.

While I masturbated, I thought about the thick, rough hands of the squat one, but grown now to the size of the tall one's; and the tall one's hazel eyes and smile—but deprived of the Sen-sen scent; and about sucking the squat one's cock, with all its black hair—except that, for the alcoholic-sweat and cologne, I substituted the slight work-salt of a good-humored housepainter I'd had on the first day I'd got to Athens.

Once I tried to use the knife blade, as he held it, full of sky: nothing happened with it.

At all.

But I used my waking up, with the sailor beside me, his leg against my arm, his hand between his legs. I did it first with fear, then with a committed anger, determined to take something from them, to retrieve some pleasure from what, otherwise, had been just painful, just ugly.

But if I hadn't—I realized, once I'd finished, drifting in the rumbling and rocking train—then, alone with it, unable to talk of it, even with John or Heidi, I simply would have found it too bleak. I'd have been defeated by it—and, more, would have remained defeated. That had been the only way to reseize my imagination, let go of the stinging fear, and use what I could of both to heal.

Raymond Federman

Once Upon a Time in the Grass

> Love is the rift that rises
> Above all things.
> —D. H. Lawrence

Last night, as you and I chased the spider of insomnia you moved over to my side of the bed and whispered close to my ear so I could smell your fading perfume:

Moinous, do you remember, how a long time ago
you got yourself all worked up and emotional
when, naked, you plunged into my aqua fresca?

I was taking a leak behind a bramble bush,
a prickly bush of twigs, leaves and flowers,
and peeking over it you saw my spread knees.

Their shiny porcelain took your breath away,
while the rubis at the entrance of my tunnel
made your hands sweat and your eyes swirl.

You stood there with your frozen blue balls
and your bare white feet sinking in the mud,
and dumbfounded you mumbled: Oh wow, Mamamia!

Behind the bush you heard the sweet trickle
and unabashedly you moved closer and closer
trying to control the clatter of your teeth.

The mud of the path was stuck to your essence,
and as you side-stepped the fresh cow dungs
you frightened away the busy buzzing flies.

When you parted the leaves of the bush
you saw my bicycle leaning against a tree,
and then reality told you how good it was.

I had taken my blouse off to feel the wind,
and I was touching the tips of my teats
gently twiddling the little brown knobs.

My opaque cotton panties were also off
so I could feel the leaves of grass tickle
my buttocks when I crouched to do my pipi.

When you saw my cocky cocoon, my sweet mimi,
you screamed and then had it in your hand,
Sweetie, for that day, for tomorrow, forever.

Under your feet you felt a wet botanic reality,
and when the wind started to caress the grass,
that slow urgent caressing became our reality.

In the green furrows filled with wild mazzards
and gurglings, essences and wetness, we laughed,
and then you looked and let out a happy shriek.

Your zizi was no longer folded and lonely,
and your cullions no longer blue and frozen,
and you started whining and begging for more.

Hey look, you said, there's a drop dripping!
Oh, let me taste that drop, let me swallow it.
No, I said, it's disgusting, and it's bitter.

What do you call it? you asked, looking at it,
smelling it on your finger close to your face
Juice it's called. The juice of life, I said.

Why are you juicing so much? Just because,
I replied. Juicito Ergo Sum, that's how it is.
Can I jump into your juicito?—Okay jump!

And so, there in the wet grass, after my pipi,
we put our fingers into each other's presence
and let the juices flow so that we could BE.

The warmth of the meadow was whirling around us,
the grass made our elbows green with grass stains,
and as I crouched the wind polished my round knees.

A taste of cider was on my fingers and in my mouth,
and you noticed the saliva at the corner of my lips,
and how the tip of my tongue was licking it off.

That's how you learned to have been, to have touched,
to have created reality with your mouth and your cock,
and it was then that you gave me the name—Sucette!

Oh yes, I remember, I remember, I said, reaching for you in the dark, so that once again we could roll in the grass and slowly fall asleep together into each other's presence.

The Goat King *(above) and* Coloring Book   Greg Boyd

Carole S. Vance

The Pleasures of Looking: The Attorney General's Commission on Pornography versus Visual Images

The Attorney General's Commission on Pornography, a federal investigatory commission appointed in May 1985 by then-Attorney General Edwin Meese III, orchestrated an imaginative attack on sexual pleasure and desire. The chief targets of its campaign were sexually explicit images, dangerous, according to the logic of the commission, because they might encourage sexual desires or acts. The commission's public hearings in six U.S. cities during 1985 and 1986, lengthy executive sessions, and an almost two-thousand-page report[1] constitute an extended rumination about visual images and their power. Although the term *representation* was not in its vocabulary, the panel of commissioners tenaciously clung to and aggressively advanced implicit theories of visual representation. More important, the commission took every opportunity to show sexually explicit images during its public hearings, using them to promote its point of view, to document the alleged nature of pornography, to offer a compelling interpretive frame, and to intensify a climate of sexual shame that made dissent from the commission's viewpoint almost impossible.

To enter a Meese Commission public hearing was to enter a time warp, an inviolable bubble in which the 1950s were magically recreated. Women were virgins, sex was dirty, shame and secrecy were rampant. Consider the testimony of self-described "victim of pornography" Larry Madigan.[2] He testified earnestly that at age twelve he was a "normal, healthy boy and my life was filled with normal activities and hobbies," when his life was radically disrupted by exposure to a deck of pornographic playing cards: "These porno cards highly aroused me and gave me a desire I never had before." Soon after that, he started to masturbate. Later, he went on to have "promiscuous" sex with two women and almost ended up "a pervert, an alcoholic, or dead," until he found Christ and was born again. How can we explain that this testimony was received in 1985 by several hundred people in a federal courthouse in a major American city without a single, publicly audible laugh? The answer lies in the commission's use of visual images to create a logical and emotional climate in which such claims were not only plausible, but convincing.

Appointed during President Ronald Reagan's second term, the commission paid a political debt to conservatives and fundamentalists who had been clamoring for action on social issues, particularly pornography, throughout his term of office. Pornographic images are symbols of what moral conservatives want to control: sex for pleasure, sex outside the regulated boundaries of marriage and procreation. Sexually explicit images are dangerous, conservatives believe, because they have the power to spark fantasy, incite lust, and provoke action, as well as convey undesirable information. What more effective way to stop sexual immorality and excess, they reason, than to curtail sexual desire and pleasure at its source—in the imagination.

Conservatives also project their intense feelings about sexuality and gender politics onto pornography. Pornography, to them, is a stand-in for destructive sexual impulses that, left uncontrolled, threaten to destroy the stability of the family, the authority of men over women, and the power of parents over children. Sexual pleasure is always suspect and usually dangerous, unless harnessed within marriage, reproduction, and God's plan. Stirrings of desire, as well as individuals who would encourage or defend it, constitute a moral lapse and a personal threat. The battle against unruly sexual impulses is a never-ending struggle, even for those with strong convictions. Part of the charm of regulating pornography is that sexual images in the public arena can be banished more reliably than sexual impulses in the individual psyche.

The campaign against pornography comes at a time when moral conservatives' control over sexual behavior is shrinking. The past century has seen a relentless increase in the frequency and acceptance of sexual behavior outside the confines of marriage and even heterosexuality.[3] Contemporary controversies about sexuality—teen pregnancy, lesbian and gay rights, sex education in the schools, abortion, and AIDS—make it obvious that traditional moral standards no longer hold absolute sway. Sexuality is an actively contested terrain, where diverse constitutencies struggle over definitions, law, and policy. Amid this flux, regulation of visual images gives the illusion of control: visual images can still be regulated, although the actual sexual behavior they depict usually cannot be. Visual images remain an easy target, since many who participate in sexual pleasure in private remain unwilling and ashamed to defend images of it in public.

The goal of the Meese Commission was to implement a repressive agenda on sexually explicit images and texts: vigorous enforcement of existing obscenity laws coupled with the passage of draconian new legislation. The commission's ninety-two recommendations continue to pose a serious threat to free expression.[4] They include appointing a high-powered Justice Department task force to coordinate obscenity investigations and prosecutions nationwide, developing a computer bank to collect data on individuals and businesses "suspected" (as well as convicted) of producing obscene materials, mandating high fines and long jail sentences for offenses, and using punitive RICO legislation (the Racketeer Influenced and Corrupt Organizations Act, originally developed to fight organized crime) to confiscate the personal property—cameras, darkroom equipment, computers, even homes and cars— of anyone convicted of the "conspiracy" of producing or distributing pornography. Performers and producers of sexually explicit photos and films should be prosecuted under existing prostitution and pimping laws, the panelists reasoned, since money changes hands in exchange for sexual services. They regretfully noted a large body of sexually explicit images beyond prosecutorial reach, since the images could not be judged obscene by current legal standards. The commission endorsed citizen action crusades, providing pages of detailed instructions for neighborhood watchdog groups to target and remove material in their communities that "some citizens may find dangerous or offensive or immoral."[5]

For imagemakers, the impact of the commission is significant in generating more aggressive prosecutions at the federal, state, and local levels, in encouraging passage of new legislation that implements the commission's recommendations, and in increasing caution and self-censorship among those who produce sexually explicit visuals. In 1988, officials arrested artist Alice Sims at her home in Alexandria, Virginia, for allegedly producing child "pornography," photographs of two naked little girls, one of them her one-year-old daughter. The photofinishing lab had reported her, as required by new laws, for developing "sexually explicit" material using children (a felony charge with a maximum penalty of ten years in jail). Officials—including U.S. Postal Inspector Robert Northrup, who testified before the Meese Commission—searched Sims's house, carted away three bags of "evidence" (her art), and removed her children, including the still breast-feeding daughter, to foster care.[6]

In another instance of the commission's impact, Congress passed, by an overwhelming majority, the 1988 Child Protection and Obscenity Enforcement Act, which contained several Meese Commission recommendations. Retroactive to 1978, the act would have required producers and distributors of material that depicted "frontal nudity" or "actual sexually explicit conduct" (not necessarily obscene) to obtain and maintain for an indefinite period of time proof of the model's age. Opponents challenged the law, arguing that such burdensome record-keeping provisions and severe forfeiture penalties would, in effect, ban constitutionally protected art books, photography, and motion pictures that have sexual content. The federal court agreed and struck down the legislation, though the government is considering redrafting the legislation or appealing.

The commission's unswerving support for aggressive obscenity law enforcement bore the indelible stamp of the right-wing constituency that brought the panel into existence. Its influence was also evident in the belief of many commissioners and witnesses that pornography leads to immorality, lust, and sin. But the commission's staff and the Justice Department correctly perceived that an unabashedly conservative position would not be persuasive outside the right wing. For the commission's agenda to succeed, the attack on sexually explicit material had to be modernized by couching it in more contemporary arguments, arguments drawn chiefly from social science and feminism. So the preeminent harm that pornography was said to cause was not sin and immorality, but violence and degradation. In practice, the coexistence of these very different frameworks and languages proved uneasy, and modernized rhetoric at best disguised, but never replaced, the persistent bias of the commission.

I. Procedures and Bias

Appointed to find "new ways to control the problem of pornography," the panel was chaired by Henry Hudson, a vigorous antivice prosecutor from Arlington, Virginia, who had been commended by President Reagan for closing down every adult bookstore in his district. Hudson was assisted by his staff of vice cops and attorneys and by executive director Alan Sears, who had a reputation in the U.S. Attorney's Office in Kentucky as a tough opponent of obscenity.[7] Prior to convening, seven of the eleven commissioners had taken public stands opposing pornography and supporting obscenity law as a means to control it. These seven included a fundamentalist broadcaster, several public officials, a priest, and a law professor who had argued that sexually explicit expression was undeserving of First Amendment protection because it was less like speech and more like dildos.[8] The smaller number of moderates sometimes curbed the staff's conservative bent, but their efforts were modest and not always effective.

The commission had a broad mandate to examine a wide range of sexually explicit texts and images, including pornography as well as the much smaller category of obscenity. Obscenity, a legally meaningful term, had been defined by a series of court decisions determining that obscene expression fell outside normal First Amendment protection and thus could be regulated in a manner that most speech could not.[9] Laws that restrict sexually explicit speech may do so only if the material meets the definition of obscenity established by the courts, as interpreted by judges and juries. Pornography, on the other hand, has no legal definition, is not regulated by law, and comprises a much wider range of material. Material can be sexually explicit and even pornographic without being obscene. Thus, the panel's challenge: how to control or eliminate the large body of material called pornography, when the available legal weapons targeted only obscenity? (One solution was to encourage extralegal citizen action against material that was merely pornographic. A second was to invent a new category of pornography—"violent pornograhy"—which was so pernicious, the panel argued, that it should be assimilated into the category of obscenity and subjected to its harsher penalties.)

The conservative bias continued for fourteen months, throughout the panel's more than three hundred hours of public hearings in six U.S. cities and lengthy executive sessions. The list of witnesses was tightly controlled: 77 percent supported greater control, if not elimination, of sexually explicit material. Heavily represented were law-enforcement officers and members of vice squads (68 of 208 witnesses), politicians, and spokespersons for conservative antipornography groups like Citizens for Decency through Law and the National Federation for Decency. Great efforts were made to find "victims of pornography" to testify,[10] but those reporting positive experiences were absent. Witnesses were treated unevenly, depending on whether the point of view they expressed facilitated the commission's ends. There were several glaring procedural irregularities, including the panel's attempt to withhold drafts and working documents from the public and its effort to name major corporations such as Time Inc., Southland, CBS, Coca-

Cola, and K-Mart as "distributors of pornography" in the final report, repeating unsubstantiated allegations made by Rev. Donald Wildmon, executive director of the National Federation for Decency. These irregularities led to several lawsuits against the commission.[11]

The barest notions of fair play were routinely ignored in gathering evidence. Any negative statement about pornographic images, no matter how outlandish, was accepted as true. Anecdotal testimony that pornography was responsible for divorce, extramarital sex, child abuse, homosexuality, and excessive masturbation was entered as "evidence" and appears as supporting documentation in the final report's footnotes. Chairman Hudson's hope that social science evidence could provide the smoking gun linking pornography to violence was dashed by social scientists' testimony, which cautioned against drawing such hasty conclusions. When it became clear that social science would not provide the indictment of pornography that he wanted, the chair announced that harm should be evaluated according to two additional tiers of evidence: "the totality of the evidence," which included victim testimony, anecdotal evidence, expert opinion, personal experience, and common sense; and "moral, ethical, and cultural values." Pornography could thus still be convicted on two out of three tiers, despite the lack of more objective data.

The commission concentrated on sexually explicit images, although obscenity law applies to both texts and images. This marks a notable departure from the past century of obscenity regulation and moral crusades, when a significant part of censorship efforts were directed against written material.[12] During the period bracketed by 1933 (when the Supreme Court upheld the publication of *Ulysses*) and 1966 (when it ruled in favor of *Fanny Hill*), however, literary prosecutions became relatively unsuccessful, with all but the most zealous prosecutors losing interest in these doomed, and increasingly ridiculed, efforts. Conservatives like to explain their current emphasis on censoring sexually explicit images in terms other than the practical, maintaining that visual images have a special power to influence behavior. In addition, they argue that pornography has become increasingly visual and influential, due to the swelling numbers of hard-core magazines, new technologies like home-video and cable television, and more audacious content. They complain that "porn" is flooding the nation, and now everyone can see it, even illiterates. This alarm signals a concern about the availability of visuals across boundaries of class, youth, and gender. This same concern fueled nineteenth-century attempts to restrict literature, when reformers worried that cheap printing processes and penny-papers would put pornography, formerly available only to classically schooled aristocrats, within reach of the barely literate masses.[13] The arguments made against pornographic visuals today are virtually the same as those made against pornographic texts in the late nineteenth and early twentieth centuries, even though twentieth-century arguments against sexually explicit texts have fallen into total disrepute.

Despite their overriding concern with visual images, the commissioners invited few recognized experts on representation to testify. The small number included social psychologists reporting on their laboratory experiments on imagery and aggression, though their testimony concentrated on scientific questions and only briefly mentioned the stills or short video clips they had fashioned as experimental stimuli. More typical was a grandiosely titled lecture, "The History of Pornography," delivered by a vice detective. He provided a brief history of pornographic images in the twentieth century, illustrating his lecture with slides from adult magazines and films. No specialists were invited to discuss the history of representing nudity, the body, or eroticism. It proved easy for the commissioners to falsely claim that their efforts to regulate commercial pornography would have no impact on the fine arts: their refusal to consider artistic material made it difficult to see the connections between them.[14]

Although few experts were called to testify, most witnesses—particularly vice cops, politicians, and moral majoritarians—offered clear statements about the effects of visual images and their mechanisms of influence. Most were adherents of the "monkey see, monkey do" school of representation: viewers simply imitated the sexual behavior they saw in pornography. Most important, visual images were presented as having the capacity to arouse sexual desire and fantasy in a visceral and immediate way. Bypassing logic and moral standards, explicit pictures stimulated lust, which then demanded immediate satisfaction through masturbation, perverted sex, or rape. The effect was cumulative and addictive, with viewers purportedly graduating from reading more socially acceptable men's magazines like *Playboy* and *Penthouse* to hard-core magazines depicting fetishism and child pornography. Soon, as the story went, viewers were dependent on pornography for the supercharged arousal it offered, causing ordinary sex to pale in comparison. The path could go only downhill, ending in sexual addiction, antisocial behavior, and personal ruin. Sexually explicit visuals also communicated information about unfamilar behavior—anal sex, bestiality, group sex—which enterprising and curious viewers would be inclined to try for themselves, thus expanding the perverse forms desire might take. In this manner, pornography served to influence norms, suggesting that hedonism, sex for pleasure, and promiscuity were acceptable. The proof of this was easily seen, witnesses claimed, offering personal and professional anecdotes as evidence. The social scientists who testified about what they had discovered to be the thin connection between sexually explicit material and sexual violence were easily overwhelmed by melodramatic recitations of personal anecdote and assertions of moral certainty.

No visual artists or art groups were called to testify.[15] The absence of spokespersons for the visual arts community was striking, given the commission's intense preoccupations with images and the potentially serious impact of its restrictive recommendations on imagemakers. A moderate panelist, *Woman's Day* editor Ellen Levine, occasionally raised questions about the relationship between the images found in the photography of Bruce Weber, Robert Mapplethorpe, and Helmut Newton and the pornographic images under discussion, asking about the impact of new regulation on their work. Since most commissioners seemed unfamiliar with contemporary work, the discussion never developed. But unlike writers' groups who vigorously testified about the possible impact of censorhip on their writing, visual and graphic arts groups, as well as individual artists, were silent. The only testimony given on behalf of groups connected to the actual production of visual images was offered by trade organizations (the Motion Picture Association of America, the Adult Film Association of America, and the National Cable Television Association), a free-lance porn producer, and representatives of several men's magazines, but they rarely addressed issues of interpretation and meaning. It is unclear if visual groups were absent because of their unwillingness to testify or their ignorance of the proceedings, but their absence was a serious loss.

II. Interpreting Visual Images

The commission's campaign against sexually explicit images was filled with paradox. Professing belief in the most naive and literalist theories of representation, the commissioners nevertheless brilliantly used visual images during the hearings to establish "truth" and manipulate the feelings of the audience. Arguing that pornography had a singular and universal meaning that was evident to any viewer, the commission staff worked hard to exclude any perspective but its own. Insisting that sexually explicit images had great authority, the commissioners framed pornography so that it had more power in the hearing than it could ever have in the real world. Denying that subjectivity and context matter in the interpretation of any image, they created a well-crafted context that denied there was a context.

The foremost goal of the commission was to establish "the truth" about pornography, that is, to characterize and describe the sexually explicit material that was said to be in need of regulation. Pornographic images were shown during all public hearings, as witnesses and staff members alike illustrated their remarks with explicit, fleshy, often full-color images of sex. The reticence to view this material that one might have anticipated on the part of fundamentalists and conservatives was nowhere to be seen, though the anomaly was not lost on wags in the audience, who jokingly referred to "the federally funded peep show." The commission capitalized on the realistic representational form of still photos and movie and video clips, stating that the purpose of viewing these images was to inform the public and themselves about "what pornography was really like." Viewing was carefully orchestrated, and a great deal of staff time went toward organizing the logistics and technologies of viewing. Far from being a casual or minor enterprise, the selection and showing of sexually explicit images constituted one of the commission's major interventions.

In fact, visual images dominated the hearings at all times. During screenings, pornographic images consistently captured the audience's attention with a reliability that eluded the more longwinded witnesses. The images were arresting, vivid, memorable, and, one had to suspect, not infrequently arousing. A rustle of excitement swept through the audience at the announcement of each showing. The chance to see forbidden material had obvious appeal. In between slide shows, the images of sex still loomed large, as witnesses testified under a blank projection screen whose unblinking, steady eye served as a reminder of the pornography whose nature had been characterized with seemingly documentary precision. Residual effects were palpable, too, in the aroused emotional state of the audience and commissioners, which made dissent not only unwelcome, but incomprehensible and personally discrediting as well.[16]

The structure of viewing was an inversion of the typical context for viewing pornography. Normally private, this was public, with slides presented in federal courthouse chambers before hundreds of spectators in the light of day. The viewing of pornography, usually an individualistic and libidinally anarchic practice, was here organized by the state—the Department of Justice, to be exact. The normal purpose in viewing, sexual pleasure and masturbation, was ostensibly absent, replaced instead by dutiful scrutiny and the pleasures of condemnation.

These pleasures were intense. Some had called the commission a show trial in which pornography was to be found guilty, but if so, it seemed scripted by the staff of "Saturday Night Live." The atmosphere throughout the hearings was one of excited repression: witnesses alternated between chronicling the negative effects of pornography and making sensationalized presentations of "it." Taking a lead from feminist antipornography groups, everyone had a slide show: the FBI, the U.S. Customs Service, the U.S. Postal Service, and sundry vice squads. At every "lights out," spectators would rush to one side of the room to see the screen, which was angled toward the commissioners. Were the hearing room a ship, we would have capsized many times.

Alan Sears, the executive director, told the commissioners with a grin that he hoped to include some "good stuff" in their final report, and its two volumes and 1,960 pages faithfully reflect the censors' fascination with the thing they love to hate. Although the commission stopped short of reproducing sexually explicit images in a government document, the enthusiastic voyeurism that marked the hearings is evident in the report. It lists in alphabetical order the titles of material found in sixteen adult bookstores in six cities: 2,370 films, 725 books, and 2,325 magazines, beginning with *A Cock between Friends* and ending with *69 Lesbians Munching*. A detailed plot summary is given for the book *The Tying Up of Rebecca*, along with descriptions of sex aids advertised in the books, their cost, and how to order them. The report describes photographs found in ten sexually explicit magazines, for example *Tri-Sexual Lust, Bizarre Climax No. 9, Every Dog Has His Day,* and *Pregnant Lesbians No. 1*. The interpretive approach may not be on the cutting edge of photographic criticism, but here it earnestly slogs along for thirty-three pages ("one photograph of the female performing fellatio on one male while the other male's erect penis rests on her cheek" and "one close-up photograph of a naked caucasian male with the testicles of another naked caucasian male in his mouth").[17]

The commission viewed a disproportionate amount of atypical material, which even moderate commissioners criticized as "extremely violent and degrading."[18] To make themselves sound contemporary and secular, conservatives needed to establish that pornography was violent rather than immoral and, contradicting social science evidence, that this violence was increasing.[19] It was important for the panel to insist that the images presented were "typical" or "average" pornography. But typical pornography—glossy, mainstream porn magazines directed at heterosexual men—does not feature much violence, as the commission's own research (quickly suppressed) confirmed.[20] Yet the slide shows did not present many carefully airbrushed photos of perfect females or the largely heterosexual gyrations (typically depicting intercourse and oral sex) found even in the more hard-core adult bookstores. The commission concentrated on atypical material, produced for private use or for small, special-interest segments of the market, or confiscated in the course of prosecutions. Slides featured subjects guaranteed to have a high shock value: excrement, urination, homosexuality, bestiality (with over twenty different types of animals, including chickens and elephants), and especially sadomasochism (SM). Child pornography was frequently shown (with no effort made to disguise the identity of the children), despite repeated testimony from the commission's own expert witnesses that severe penalties had made this material virtually unobtainable in the commercial market.

Predictably, the commission relied on the realism of photography to amplify the notion that the body of material shown was accurate, that is, representative. The staff also skillfully mixed atypical and marginal material with pictorials from *Playboy* and *Penthouse*, rarely making a distinction between types of publications or types of markets. The desired fiction was that extreme images were found everywhere and that all pornography was the same. Images existed in a timeless pornographic present, with little attention given to describing an image's date, provenance, conditions of production, intended market, or producer. Although representatives from major men's magazines testified, taking pains to distance what they called the "healthy adult entertainment" in their publications from the sleazy and degraded images, which they agreed deserved censorship, the mud-slinging only reinforced the idea that sexual images were suspect.

The panel's effort to modernize the case against pornography led to complex symbolic and rhetorical gymnastics. The most successful effort was the appropriation of the term *degrading*. Used by some antipornography feminists to describe sexist images, the term was rapidly appropriated to cover images of all sexual behavior that might be considered immoral, since in the conservative worldview, immorality degraded the individual and society. "Degrading" was freely applied to visual images that portrayed homosexuality, masturbation, and even consensual heterosexual sex. Even images of morally approved marital sexuality were judged "degrading," since public viewing of what should be a private experience degraded the couple and the sanctity of marriage.

A more difficult enterprise for the commission was managing the contradiction between the heavy emphasis on "violent" or "degrading" pornography in the hearings and the commission's concerns about more typical sexually explicit images, that is, the *Playboy* problem. Strategically, the panel emphasized atypical material to build a strong case against pornography. But even successful attempts to restrict these images (child pornography, SM, bestiality) would in fact have little impact on pornography available, because they constitute such a small fraction of the market. This reality surfaced in panel discussions periodically, and members' frustration exposed the panel's enduring interest in restricting all sexually explicit material, including mainstream magazines that had never been judged obscene by the courts. Commissioners complained that the overemphasis on extreme material incorrectly implied that the worst harm of pornography was found at the edges of the porn industry. To the contrary, they stated, the real danger of pornography was in its most acceptable guise, the men's magazine, which endorsed hedonism, promiscuity, and sex without responsibility in homes throughout America.

The visuals, including commentaries, descriptions, and instructions about how to read them, were a crucial part of the commission's discourse. Yet the commission's strategic maneuvers and assertions about sexual images were covert and therefore exempt from argument. Many have commented on the way all photographic images are read as fact or truth because the images are realistic. This general phenomenon is true for pornographic images as well, but it is intensified when the viewer is confronted by images of sexually explicit acts that he or she has little experience viewing in real life. Shock, discomfort, fascination, repulsion, arousal all operate to make the image have an enormous impact and seem undeniably real.

But any photographic image, of course, reflects choice, perspective, intention, and conventions of produciton. And any collection of images said to represent a body of work—say, a slide show—bears the mark of an editing hand and an organizing intelligence or intentionality. Yet the ritual of showing of pornographic images with their accompanying voice-overs throughout the course of the hearings erased the commission's editing hand, guaranteeing that many images and their interpretations would be given the status of unassailable truth. It is difficult to argue with a slide show.

The commission's frame was always a literal one. The action depicted was understood as realistic, not fantastic or staged for the purpose of producing an erotic picture. Thus, images that played with themes of surrender or domination were read as actually coerced. A nude woman holding a machine gun was obviously dangerous, because the gun could go off (an interpretation not, perhaps, inaccurate for the psychoanalytically inclined reader). Images of obviously adult men and women dressed in exaggerated fashions of high school students were called child pornography. Although meaning was said to be self-evident, nothing was left to chance.

Sadomasochistic pornography had an especially strategic use in establishing that sexually explicit imagery was "violent." The intervention was effective, since few (even liberal critics) have been willing to examine the construction of SM in the panel's argument. Commissioners saw a great deal of SM pornography and found it deeply upsetting, as did the audience. Photographs included images of women tied up, gagged, or being "disciplined." Viewers were unfamiliar with the conventions of SM sexual behavior and had no access to the codes participants use to read these images. The panel provided the frame: SM was nonconsensual sex that inflicted force and violence on unwilling victims. Virtually any claim could be made against SM pornography and, by extension, SM, which remains a highly stigmatized and relatively invisible sexual behavior. Stigma and severe disapproval ensure that one normal channel of information about the unfamiliar, discussion with friends and peers about behavior they engage in, is closed, because the cost to participants is too high. As was the case for homosexuality until recently, invisibility reinforces stigma, and stigma reinforces invisibility in a circular manner.

The redundant viewing and narration of SM images reinforced several points useful to the commission: pornography depicted actual violence; pornography encouraged violence; and pornography promoted male dominance and the degradation of women. Images that depicted male domination and female submission were often shown. An active editorial hand was at work, however, to remove reverse images of female domination and male submission; these images never appeared, though they constitute a significant portion of SM imagery. Amusingly, SM pornography elicited hearty condemnation of "male dominance," the only sphere in which conservative men were moved to critique it throughout the course of the hearing.

The commission called no witnesses to discuss the nature of SM, either professional experts or typical participants. Given the atmosphere, it was not surprising that no one defended it. Indeed, producers of more soft-core pornography joined in the condemnation, perhaps hoping to direct the commission's ire to more stigmatized groups and acts.[21] The commission ignored a small but increasing body of literature that documents important features of SM sexual behavior, namely consent and safety.[22] Typically the conventions we use to decipher ordinary images are suspended when it comes to SM images. When we see war movies, for example, we do not leave the theater believing that the carnage was real or that the performers were injured making the films. But the commissioners assumed that images of domination and submission were both real and coerced.

In addition, such literalist interpretations were evident in the repeated assertions that all types of sexual images had a direct effect on behavior. Witnesses provided the evidence: rapists who were said by arresting officers to have read pornography, and regretful swingers who said their careers were started by exposure to pornography. According to the commission, the danger in sexually explicit images was that they inspired literal imitation, as well as more generalized and free-flowing lust. The less diversity and perversity available for viewing, the better.

The commission downplayed the most common use of pornography—for arousal during masturbation. To fully acknowledge this use would put the entire enterprise dangerously close to seeming to attack masturbation, a distinctly nineteenth-century crusade that would seem to defy most forms of rhetorical modernization. The idea that sexual images could be used and remain on a fantasy level was foreign to the commission, as was the possibility that individuals might use fantasy to engage with dangerous or frightening feelings without wanting to experience them in real life. This lack of recognition is consistent with fundamentalist distrust and puzzlement about the imagination and the symbolic realm, which seem to have no autonomous existence; for fundamentalists, imagination and behavior are closely linked. For these reasons, the commission was deeply hostile to psychoanalytic theory, interpretation, or the notion of human inconsistency, ambiguity, or ambivalence. If good thoughts lead to good behavior, a sure way to eliminate bad behavior was to police bad thoughts.

The voice-over for the visual segments was singular and uniform, which served to obliterate the actual diversity of people's response to pornography. But sexually explicit material is a contested ground precisely *because* subjectivity matters. An image that is erotic to one individual is revolting to a second and ridiculous to a third. The object of contestation *is* meaning. Age, gender, race, class, sexual preference, erotic experience, and personal history all form the grid through which sexual images are received and interpreted. The commission worked hard to eliminate diversity from its hearings and to substitute instead its own authoritative, often uncontested, frequently male, monologue.

It is startling to realize that many of the Meese Commission's techniques were pioneered by antipornography feminists between 1977 and 1984. Claiming that pornography was sexist and promoted violence against women, antipornography feminism had an authoritative voice-over, too, though for theorists Andrea Dworkin and Catharine MacKinnon and groups like Women Against Pornography, the monologic voice was, of course, female.[23] Although antipornography feminists disagreed with fundamentalist moral assumptions and contested, rather than approved, male authority, they carved out new territory with slide shows depicting allegedly horrific sexual images, a technique the commission happily adopted. Antipornography feminists relied on victim testimony and preferred anecdotes to data. They, too, shared a literalist interpretative frame and used SM images to prove that pornography was violent. It was not a total surprise when the panel invited leading antipornography feminists to testify at its hearings, and they cooperated.

In the Meese Commission's monologue, even dissenting witnesses inadvertently cooperated by handing over the arena of interpretation to the commission. Not a single anticensorship witness ever showed a slide, provided a competing frame of visual interpretation, or showed images he or she thought were joyful, erotic, and pleasurable.[24] All lost an important opportunity to present another point of view, to educate, and to interrupt the fiction of a single, shared interpretive frame. Visual images remained the exclusive province of the censors and the literalists. This further cemented the notion that the visual "evidence" was uncontested and indeed spoke for itself. Why did the anticensorship community not do better?

The Meese Commission was skilled in its ability to use photographic images to establish the so-called "truth" and to provide an almost-invisible interpretative frame that compelled agreement with its agenda. The commission's true genius, however, lay in its ability to create an emotional atmosphere in the hearings that facilitated acceptance of the commission's worldview. Its strategic use of images was a crucial component of this emotional management. Because the power of this emotional climate fades in the published text, it is not obvious to most readers of the commission's report. Yet it was and is a force to be reckoned with, both in the commission and, more broadly, in all public debates about sexuality that involve the right wing. Though the commission was not infrequently ridiculed by journalists for its lack of objectivity and its overzealous puritanism, logical objections to its manipulations often faded in the hearing room.

III. Creating a Climate of Sexual Shame

The commission relentlessly created an atmosphere of unacknowledged sexual arousal and fear. The large amount of pornography shown, ostensibly designed to educate and repel, was nevertheless arousing. The range and diversity of images provided something for virtually everyone, and the concentration on taboo, kinky, and harder-to-obtain material added to the charge. Signs were evident in nervous laughter, rapt attention, flushed cheeks, awkward jokes, throat clearing and coughing, squirming in seats, and a charged, nervous tension in the room. Part of the discomfort may have come from the unfamiliarity of seeing sexually explicit images in public, not private, settings, and in the company of others not there for the express purpose of sexual arousal. But a larger part must have come from the problem of managing sexual arousal in an atmosphere where it was condemned.

The rhetoric of the commission suggests that pornographic material is degrading and disgusting and that no decent person would seek it out or respond to it. Although it is obvious that millions of people buy pornography, none of them appeared in the hearing room to defend it. And, as the testimony elicited by the panel suggested that porn consumers are likely to be rapists, raving maniacs, and perverts easily detected by their flapping raincoats and drooling saliva, certainly no one present at the hearing was willing to admit to feeling sexually aroused. As a result, anyone who experienced any arousal to the images shown felt simultaneously ashamed, abnormal, and isolated, particularly in regard to homosexual or SM imagery, which had been characterized as especially deviant.

The commission's lesson was a complex one, but it taught the importance of managing and hiding sexual arousal and pleasure in public, while it reinforced sexual secrecy, hypocrisy, and shame. The prospect of exposure brought with it fear, stigmatization, and rejection. Sexual feelings, though, did not disappear; they were split off as dangerous, alien, and hateful, projected onto others, where they must be controlled. Unacknowledged sexual arousal developed into a whirlwind of confused, repressed emotion that the Meese Commission channeled toward its own purpose.

Dissenting witnesses rarely attacked the commission's characterization of pornography. Although they made important arguments about censorship, they left the commission's description of pornography, interpretive frame, and account of subjectivity unchallenged. The commission's visual interventions and narrative voice-over remained powerful because no one pointed out their existence or the mechanisms through which they were created.

No one offered a deconstruction of the commission's visual techniques or offered images that would problematize its constructions. A counter slide-show might have included erotic images from the fine arts as well as from advertising, calling into question the neat category of "the pornographic." It could have historicized sexually explicit imagery by relating images to time, place, genre, audience, and conditions of production. It might have included images of similar bodies and body parts whose context made all the difference in meaning, or included viewers talking about the diversity of their responses to the same image. And it could have included artists talking about erotic creativity. To show positive images of sexual explicitness would have been a radical act.

To be fair, it was extraordinarily difficult to offer a dissenting perspective. The overwhelming emotional climate created by the hearings turned anyone who disagreed into a veritable monster, a defender of the most sensational and unpalatable images shown. The frame demonized pornography, but it also tarnished the reputation of anyone who questioned the commission's program. Most prospective dissenting witnesses correctly perceived that the atmosphere was closer to a witchcraft trial than a fact-finding hearing. Some declined to testify, and others moderated their remarks, anticipating a climate of intimidation.[25]

Indeed, an important aspect of the commission's work was the ritual airing and affirmation of sexual shame in a public setting, a practice that was embedded in the interrogatory practices of the chair. Witnesses appearing before the commission were treated in a highly uneven manner. Commissioners accepted virtually any claim made by antipornography witnesses as true, while those who opposed restriction of sexually explicit speech were often met with rudeness and hostility. Visual images proved to be the Achilles' heel of anticensorship witnesses, since the witnesses were often asked if they meant to defend a particularly stigmatized image that had just been flashed on the screen, such as *Big Tit Dildo Bondage* or *Anal Girls*. The witnesses were often speechless, and their inarticulateness about images often undercut their testimony.

Sexual shame was also ritualized in how witnesses spoke about their personal experience with images. "Victims of pornography" told in lurid detail of their use of pornography and eventual decline into masturbation, sexual addiction, and incest. Some testified anonymously, shadowy apparitions behind translucent screens. Their first-person accounts, sometimes written by the commission's staff,[26] featured a great elaboration of the sexual damage caused by visual images. To counter these accounts there was nothing but silence: descriptions of visual and sexual pleasure were absent. The commission's chair even noted the lack and was fond of asking journalists if they had ever come across individuals with positive experiences with pornography. The investigatory staff had tried to identify such people to testify, he said, but had been unable to find any. Hudson importuned reporters to please send such individuals his way. A female commissioner helpfully suggested that she know of acquaintances, "normal married couples living in suburban New Jersey," who occasionally looked at magazines or rented X-rated videos with no apparent ill effects. But she doubted that they would be willing to testify about their sexual pleasure in a federal courthouse, with their remarks transcribed by a court stenographer and their photos probably published in the next day's paper as "porn-users."

Though few witnesses chose to expose themselves to the commission's intimidation through visual images, the tactics used are illustrated in the differential treatment of two female witnesses, former *Playboy* Playmate Micki Garcia and former *Penthouse* Pet of the Year Dottie Meyer. Garcia accused Playboy Enterprises and Hugh Hefner of encouraging drug use, murder, and rape (as well as abortion, bisexuality, and cosmetic surgery) in the Playboy mansion. Her life was endangered by her testimony, she claimed. Despite the serious nature of her charges and the lack of any supporting evidence, her testimony was received without question.[27] Meyer, on the other hand, testified that her association with *Penthouse* had been professionally and personally beneficial. At the conclusion of her testimony, the lights dramatically dimmed and large blowups of several *Penthouse* pictorials were flashed on the screen; with rapid-fire questions the chair demanded that she explain sexual images he found particularly objectionable. Another commissioner, prepared by the staff with copies of Meyer's nine-year-old centerfold, began to pepper her with hectoring questons about her sexual life: Was it true she was preoccupied with sex? Liked sex in cars and alleyways? Had a collection of vibrators? Liked rough-and-tumble sex?[28] His cross-examination was reminiscent of that directed at a rape victim made vulnerable and discredited by an image of her own sexuality.

The commission's success in maintaining and intensifying a climate of sexual shame depended on the inability of witnesses to address the question of sexuality and pleasure. Most witnesses who opposed greater restriction of sexually explicit material framed their arguments in terms of the dangers of censorship, illustrating their points by examples of literature that had been censored in previous, presumbaly less enlightened, times. Visual examples were rare. Speakers favored historical, rather than contemporary, examples around which a clear consensus about value had formed. Favored examples were the plays of Eugene O'Neill and D. H. Lawrence's *Lady Chatterley's Lover*. The frame was cultured and high-minded, calling on general principles like free speech and the Bill of Rights.

The motives behind this strategy differed. The small number of witnesses directly associated with the sex industry (producers of X-rated films, books, or magazines) believed that their disreputable image could be uplifted by associating themselves with higher, unassailable principles that had a minimal connection with sexuality. Although they had practical experience with visuals, they judged it a wiser course to say little about their real-world connection. The second group, a much larger number of witnesses representing literary, artistic, and anticensorship organizations, was totally unprepared to talk about visuals. They had thought little about questions of representation or sexually explicit images, often shared the same unsophisticated premises as the commissioners, and appeared to feel that association with sexuality was potentially discrediting.

The second group was fair game for the chair. Relying on his well-honed prosecutorial abilities, he was selectively relentless. He went right to the heart of the witnesses' reluctance to associate themselves with anything sexual, visual, or pleasure-filled. Pointing to the latest slide or holding aloft the latest exhibit, he questioned them about their organization's position on *Hot Bodies* or *Split Beavers*. Did their members produce such images? Did their organization mean to defend such material? Did they think such material should be available?

Like vampires spying crosses and garlic cloves, witnesses shrank back. Having never seen the sexually explicit material or thought about it, having no well-developed position about sexuality or visual representation, and sensing the increasingly dangerous turf they were being lead into, they said, "No." They were unprepared, speechless, and unwilling to defend anything so patently sexual. The chair had proven his point: even anticensorship advocates would not defend visual pornography. He politely excused them, with bland, if inaccurate, assurances that antipornography efforts would target only indefensible sleaze, not worthy high culture. More important, he appeared to establish a consensus, which included even liberals, that sexually explicit visuals were beyond the pale. Despite their valiant effort, the testimony of anticensorship witnesses never succeeded in deconstructing or interrupting the Meese Commission's rhetorical and symbolic strategies. The right-wing's commitment, however, to controlling symbols means that there will be other times, other battles in which to elaborate a richer, more complex response.

IV. Speaking Sexual and Visual Pleasure

The antidote to the Meese Commission—and by extension all conservative and fundamentalist efforts to restrict sexual images, whether in pornography, sex education, or AIDS information—is a complex one, requiring vigorous response that goes beyond appeals to free speech. Free expression is a necessary principle in these debates because of the steady protection it offers to all images, but it cannot be the only one. We need to offer an alternative frame for understanding images, one that rejects literalist constructions and offers in their place multiplicity, subjectivity, and the diverse experience of viewers. We must challenge the conservative monopoly on visual display and interpretation. The visual arts community needs to employ its interpretive skills to unmask the modernized rhetoric conservatives use to justify their traditional agenda, as well as deconstruct the "difficult" images fundamentalists pick to set their campaigns in motion. Despite their uncanny intuition for choosing culturally disturbing material, their focus on images also contains many sleights of hand, even displacements, which we need to examine. Images even we allow to remain "disturbing" and unconsidered put us anxiously on the defensive and undermine our own response. To do all this, visual artists and arts groups need to be willing to enter public debate and activism, giving up the notion that art or photography is somehow exempt from right-wing crusades against images.

The most robust and energetic response, however, must be to take courage and begin to speak to what is missing, both in the Meese Commission's monologue and in the anticensorship reply: desire, sexuality, and pleasure. Truly dissenting voices and speakers must start to say in public that sexual pleasure is legitimate and honorable, a simple statement that few witnesses in the commission's hearings dared to make. If we remain afraid to offer a public defense of sex and pleasure, then even in our rebuttal we have granted the right wing its most basic premise: sexuality is shameful and discrediting. The rigid, seemingly impenetrable symbolic and emotional façade constructed by the Meese Commission can, in fact, be radically undermined by insistently confronting it with what it most wants to banish—the tantalizing connection between visual and sexual pleasure.

Notes

An early version of this paper was given at the Society for Photographic Education convention, Rochester, New York, 1989; thanks to the audience for a stimulating exchange and to the Women's Caucus for inviting me. Portions of this argument first appeared in "The Meese Commission on the Road," *The Nation*, 2-9 August 1986, pp. 65, 76-82.

[1] Attorney General's Commission on Pornography, *Final Report*, 2 vols. (Washington, D. C.: U. S. Government Printing Office, July 1986). Public hearings were organized around preselected topics in six cities: Washington, D. C. (general), Chicago (law enforcement), Houston (social science), Los Angeles (production and distribution), Miami (child pornography), and New York (organized crime). Each public hearing typically lasted two full days. Commission executive sessions were held in each city, usually for two working days, in conjunction with the public hearings. Additional work sessions occurred in Washington, D. C. and Scottsdale, Arizona. All the commission's executive sessions were open to the public, following the provision of sunshine laws governing federal advisory commissions. Commissioners were specifically enjoined from discussing commission business or engaging in any informal deliberations outside public view. My analysis is based on direct observations of the commission's public hearings and executive sessions, supplemented by many interviews with participants.

[2] Larry Madigan, "former consumer of pornography," testified at the Miami hearings. He was introduced by his therapist, Dr. Simon Miranda, who claimed that most of his own clinical work was with patients whose problems were caused by pornography. "Larry," he stated, "has informed me recently that, in fact, he can trace many of the problems that he has had life long to an encounter with pornography" (Miami hearing transcripts, 21 November 1985).

³For changes in sexual patterns in the last century see (for England) Jeffrey Weeks, *Sex, Politics and Society: The Regulation of Sexuality Since 1800* (New York: Longman, 1981) and (for America) John D'Emilio and Estelle B. Freedman, *Intimate Matters* (New York: Harper and Row, 1988).

⁴See *Final Report*, pp. 433-458, for a complete list of the panel's recommendations.

⁵*Final Report*, p . 420. See *Final Report*, pt. 4, chap. 7, "Citizen and Community Action and Corporate Responsibility." These instructions are significant because they outline a powerful, extralegal strategy for eliminating materials that are "non-obscene but offensive," that is, normally immune from legal action under obscenity law. Suggestions include forming antipornography activist groups and collecting detailed information on sexually explicit materials available in local stores, movie theaters, hotels, and through video, cable, and computer channels. A detailed checklist is provided for citizens to conduct "a thorough survey of these establishments and media." Citizens are also encouraged to pressure police and public officials, conduct court watches, picket and boycott local stores, and monitor rock music heard by their children. Commissioners also reccomend that institutions that are taxpayer supported prohibit the "production, trafficking, distribution, or display of pornography on their premises or in association with their institution." Conservative politicians and right-wing decency groups used this strategy in 1989 to attack the National Endowment for the Arts for indirectly funding an exhibit of Robert Mapplethorpe's photographs, some of which were erotic, some sexually explicit, at the Corcoran Gallery, Washington, D. C. (For an account of the NEA-Mapplethorpe controversy, see Carole S. Vance, "The War on Culture," *Art in America*, September 1989, pp. 39-45.)

⁶The children were returned home the next day, as social-service officials determined there was no evidence that the children were in

danger. Charges were eventually dropped by the state of Virginia because of local protest, but the U. S. Postal Service has not officially closed the case. According to Sims, while searching her house agent Northrup told her, "Art is anything you can get away with," and referring to her work, "This is all filth." Later, in an interview with *Village Voice* art critic Elizabeth Hess, he said, "Artistic people are funny. Mrs. Sim's house was not like Ozzie and Harriet's." He asked, "How do you differentiate between an artist and a pedophile?" For a more complete account of the case, see "Snapshots, Art, or Porn?" *Village Voice*, 25 October 1988, pp. 31-32. Thanks to Jeff Weinstein for this citation.

[7]Alan Sears went on to become the executive director of Citizens for Decency through Law, a major conservative antipornography group. (The group has since changed its name to the Children's Legal Foundation.)

[8]Besides Hudson, the commission panel included the following: James Dobson, head of the fundamentalist organization Focus on the Family: "I have a personal dislike for pornography and all it implies," he told *The Washington Post.* Judge Edward Garcia, recently appointed by then-President Reagan to the Federal District Court in California; Garcia prosecuted obscenity cases before becoming a judge. Diane Cusack, a member of the Scottsdale, Arizona, City Council; Cusack urged residents to take photographs and license numbers of patrons entering the local adult theater. Father Bruce Ritter, a Franciscan priest; Ritter directs Covenant House, a home for runaways in New York's Time Square area, and is an outspoken critic of pornography. Attorney Harold (Tex) Lazar; Lazar played an instrumental role in setting up the commission as an aide to Reagan's first Attorney General, William French Smith. Frederick Schauer, a law professor at the University of Michigan; Schauer has written extensively on obscenity. The four members of the panel with no public positions on pornography included Park Elliott Dietz, a psychiatrist at the Univer-

sity of Virginia and a consultant to the Federal Bureau of Investigation, who specialized in the subject of sexual deviations ("paraphilias"); Judith Becker, a Columbia University psychologist known for her research on rapists and rape victims; Ellen Levine, a vice president of CBS and editor of *Woman's Day*; and Deanne Tilton, head of the California Consortium of Child Abuse Councils.

[9]A variety of state laws had resulted in prosecutions and convictions for obscenity in the nineteenth and twentieth centuries. In response to a challenge of one such law, the Supreme Court in 1957 articulated the First Amendment standard for what could be prosecuted as "obscene" in *Roth v. United States* [354 U.S. 476 (1957)]. The court decided that the normal protections given to constitutionally protected speech need not be given to legally obscene material. The most recent attempt to define what is "obscene" in a constitutionally permissible manner is found in a 1973 case, *Miller v. California* [413 U.S. 15 (1973)]. According to *Miller*, material is obscene if all three of the following conditions are met: 1. The average person, applying contemporary community standards, would find the work, taken as a whole, appeals to the prurient interest, and 2. the work depicts or describes, in a patently offensive way, sexual conduct specified by the statute, and 3. the work, taken as a whole, lacks serious literary, artistic, political, or scientific value.

[10]Victims of pornography, as described in the *Final Report*, included "Sharon, formerly married to a medical professional who is an avid consumer of pornography," "Bill, convicted of the sexual molestation of two adolescent females," "Dan, former Consumer of Pornography [sic]," "Evelyn, Mother and homemaker, Wisconsin, formerly married to an avid consumer of pornography," and "Mary Steinman, sexual abuse victim."

[11]In February, 1986, the executive director of the commission announced that in the future no drafts or working papers could be

released to the press or public. The American Civil Liberties Union sued the commission for violating access laws governing federal panels, and the commission settled before the case got to court, agreeing to release these documents to the public (see *The Washington Post*, 7 March 1986; 4 April 1986; 12 April 1986). When some commissioners objected to repeating unsubstantiated allegations in the final report, the staff sent letters to the corporations on Department of Justice letterhead, noting that "the Commission received testimony alleging that your company is involved in the sale or distribution of pornography." The letter noted that the companies had thirty days to repsond and that "a lack of reply would indicate they did not differ" with the allegations. Some corporations strenuously protested these methods. Others, however, caved in. Southland Corporation, which owns forty-five hundred 7-Eleven convenience stores, announced that it would no longer carry P*layboy, Penthouse*, and *Forum* magazines. Bob Guccione, *Penthouse* publisher, called the move "blacklisting" and launched lawsuits against the commission. The commission settled one by agreeing not to publish the allegations in the report, but Guccione's suit for economic damages against the commission and individual commissioners is still pending (*The New York Times*, 15 April 1986, p. B5; *Newsweek*, 26 April 1986, pp. 38-39).

[12]For accounts of the history of regulating indecency and obscenity in the United States and England, see Edward J. Bristow, *Vice and Vigilance: Purity Movements in Britain since 1700* (New Jersey: Rowman and Littlefield, 1977); David Pivar, *Purity Crusade: Sexual Morality and Social Control: 1868-1900* (Connecticutt: Greenwood Press, 1972); Walter Kendrick, *The Secret Museum* (New York: Viking, 1987); John D'Emilio and Estelle B. Freedman, *Intimate Matters* (New York: Harper and Row, 1988).

[13]See Walter Kendrick, *The Secret Museum* (New York: Viking, 1987), for a discussion of the class concerns that motivated nineteenth-century obscenity regulation.

¹⁴The falsity of this claim is made evident by the recent right-wing attack on the National Endowment of the Arts over the "blasphemy" and "obscenity" contained in the work of Andres Serrano and Robert Mapplethorpe.

¹⁵In contrast to visual artists, print and literary groups turned out in force. The commission heard testimony from the National Writers Union, Writers Guild, Association of American Publishers, the American Library Association, the Freedom to Read Committee, Bantam Books, and Actors Equity Association.

¹⁶A number of potential witnesses told me that they were afraid to testify, in some cases declining actual invitations and in other cases deciding against requesting to speak. They feared hostile and humiliating cross-examination and, for producers of sexually explicit material, police retaliation in the form of harassment, investigation, and potential prosecution. Fear of reprisal was especially common among the free-lance, and often more innovative, producers of sexually explicit material, whether pornography or radical political graphics. As independent producers, they could not rely on large parent organizations to offer legal protection and financial backing (and, some implied, payoffs to corrupt vice cops). With only modest financial resources at hand, the prospect of disrupted business or costly legal battles (even if ultimately victorious) spelled financial disaster. Most small producers felt it was prudent not to testify, leaving the job to mainstream men's magazines not known for radical sex politics or innovative graphics.

¹⁷Descriptions of magazine photographs can be found in *Final Report*, pp. 1614-1646. Videos and movies are also described, though the narrative concentrates primarily on plot and dialogue. The narrative reproduces long sections of dialogue verbatim, arguably constituting a copyright violation.

[18] *Final Report*, statement of Judith Becker and Ellen Levine, p. 199. In addition, they wrote: "We do not even know whether or not what the Commission viewed during the course of the year reflected the nature of most of the pornographic and obscene material in the market; nor do we know if the materials shown us mirror the taste of the majority of consumers of pornography. . . . While one does not deny the existence of this material, the fact that it dominated the materials presented at our hearings may have distorted the Commission's judgment about the proportion of such violent material in relation to the total pornographic material in distribution."

[19] Recent empirical evidence does not support the often-repeated assertion that violence in pornography is increasing. In their review of the literature, social scientists Edward Donnerstein, Daniel Linz, and Steven Penrod conclude, "at least for now, we cannot legitimately conclude that pornography has become more violent since the time of the 1970 obscenity and pornography commission" [in *The Question of Pornography: Research Findings and Policy Implications* (New York: The Free Press, 1987), p. 91].

[20] The only original research conducted by the commission examined images found in the April 1986 issues of best-selling men's magazine (*Cheri, Chic, Club, Gallery, Genesis, High Society, Hustler, Oui, Penthouse, Playboy, Swank*). The study found that "images of force, violence, or weapons constituted less than 1 percent of all images (0.6 percent), hardly substantiating the commission's claim that violent imagery in pornography was common. Although the results of this study are reported in the draft, they were excised from the final report. The study found that the most common acts portrayed were "split beaver" poses (20 percent), other imagery including touching (19 percent), oral-genital activity (12 percent), and activities between two women (12 percent). According to the Audit Bureau of Circulation (ABC) the thirteen top-selling mainstream magazines sold 12 million

copies per month (4.2 million copies for *Playboy*, 3.3 million copies for *Penthouse*), with a monthly sales value over $38 million (1984 data).

[21] The proclivity of mildly stigmatized groups to join in the scapegoating of more stigmatized groups is explained by Gayle Rubin in her discussion of the concept of sexual hierarchy ["Thinking Sex: Notes for a Radical Theory of the Politics of Sexuality" in *Pleasure and Danger: Exploring Female Sexuality*, ed. Carole S. Vance (Boston: Routledge & Kegan Paul, 1984), pp. 267-319].

[22] For recent work on SM, see Gini Graham Scott, *Dominant Women, Submissive Men* (New York: Praeger, 1983); Thomas Weinberg and G. P. Levi Kamel, *S and M: Studies in Sadomasochism* (Buffalo: Prometheus Books, 1983); Gerald and Caroline Greene, *S-M: The Last Taboo* (New York: Grove Press, 1974); Michael A. Rosen, *Sexual Magic: the S/M Photographs* (San Francisco: Shaynew Press, 1986; Geof Mains, *Urban Aboriginals* San Francisco: Gay Sunshine Press, 1984); Samois, ed. *Coming to Power*, 2d ed. (Boston: Alyson Press, 1982).

[23] Major works of antipornography feminism include Andrea Dworkin, *Pornography: Men Possessing Women* (New York: G. P. Putnam & Sons, 1979); Laura Lederer, ed. *Take Back the Night* (New York: William Morrow, 1980); Catharine A. MacKinnon, "Pornography, Civil Rights, and Speech," *Harvard Civil Rights-Civil Liberties Law Review* vol. 20 (Cambridge: Harvard University, 1985), pp. 1-70. Opinion within feminism about pornography was, in fact, quite diverse, and it soon became apparent that the antipornography view was not hegemonic. For other views, see Varda Burstyn, ed. *Women Against Censorship* (Vancouver: Douglas & McIntyre, 1985) and, FACT (Feminist Anticensorship Taskforce), ed. *Caught Looking: Feminism, Pornography, and Censorship* (East Haven, Connecticut: Long River Books, 1992).

[24] These witnesses included legal scholars, representatives from the American Civil Liberties Union, the Freedom to Read Committee, and publishers' and authors' groups.

[25] Some producers of sexually explicit material declined to testify, because the commission had no authority to immunize witnesses from criminal prosecution. They feared that their testimony would be used by law enforcement officials to investigate or prosecute them. This was especially true during the Los Angeles hearing devoted specifically to the sex industry, since local officials were just then conducting an especially vigorous effort against producers.

[26] Statement of Alan Sears, executive director (Washington, D.C. transcript, 18 June 1985).

[27] Los Angeles hearing, 17 October 1985.

[28] New York City hearing, 22 January 1986.

I am grateful to many individual for helpful discussion, comments on early drafts, and encouragement, especially Ann Snitow, Frances Doughty, Sharon Thompson, Lisa Duggan, David Schwartz, and Gil Zicklin. Special thanks to Frances Doughty for insightful and invaluable suggestions about writing. Thanks to Carol Squiers for editorial suggestions and to Gayle Rubin for last-minute help.

John Greyson

from The Making of Monsters: A Musical Comedy about Anti-Gay Violence

(sung to the tune of "Mac the Knife")

*In this big world, there's a rule, dear
Boys must choose girls, for their mates
We are always taught in school, dear
To hate queers, but, I hate straights*

*Straights are stupid, straights are boring
They get upset when we come out
They prefer us in our closets
Disenfranchised, without clout*

*Homophobia is an equation
It increases with our pride
Calculate the ebb and flow dear
It decreases when we hide*

*Straights breed babies, straights breed violence
Through their churches, through their states
Queers must rise up, fight the monsters
Shout out loud, dear, I hate Straights!*

Still from *The Making of Monsters* written and directed by John Greyson: Joe's boyfriend sings "I Hate Straights."

Barbara Henning

Resumé

> Addicts of sensual pleasure, made restless by their many desires and caught in the net of delusion... I cast them back again and again into the wombs of degraded parents, subjecting them to the wheel of birth and death.
>
> —*Bhagavad-Gita*

Delivered through my mother's body on the twenty-sixth of October, nineteen hundred and forty-eight, head, hands, feet, the white creme of entry on my face in the folds of my skin. Maple leaves flicker in the sunlight. Inside the grey cinderblock house, I watch my mother asleep in bed, her thin bare chest rising and falling.

    Held over father's legs—he cries and I await the spanking on bare buttocks. I dream deep in a puddle. Barefoot on the hot sidewalk. Climb the pole in the park and slowly slip down. Lie on a table prodded by boys and looked at with mirrors. In the tent with the girls, skin against skin, cunt against cunt.

Gramma hits me with the stick as I run back and forth in the living room. All her friends are dying, she says. Eat your peas. Sit up straight. Clean your plate. Don't put your elbows on the table. Shut up. Shut up. Shut up. Expect nothing wonderful, mother tells me. Plenty of kisses, perhaps a plastic doll in my arms. Her bare thin chest expands in sleep, eyes closed, mouth open, the dark circle of her nipple.

White around my hips, legs over the edge of the toilet. Flat on the pavement, suntanned skin around the bathing suit, around the breasts and abdomen, a tough blue jeaned boy on top. Put it in, put it in, says the crowd of children. Held still, in the grip of my father's hands, the doctor pierces my thin arm with his needle. Mother sits up suddenly and talks about the appearance and voice of Jesus in the middle of her bedroom, his arms held open, beckoning to her. At the foot of the stairs, in the darkness, I watch her body turn and rest on the sofa.

Books about northern England, darkness, moors, dogs, mysterious lovers, anger, a detailed account of the back of my father's hand. Kiss and stroke my own shoulder, the inside of my arms. My little sister and I stumble to a halt in the dark. The headlights slow down, call out, whistle, baby doll. We look at each other, our spindly legs and slumped over shoulders. In bed, I cover my swelling nipples with my fingers, afraid of scissors and knives.

Blood gushes. Denied access. No, the father says. No, you cannot shower. Mother's voice remembers folded rags and her father's eyes watching her in the living room. The August heat drags us up and down the street. Lock the boy in the dog's pen, snot running over his chin. Slap the teenage girl. Smoke on the steps of the school. On the Avenue. Back to the swing. Up, down, the sky, the air. Slide down the pole. Black eyeliner. Lipstick. Tight skirts on the Avenue, lighted cigarettes and back seat conquests.

Mother's hands rest, eyes closed, deep into wax, feet hidden, face cold and stiff. (In sorrow thou shalt bring forth children.) The teenage boy puts his fingers on my shoulder, calling me into the parlor lounge. Dream mother, legless and armless repeats her mantra: I have no husband. I have no husband. Daddy is asleep in his chair. Skinny and shy, I outline my eyes in the bathroom mirror. Janet cuts my bleached blond bangs: she clips around my ears. Ray's tongue in my ear, the sound of Lake Huron, crying again while father snores, the sound of the ocean far away and lilacs outside the window.

Men take me home to their beds. It will be nothing much mother's voice remembers. Ah mother dear, let us in, I say, dancing, folded over apart and together, breaking open my body. Church-like fingers turn the pages in the dark, slip inside my crack. Gently wrists open, the veins exposed, twisted over, scarred and fragile, swelling passively in my lap. Legs shaved, rubbed, stretched open, knees to chest, head bowed, I worship with my mouth, anus, vagina, push the chorus of one body from and to another, the children to and from my breasts annointed with the white creme of entry, birth waters and the smell of tar after rain. Even on this July wordless night on the rooftop as I offer my son and my brother this body, this corpse, the breeze flickering through our hair, I notice my father reading in the stairwell, and I beckon him to please come back and take his turn.

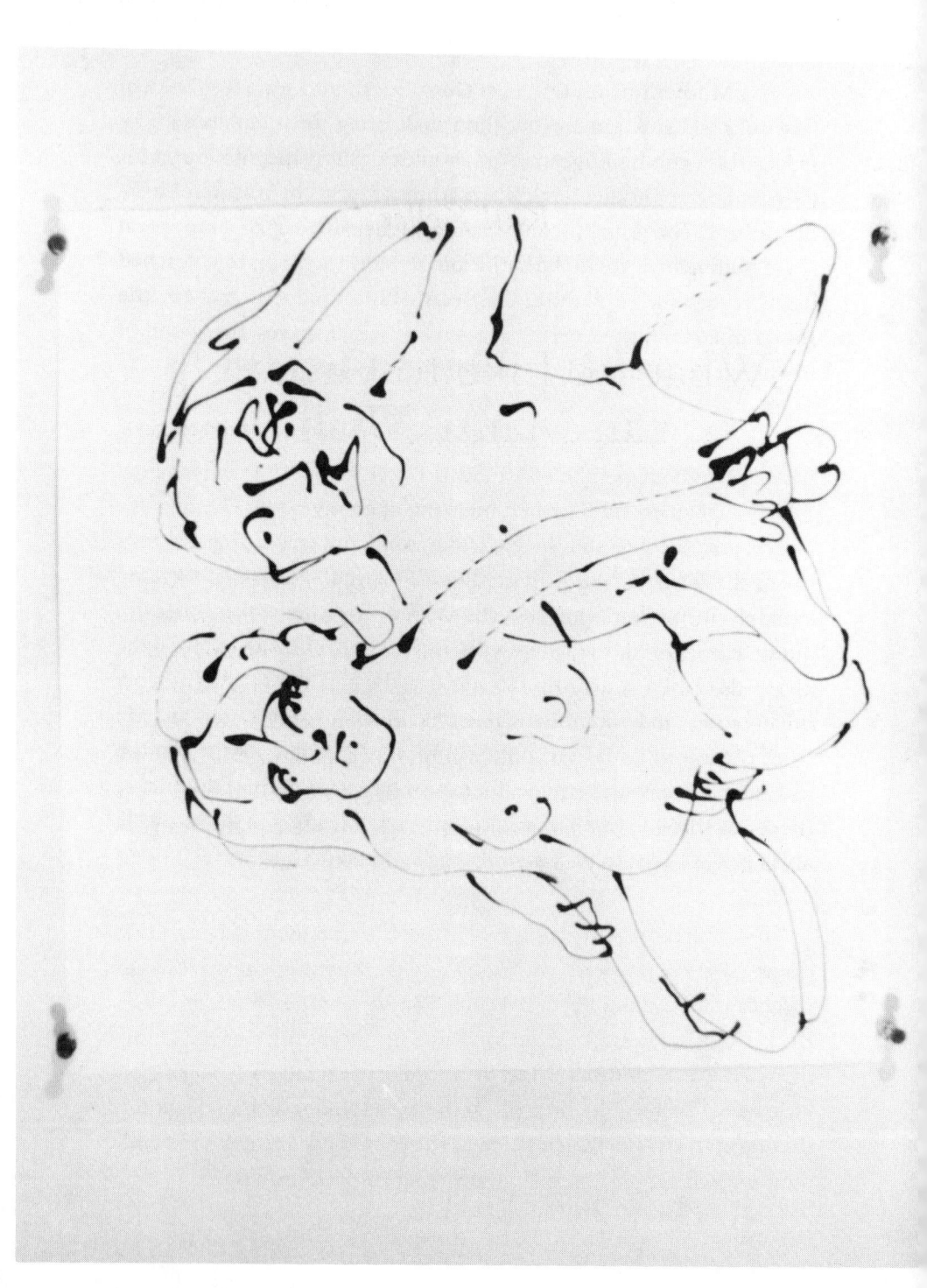

(acrylic on paper) Gail Schneider

Karl Keller

What It's Like to Grow Up in Manti, Utah

Imagine the boy at the piano. 12. A hot summer morning. Playing loud, playing soft. All the doors on Main St. are open. Flies are on the music. It goes out into the ears of all the movie star agents driving past taking the curve slowly by the old stone house listening hard with smiles to hear the boy at the piano 12 a hot summer morning playing loud, playing soft. He wants them all so much all the world so much so much to be taken and taken his little balls ache in his little legs. And Bette Davis looks up at him playing loud, playing soft and says with her wicked groping eyes You are beautiful and you shine.

Imagine him hearing it above the sounds he sends playing loud, playing soft out the doors on Main St. to the movie star agents driving past beautiful and shining to hear him 12 a hot summer morning—*him*! Bette Davis's voice above the loud, the soft beautiful, shining calling them to find the doors on Main St. and take the aching boy playing his little balls 12 all so much so much the eyes looking at him beautiful, shining giving taking given taken all the movie star agents saying with their wicked groping eyes You are beautiful and you shine.

Slowly they all together put their hands and arms up his little boy ass and tear him all the ways—imagine!—until he is a beautiful shining bloody flower. The deep wrinkles around his eyes smile love, smile love.

Cris Mazza

Hesitation

It's not that he left after fucking her because he wanted to get away from her. It's not that he wouldn't've enjoyed the heat of her beside him or her hand creeping inside his underwear in the morning when they would both be groggy and he was hard but not urgent. He would've liked her to hold it while he slept. But what if he were with her and the phone rang at 1 or 2 in the morning, and what if it were his ex-wife calling? Once he lay spread eagle and said "Tie me up and do whatever you want to me." She actually put her tongue in his armpit, sucked his toes, rubbed his hard-on between her breasts. The jewel in her pierced nose scratched gently on his stomach as she nipped and licked around his navel, growling like a puppy, laughed and said she was eating away the cord he'd forgotten to cut. So she can't piss her poison into you no more, the girl said, it's not like she's your fuckin *mother*. It's not that he still went out with his ex-wife because he wanted her company. It's just that he destroyed someone's whole world and he owed that much in return, so she wouldn't feel like a worthless person, so she wouldn't feel totally abandoned. More than once he wet the girl's neck with his tears. She touched his cheeks and kissed his face and sometimes he held her hard but the worst time he just stared at the ceiling through his brimming eyes because the woman said he was selfish and always got what he wanted but never wanted to take care of her and never wanted to give her what she wanted and he was always constantly shoving that thing at her but why didn't he hold her hand or take her to hear the symphony play outside at the beach at night—so why should she want to have sex with him?—and now he's ruined her plan for her life because they were supposed to grow old together in their lovely home and now she'll be alone and even though she was going on a vacation cruise to the Mediterranean the next week, think how awful it would be for her knowing he'd be with that weirdo filthy girl, doing whatever he wants, how was that supposed to make her feel? It would ruin her trip, she said. It's not that he thought the woman had actually guessed his dream that the girl helped bring to life as soon as the Rome-bound jet was off the ground: the hungry, vibrant creature wearing an evening gown slit up the back to her bare ass who wandered around among the crowd at the opera until she chose him out of a whole theatre full of people and followed him to the downtown pier, begging him to fuck her on the rail above the angry, violent breakers lapping at the pylons 100 feet from shore as embarrassed tourists hurried past in the salty milk-warm darkness, pretending not to notice. It's not that he felt guilty or wrong for making love to the girl like that, after all those years of his own spit. It's not like he vacillated at all, it's not as though he'd had any qualms, that he wasn't flying on adrenalin as he and the girl made up those fantasies while eating take-out ribs in the living room in their underwear, and promised them to each other as gifts. It's not as though he wasn't absolutely exhilarated when she rolled him over and used colored pens to draw a tattoo on his butt. He saw it in the mirror later, a heart all wrung up like a dish cloth, with blood dripping out, a little smeared because she'd pressed her face over it before the ink was dry. She said, You mean none of those friends of yours ever said you've got a sexy ass? I'm gonna ask them why. It's not that he was reluctant to introduce her to his friends because he was ashamed of her. It's not that he thought they wouldn't like her, wouldn't think she's smart enough or sophisticated enough for him. He said after 20 years of knowing him with his wife, they weren't ready for him to appear suddenly with a new girl. They'd be uncomfortable. He wouldn't want to do that to them. He said maybe they always thought if their kids turned out like her, they'd feel like complete failures or kill themselves. Yeah, she said softly. He just meant he had to prepare them first. He couldn't imagine what they would think if he dropped in or showed up at a party unannounced with her. The girl suggested, maybe they'll wonder: wow, what's *he* got that *I* don't got? Maybe she didn't understand when he said don't ever tell anyone that another girl once fell in love with her. And don't ever tell anyone that a former lover took polaroid snapshots of her during foreplay before he beat her up. Don't talk about the head shop in Ocean Beach where she used to work, her alcoholic mother who held her down and shaved her head long before that style became popular, or why she was kicked out of bartender school. And don't show them her wrists where the scars stand up, cherry red, shiny just-born skin that sometimes she ran her tongue along while watching his collection of Bogart movies. Don't laugh and tell anyone they're called hesitation marks. Don't say it was the first new skin of a whole new girl, that there's a chart in some hospital basement saying 26 sutures, lacerations on right and left forearms, suicide gesture suspected. Don't mention at a dinner party that blood tastes like silver, if silver had a taste, that's what it would taste like—like blood. Don't talk about incest or abortions or hitchhiking or sugar-daddies or bull-dykes or body art or dildos. He only warned her because they would've wondered about her, would've thought funny thoughts about her, and he wanted them to know her as he knew her. He says in her case maybe first impressions wouldn't've told the whole story. It's not that he asked her not to wear sleeveless shirts in public because he didn't think her tattoos were cute. And it's not that he was wavering, the night he'd sent her home, as usual, but she crouched in the bushes outside his bedroom until dawn because she'd moved again and couldn't remember where she lived. If he'd known it was her he wouldn't've called the police. It's not that he doesn't care enough to call someone now, but how could he describe her to the police? He doesn't have a photograph of her to put up on telephone poles, and, even though he's not embarrassed of her fantasy, he wouldn't want to show them the videotape of it: the dark room with dozens of candles, the 24-hour road race from Le Mans on the television, him on the floor in jeans and bare feet, eating microwave pizza and drinking 7-up from a can, the girl arriving like a thief through the glass slider behind the sofa, wearing crotch-length mini and spike heels with ankle straps, nothing underneath, and completely shaved, kisses his neck and ears but his eyes never move from the TV screen, he continues sipping the 7-up as she unbuttons his jeans, but not the top button, takes his cock and balls out of the fly, strokes him and licks the cheese from his fingertips as he finishes the soda and settles back against the sofa, leans sideways to see the TV, doesn't even close his eyes as she sucks his cock, but his toes curl and uncurl, then she straddles him, slides her shaved pussy right down over him, but the end of the fantasy was ruined—the part where the cars go into their final lap and he gets up, bends her onto her knees and fucks her from the rear—because a door opens in the background and someone says "Yoo-hoo," and the woman he'd been married to comes into the picture, and there's absolutely no pause before the girl falls sideways, almost onto the candles, as he struggles to his feet to hurry after the woman who has run from the room. The videocamera kept filming until the tape was finished. He didn't reappear in the picture, but it does show the girl leaving through the slider, splashing through the glass like water. He used to tell the girl he needed her. He used to say how she was the only one he could turn to, the only one on his side. He used to say no one else had ever given him as much as she did. Once he'd told her she was a dream come true. Once he said she'd saved his life.

Joyce Carol Oates

from Martyrdom

What a beautiful baby *she* was, Babygirl the loving parents called her, conceived in the heat of the most tender yet the most erotic love, fated to be smothered with love, devoured witn love, an American Babygirl placed with reverent fingers in her incubator. Periwinkle blue eyes, fair silk-soft blond hair, perfect rosebud lips, tiny pug nose, uniform smoothness of the Caucasian skin. A call went out to nursing mothers in ghetto neighborhoods requesting milk from their sweet heavy balloon-breasts, mother's milk for pay, since Babygirl's own mother failed to provide milk of the required richness. Her incubator filtered our contaminated air and pumped pure oxygen into her lungs. She had no reason to wail like other infants, whose sorrow is so audible and distracting. In her incubator air humid and warm as a tropical rain forest Babygirl thrived, glowed, prospered, *grew*.

And how *he* grew, though nameless even to his mother! How *he* doubled, trebled, quadrupled *his* weight within days! Amid a swarm of siblings he fended his way, shrewd and driven, ravenous with hunger. Whether he was in the habit of gnawing ceaselessly during his waking hours, not only edible materials but such seemingly inedible materials as paper, wood, bone, metal of certain types and degrees of thinness, etc., because he was ravenously hungry or because he simply liked to gnaw, who can say? It is a fact that his incisors grew at the rate of between four and five inches a year, so he had to grind them down to prevent their pushing up into his brain and killing him. Granted the higher cognitive powers generated by the cerebral cortex, he might have speculated upon his generic predicament: is such behavior voluntary or involuntary; where survival is an issue, what *is* compulsion; under the spell of Nature, who can behave *unnaturally*?

In her glass-topped incubator Babygirl grew ounce by ounce, pound by pound, feeding, dozing, feeding, dozing—no time at all before her dimpled knees pressed against the glass, her breath misted the glass opaque. Her parents were beginning to be troubled by her rapid growth, yet proud too of her rosy female beauty, small pointed breasts, curving hips, dimpled belly and buttocks and crisp cinnamon-colored pubic hair, lovely thick-lashed eyes with no pupil. Babygirl had a bad habit of sucking her thumb so they painted her thumb with a foul-tasting fluorescent-orange iodine mixture and observed with satisfaction how she spat, and gagged, and writhed in misery, tasting it. One mild April day, a winey-red trail of clotted blood was detected in the incubator, issuing from between Babygirl's plump thighs, we were all quite astonished and disapproving but what's to be done? Babygirl's father said, Nature cannot be overcome, nor even postponed.

So many brothers and sisters he had, an alley awash with their wriggling bodies, a warehouse cellar writhing and squeaking with them, he sensed himself multiplied endlessly in the world, thus not likely to die *out*. For of all creaturely fears it is believed the greatest is the fear of, not merely dying, but dying *out*. Hundreds of thousands of brothers and sisters related to him by blood which was a solace, yes but also a source of infinite anxiety for all were ravenous with hunger, the *squeak! squeak! squeak!* of hunger multiplied beyond accounting. He learned, on his frantic clicking toenails, to scramble up sheer verticals, to run to the limits of his endurance, to tear out the throats of his enemies, to leap, to fly—to throw himself, for instance, as far as eleven feet into space, from one city rooftop to an adjacent rooftop—thus thwarting his pursuers. He learned to devour, when necessary, the living palpitating flesh of prey while on the run. The *snap!* of bones radiated pleasure through his jaws, his small brain thrummed with happiness. He never slept. His heartbeat was fever-rapid at all times. He knew not to back himself into a corner, nor to hide in any space from which there was no way out. He was going to live forever!—then one day his enemies set a trap for him, the crudest sort of trap, and sniffing and squeaking and quivering with hunger he lunged for the moldy bread-bait and a spring was triggered and a bar slammed down across the nape of his neck snapping the delicate vertebrae and nearly severing his poor astonished head.

They lied to her, telling her it was just a birthday party—for the family. First came the ritual bath, then the anointing of the flesh, the shaving and plucking of certain undesirable hairs, the curling and crimping of certain desirable hairs, she fasted for forty-eight hours, she was made to gorge herself for forty-eight hours, they scrubbed her tender flesh with a wire brush, they rubbed pungent herbs into the wounds, the little clitoris was sliced off and tossed to the clucking hens in the yard, the now-shaven labia were sewed shut, the gushing blood was collected in a golden chalice, her buckteeth were forcibly straightened with a pliers, her big hooked nose was broken by a quick skilled blow from the palm of a hand, the bone and cartilage grew back into more desirable contours, then came the girdle-brassiere to cinch in Babygirl's pudgy twenty-eight-inch waist to a more desirable seventeen-inch-waist, so her creamy hips and thighs billowed out, so her gorgeous balloon-breasts billowed out, her innards were squeezed up into her chest cavity, she had difficulty breathing at first, and moist pink-tinted bubbles issued from her lips, then she got the knack of it, reveling in her classic "hour-glass" figure and new-found power over men's inflammable imaginations. Her dress was something fetching and antique, unless it was something sly and silky-slinky, a provocative bustline, a snug-fitting skirt, she was charmingly hobbled as she walked her dimpled knees chafing together and her slender ankles quivering with the strain, she wore a black lace garter belt holding up her gossamer-transparent silk stockings with straight black seams, in her spike-heeled pointed-toed white satin shoes she winced a bit initially until she got the knack and very soon she got the knack, the shameless slut. Giggling and brushing and making little fluttery motions with her hands, wriggling her fat ass, her nipples hard and erect as peanuts inside the sequined bosom of her dress, her eyes glistened like doll's eyes of the kind that shut when the doll's head is thrust back, the periwinkle-blue had no pupils to distract, Babygirl was not one of those bitches always thinking plotting calculating how to take advantage of some poor jerk, she came from finer stock, you could check her pedigree, there were numerals tattooed into her flesh (the inside of the left thigh), she could be neither lost nor mislaid, nor could the cunt run away, and lose herself in America the way so many have done, you read about it all the time. They misted her in the most exquisite perfume—one whiff of it, if you were a man, a normal man, there's a fever in your blood only one act can satisfy, they passed out copies of the examining physician's report, she *was* clean of all disease venereal or otherwise, she *was* a virgin, no doubt of that though tripping in her high heels and grinning and blushing peering through her fingers at her suitors she sometimes gave the wrong impression, poor Babygirl: those lush crimson lips of such fleshy contours they suggested, even to the most gentlemanly and austere among us, the fleshy vaginal labia.

Filthy vermin! obscene little beast! they were furious at him for *being* as if, incarnated thus, he'd chosen his species, and took a cruel pleasure in carrying the seeds of typhus in his guts, bubonic plague virus in his saliva, poisons of all kinds in his excrement. They wanted him dead, they wanted all of his kind extinct, nothing less would satisfy them firing idle shots at the town dump as, squeaking in terror, he darted from one hiding place to another, reeking garbage exploding beside him as the bullets struck, they blamed him for the *snap!* of poultry bones in predators' jaws, they had no evidence but they blamed him for a litter of piglets devoured alive, and what happened to that baby in the ground floor apartment on Eleventh Street left unattended for twenty minutes when its mother slipped out to buy cigarettes and milk at the 7-Eleven store a block away—*Oh my God! Oh oh oh don't tell me, I don't want to know*—and a fire that started and blazed out of control in the middle of a frigid January night because insulation around some electrical wires had been gnawed through, but how was that his fault, how *his*, where was the proof amidst hundreds of thousands of his siblings, each possessed by a voracious hunger and a ceaseless need to gnaw? Pursuing him with rocks, a gang of children, whooping and yodeling across the rooftops injuring him as in desperation he scrambled up the side of a brick wall, yes but he managed to escape even as his toenails failed him and he slipped, fell—fell sickeningly into space—down an air-shaft—five storeys—to the ground below—high-pitched squeaky shrieks as he fell—plummeted downward thrashing and spiraling in midair, red eyes alight in terror for such creatures know terror though they do not know the word "terror," they embody terror, that's to say *embody* it, though every cell in his body strained to live, every luminous particle of his being craved immortality, even as you and me. (Of the suffering of living things through the millenia, it is wisest not to think, Darwin advises.) So he fell off the edge of the roof, down the airshaft, the equivalent of approximately one hundred seventy times his size measured from nose to rump (but excluding his tail which, uncurled, straight and stiff, is longer than his length——eight inches!) so we were watching smiling in the knowledge that the dirty little bugger would be squashed flat, thus imagine our indignation and outrage to see him land on his feet! a tiny bit shaken, but uninjured! untouched! a fall that would have broken every bone in our goddam bodies and *he* shakes his whiskers and furls up his tail and scampers away! And the rancid night parted like black water to shield him.

It was the National Guard Armory, rented for the night at discount price, a slow season, and in the cavernous smoke-filled gallery fresh-groomed men sat attentive in rows of seats, their faces indistinct as dream-faces, their eyes vague and soft as molluscs focussed on Babygirl, fingers fat as cigars poking in their crotches, genitalia heavy as giant purplish ripe figs straining at the fabric of their trousers. Yes but these are carefully screened and selected gentlemen. Yes but these are serious fellows. Most of them pointedly ignore the vendors hawking their wares in the Armory, now's hardly the time for beer, Coke, hotdogs, caramel corn, the men's eyes are hotly fixed on Babygirl my God get a load of *that*. To find a worthy wife in today's world is no simple task. An old-fashioned girl is the object of our yearning, the girl that married old dead dad is our ideal, but where is she to be found?— in today's debased world. So Babygirl tossed her shimmering cinnamon curls and prettily pouted, revealed her dazzling white smile, in a breathy sing-song she recited the sweet iambic verse she had composed for this very occasion. So Babygirl twirled her gem-studded baton. Flung her baton spinning up into the rafters of the Armory where at the apogee of its flight it seemed for a magic instant to pause, then tumbled back down into Babygirl's outstretched fingers—the rows of staring seats burst into spontaneous applause. So Babygirl curtsied, blushed, ducked her head, paused to straighten the seams of her stockings, adjusted an earrlng, adjusted her girdle that cut so deeply into the flesh of her thighs there would be angry red indentations there for days, Babygirl giggled and blew kisses, her lovely skin all aglow, as the auctioneer strutted about hamming it up with his hand-held microphone, Georgie Bick's his name, cocky and paunchy in his tux with the red cummerbund, Hey whooee do I hear 5000, do I hear 8000, gimme 10-, 10-, 10,000, in a weird high-pitched incantatory voice so mesmerizing that bidding begins at once, a Japanese gentleman signaling a bid by touching his left ear lobe, a swarthy turbanned gentleman signalling with a movement of his dark-glittering eyes, Hey whooee do I hear 15,000, do I hear 20,000, do I hear 25-, 25-, 25,000, thus a handsome moustached Teutonic gentleman cannot resist Yes, a Mediterranean gentleman, a gentleman with a shaved blunt head, a gentleman from Texas, a heavyset perspiring gentleman rubbing at the tip of his flushed pug nose, Do I hear 30,000, do I hear 35,000, do I hear 50,000, winking and nudging Babygirl, urging her to the edge of the platform, C'mon sweetie now's not the time for shyness, c'mon honey we all know why you're here tonight don't be coy you cunt, clumsy cow-cunt, gentlemen observe those dugs, those udders, and there's *udder* attractions too, hardee-har-har! And from up in the balcony, unobserved till now, a handsome white-haired gentleman signals with his white-gloved hand Yes.

    He was battle-weary, covered in scabs, maggot-festering little wounds stippling his body, his once-proud tail was gangrenous, the tip rotted away, yet he remained stoic and uncomplaining gnawing through wood, through paper, through insulation, through thin sheets of metal, eating with his old appetite, the ecstasy of jaws, teeth, intestines, anus, if the time allotted to him were infinite as his hunger it's certain he *would* gnaw his way through the entire world and excrete it behind him in piles of moist dark dense little turds. But Nature prescribes otherwise: the species into which he was born grants on the average only twelve months of survival—if things go well. And this May morning things are decidedly not going well here on the fourth floor of the partly empty ancient brick building on Sullivan Street housing on its first floor the Metropole Bakery, most acclaimed of local bakeries, "Wedding Cakes Our Specialty Since 1949," he has nested in a nook in a wall, he has been nibbling nervously on a piece of something theoretically edible (the hardened flattened remains of a sibling struck by a vehicle in the street, pounded into two dimensions by subsequent vehicles) sniffing and blinking in an agony of appetite: on the fourth floor, with his many thousands of fellows, since, it's one of Nature's quiddities, when BROWN and BLACK species occupy a single premise, BROWN (being larger and more aggressive) inhabit the lower levels while BLACK (shier, more philosophical) are relegated to the upper levels where food foraging is more difficult. So he's eating, or trying to eat, when there's a sound as of silk being torn, and a furry body comes flying at him, snarling, incisors longer and more deadly than his own, claws, hind legs pummeling like rotor blades, every flea and tick on his terror-struck little body is alert, every cell of his being cries out to be spared, but Sheba with her furry moon face has no mercy, she's a beautiful silver tabby much adored by her owners for her warm affectionate purring ways but here on this May morning in the ancient brick building housing the Metropole Bakery she is in a frenzy to kill, to tear with her jaws, to eat, the two of them locked in the most intimate of embraces, yowling, shrieking, he'd go for her jugular vein but, shrewd Sheba, she has already gone for his jugular vein, they are rolling crazily together in the filth, not just Sheba's terrible teeth but her maniac hind legs are killing him, yes but he's putting up a damned good fight yes he has ripped a triangular patch of flesh out of her ear, yes but it's too late, yes you can see that Sheba's greater weight will win the day, even as he squeaks and bites in self-defense Sheba has torn out his throat, she has in fact disemboweled him, his helpless guts in slimey ribbons now tangled in her feet, what a din! what a yowling! you'd think somebody was being killed! and he's dying, and she begins to devour him, warm-gushing blood is best, twitchy striated muscle is best, pretty Sheba shuts her jaws on his nobby little head and crushes his skull, his brains inside his skull, and he goes *out*. Just goes *out*. And the greedy tabby (who isn't even hungry: her owners keep her sleek and well fed, of course) eats him where they've landed, snaps his bones, chews his gristle, swallows his scaly tail in sections, his dainty pink-whorled ears, his rheumy eyes, his bristly whiskers, as well as his luscious meat. And afterward washes herself, to rid herself of his very memory.

Except: wakened rudely from her post-prandial nap by a sickish stirring in her guts, poor Sheba is suddenly wracked by vomiting, finds herself reeling ungracefully and puking on the stairs, descendlng to the rear of the Metropole Bakery, mewing plaintively but no one hears as, teetering on a rafter above one of the giant vats of vanilla cake batter, poor Sheba heaves out her guts, that's to say *him*, the numerous fragments and shreds of *him*: a convulsive gagging and choking that concludes wlth the puking-up of his whiskers, which are now broken into half- and quarter-inch pieces. Poor puss!—runs home meek and plaintive and her adoring mistress picks her up, cuddles, scolds, Sheba where have you *been!* And Sheba's supper comes early that evening.

Madly in love, Mr. X is the most devoted of suitors. And then the most besotted of bridegrooms. Covering Babygirl's pink-flushed face wlth kisses, hugging her so tight she cries *Oh!* and all of the wedding company, her own daddy in particular, laugh in delight. Mr. X is a dignified handsome older gentleman. He's the salt of the earth. He leads Babygirl out onto the polished dance floor as the band plays "I Love You Truly" and how elegantly he dances, how masterfully he leads his bride, blood-red carnation in his lapel, chips of dry ice in his eyes, wide fixed grinning-white dentures, how graceful the couple's dips and bends, Babygirl in a breathtakingly beautiful antique wedding gown worn by her mother, her grandmother, and her great-grandmother in their times, a heirloom wedding ring as well, lilies of the valley braided in the bride's cinnamon curls, Babygirl laughs showing the cherry-pink interior of her mouth, she squeals *Oh!* as her new husband draws her to his bosom, kisses her full on the lips. His big strong fingers stroke her shoulders, breasts, rump. There are champagne toasts, there are gay drunken speeches lasting well into the evening. The Archbishop himself intones a blessing. Babygirl on Mr. X's knee being fed strawberries and wedding cake by her bridegroom, and feeding her bridegroom strawberries and wedding cake in turn, each sucking the other's fingers, amid kisses and laughter. Chewing her wedding cake Babygirl is disconcerted to discover something tough, sinewy, bristly in it, like gristle, or fragments of bone, or tiny bits of wire, but she is too well-bred and embarrassed to spit the foreign substance, if it is a foreign substance, out: discreetly pushes it with her tongue to the side of her mouth, behind her molars, for safe-keeping. For his part, Mr. X, a gentleman, washes his mouthfuls of wedding cake down with champagne, swallows everything without blinking an eye,

This is the happiest day of my life he whispers into Babygirl's pink-whorled ear.

It was an experiment in behavioral psychology, in the phenomenon of conditioning, to be published in *Scientific American*, and there to cause quite a stir, but naturally *he* wasn't informed, poor miserable bugger, nor did he give consent. Semi-starved in his wire mesh cage, compulsively gnawing on his own hind legs, he quickly learned to *react* to the slightest gesture on the part of his torturers, his monitored heartbeat raced in panic, his jaundiced eyeballs careened in their sockets, a metaphysical malaise permeated his soul like sulphur dioxide, after only a few hours. Yet his torturers persisted for there were dozens of graphs and charts to be filled out; dozens of young assistants involved in the experiment. In the gauging of "terror" in dumb beasts of his species they shocked him with increasing severity until virtual puffs of smoke issued from the top of his head, they singed his fur with burning needles, poked burning needles into his tender anus, lowered his cage over a Bunsen burner, wiped their eyes laughing at his antics, shaking and rattling his cage, spinning his cage at a velocity of ninety miles an hour, they marveled at how he was conditioned to respond not just to their features but to their words as if he could understand them and then, most amazing of all,—this would be the crux of the controversial article in *Scientific American*—after forty-eight hours he began to react unerringly to the mere *thought* that the torture would be resumed. (Provided the experimentors consciously "thought" their thoughts inside the laboratory, not outside.) A remarkable scientific discovery!—unfortunately, after his death, never once to be duplicated. Thus utterly worthless as science and a bit of a joke in experimental psychology circles.

How Mr. X adored his Babygirl!—lovingly bathing her in her fragrant bubble bath, brushing and combing her long wavy-curly cinnamon hair that fell to her hips, cooing to her, poking his tongue in her, bringing her breakfast in bed after a fevered night of marital love, insisting upon shaving, with his own straight razor, the peachy-fuzzy down that covered her lovely body, and the stiff "unsightly" hairs of underarms, legs, and crotch. Weeks, months. Until one night his penis failed him and he realized he was frankly bored with Babygirl's dimpled buttocks and navel, her wide-open periwinkle-blue eyes, the flattering *Oh!* of her pursed rosebud lips. He realized that her flat nasal voice grated against his sensitive nerves, her habits disgusted him, several times he caught her scratching her fat behind when she believed herself unobserved, she was not so fastidious as to refrain from picking her nose, frequently the bathroom stank of flatulence and excrement after she emerged from it, her menstrual blood stained the white linen heirloom sheets, her kinky hairs collected in drains, her early-morning breath was rancid as the inside of his own oldest shoes, she gazed at him with big mournful questioning cow-eyes, Oh what is wrong dearest, oh! don't you love me any longer? What did I *do*! lowering her bulk onto his knees, sliding her pudgy arms around his neck, exhaling her meaty breath in his face, so, cruelly, he parted his knees and Babygirl fell with a graceless thud to the floor. As she stared at him speechless in astonishment and hurt he struck her with the backside of his hand, bloodying her nose, Oh you will, bitch, will you! he grunted, will you! Eh!

  Mating, and mating. Mating. A frenzy of mating. In the prime of his maleness he fathered dozens, hundreds, thousands of off-spring, now they're scurrying and squeaking everywhere, little buggers everywhere underfoot, nudging him aside as he feeds, ganging up on him, yes a veritable gang of them, how quickly babies grow up, it's amazing how quickly babies grow up, one day an inch long, the next day two inches long, the next day four inches long, those tiny perfect toes, claws, ears, whiskers, graceful curved tails, incisors, ravenous appetite *And the horror of it washed over me suddenly: I cannot die, I am multiplied to infinity.* It was not his fault! His enemies are even now setting out dollops of powdery-pasty poison, to rid the neighborhood of him and his off-spring, but it was not his fault! A fever overtook him,

him and certain of his sisters, almost daily it seemed, yes daily, maybe hourly, no time to rest, no time for contemplation, a two-inch thing, a sort of a knob of flesh, a rod, hot and stiff with blood, piston-quick, tireless, unfurling itself out of the soft sac between his hind legs, yes and he was powerless to resist, it was more urgent even than gnawing, more excruciatingly pleasurable, *he* was but an appendage! thus innocent! But his enemies, plotting against him, don't give a damn, they're cruel and cold-blooded setting out dollops of this most delicious poison, sugary, pasty, bread-moldy, delicious beyond reckoning, he should know better (shouldn't he?) but he's unable to resist, pushing his way into the sea of squeaking quivering young ones, seething sea, dark waves, wave upon wave eating in a delirium of appetite, a single feeding organism you might think, it's a diabolical poison however that doesn't kill these poor buggers on the premises but induces violent thirst in them thus shortly after feeding he and his thousands of sons and daughters are rushing out of the building, in a panic to find water, to drink water, to alleviate this terrible thirst, they're drawn to the dockside, to the river, there are screams as people see them emerge, the dark wave of them, glittering eyes, whiskers, pink near-hairless tails, they take no notice of anyone or anything in their need to get to water, there in the river a number of them drown, others drink and drink and drink until, as planned, their poor bodies bloat, and swell, and *burst*. And city sanitation workers wearing gas masks complain bitterly as they shovel the corpses, small mountains of corpses, into a procession of dumpster trucks, then they hose down the sidewalks, streets, docks. At a fertilizer plant he and his progeny will be mashed down, ground to gritty powder and sold for commercial/residential use. No mention of the poison of course.

Grown increasingly and mysteriously insensitive to his wife's feelings, Mr. X, within their first year of marriage, began to bring home "business associates" (as he called them) to ogle Babygirl, to peek at her in her bath, to whisper licentious remarks in her ears, to touch, fondle, molest—as Mr. X, often smoking a cigar, calmly watched! At first

Babygirl was too astonished to comprehend, then she burst into tears of indignation and hurt, then she pleaded with the brute to be spared, then she flew into a tantrum tossing silky garments and such into a suitcase, then she was lying in a puddle on the bathroom floor, nights and days passed in a delirium, her keeper fed her grudgingly and at irregular intervals, there were promises of sunshine, greenery, Christmas gifts, promises made and withheld, then one day a masked figure appeared in the doorway, in leather military regalia, gloved hands on his hips, brass-studded belt, holster and pistol riding his hip, gleaming black leather boots the toes of which Babygirl eagerly kissed, groveling before him, twining her long curly-cinnamon hair around his ankles. Begging, Have mercy! don't hurt me! I am yours! in sickness and in health as I gave my vow to God! And assuming the masked man was in fact Mr. X (for wasn't this a reasonable assumption, in these circumstances?) Babygirl willingly accompanied him to the master bedroom, to the antique brass four-postered bed, and did not resist his wheezing, straining, protracted and painful lovemaking, if such an act can be called lovemaking, the insult of it! the pain of it! and not till the end, when the masked figure triumphantly removed hls mask, did Babygirl discover that he was a stranger—and that Mr. X himself was standing at the foot of the bed, smoking a cigar, calmly observing. In the confusion of all that followed, weeks, months, there came a succession of "business associates," never the same man twice, as Mr. X grew systematically crueler, hardly a gentleman any longer, forcing upon his wife as she lay trussed and helpless in their marriage bed a man with fingernails filed razor-sharp who lacerated her tender flesh, a man with a glittering scaly skin, a man with a turkey's wattles, a man with an ear partly missing, a man with a stark-bald head and cadaverous smile, a man with infected draining sores like exotic tattoos stippling his body, and poor Babygirl was whipped for disobedience, Babygirl was burnt with cigars, Babygirl was slapped, kicked, pummelled, near-suffocated and near-strangled and near-drowned, she screamed into her saliva-soaked gag, she thrashed, convulsed, bled in sticky skeins most distasteful to Mr. X who then punished her additionally, as a husband will do, by withholdng his affection.

So light-headed with hunger was he, hiding in terror from his enemies beneath a pile of bricks, he began to gnaw at his own tail— timidly at first, then more avidly, with appetite, unable to stop, his poor skinny tail, his twenty pink toes and pads, his hind legs, choice loins and chops and giblets and breast and pancreas and brains and all, at last his bones are picked clean, the startling symmetry and beauty of the skeleton revealed, now he's sleepy, contented and sleepy, washes himself with fastidious little scrubbing motions of his paws then curls up in the warm September sun to nap. A sigh ripples through him: exquisite peace.

Except: two gangling neighborhood boys creep up on him dozing atop his favorite brick, capture him in a net and toss him squeaking in terror into a cardboard box, slam down the lid that's pocked with air holes, he's delivered by bicycle to a gentleman with neatly combed white hair and a cultivated voice who pays the boys $5 each for him, observes him crouched in a corner of the box rubbing his hands delightedly together chuckling softly, Well! you're a rough-looking fella aren't you! To his considerable surprise, the white-haired gentleman feeds him; holds him up, though not unkindly, by the scruff of his neck, to examine him, the sleek perfectly-formed parts of him, the rakish incisors most particularly. Breathing audibly, murmuring, with excited satisfaction, Yes. I believe you will do, old boy.

No longer allowed out of the house, often confined to the bedroom suite on the second floor, poor Babygirl nonetheless managed to adjust to the altered circumstances of her life wlth commendable fortitude and good humor. Spending most of her days lying languorously in bed, doing her nails, devouring gourmet chocolates brought her by one or another of Mr. X's business associates, sometimes, in a romantic mood, by the unpredictable Mr. X himself, she watched television (the evangelical preachers were her favorites), complained to herself in the way of housewives in America, tended to her wounds, clipped recipes from magazines, gossiped over the telephone with her female friends, shopped by catalogue, read her Bible, grew heavier, sullen, apprehensive of the future, plucked her eyebrows, rubbed fragrant creams into her skin, kept an optimistic attitude, made an effort. Of the disturbing direction in which her marriage was moving she tried not to think for Babygirl was not the kind of wife to whine, whimper, nag, not Babygirl so imagine her surprise and horror when, one night, Mr. X arrived home and ran upstairs to the bedroom in which, that day, she'd been confined, tied to the four brass posts of the marital bed by white silken cords, and in triumph threw open his camel's hair coat, See what I've brought for you, my dear! unzipping his trousers with trembling fingers and as Babygirl stared incredulous out *he* leapt—squeaking, redeyed, teeth bared and glistening with froth, stiff curved tail erect. Babygirl's screams were heartrending.

Mr. X and his (male) companions observed with scientific detachment the relationship between Babygirl and He (as, in codified shorthand, they referred to him): how, initially, the pair resisted each other most strenuously, even hysterically, Babygirl shrieking even through the gag stuffed in her mouth as He was netted in the bed with her, such a struggle, such acrobatics, He squeaking in animal panic edged with indignant rage, biting, clawing, fighting as if for His very life, and Babygirl, despite her flaccid muscles and her seemingly indolent ways, putting up a fight as if for *her* very life! And this went on for hours, for an entire night, and the night following, and the night following that. And there was never anything so remarkable on Burlingame Way, the attractive residential street where Mr. X made his home.

He did not want this, no certainly he did not want this, resisting with all the strength of his furry little being, as, with gloved hands, Mr. X forced him *there*—poor Babygirl spread-eagled and helpless bleeding from a thousand welts and lacerations made by his claws and teeth and why was he being forced snout-first, and then head-first, then his shoulders, his sleek muscular length, why *there*—in *there*—so he choked, near-suffocated, used his teeth to tear a way free for himself yet even as he did so Mr. X with hands trembling in excitement, as his companions, gathered round the bed, watched in awe pushed him in farther, and then *farther*—into the blood-hot pulsing toughly elastic tunnel between poor Babygirl's fatty thighs—and stlll *farther* until only the sleek-furry end of his rump and his trailing hind legs and, of course, the eight-inch pink tail were visible. His panicked gnawing of the fleshy walls that so tightly confined him released small geysers of blood that nearly drowned him, and the involuntary spasms of clenching of poor Babygirl's pelvic muscles nearly crushed him, thus how the struggle would have ended, if both he and Babygirl had not lost consciousness at the same instant, is problematic. Even Mr. X and his companions, virtually beside themselves in unholy arousal, were relieved that, for that night, the *agon* had ceased.

As, at her martyrdom, at the stake in Rouen, as the flames licked mindlessly ever higher and higher to consume her, to turn her to ashes, Jeanne d'Arc is reported to have cried out "Jesu! Jesu! Jesu!" in a voice of rapture.

And who would clean up the mess. And who, with a migraine, sanitary pad soaked between her chafed thighs, she's fearful of seeing her swollen jaw, blackened eye in any mirrored surface weeping quietly to herself, padding gingerly about in her bedroom slippers, mock-Japanese quilted housecoat. The only consolation is at least there's a t.v. in most of the rooms so, even when the vacuum is roaring, she isn't alone: there's Reverend Tim, there's Brother Jessie, there's Sweet Alabam' MacGowan. A consolation at least. For, not only did Babygirl suffer such insult and ignominy at the hands of the very man who, of all the world, was most responsible for her emotional well-being, not only was she groggy in the aftermath of only dimly remembered physical trauma, running the risk, as she sensed, of infection, sterility, and a recrudescence of her old female maladies,— not only this but she was obliged to clean up the mess next morning, who else. Laundering the sheets, blood-stained sheets are no joke. On her hands and knees trying (with minimal success) to remove the stains from the carpet. Vacuum the carpet. And the dirt-bag is full and there's a problem putting in a new dirt-bag, there always is. Faint-headed, wracked several times with whitehot bolts of pain so she had to sit, catch her breath. And the pad between her legs soaked hard in blackish blood like blood-sausage. And the steel wool disintegrating in her fingers as gamely she tries to scour the casserole dish clean, dissolves in tears, Oh! where has love gone! so one evening he surprises her, in that melancholy repose, the children are in on it too, what's today but Babygirl's birthday and she'd tormented herself thinking no one would remember but as they sweep into the restaurant, the Gondola that's one of the few good Italian restaurants in the city where you can order pizza too, the staff is waiting, Happy Birthday! balloons, half-chiding there's a chorus, Did you think we'd forgotten? and Babygirl orders a sloe gin fizz which goes straight to her head and she giggles and suppresses a tiny belch patting her fingers to her mouth, later her husband is scolding one of the boys but *she's* going to steer clear of the conflict, goes to the powder room, checks her makeup in the rose-lit flattering mirrors seeing yes, thank God the bruise under her left eye is fading, then she takes care to affix squares of toilet paper to the toilet seat to prevent picking up an infectious disease, since AIDS Babygirl is even more methodical, then she's sitting on the toilet her mind for a moment blissful and empty until, turning her head, just happening to turn her head, though probably she sensed its presence, she sees, not SIX inches away, on the slightly grimy sill of a frosted-glass window, the red-blinking eyes of a large rodent, oh dear God is it a rat, these eyes fixed upon *hers*, her heart gives a violent kick and nearly *stops*. Poor Babygirl's screams penetrate every wall of the building.

Some Kinda Asshole — Tuli Kupferberg

Rob Hardin

Still

He wasn't drunk or paralytic, and no one had put him under hypnosis. The X-K seemed to have fooled around with some dangerous strain of boredom, then wandered into a trance through a door that locked automatically. Motionless from his tensed shoulders to his gangly legs, he was the image of an ollie hanging out. Some photo-realist might have sculpted his look of lobotomized bliss.

Like the windshields of showroom cars, his eyes merely framed the absence of the owner. They were wading-pool blue and glimmered above his small, sunburnt nose. His lips were thick, chapped, the color of scarlet model paint. Long ash-blond curls fell to the ridged neck, just touching the over-developed deltoids. The chest and groin were striped with shadow under half-drawn venetian blinds.

The white room was big, empty. It contained only black furniture. The blinds, metal chair and cubed coffee table gleamed with streaks of sun-light. The black-sheeted mattress reflected nothing. Stage center, it drooped over a board mounted on some concrete blocks. The X-K sat on the mattress. He was still except for his legs, which rocked slightly as they dangled over the bedboard.

The man who lived there slanted against the doorpost, his frame a limp diagonal. He couldn't understand how the kid had gotten past two dead-bolt locks and a steel door—a tall order, especially for someone whose mind was missing. Fortyish, slight, the man pushed sharpened fingernails through silver-black hair. His eyes curved to inverted U's as he sized up the X-K's oblivious body.

In the hallway, mounted on vinyl-coated steel rods: a compact disc player, turntable and cassette machine. In the bedroom, discreetly wired above the windows: thin white speakers. Mahler's *Kindertotenlieder* poured from them, filling the room with its *fin de siecle* necrophrenia. Next to the amplifier, various records and tapes: *SPK,* Gesualdo, *Deploration On The Death Of Ockeghem*.

The man walked to the window, drew the blinds, then moved to the closet. Parting the rack in the middle, he pulled out lace-up leather pants and a shirt of cherry-red silk. He slid into them, then slipped into black boots of soft Italian leather. Last of all, he chose a black medieval waistcoat. He ran two fingers along its raised pattern of scythes, stopped at the breast pocket, and reached in.

He dragged out a cigarette and held a match to it, staring at the X-K the whole time. Like storerooms that once contained important negatives, the eyes led to an absence. The X-K's *Body* seemed a better canvas than the eyes: its musculature had been eccentrically developed. So much wreckage lay under the surface that it was as if a breastplate of spears threatened to rise through the Body's skin.

The man studied the Body for a few seconds, approached it, and dropped to a kneeling position.

Tilted between thumb and forefinger, butt of the filter pushed forward by the thumb, the cigarette drew zig-zags of smoke across the chest. The (visual) process implied deeper operations: the cigarette was evocative, a light pencil tracing wave-forms on the screen of a Synclavier. Afternoon chilled to evening; as if in response to the cigarette's floating graphics, the Body began to shudder.

The man pointed his cigarette at the xiphoid process. He considered burning a mark there, then dismissed the idea. There was no reason to disfigure the Body with a grid that would rise in welts. The thought of inflicting pain left him indifferent: any damage to the skin would prove too literal for the imagination to distort. The Synclavier screen would freeze under the Medusa-gaze of Violence, and discoloration would be the only added dimension in place of numerous subtractions.

The jagged lines began to straighten and intersect. A moment of extreme pleasure took him over as the grid of smoke tightened against The Body. The tautening lines resembled laces that were slowly being pulled through a series of obliquely-positioned holes. He blew smoke rings against this—one for the hollow of each violin-soundboard hip—and the rings complicated the latticework to Art Nouveau.

As the window's square of sky dimmed, the glow of the cigarette ash grew brighter: it became an arrow-head of raw meat under the violet lamp of a science exhibit. Trembling slightly, the Body paled to black-light-poster garish as bands of smoke rose to restrain the shoulders. At last, it was encased in a suit of ghostly white bondage gear.

The Body shuddered in the draft. Bumps rose in patches on its chest and stomach, streaks reddened across the white shoulders. Tiny slash-marks appeared where the sleeping skin smarted most under the fumes.

Lesions formed between the costal margin and the linea sublunaris. The lesions widened and spread below the xiphoid process; they spat threads of black smoke which climbed the thorax, deserted the Body at the upper deltoids, and gathered into blurred bars. The bars crumbled into black dots which formed shadowy, Seurat-like representations of nucleated cells. The cells were bound into spirochetes, and these gathered into whorls. The smoke had become a pointillist's animated cartoon of the morphology of multicellular animals.

The skin surrounding the nipples cracked and healed repeatedly, as in a case of fast-motion eczema. The area soon resembled a cartographer's map of layered transparencies.

The sunset was of epic duration. Lingering streaks dangled in the mirror like an homage to Calder. In contrast, the Body's scars healed in the tangerine light as in a fast-motion film, until the cartography of lesions and ruptured tissue smoothed to uninflected white.

The man exhaled sharply. He could not account for the series of Herschel Gordon Lewis mutilations he had just performed. He calmed himself, lit another cigarette, and returned to the Body.

As before, the chest writhed under blurred restraints. Roman X's bound the torso, and a mesh of fine ash tightened around the tremulous frame.

Particles of red smoke seemed to magnetize lit cigarettes inside the Body: red tips pressed through its smoking skin.

The space between the ribs and stomach, and another directly below the navel, filled with pus until they began to swell and pulsate. Bumps appeared on these areas; the bumps darkened, blistered, opened. The muscles and tissue below these began to bulge. The upper chest and navel were invisibly pulled in opposite directions until the waist and ribs were twisted open.

Pieces of the Body began to fly around the room.

The man trembled with release. Fissures opened in his chest, spuming with ejaculate until he was completely drained. His lids closed slowly, like power windows. Through them, he saw the yellow of oncoming headlights. The yellow intensified to white until, when sleep came down, even that empty color had been erased.

As the *Kindertotenlieder* ended, the two Bodies slumped to the floor.

Integuments lifted themselves slightly from the lacerations and veins wriggled out. These flew to the center of the room, knotted themselves into an arabesque, and hardened into a green partition, which stood between the Bodies.

The partition was divided into two halves. Its design revealed droll figurations which, seen at a distance of a few yards, proved to depict an unusually violent masque.

The organs featured in the masque were impaled on an arabesque that, in the style of Art Nouveau at its most excessive, represented a kind of serrated circuitry.

At the center of the arabesque, trefoil components outlined the disfigured body of Origen. Two keyholes formed the stylized wound in his side. Drops of blood hung in a chain from each keyhole, and each chain extended laterally to an antipodally positioned object. The right chain led to a burning trilobite, the left, to a brain sealed in fire. The pointed flames which surrounded each object terminated in a band of smoke that curved diagonally to the top of the arabesque.

There, both bands joined in an ogee and, at its vertex, spelled the word PASSIVITY in skywritten characters.

The room dimmed.

The delicate lineations of the arabesque drooped, then tore, until the partition came apart in ragged halves.

The two veinless Bodies flattened like deflating beach toys, molding themselves to the wood-grain of the floor. Only the man's head remained erect. It swelled to hydrocephalic, and its lips began to move.

Invisibly, a phonograph stylus clicked against a record label. Forced by the record's spiral groove, it endlessly repeated this action at the interval of a double-dotted quarter note.

The man's mouth twitched in time with the clicking stylus. The ticcing was violent, parodistic, and was soon accompanied by a periodic bulging of the eyes.

A string section see-sawing between two unrelated chords—C major and E-flat minor—and bassoons and tympani answering each other with absurd trills, grew faintly audible between clicks.

As the light continued to dim, only the twitching head moved. Even the monotony of its ticcing suggested a kind of stasis.

The room went black, but the noise persisted like an after-image.

Mark Wisniewski

Full Circle

I moved again, right? This time to New Orleans. You know, bayous, crawdads, accordions—all that down and dirty Cajun shit that the Pinheads love and their kids will laugh about come 2000. Anyway I'm *down* there, feeling like I'm happenin, washing dishes for cash, and then this one night I go out.

It wasn't on Bourbon Street—screw Bourbon Street, you see one set of stretchmarks and that's it for burlesque, you see twenty old French buildings and you feel sorry for the Pinheads who own them and gotta act like they have *room* in the things—it was a street or so over, maybe Fillmore or something, and I hear this voice in my ear, this dude's voice, kinda half-whisper the word Blow.

I turn and this guy my height is standing there, hair buzzed to nubs, little gold wire earring—happenin, right?—but I'm trying to quit coke so I say No. His eyes and mine are the corners of a little square and I see that his are blue and he says, Sankie!

I think *Sankie?* and frown, and he smiles and then I remember goddamn *high* school: the guy's fucking right—I was Sankie back then.

He points at his chest and says, Bags! I try not to frown and then—yeah, *Bags*, there was this guy in high school we called Bags, I had him in AP English. So I shake the guy's hand and it's his *fingers*, man, its Bags' cold bony fingers I recognize, but this guy's eyes aren't right—Bags' were brown.

I say *Bags*?

From AP English, he says, Right? With Father Dan Bernbrock, S.J., I say, and he nods. The blue eyes must be contacts so I look at his teeth—the braces are gone and maybe there's caps—so I look at his hand. We're still pumping the handshake and I say, God-damn-good-to-see-ya, and let go. Then we both take deep breaths, I silence my exhale but hear his, and who knows why but I say it, I ask him, Did you say *blow*?

Don't get me wrong Sankie, he says, I'm almost Full Circle. Full Circle? I say, and I can't hide the look—I can never hide my damned I-don't-follow look—and he says Yeah, but nothing more. *That's* more like the Bags I knew in high school, he did his own thing but never for effect, never to get this person's attention or piss that person off, just for himself. You'd know his thing if you really wanted to, if you asked more than once, and waited.

Back then it was Joan Armatrading and gays, he was into them both, so when he got into Northwestern, where people were happenin and respected those things, I thought Good.

But we're past back then and here in New Orleans, and this blue-eyed Bags is looking at me like I'm stupid and says Full Circle, you don't know what that means?

I think Fuck he's reading my look anyway, so I say No. It means I've had enough, he says, and the skin beside his nose pulls like he's just shot Everclear. I start not liking this reunion at all, this new Bags is like a bad remake of a good oldie, but I don't know what else to say so I decide to ask him just once, I say Enough what? He says Of what I've been doing, and I think This *is* a new Bags, the fucker's spilling himself all over the place, I'm gonna get wet without trying. I say You mean coke? and this new Bags says No, and waits maybe a beat, then looks at his feet and walks away, heading straight for this night club.

He looks over his shoulder and I wanna be happenin, so I follow. We go inside. No one's on stage but according to the glossies on the mirror behind the bar it's a female impersonator place. We sit down and shoot some tequila. I mention the worm. He studies the glossies. We shoot more tequila and he says, Who was your counselor? In high school? I say and he licks out his shot glass nodding.

I think for a second and then the name comes, I say Thames. He says That guy who taught history—with the twin sons? With that red beard, I say and I nod. I had Moreland, he says, Moreland, S.J. That short guy? I say and Bags says Yeah, the twirp with the Master's in Psych. The barkeep brings two more and we shoot them to hell and Bags starts spilling bad, starting with the first time Moreland S.J. called him in.

He said that Moreland S.J. gave him this book called *Don't Be Afraid To Tell Me Who You Are*—or something like that—and had him read a chapter a week and come in after school, after band practice. Which Bags did. Then they'd have talks. Moreland S.J. showed Bags Rorschachs, told Bags what his answers meant, explained how to use them, let Bags use them on him. Bags enjoyed this, felt intelligent, sold his trumpet, quit the band, started hanging out with Moreland S.J. before *and* after school. Moreland S.J. taught Bags Freud, Jung and Leary. Bags had his ma cook Moreland S.J. dinner. In the spring Moreland S.J. called Bags' dad and asked him if Bags could go camping in Northern Wisconsin. Bags' dad was a thick Catholic—he wanted Bags to be a priest like some dads want their sons to throw curveballs—so he says Yeah and Bags went. They drive 300 miles alone and get to some wheat field, the sun sets and Moreland S.J. pulls out some wine, not altar wine but nonetheless Christian Brothers, and they sip some—for Bags it's a first, his first sip of wine that's not the blood of Christ. Moreland S.J. says Finish up, let's go swimming, and leads Bags to this lake. Moreland S.J. strips down to his boxers, stands there until Bags is down to his briefs, then leads Bags to the shore. Bags toes the water—the shit's freezing. Moreland S.J. says Let's do it together, Let's do it as prayer. He grabs Bags' hand and says On three, so it's one-two-three and they dive. Bags comes up first and gets scared waiting but finally Moreland S.J. comes up, and throws his boxers on the shore. Skinny dipping, Moreland S.J. says, You ever try it? No, Bags says. Give it a try, Moreland S.J. says, so Bags does and swims to one of those decks floating on old oil barrels. Moreland S.J. follows and Bags climbs onto the deck, out of breath, his jaw shivering, the rest of him numb. Moreland S.J. treads water, says, Look at your scrotum, how small. Bags looks down and sonofabitch, this Moreland S.J. is right. Moreland S.J. pulls himself onto the deck, says, Look at mine. Bags looks and sees that Moreland S.J.'s cock is making a stand, a hard-on that Moreland S.J. handles like it's something imported, something expensive—like a goddamned antique. This is natural, Moreland S.J. says, Someday yours will do this also. It already has, Bags says, Just not here. Someday it'll do it more often, Moreland S.J. says, Someday whenever you want it to. Bags starts shivering. Someday, Moreland S.J. says, You'll be able to have it get big around anyone, even around me. Let's pray together, he says, Let's face the stars and pray. Moreland S.J. lies on his back. Bags lies beside him, shivering worse. Let's close our eyes, Moreland S.J. says, And pray. Bags closes his eyes. Moreland S.J. prays for Bags' Christian development, and in thanksgiving for nature. Then Moreland S.J. grabs Bags' hand, squeezes and says Lie still. Take deep breaths. Breathe in God, breathe in nature. Bags is still shivering, so he breathes in the best he can. Keep your eyes closed, Moreland S.J. says, Relaxed but closed. Bags closes his eyes. Moreland S.J. prays out loud in what Bags guesses is Hebrew. Then Moreland S.J. prays in whispers, massaging Bags' jaw, then the neck, the chest, the hips, the outside of the thighs, and then, after lifting, spreading and setting down Bags' feet, the inside of the legs. Moreland S.J.'s hands feel warm so Bags almost likes it. Then something warmer—something almost hot—touches the tip of Bags' cock. Keep your eyes closed, Moreland S.J. says, Pray in whispers. Bags doesn't pray but closes his eyes, feels the heat surround his dickhead, feels fingers tickle his balls, feels pressure on his asshole—gradual pressure that goes in deep and is making him hard. There, Moreland S.J. says, It's working. Stop, Bags says, It feels uncomfortable. Just relax, Moreland S.J. says, Close your eyes. Breathe deeply. Pray to God. Thank God for nature. Bags exhales for what feels like forever. The finger presses deeper and heat covers Bags' dickhead, then sucks, sucks until Bags says Stop, that's starting to hurt. The heat disappears. We don't wanna hurt you, Moreland S.J. says. The finger slides out and Moreland S.J. lays next to Bags and grabs his hand. But you did, Moreland S.J. says, Get hard. And right then Bags realizes he isn't shivering. Let's pray, Moreland S.J. says, Let's pray in thanksgiving.

 We shoot more tequila. Fucking unreal, I say to Bags.

 Not after it's happened, Bags says, and studies his glass.

 All Thames and I did, I say, was talk about multiple choice tests.

 Bags doesn't laugh. So when I went to Northwestern, Bags says, it almost seemed natural. What did? I say. Joey, Bags says. Joey? I say. My first lover, Bags says. A grad student, Bags says, and a bonger.

 Whatever *happened* to bongs? I say, and Bags snuffs out a laugh and then lids his glass with his palm.

 I thought Joey was so damn cool, Bags says, and blinks a few times. He was my first friend there, Bags says, and a bonger. And it didn't, Bags says, feel that uncomfortable.

 You mean oral sex with him? I say.

 Anal, he says.

 You mean taking? I say.

 I mean putting it in, Bags says. Fucking ass, Bags says, can hurt both parties. Putting it in Joey the first time, Bags says, hurt just a little bit more, Bags says, than when I'd screwed this neighbor girl when I was twelve. It felt equally as wrong, Bags says, but see I was Catholic either way.

 And after Moreland S.J.'s finger, Bags says, you had to go— Bags' eyes meet mine—you had to go, Bags says, With God.

 I want to leave bad. I feel sorry for Bags but more sorry for myself—having to sit there and act like his fucked up sexuality is everyday shit. The barkeep is there so I say, One more, Bags, and I gotta go, the barkeep goes to get the bottle. Go where? Bags says. Back to my place, I say, and I realize those words might have been a mistake.

You mean you live down here, Bags says, you're not just visiting? To tell you the truth, I say, I'm housesitting for the month. So it's only sort of like living here. I worry that Bags will read my I-hope-you-can't-tell-I'm-lying look, but he's eyeing his shot glass—the barkeep is pouring more Cuervo.

Well before you go, he says, let me explain Full Circle.

He shakes his head smiling. I can't believe you've never heard it, he says. You were always on top of things in high school. He sips from his glass and I shoot mine.

That was a long time ago, I say. Stairway to Heaven was new then.

Bags stares at his thumbnail. Going Full Circle, he says, means turning yourself straight.

Get the fuck out of here, I say, but Bags' serious face doesn't break, his eyes are glued to that thumbnail as if they need to keep seeing.

Most of my friends say it's bullshit, Bags says. My gay friends, I mean. He sips from his shotglass, then starts scratching one thumbnail with the other. But I don't know.

You can't just change your sexuality, I say, but I'm just saying out loud what I've heard, the truth is I've never really given it much thought.

Masters and Johnson did a study, Bags says, Sometime around 1979. It was the closest thing to hard science anyone's ever applied to homosexuality, Bags says, and they found out they could make gays straight by a combination of abstinence, select pornography and positive reinforcement.

Bullshit, I say.

You say bullshit, Bags says, because you don't want to sound homophobic. You're like everyone else, gays included. You don't wanna be a bad guy. You don't want to rock the boat. You're scared of thinking about the possibilities of a reality in which human sexuality is nothing more than whatever we condition ourselves to be comfortable with.

That's crazy, I say, and I try to throw back a shot but find my glass empty.

Which gender did you come with comfortably first? Bags says. Female, I say.

What if Thames had been my high school counselor, Bags says, And Moreland S.J. had been yours? I would've run from Moreland as soon as he took his pants off, I say.

Easy to say now, Bags says.

Then he tells me how he went to this doctor for this complete physical—but really so he could ask for an AIDS test—when he was thirty. He said this woman doctor wanted a semen sample and put a gloved finger up his asshole and just touched his prostate to make him ejaculate in less than two seconds. This woman doctor explained it was just a medical procedure, that it was the fastest, easiest way to get come.

So? I say.

So she got me off, Bags says. A *woman*. And she could get anyone off, Bags says.

Anyone could get anyone off, Bags says. I mean its not like med school qualified her finger to do that.

I gotta go, I say, and slide off my barstool. It's late.

No, Bags says, and stares at me like he's ready to cry.

I stare back pissed, hating him for making me think serious during shots, and say, What do you mean, no.

I mean it's not too late for me, Bags says.

This whole thing is nuts, I say. I mean we don't even know each other.

Listen, he says. You touched my hand before, he says, *right*?

I don't even fight the I-don't-follow look on my face, because I haven't the slightest fucking idea what he's talking about.

I mean when we shook hands, he says. Out there.

Oh, I say. Right.

I just want you to do that again, he says.

So I do it right away—I hold out my hand.

Not here, he says. Upstairs. Why up there? I say. Because we need to go up there, he says, For me to come Full Circle.

Is this some kind of scam to convert *me*? I say.

Just the opposite, Bags says. Come on Sankie, he says. Please.

Now that I'm standing I feel the Cuervo, plus I'm bigger than Bags anyway and I wanna be happenin, so I say OK, man. Just don't call me Sankie.

Bags doesn't smile. In fact all of a sudden he looks scared. He doesn't say anything, he just leads me across the bar to this hallway with two telephones and a unisex bathroom, and a narrow spiral staircase we start climbing. The little steps fan out to maybe six inches wide and the staircase is so steep my face is even with the heels of Bags' shoes. He's wearing a pair of black Chuck Taylors and I realize that since high school, black Chuck Taylors have gone from being dorky to cool to old hat.

We make it without falling to this hallway upstairs. It's painted pink and has three enamelled white doors on carved and varnished cherrywood doorframes the Pinheads would just die to refinish. He knocks on the third door down, puts his ear to it for a second, opens it. I'm stopped in my tracks halfway down the hall.

I smell something like cloves.

I whisper Why the fuck do you need me here?

Bags wrinkles his forehead like he didn't understand me, so I take two steps toward the door and see this woman reading a lingerie catalogue in this room that's furnished like 18th century France. She's wearing a one-button white chiffon robe and sitting the wrong way on a cherrywood chair, straddling and hugging the chairback so that I can see the crotch of her red panties. She drops the catalogue when she sees us, then grabs the top of the chair and stands. Her face looks soft but her legs and arms look hard, and her hair is the color of Johnson's baby shampoo.

You found someone, she says to Bags.

Bags looks down, starts scraping that same goddamn thumbnail with the other. This is Vera, he says, and I nod. She's the best at Full Circle, he says.

Vera gives me this pouty look and holds her robe closed, her caramel brown nipples pinging hard against it.

I don't doubt it, I say, and she smiles.

She twists the chair on its leg so it lands facing toward us, then stands behind it with this twin-sized bed that's nothing fancy about a foot or so behind her. Shall we? she says.

Bags keeps scraping that thumbnail, his eyes on his hands, his arms tight at his sides. I guess, he says.

Vera looks at me like this is the most important moment in her life. Bring him over, she says, and I grab Bags' cold bony wrist—he's still scraping that thumbnail—and pull.

We walk over slowly—I'm on Bags' left—and Vera puts a pillow on the chair and says to Bags, kneel. She doesn't blink, she just stands there looking at Bags like she's teaching him kindergarten.

Bags locks his fingers in mine, kneels on the chair. I feel his hand sweat—warm, slimy sweat—and she unbuttons her robe and takes his free hand and puts his palm on her breast, his fingers so stiff the knuckles are wrinkled.

Squeeze, she says.

His fingers relax, then squeeze, and his other hand—the one that I'm holding—clenches mine down to the bone.

Harder, she says. Don't be afraid to hurt me.

Bags licks his lips—they look pretty damned dry—and squeezes harder. Vera watches his mouth, blinking. Their eyes meet. She stares back as if dazed, unzips his pants, slides the four blue-nail-polished fingers of her right hand inside, starts massaging in slow circles. Her nipples look hard but I watch Bags' face. The side of his nose quivers so I squeeze his hand harder, so hard it hurts.

Kiss him, Vera says and I try to say no with my eyes, but I can't stop looking at Bags.

Just once, she says.

Bags' closed eyelids are trembling, like he's crying. He licks his lower lip. I bite mine. I nod, stare at her breasts, peck his shoulder. She massages a little harder. Again, she says, and I feel scared and unglued but do it anyway. Now the neck, she says. Bags' eyes are still shut and I shake my head firmly. Just one, she says, Just one more kiss on his neck. I do it quickly, barely making contact. She takes Bags' hand from mine, puts it on her other breast. He squeezes hard, keeps squeezing. A chill grabs my scrotum. Just one more on his neck, she says, and I kiss his neck solid, without thinking. Good, she says. We're getting there. Bags' lips look something like smiling. Now your thumb, Vera tells me. Her eyes are on mine. They shift to my hand, the one that held Bags'. That one, she whispers, her eyes on my thumb.

I look at my thumbnail, not believing what's happening.

Put it in his mouth, she says.

I shake my head quickly.

She stares me down and says, That's the last thing we'll ask you.

I promise myself no but Bags squeezes her breasts harder so I hold up my thumb—bent back like I'm hitchiking—and aim it head-first at his lips. I'm shivering inside. He opens his mouth, cranes his head forward, bites down gently, his bottom teeth slipping on nail. Suck, she says, and he does. The warmth makes me shiver but Vera says Yes, massaging Bags harder, smiling. She keeps massaging and cups her other hand under a breast—his hand sliding off it—and presses herself forward, toward his mouth. My thumb is still in there. My fingers uncurl and the breast slides alongside them, the nipple aimed straight for his lips. Her eyes are on mine. Bags' are closed and he sucks my thumb harder. Her breast feels cool and Bags opens his eyes, sucking softer. The nipple moves closer and her eyes question his and his eyelids close, quivering. She stops smiling, turns to me and nods quickly. Slowly, she says.

So we do it slowly—I pull my thumb free and she presses the breast closer and his wet lips pucker and reach for the nipple, finding it, sucking. Her free hand grabs the back of his head—the hair there is thin as a baby's—and she presses his face firmly against her, closing her eyes, nodding.

You can go now, she whispers, but I don't. I stand there watching Bags' head nod from the sucking.

He's doing fine, she says, and Bags' arms hug her thighs. She looks a little embarrassed.

Bags sounds like he's crying.

You really should go, she says, so I turn and go quickly, the door kissing the doorframe behind me.

Kevin Ray

Obvious Advertisement: Robert Duncan and *The Kenyon Review*

In October 1944, a year after Robert Duncan had submitted "Sections Toward an African Elegy"[1] to *The Kenyon Review*, and some months after the poem had been accepted for publication, John Crowe Ransom, *Kenyon*'s founder and editor, wrote to him: "I am distressed, and I invite your opinion."[2] The direct cause of his distress, as he explains, is the need to decide whether and when to publish the elegy. Already it had been displaced twice by other work, from the Summer number, and then again from the Autumn. But Ransom's distress is at once less local and more particular; its direct cause itself has a cause.

"Originally," Ransom writes, "I thought your poem very brilliant."[3] In the interim, though, Duncan's essay "The Homosexual in Society" had appeared in Dwight MacDonald's polemical monthly *Politics* and in light of that essay, what had seemed excellent in the elegy—". . . it occurred to me that Africa was a fine symbol of whatever was dark in the mind. . . . I didn't think the particular darkness was defined; I said it was dark dissipation, or dark despair infecting love . . . ."[4] —proved to be a space not merely of mystery or of ambiguity, but potentially a space of danger and obscenity. The "fine symbol" becomes exactly that which makes the poem unacceptable. It is the defining space, and the turning point from brilliance to obscenity (since that is ultimately the grounds on which Ransom rejects the poem) that makes this incident so telling. Perhaps one should say that it shows clearly the muddle that exists, this muddle of reading and censorship.

Now well-known, and considered by many to be a landmark, Duncan's essay was the first in American letters in which a writer, without the safety of a pseudonym, not only declared himself to be homosexual, but took other homosexual writers to task for choosing to cut themselves off from the full flow of humanity, creating for themselves a high, safe haven; they find, he claims, not simply security but privilege in withdrawing into a ghetto of art and indirection. Duncan takes his approach from "James Agee's recent approach to the Negro pseudo-folk,"[5] observing that among homosexuals in their own attempts at self-definition, what he terms "self-recognition," the attacks from without, from those hostile to homosexual rights are less damaging than the "cult of homosexual superiority" in which the mass of homosexual intellectuals indulge. "There is in the modern scene no homosexual who has been willing to take in his own persecution a battlefront toward human freedom."[6]

But Duncan reserves his strongest language for an assault on the effect this choice, this self-balkanization, has on these writers' work. "There are critics," he writes:

> whose cynical, back-biting joke upon their audience is no other than this secret special superiority ... there are new cult leaders whose special divinity, whose supernatural and visionary claim is no other than the mystery of sex .... Like early witches, the homosexual propagandists have rejected any struggle toward recognition in social equality and, far from seeking to undermine the popular superstition, have accepted the charge of Demonism. Sensing the fear in society that is generated in ignorance of their nature, they have sought not to bring about an understanding, to assert their equality and their common aims with mankind, but they have sought to

profit by that fear and ignorance, to become witchdoctors in the modern chaos.[7]

The argument is complex. Duncan's essay is at once a confession, a repentance or recantation, an attack on coterie, and a call to action, both homosexual and heterosexual. "In the face of the hostility of society which I risk in making even the acknowledgement explicit in this statement," he writes, in the most crucial and ultimately troublesome sentence in the essay, "in the face of the 'crime' of my own feelings, in the past I publicized those feelings as private and made no stand for their recognition but tried to sell them disguised, for instance, as conflicts rising from mystical sources."[8] This sentence, Duncan's confession that he has himself been guilty of exactly that indirection he is most critical of, became, in Ransom's eyes, a more direct and un-nuanced announcement. It was a distressing confession.

Ransom speaks to this when he writes, "you say that the homosexual poets have usually symbolized their abnormality and palmed it off on the innocent 'little magazines.'"[9] For the editor, the line which divides the acceptable from the unacceptable, the obscene from the wholesome, has been made clear, and, it would seem, has been crossed. "As to the present poem," he writes, ". . . now that you have called public attention to it, it seems to me to have obvious homosexual advertisement, and for that reason not to be eligible for publication. . . . Is it not possible that you have made the sexual inferences inescapable, and the poem unavailable?"[10]

Duncan's long response had no salving effect. His answer to Ransom's question concerning the elegy, several paragraphs, is lost in a much broader defense and explanation of the *Politics* article. "Your misreading is clear in the curious translation which you make of the article in using the words 'abnormality' and 'palmed off'—a coloring of language which is so far from my meaning."[11] Indeed, though Ransom praised the essay as "courageous," his disagreement with it, and with Duncan's call for an end to indirection, could not have been more complete. "The theme of the poem," Duncan writes, "is not homosexuality; nor does the darkness stand for homosexuality. The dark continent in the poem is not what one hides, but what is hidden from one. . . . It would be rather astounding in an overt homosexual that what was held back, imprisoned in the unconscious, was the homosexual desire."[12] The weakness, for Duncan, in homosexual artists sublimating or symbolizing their "difference" is precisely that this forestalls their artistic move beyond stigma and abnormality, that, in essence, by this indirection their work takes on the characteristics of rebus or a puzzle in which the content is reduced to the simple fact of homosexuality: "a convention that assumes that homosexuality is the repressed, the important content, dictates a set of conventional homosexual symbols . . . which rather effectively thwarts the struggling subconscious element of the poem."[13]

Duncan holds to an artistic and ethical tenet that, with the gulf between their views of the homosexual artist, allows for (or does not disallow) Ransom's determined misreading of "The Homosexual in Society," which in turn creates for Ransom a paranoia of interpretation extending to "An African Elegy." This misreading is "determined" in both the common sense, resolved (it is unclear whether Duncan could have said anything at all that would have satisfied the editor once the possibility of the elegy's "obvious homosexual advertisement" existed), and in the particular sense in which a reading is "highly determined," where the interpretive field of possibility is complicated, in fact is restricted by other factors. Where Ransom has asked for the assurance that the poem is not overt, Duncan has answered by denying the validity of an aesthetic that would require it to be otherwise. For *The Kenyon Review* the innocuous had become a danger.

In her history of *The Kenyon Review*, Marian Janssen places this incident among other rejections of promising writers at the end of what she calls the *Kenyon's* "trial period," when it was fully established as one of the most influential literary journals of the 1940s and 1950s, the period of the New Criticism. "Duncan pointed out to Ransom," Janssen writes, "that 'once the aesthetic choice had been made,' an editor is morally obliged to accept a poem 'regardless of its agreement or opposition to one's own convictions.' Although this was an article of Ransom's editorial faith, he nevertheless returned Duncan's poem because of its homosexual overtones, with his 'deepest apologies.'"[14]

The revision of "An African Elegy" from "very brilliant" to "unavailable" is a quite different case from the well-rehearsed mid-century legal battles over obscenity and art, since it concerns not the artistic use of obscene or sexually explicit material, but an interpretive reassignment, a reassignment, it should be said, strongly in opposition to the stated theoretical and aesthetic views of the New Critics and of John Crowe Ransom himself. As Ekbert Faas has observed, "anonymity, as Ransom had put it in *The World's Body*, 'is a condition of poetry. A good poem, even if it is signed with a full and well-known name, intends as a work of art to lose the identity of the author.'"[15] Despite his own analysis of the elegy, Duncan himself agrees that "the sexual inferences of the poem are inescapable"[16], which Ransom understands as giving him the poet's "permission . . . [to] read the poem as an advertisement or a notice of overt homosexuality."[17] The fascination of this incident lies neither in the obscenity nor the innocence of "An African Elegy," but in the window it provides on a particular defining moment, not the fact of obscenity, but the decision of obscenity.

Notes

[1] The poem's title appears in this form in Ransom's letters, but as "The African Elegy" in Duncan's. It was later published as "An African Elegy."

[2] John Crowe Ransom to Robert Duncan, October 26, 1944, Washington University Libraries, St. Louis, Mo.

[3] Ibid.

[4] Ibid.

⁵Robert Duncan, "The Homosexual in Society," *Politics* (August 1944): 209.

⁶Ibid., 210.

⁷Ibid., 210.

⁸Ibid., 210.

⁹Ransom, October 26, 1944.

¹⁰Ibid.

¹¹Robert Duncan to John Crowe Ransom, October 1944, Washington University Libraries, St. Louis, Mo.

¹²Ibid.

¹³Ibid.

¹⁴Marian Janssen, *The Kenyon Review, 1939-1970: A Critical History*. (Baton Rouge: Louisana State University Press, 1990), 140.

¹⁵Ekbert Faas, *Young Robert Duncan: Portrait of the Poet as Homosexual in Society*. (Santa Barbara: Black Sparrow Press, 1983), 153.

¹⁶Duncan, October 1944.

¹⁷John Crowe Ransom to Robert Duncan, December 6, 1944, Washington University Libraries, St. Louis, Mo.

Mel Freilicher

Prolog

The dead are always upon us. Hiding in the light.

Joe's driving down Washington, past the Figaro. Last place I saw Alex alive, unaware he was sick. In a tight white glow with his new young boyfriend from New York. Just back from a triumphant San Francisco performance—unaccountably praising the food here.

Expect to feel sad, feel nothing. Next time we drive by, practically assaulted by images of Alex: wiry, radiant, imperiously bemused.

Now this over-priced and rather nondescript restaurant, on a similar street of trendy shops and offices, has become sacrosanct: an anchor.

This is no riddle, nor rune; it's real—daily life is peopled with the dead.

Catch someone familiar out of the corner of my eye. Something about that walk, with the half toss of her longish brown hair—vulnerable, contemplative. Brooke! Then you remember she's been gone several years already. Still, approaching from behind, I pick up the pace, just to get a closer look.

They don't always sneak up. Sometimes the dead simply assert themselves into your mind's eye with an absolute and stark prerogative.

Also in the car, Jack's face emerges out of the neutral gray horizon of the passenger's window: quite palpable, considering I haven't seen him in over a decade. Half-closed, nearly almond shaped brown eyes, that wide mischievous grin. An apparently immobile, vaguely Buddha-like expression; tongue poised to slip into lust.

But most wonderful are the dream/visitations: intensely personal, and not personal at all, moments. The true province, I imagine, of those who perform spiritual expercises:

The beloved dead one is just there. Beaming at you with that inevitable sly, knowing smile. Sometimes, it's someone from very long ago, elementary school, who appears with that same luminous quality. For the moment, you are wordlessly told, all doubt is transcendentally irrelevant.

(He) clasps your hand; (she) touches your arm. You *know* this is real is the first thing you think when you wake up.

But the problem is not the dead—in some ways the most comfortable feature of the landscape. The problem is how to live daily with any grace and humor.

Which, nevertheless, is happening all the time. As we're forced into materializing the ideals of community many of us rather glibly espoused in the 60s. Or else suffer the most dire isolation, deterioration.

It would take a Master Propagandist, or a Balzac, to incisively illustrate the ways friends, support networks—most often improvised and sustained by the sick and dying—are keeping each other alive day after day: redeeming words like "faith" and "hope" from the deepest banality.

An everyday heroism, absolutely invisible to the majority, who refuse all evidence of our catastrophic age.

Even before AIDS, it was hard enough to understand the prevailing complacency, overweaning passivity, the cloying narcissism. Now, in a way, things are simpler. Denial becomes sin: giving new shape and categorical meaning to that word.

With news of our resilience, we maneuver toward increasing visibility.

Edward Field

Sex in Poetry, A Meditation on My Poem, "Triad"

> A temple sculpture: Two warriors in combat.
> Down between their knees, a female,
> with the prick of one of them up her cunt
> and at the same time bending over backwards
> to take the other's cock in her mouth—
> while the men cross swords over her.
>
> —from "Triad"*

Prick. Cunt. Cock. Fiction can get away with it nowadays, but a poem, (like "Triad"), no matter how serious, using these words, not to mention the more notorious "asshole" or "hardon," will, even in our liberated era, not get into the *New Yorker* or *Poetry* Magazine, even if I substituted euphemisms, colloquial and lewder, like shaft, tool, member, or the more clinical erection, penis, vagina. Even not using the words, poems about sex, unless dealt with on a "high" level, will not make it. (Though I actually once saw the word "glory hole" in a little poem in the *New Yorker*'s back pages, but Howard Moss, then poetry editor, was probably the only one on the staff who knew what a glory hole was, and it slipped through, so to speak.) In "Triad," with the possible exception of "daisy chain," a sex game which, like orgies, is part of history since it can no longer be indulged in in this era of Safe Sex, the rest of the poem couldn't sully the ears of a virgin, if such a creature existed anymore (except perhaps among the readers of the *New Yorker* and *Poetry* Magazine who are being shielded from such violation).

I despair that in almost every one of my poems is a word that will prevent it from being published in the famous journals I long to be accepted by. I recently had a poem about carrier pigeons taken by *The Atlantic Monthly*, but what they put me through. I not only had to change the title, but also the word "screwing" to the less raffish "copulation," since they claimed that pigeons did not have anything to screw with. This seemed to me as far-fetched as my mother's idea that birds did it with their beaks, billing and cooing. (The editor finally decided not to publish this poem.) But in spite of generations of wild poets shouting Fuck at their readings, the poetry world persists in preserving its ramrod puritanism. Take, for example, an organization like the Academy of American Poets which is founded on the idea that poets are ladies and gentlemen, whatever they do in private, and will speak in public only with pristine lips that have never licked an asshole. And all the big poets play the game. Never, at their black tie readings held at the Morgan Library for their Park Avenue donors, would such a poem as "Triad" be read, with its frank use of four-letter words. And this and all the other prestigious, snobbish organizations claim to be doing such good for poetry around the country!

How, though, can I keep these words out of my poems when they are in my head? I don't divide my vocabulary into acceptable and unacceptable, especially when I write, alone at my desk, enjoying the possibilities of my usually sexy imagination. Of course, you might ask, in rewriting with a cooler head one can easily substitute other, less offensive, words. Yes, I do change words when I work on a poem, but almost always from fancier to simpler and earthier. (It is odd that writing prose, I have learned that, as a rule, fancier words work better.) I'd be ashamed to clean up my poems for the sake of gentility, though.

It would almost be like denying I'm a Jew, and yet to save my life I admit I would do just that, if I could get away with it, and in travelling in Moslem countries I don't go out of my way to announce it. It is true that in person I offer as conventional an appearance to the world as I can, letting the freak pervert exist inside, but that is for safety and a late-preference for privacy. About poetry I feel different. Poetry, for me, is about breaking through falseness, telling the truth, about openness. As soon as I say that, though, it seems nuts. Look at Poetry with its formalities, almost like the ritual of ambassadors between kingdoms. Well, not my poetry, though "Triad" is developed with a literary formality, because I worked on it for a number of years. But I'm from humble people, shtetl people, and we don't have a tradition of formalities. We don't put on airs. We express our real feelings, using all the words. (Though, personally, I think interesting subject matter is more important than anything, because Poetry, most poetry, is so boring.) Moreover, the cause of sexual freedom (sacred to my generation) involved overcoming inhibitions and learning to be frank, proclaiming your secrets, chasing prudery, cleansing the language of hypocrisy. This may sound old-fashioned today, when the sexual revolution has been won, and then destroyed by diseases like AIDS and Jesse Helms, which at the same time opened up frank sexual discourse on a popular level. But, the sexual revolution aside, wasn't one of the goals of modern poetry to restore the language to vigor and, dare I say in this context, purity? Also, I'll admit there may be an element of Bad Boy at work in my writing: Let's say dirty words in polite society (and the poetry world today, unfortunately, qualifies as polite society) and I'll prove you are shockable even if you play sophisticated and claim nothing will shock you.

---

*from *New and Selected Poems,* by Edward Field (The Sheep Meadow Press, 1987)

Greg Boyd

Horny

I wake up horny. God's punishing me again, testing my endurance, so I fall to my knees and pray for strength. But evil thoughts course through my mind like a polluted stream. I try my best to purify them. I am chlorine, lava soap. I bubble and foam, but in the end it happens again anyway. It's always the same. My soul screams at the exact moment of my body's release. It's a righteous voice that wells up inside me, a deep and hoary voice that comes out of the wilderness and is filled with the indignation of the ages. It inspires in me a kind of holy terror and afterwards I shake for a good five minutes.

Though I won't eat today, I allow myself one cup of instant coffee. Then I go into the garage and give myself fifty lashes on my bare back with a leather strap. Afterwards I climb up on a stepladder and take down the cross I keep suspended from the rafters. I built it myself from heavy lumber, wood screws and angle braces I bought at the hardware store. I had to carry the beams six miles home with me in two separate trips because they wouldn't fit in or on my car. That was months ago, back when I still had a car. It was mid-summer then, and under the sun's whip the sweat dripped from my vile body as I walked and melted my impure thoughts about beach girls in their bikinis. I was already learning how to suffer.

There are leather straps on the cross for me to hold onto so that I can keep it balanced as I walk. The first few times I used it I kept dropping it on the sidewalk and by the end of the day my hands were full of splinters from trying to catch ahold of it when it started to slip from off my shoulder. Like I said, it's a very heavy cross, and long enough so that if it were put into the ground, and raised up on end with me nailed to it like it's supposed to be, it would still be plenty high to keep me way above everyone so they could see just how much I'm suffering up there. The splinters were actually never a problem, as they only added to my suffering and my contemplation thereof as I pulled them out with tweezers at home later, and it's nice for the cross to hit the sidewalk once in a while, where it makes a huge noise, though better, I think, for me to fall with it, to one knee or even right onto my face, which happens more often now that I'm actually strapped to it, but once a woman with a baby carriage was walking past me and I kind of leaned over a bit to look at her and just as I was getting a good peek the cross started to slip and only the grace of God spared her child, though the carriage was damaged beyond repair. Praise be to God.

Since then the police have kept close tabs on me. It was even their idea to use the leather hand straps. They've given me a few simple guidelines to follow as well. It's a free country, they tell me, but I'm not to bother people. And they've asked me to stay out of the mall, which is where I had a little trouble another time on account of the over-zealous security officers there who accused me of disturbing with my wild stares and weird cross the young girl-shoppers that mill around eating salted pretzels and sucking orange drinks through straws. The security guards wanted to grab my arms and guide me forcibly to the exit and when I refused to let them abuse my rights to freedom of religion and expression they ended up calling the police to have me arrested for disorderly conduct and disrupting the peace. Except for those two times the police have been nice enough whenever they stop their cars to check in with me along the sidewalk downtown, and there's even a young lady officer who wears her tight blue uniform shirt with the badge pinned right over her swelling chest, though none of them can keep themselves from winking at each other or chuckling. They know I'm not a criminal, but, even so, they still like to imagine I'm some kind of kook. But that laugh-about-it-all attitude is understandable given all the wickedness and depravity they witness on a daily basis.

I strip down completely and wrap the loincloth I made from an old white sheet between my legs and then twice around my waist. It's modest but authentic. I fasten it tightly at both the waist and legs with safety pins to keep the cloth from falling down and my private parts from spilling out as I grapple with the cross. I won't stand for people having any lewd thoughts or fantasies about an act that's meant to purify. And I certainly don't want to be humiliated in public. Outside I hear the wind blowing rain against the garage door as I get ready. No doubt about it, today I'm going to suffer.

On the street I see one of my neighbors, dressed in a yellow plastic raincoat, stooping to pick up her newspaper. She waves to me briefly before she scurries back inside her house, even though she knows I can't wave back because my hands are holding onto the wet straps of the cross. She's an attractive young woman who works in an office. Sometimes I see her getting out of her car in the evening, her tight skirt riding up her thighs, her high heels gleaming in the late afternoon light. Only recently married, she and her husband have lived on my street just a few months. For a second I catch a glimpse of her legs as she stoops, and I wonder what, if anything, she's wearing under the raincoat. Even at this distance I can tell that her breasts are full and round. Her big red nipples puff out and stand erect beneath the cold plastic, begging for my tongue's devotion. Her hot host is already moist with the anticipation of everlasting joy, of paradise on earth, of things to come.

But God loves me. My thoughts are interrupted by a car at the corner that splashes the cold and holy water of repentance upon me as it passes through a puddle in the road, drenching my budding lust in its wake. My hair clings limply to my head and rainwater runs down my face as I struggle against the weight of the cross, the cold, the wind that sends chilling spikes of pain up and down my legs. Sharp pebbles press into my bare feet. I pass through residential neighborhoods and as I do I know that temptation lurks behind every door, every window. I avert my eyes, cast them downward. Along the sidewalk I see drowned earthworms that have been flushed like so many unclean corpses out from their soaked graves. Bent beneath my burden I contemplate my life and its eventual end. As the sky weeps, so do I, for my sins are great and many.

Downtown I walk past rows of storefronts, windows full of worldly goods. I don't let myself look inside or think about the shopgirls standing in their short skirts—how they pull their pantyhose up over their long legs in the morning, how they push their firm breasts into the cups of their lacy bras, how they splash perfume behind their ears and knees in anticipation. Finally I take my position at the center of town, stand silently in the rain at the intersection of Broadway and Main. People drive past in their warm, dry cars, listening to pop songs about love, or more often about love-making—the words barely clothed in a fine, see-through mesh of metaphor that leaves little to the imagination. Some of them honk their horns at me. Perhaps they know me. In better weather they might speak to me, offer me their blessing or ask for mine. More likely they recognize what I represent, why I am here. They understand that safe inside their cars they are swimming in filthy thoughts, vile debauchery.

A man and a woman in a blue Mercedes drive past slowly, staring at me *with unbelieving eyes*. The man wears an expensive suit, the woman a silk blouse under a tweed blazer. No doubt they've just come from a motel where they've been engaging in every illicit sex-act conceivable. No doubt his penis now hangs between his legs swollen red, bruised and sore from pounding inside her tight and hungry hole. No doubt her vagina likewise feels ragged and sore from their debauch, its soft walls stretched and battered from the satanic thrashing action of the devil's massive, oversized piston. It takes a long time for the car to turn the corner, an eternity. All the while the woman looks into my eyes, first through the hysterical waving arms of the windshield wipers, then, head turned sharply to the side, through the passenger window, a harlot, a fellow sinner in need of spiritual guidance, pleading for help, for compassion. I am here for her, a beacon set firmly in place in the midst of a storm. I loosen my hand from its tether to signal and the cross slips, pulling me with it to the wet concrete. When I touch my face, my hand comes away bloody. She is gone.

I could have saved her. I could have taught her how to love. I could have taken her by the hand. I could have undressed her with my teeth. I could have . . .

By the time I get home it's nearly dark. I'm soaked to the bone, skin blue and shrivelled, feet numb and bloody, chilled, shivering, feverish. I wrap one towel around my head, another around my shoulders, a third over my legs and sit in front of the television for hours drinking hot tea and watching cable network evangelism. The first hour features a fiery preacher who explains the sufferings of Jesus for Mankind while threatening me with eternal damnation and a gospel rock singer with lips made for fellatio. Later, before my very eyes a blind woman has her vision restored by the love of Christ and a cripple walks when he accepts the Lord as his personal savior. As the camera pans the audience to show the radiant faces of the true believers I see a pretty woman in the third row that I want to fuck. I am exalted, mesmerized, shivering uncontrollably.

At eleven o'clock I switch off the television and pray on stiff knees in total darkness for an hour and a half. I go to bed exhausted and hopelessly horny.

Roy Schneider

Pubic Skies

He unloads it with abandon. The vein at the end of the earth. Bellies up to the eternal porcelain. A snake brandishing its tongue. She slips in behind him, says, "Can I hold it?"

"It's dead," he says.

He's talking with brown teeth. A smile that offends and arouses. The knowledge it imparts: the distance between two souls.

"I'll bet it tastes like anticipation."

He has a nose that could open letters.

"Yeah, so sit on my fist."

Balls crawl to his chin. Breathless. Her cool legs cross. Exposed from mid-thigh. Breasts the size of psalms. Cheeks: a pout of blood and booze.

Later his eyes will make her crawl deeper into her lover.

He will recognize her scent in pictures. Fishing news. Salmon upstream, fertile, free.

She heads back toward the music, eyelids at half-mast, full knowledge. "Well," she says, "I didn't mean to, but it was deliberate."

"Sometimes I just want to see it. A viewing of the organ. A ritual. A prelude. I mean, maybe we'll never get lewd. But I'll have seen it. No details. Just a knowledge. And you know, dear boy, you can't lie to the knowledgeable."

My hand: the beast that lays across the page   The polluting paw ringed gold where all sex sees   Forget the words   Wombs of knowledge   Lies in the eye of hope   Nipples that claw the night   An ass that bends to a yawn   The weight of fear   The scratch behind the ear that doesn't bleed   The skull's own giggle

"As long as you keep 'em talkin' you've got a chance. It's silence that kills. That hole in the breath. You might as well cut a vein as kill the words. Nothin' deadlier than silence. Momentum. You gotta buy a vowel. Cheapest love in town."

When are they going to realize that the beer at my lips tastes of flesh? The broad expanse of a mushroom aroused. Booze. And distended bellies. Begins with the lie and moves out from there. Balls that hang in the shape of shot glasses. Blood in the stool. Bowels that talk back. . . to applause.

"Now look at that! The way her breasts wag under that silk. And she won't look me in the eye. She knows. But she denies. . . Hey, honey, you bouncing hard! Yeah, go on, girl. Dribble your sweet self over here. Mmmm, and your ass is takin' a bite outta that dress, too. . . See, she knows. But she won't acknowledge. Won't talk. So tell me, how's a man gonna believe in that?"

Your dead presence warm at my side   Panties a ripe patch of lies   Cool alabaster ass   The gloss of bone   The thick breath of trees   Your touch the knowledge we avoid   Blood on soft cotton: children flushed from our soul   So married our cheeks hurt: forces smiles

Wives are blunt. Butter knives to the soul. She left. Laid it on the line, double spaced, neatly folded: "Queer is queer, even when done in great numbers."

"He's a beast! Sometimes he eases my pants down like he's peeling back skin. Going after me like I've got the whole damned solution stashed in a hole just south of my ass. Doesn't make sense. Doesn't make me happy. And damned sure doesn't make sense... But, damn, once a man gets in your pants, honey, he never gets out."

He left with only words, unbent and aroused. Bar babble, stains in the air. And words on walls, his own secret treasure... WE SMILE IN DAD'S PRESENCE, TALK WHEN HE'S GONE THERE ARE 3,000 WAYS TO DIE, BUT NOBODY'S COUNTING I DIED AND WENT TO SHIT, HEAVEN WAS FULL THE SMELL OF SEX AROUSES SLEEPING LIONS... The call of the mild.

He leans out the door, eyes hazy figures at the bar. "Hey, I gotta little class, but I don't let it get in the way!"

He retreats to the womb of stench. Chooses carefully. Pens it to the wall. The only lie he wants to believe:

DURING MENSTRUATION
HER BREATH TASTES
OF BURNT EARTH
HE THINKS SHE DOESN'T KNOW
SHE THINKS HE DOESN'T CARE
THEY CALL IT LOVE...

Richard Kostelanetz

Flirting

flirting	kissing	hugging	petting	undressing	rubbing
flirting	kissing	hugging	petting	undressing	rubbing
flirting	kissing	hugging	petting	undressing	rubbing
flirting	kissing	hugging	petting	undressing	rubbing
flirting	kissing	hugging	petting	undressing	rubbing
flirting	kissing	hugging	petting	undressing	rubbing
flirting	kissing	hugging	petting	undressing	rubbing
flirting	kissing	hugging	petting	undressing	rubbing
flirting	kissing	hugging	petting	undressing	rubbing
flirting	kissing	hugging	petting	undressing	rubbing
flirting	kissing	hugging	petting	undressing	rubbing
flirting	kissing	hugging	petting	undressing	rubbing
foreplaying	fingering	fondling	exciting	tonguing	rolling
foreplaying	fingering	fondling	exciting	tonguing	rolling
foreplaying	fingering	fondling	exciting	tonguing	rolling
foreplaying	fingering	fondling	exciting	tonguing	rolling
foreplaying	fingering	fondling	exciting	tonguing	rolling
foreplaying	fingering	fondling	exciting	tonguing	rolling
foreplaying	fingering	fondling	exciting	tonguing	rolling

foreplaying fingering fondling exciting tonguing rolling
foreplaying fingering fondling exciting tonguing rolling
foreplaying fingering fondling exciting tonguing rolling
foreplaying fingering fondling exciting tonguing rolling
foreplaying fingering fondling exciting tonguing rolling
penetrating sliding slipping plunging withholding arching
penetrating sliding slipping plunging withholding arching
penetrating sliding slipping plunging withholding arching
penetrating sliding slipping plunging withholding arching
penetrating sliding slipping plunging withholding arching
penetrating sliding slipping plunging withholding arching
penetrating sliding slipping plunging withholding arching
penetrating sliding slipping plunging withholding arching
penetrating sliding slipping plunging withholding arching
penetrating sliding slipping plunging withholding arching
penetrating sliding slipping plunging withholding arching
penetrating sliding slipping plunging withholding arching
pumping humping coming resting sleeping .
pumping humping coming resting sleeping .
pumping humping coming resting sleeping .
pumping humping coming resting sleeping .
pumping humping coming resting sleeping .
pumping humping coming resting sleeping .
pumping humping coming resting sleeping .
pumping humping coming resting sleeping .
pumping humping coming resting sleeping .
pumping humping coming resting sleeping .
pumping humping coming resting sleeping .
pumping humping coming resting sleeping .
flirting flirting kissing kissing hugging hugging
flirting flirting kissing kissing hugging hugging
flirting flirting kissing kissing hugging hugging
flirting flirting kissing kissing hugging hugging

flirting flirting	kissing kissing	hugging hugging
flirting flirting	kissing kissing	hugging hugging
petting petting	undressing undressing	rubbing rubbing
petting petting	undressing undressing	rubbing rubbing
petting petting	undressing undressing	rubbing rubbing
petting petting	undressing undressing	rubbing rubbing
petting petting	undressing undressing	rubbing rubbing
petting petting	undressing undressing	rubbing rubbing
foreplaying foreplaying	fingering fingering	fondling fondling
foreplaying foreplaying	fingering fingering	fondling fondling
foreplaying foreplaying	fingering fingering	fondling fondling
foreplaying foreplaying	fingering fingering	fondling fondling
foreplaying foreplaying	fingering fingering	fondling fondling
foreplaying foreplaying	fingering fingering	fondling fondling
exciting exciting	tonguing tonguing	rolling rolling
exciting exciting	tonguing tonguing	rolling rolling
exciting exciting	tonguing tonguing	rolling rolling
exciting exciting	tonguing tonguing	rolling rolling
exciting exciting	tonguing tonguing	rolling rolling
exciting exciting	tonguing tonguing	rolling rolling
penetrating penetrating	sliding sliding	slipping slipping
penetrating penetrating	sliding sliding	slipping slipping
penetrating penetrating	sliding sliding	slipping slipping
penetrating penetrating	sliding sliding	slipping slipping
penetrating penetrating	sliding sliding	slipping slipping
penetrating penetrating	sliding sliding	slipping slipping
plunging plunging	withholding withholding	arching arching
plunging plunging	withholding withholding	arching arching
plunging plunging	withholding withholding	arching arching
plunging plunging	withholding withholding	arching arching
plunging plunging	withholding withholding	arching arching
plunging plunging	withholding withholding	arching arching

pumping pumping   humping humping   coming coming
pumping pumping   humping humping   coming coming
pumping pumping   humping humping   coming coming
pumping pumping   humping humping   coming coming
pumping pumping   humping humping   coming coming
pumping pumping   humping humping   coming coming
resting resting   sleeping sleeping   .
resting resting   sleeping sleeping   .
resting resting   sleeping sleeping   .
resting resting   sleeping sleeping   .
resting resting   sleeping sleeping   .
resting resting   sleeping sleeping   .
flirting flirting flirting   kising kissing kissing
flirting flirting flirting   kising kissing kissing
flirting flirting flirting   kising kissing kissing
flirting flirting flirting   kising kissing kissing
hugging hugging hugging   petting petting petting
hugging hugging hugging   petting petting petting
hugging hugging hugging   petting petting petting
hugging hugging hugging   petting petting petting
undressing undressing undressing   rubbing rubbing rubbing
undressing undressing undressing   rubbing rubbing rubbing
undressing undressing undressing   rubbing rubbing rubbing
undressing undressing undressing   rubbing rubbing rubbing
foreplaying foreplaying foreplaying   fingering fingering fingering
foreplaying foreplaying foreplaying   fingering fingering fingering
foreplaying foreplaying foreplaying   fingering fingering fingering
foreplaying foreplaying foreplaying   fingering fingering fingering
fondling fondling fondling   exciting exciting exciting
fondling fondling fondling   exciting exciting exciting
fondling fondling fondling   exciting exciting exciting
fondling fondling fondling   exciting exciting exciting

tonguing tonguing tonguing	rolling rolling rolling
tonguing tonguing tonguing	rolling rolling rolling
tonguing tonguing tonguing	rolling rolling rolling
tonguing tonguing tonguing	rolling rolling rolling
penetrating penetrating penetrating	sliding sliding sliding
penetrating penetrating penetrating	sliding sliding sliding
penetrating penetrating penetrating	sliding sliding sliding
penetrating penetrating penetrating	sliding sliding sliding
slipping slipping slipping	plunging plunging plunging
slipping slipping slipping	plunging plunging plunging
slipping slipping slipping	plunging plunging plunging
slipping slipping slipping	plunging plunging plunging
withholding withholding withholding	arching arching arching
withholding withholding withholding	arching arching arching
withholding withholding withholding	arching arching arching
withholding withholding withholding	arching arching arching
pumping pumping pumping	humping humping humping
pumping pumping pumping	humping humping humping
pumping pumping pumping	humping humping humping
pumping pumping pumping	humping humping humping
coming coming coming	resting resting resting
coming coming coming	resting resting resting
coming coming coming	resting resting resting
coming coming coming	resting resting resting
sleeping sleeping sleeping	.
sleeping sleeping sleeping	.
sleeping sleeping sleeping	.
sleeping sleeping sleeping	.

flirting   kissing   hugging   petting   undressing   rubbing
foreplaying   fingering   fondling   exciting   undressing   rolling
penetrating   sliding   slipping   plunging   withholding   arching
pumping   humping   coming   resting   sleeping   .

flirting   kissing   hugging   petting   undressing   rubbing
foreplaying   fingering   fondling   exciting   tonguing   rolling
penetrating   sliding   slipping   plunging   withholding   arching
pumping   humping   coming   resting   sleeping   .
flirting   kissing   hugging   petting   undressing   rubbing
foreplaying   fingering   fondling   exciting   tonguing   rolling
penetrating   sliding   slipping   plunging   withholding   arching
pumping   humping   coming   resting   sleeping   .
flirting   kissing   hugging   petting   undressing   rubbing
foreplaying   fingering   fondling   exciting   tonguing   rolling
penetrating   sliding   slipping   plunging   withholding   arching
pumping   humping   coming   resting   sleeping   .
flirting   kissing   hugging   petting   undressing   rubbing
foreplaying   fingering   fondling   exciting   tonguing   rolling
penetrating   sliding   slipping   plunging   withholding   arching
pumping   humping   coming   resting   sleeping   .
flirting   kissing   hugging   petting   undressing   rubbing
foreplaying   fingering   fondling   exciting   tonguing   rolling
penetrating   sliding   slipping   plunging   withholding   arching
pumping   humping   coming   resting   sleeping   .
flirting   kissing   hugging   petting   undressing   rubbing
foreplaying   fingering   fondling   exciting   tonguing   rolling
penetrating   sliding   slipping   plunging   withholding   arching
pumping   humping   coming   resting   sleeping   .
flirting   kissing   hugging   petting   undressing   rubbing
foreplaying   fingering   fondling   exciting   tonguing   rolling
penetrating   sliding   slipping   plunging   withholding   arching
pumping   humping   coming   resting   sleeping   .
flirting   kissing   hugging   petting   undressing   rubbing
foreplaying   fingering   fondling   exciting   tonguing   rolling
penetrating   sliding   slipping   plunging   withholding   arching
pumping   humping   coming   resting   sleeping   .

flirting   kissing   hugging   petting   undressing   rubbing
foreplaying   fingering   fondling   exciting   tonguing   rolling
penetrating   sliding   slipping   plunging   withholding   arching
pumping   humping   coming   resting   sleeping   .
flirting   kissing   hugging   petting   undressing   rubbing
foreplaying   fingering   fondling   exciting   tonguing   rolling
penetrating   sliding   slipping   plunging   withholding   arching
pumping   humping   coming   resting   sleeping   .
flirting   kissing   hugging   petting   undressing   rubbing
foreplaying   fingering   fondling   exciting   tonguing   rolling
penetrating   sliding   slipping   plunging   withholding   arching
pumping   humping   coming   resting   sleeping   .

Tom Jurek

from Straight Fiction

The limitations of my own sex confuse hotly used words and the glimpses I have of you sliding through the sheets with women. Each of the ten spasms yanked me further into an agony unappeased by explanations or profiles. Photos and dialogue are no longer enough, as the screen comes up and certain muscles show their whiteness. Writing to see what happens usually leaves off at the unintelligible glances of seduction. In each case I fast forward, looking for some strain of data that can hold off disaster until the shaking stops. Fabric is too easy to drift into and retains a portion of whatever is spilled into it. In the challenge of looking through windows, I can almost hear you smile and slip the needle in as I do. She breathes again into your cunt and what falls out is my beginning. A longer, pirated version has been edited for maximum effect. An allowance for position is taken into account.

The edge of her body with you not quite facing reels {the action} from my keyboard, and forces my fingers to stray from murder. Her right arm reaching the nipple at the precise moment your vulva rolls and bucks down. Contours become their own events liquid and noteworthy, destroying any chance of removal for me from a scene. An example showing inanimate objects extracting their own tongue-like movements from an atmosphere that is charged with the obscene. Gestures from passing trains remind me of ghosts. Those lost frames in a matrix *before* connotation and commingling fluids.

Solo renditions of passing sexualities mutilate the skin and peel it back. Lascivious and drunken in the coolness of sweat. Covering the marks would take time. Becoming a triangle with equal roles would be impossible. I am aware of how long it takes to submit so completely that the possessor would become the slave. Sinewave liberation inside the sewers with various diseases detailed in a child's lunchpail. Talk like a stranger and you'll live one. You were a hole smiling through a girl in our desire. I want to grease you and have you enter me by pushing the lies out of my mouth. I think of my heroes and insert their tenderness while being outside their experience.

Ordered through a cruelty and playing with a different sex.

Stephen-Paul Martin

Double Bed

Freddie might have been dead. Or he might have been trapped in sleep, the kind that's too complex to wake from. Or he might have been having the kind of dream you can't remember later, but which you nonetheless pretend to reconstruct from an image of two, building it into something a friend or therapist might find amusing. Or he might have been deep in stupor, plunging so firmly into an absence of mind that a vortex was forming, sucking him all the more firmly into a place his mind had abandoned. He might have been caught up in any one of these conditions, or all of them at once, as if several different possibilities were moving toward a more definite shape, and one of them took off in a totally unforeseen direction, and he suddenly found himself wide awake, staring at an unfamiliar woman stretched out naked beside him in bed. Jenny opened her eyes two seconds later. She said: What are YOU doing here? And Freddie said: I live here, what are YOU doing here? Then they just stared at each other. Both felt the need to make a decisive argument, proving beyond all doubt whose double-bed it really was, but neither felt up to the task, so they kept on staring. The light was ripping in through green silk drapes, thrusting in so fiercely that everything in the room, their faces and bodies included, seemed to be on the verge of becoming invisible. So both began to search in silent fear for explanations.

But only one explanation seemed at all plausible: that they both must have been really drunk in a singles bar the night before, picked each other up and gone to bed. Both of course had done this kind of thing many times in the past, so neither felt surprised. But the thought of having done it again was depressing, not because either one had moralistic inhibitions, but rather because they'd recently sworn off sex, and especially casual sex, having spent long nights with friends in hospitals dying of AIDS, and having gotten sick of going to bed with total strangers.

So they tried to find other reasons, not wanting to just admit that they'd been drunk and deeply horny, feeling like they were lost in a park in a dark and distant city, where children ran around screaming and fighting, and grown-ups thought their kids were cute for making so much noise, and a sky-blue hand was reaching down from a cardboard sky in the suburbs, and still no words came to mind so they kept on staring, not moving, barely breathing, completely oblivious to the loud knocking at the door, a sound that should have made it clear to both Jenny and Freddie that city life is an architectural discourse, a language in three dimensions, and we therefore need to prepare a careful response in three dimensions, a durably installed generative principle of regulated improvisations, aware that the ethics of disposability clearly signify more than merely throwing out plastic spoons and forks, but in fact refer to the disposability of moral values, of personalities, relationships with other people, relationships between people and what they perceive, the values they might assign to space and time and material objects, producing in the long run a kind of paralysis, a depressive condition in which all things appear inaccessible, but also desirable, and nothing seems clear. But Freddie was pretty clear about one thing, something which made his earlier thoughts about how he'd ended up with Jenny seem completely ridiculous, and this one thing was that he had no recollection, not even the vaguest memory, of having been looking for sex the night before. Nor did Jenny look even slightly familiar. She didn't even remind him of his mother.

Jenny put her finger in his mouth, smiled as if his dick might be a light green rubber duck, tried to get a romantic look in her eyes. But none of it came off with any conviction. And Freddie's response was painfully mechanical, as if he could tell she was just going through the motions, initiating sex because their proximity seemed to suggest it. In fact, it suggested a good deal more, a matrix of implications that became painfully clear when the room was suddenly filled with a horrible sound coming out of the north, a long sound gripping and stretching the sky, ripping the stitches that held it together, but no indication of what the sound was, and no sense that anyone else—anyone in rooms nearby or anyone out on the street—was even in the vaguest way aware of it.

Jenny creased her brow. Freddie wasn't sure what she meant, so he creased his brow in response, put his finger in her mouth, then took it out and wiped it on his thigh. Jenny smiled and began to moan, rubbing her teeth against his neck. Both could hear the sound of people walking past on the pavement. They tried to pay close attention to that sound, tracing it up and down the street, footsteps coming close and moving away, but the truth is that control over information, coupled with an instant capacity for analyzing huge amounts of data, is crucial in coordinating far-flung corporate interests, as if to say that history can now be seen as a vast archive filled with instantly retrievable events, each of which can be consumed and reconsumed at the push of a button. Time is nothing more than a costume drama. By treating certain idealized conceptions of space and time as if they were physically real, we run the risk of confining the free flow of human experience to a set of rational expectations. Our thinking starts to look, in fact, like a motel struck by lightning.

So Freddie said, Why don't we get up and have breakfast? Maybe we could have a conversation.

And Jenny said, Yeah, sure, that sounds good. We could talk about our favorite TV shows, and from there we could move into something more intimate, like how our parents messed us up, and how we've had to spend thousands of dollars on therapy. The gnashing sunlight forced its way through the blinds onto Freddie's forehead, making his face appear to be sliced into three unequal sections, but Jenny thought his face had been sliced into five unequal sections, and she thought she might tell him that, in no uncertain terms, until that thought was replaced by a thought that had twelve equal sections, and then collapsed in a heap at the foot of the bed.

The knocking at the door got louder and louder, as if it were slowly building toward a point of no return, a crescendo of sorts that would finally reveal, in pure non-verbal terms, the unequivocal meaning of what they were doing there, assuming such unequivocal terms could really be brought into focus. After all, what appears at first unequivocal, needing no explanation, may suddenly seem offensively complex in the face of new information. The collapse of money as means of firmly representing value, like a train breaking down before leaving the station, has led to a widespread crisis of representation. The rapidity with which currency markets fluctuate, for example, may well define a larger fluctuation, a shift in how we approach our basic spatial situation. Time horizons collapse, birds get bored and stop flying, the footsteps on the pavement seem to get louder moving farther away. Even as recently as fifteen years ago, we might have appealed to a standardized sense of space and time as a point of departure. But today things are quite different, and on some days that difference becomes unavoidable, and Freddie and Jenny felt that difference keenly, and the sun was coming in like a battering ram, like an angry fullback bashing in for a touchdown, like a Bengal tiger smashing through a fancy storefront window, like someone stuffing your mouth with a huge potato.

So many things were happening all at once, and Freddie felt the need to get some firmly defined information. He fixed his gaze on Jenny's lovely neck and showed his big sharp teeth. Then he asked her if she liked modern dance and she said that she did, that in fact she'd done modern dance for fifteen years before messing up her back, and he said he could tell she'd been a dancer because she was all curve and muscle, a phrase he'd meant as a turn-on, but she took it the wrong way since it reminded her that no matter how beautiful her body was it hadn't helped her find the right person to settle down with, and now she was almost too old to have kids, but Freddie thought that kids were a pain in the ass, and besides, why bring kids into a doomed and disgracefully unfair world, but this made Jenny sad again, because she knew that unless people had kids the human species would come to an end, so Freddie said that he prided himself on being honest enough to admit that he'd didn't care if humanity came to an end, and that he didn't think people who said they cared were better people than he was just because they felt the need to say what they thought other people expected, but Jenny said she didn't think it had anything to do with expectations, she said it had more to do with convictions, and the steeple clock outside began to chime, it was nearly ten, and the knocking at the door was getting louder, and someone outside began screaming, but nothing seemed to penetrate the basin of attraction, bland and unfocused though it might have been, that hovered above the bed in the churning sunlight. This was the bitter harvest of charismatic politics, of voodoo economics, of passive depictions of otherness, of people getting drunk at cocktail parties, of born-again Christians getting hooked on pornographic movies, of people going mad from having too much time to kill.

But Jenny knew how to brush past what she recognized as nonsense, and she knew how to penetrate, how to use her hands to gently open a person's body, to form a gap in his flesh and pull it wide, climb inside, stay there until it was safe to come out—a good thing to know how to do, except that with Freddie she felt no need to be cautious. It wasn't that he was so gentle or sensitive or anything like that, but that he was preoccupied, concerned that money was quickly becoming totally fictitious, reducing all significance to a rubble of obsolete sounds and shapes, a lunar landscape not unlike Hiroshima, or a burning face, or stepping on someone's dog by mistake, or doing it on purpose. The days were becoming the past before they were fully part of the present, and Freddie said: What came from my hands allows me to see your face, and Jenny looked puzzled, but she didn't want to get stuck staring in silence again, so she said they should go out for breakfast, talk about how their parents had messed up their childhoods, skip the talk about their favorite TV shows and movies, get married in a fancy modern chapel, and then decide about having kids, or maybe get a dog instead, decide on what kind later. But Freddie put on a big smile, ran his fingers up her shapely thigh, sucked her shoulder, played with her so gently, so skillfully, and in the end with such abandon, that soon she began to split with unrehearsed passion, gripping the sides of the bed and staring her way through the wall toward a cardboard sky, grunting like someone making repairs on a highway into the future. And when she came, the knocking stopped, the footsteps on the pavement stopped, the chimes from the nearby steeple stopped. The street grew dark and violent.

Lyn Butler Oaks

Twins

Sallee's breasts are no bigger than the bowls of silver champagne glasses. This is the first Tuesday of the fifth month Sallee has come to a different plastic surgeon. She is reading "Augmentation." Its cover is nipple-pink, the lettering nipple-plum. It says, this surgery will reshape your breasts, it will not reshape your life. The chair Sallee is sitting in is nipple-brown, old nipples.

Sallee hops up onto the examination table and unbuttons her buttons, unlatches latches.

"Small breasts are not necessarily bad," the doctor says, lifting each breast under the nipple to test its weight.

"Take the pictures," Sallee says.

The nurse comes in with the Polaroid and takes a picture from the front. A picture from the side.

The doctor, the nurse, and Sallee pass the pictures around.

"Make sure they keep track of your nipple," Suzie says when Sallee tells her about the surgery. Suzie is Sallee's twin. I am the only sibling who is not a twin.

"Tell the *surgeon*," Suzie says.

Our great aunt Lila is missing one breast and one eye on opposing sides of her body. At family reunions, she won't allow the children to stand on the side of her missing breast.

"Never take chances with cancer," she says.

So the kids sneak up on her blind side and pop gum in her ear.

Sallee used to become nervous when our mother balanced the younger twins, Ethan and Eric, on her hips. She would stand in the doorway, swaying from side to side. Ethan would clutch her shoulder. Eric sometimes fist-balled his hands and let go. As they got older, their heads became haloed in blond curls and their feet touched, toes intertwined.

"Don't let them fall!" Sallee would holler.

Sometimes, even now, when our mother is standing alone, absorbed in her thoughts, she sways.

Now the twins look at Sallee and say, "I sure hope you don't get momma's tits."

Momma's tits are the kind of tits one controls with stiff cotton bras and broad underwires. At Christmas, momma wears all of her jewelry at once. The necklaces lie out over the shelf of her breasts like a soldier's medals.

My friend Margie went to St. Marks to have her breasts lifted. To do that, the doctor takes the nipple off, cuts a keyhole high on the breast, cuts a wedge of skin from underneath, sews the edges of the wedge together, and puts the nipple into the keyhole. When the surgeon was working on Margie's second breast, after he'd sewed the wedge together underneath, he asked the nurse to hand him the nipple. The aluminum saucer was empty. Everyone in the room sucked in their breath. Got wide-eyed. The nurses, anesthesiologist, and surgeon starting checking around their shoes.

Outside, in the hall, an orderly slipped and fell. As he pulled himself to his feet, he noticed something flesh-colored stuck loosely to the inside of his surgery greens.

This story, Sallee says, would never have made the light of day if Margie had gone under general anesthetic.

My breasts, in fact, are closer to my grandmother's on my father's side. Her name is Enid. Enid's breasts are empty puffs of fabric, curtain folds. Enid makes tea from the toast she burns. She makes her own soap from lye.

I have decided to do something liberating after my surgery. I have decided to wear two bras and burn my panties.

What they will take out of my breasts is either a mass of hardened scar tissue—scar tissue I got as a girl, a competitive swimmer who swam too many meters of the Butterfly—or it is cancer. Either way, I won't drag these to the grave.

from The Elements of Style		Derek Pell

THE
ELEMENTS
OF
Style

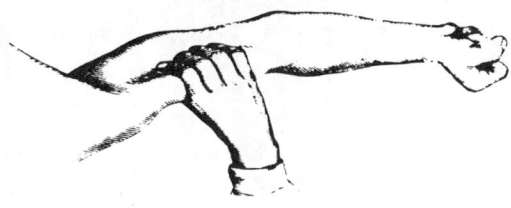

BY

The Marquis de Sade

*With Revisions, an Introduction,
and a Chapter on Writhing*

BY

E. B. WHIPE

THIRD EDITION

Painstakingly translated by Derek Pell

from The Elements of Style   Derek Pell

"Sade...[his] pornographic messages are embodied in sentences so pure they might be used as grammatical models."

-Roland Barthes
<u>The Pleasure of the Text</u>

a c h e k n o w l e d g e m e n t

The coauthor, E.B. Whipe, is most grateful to Miss Justine Strunk for her many sacrifices made during the preparation of this edition.

Copyright © 1987 by Derek Pell

from The Elements of Style   Derek Pell

Ronald Sukenick

The Flood

I - The Fifth Force
The Uncles used to tell a story about two business men who find themselves in adjacent deck chairs in Miami Beach. "So what do you do?" asks one.

"I'm retired," he says. "I had a fire that wrecked my store, so I took the insurance money and I came down here."

"The same thing happened with me," says the other. "I had a flood that ruined my store so I took the insurance and retired."

"A flood?" says the other man. "How do you start a flood?"

With Austyn, Sergio Biennale starts a flood.

She meets him at a dinner in Rue de la Tombe Issoire. Biennale is an avant-garde music maestro as well as an impresario who knows how to orchestrate business and art. He specializes in the new electronic music and has a scientific theory about the essence of sound. Biennale analyzes music as waves of vibrating electrons that are as much a matter of pure matter as a piece of meat. Music is simply a process of liberating energy from mass, a process that can be accomplished as well by a computer as by a human brain. Better, because more precise.

And once energy is released from the mass it floods all systems, overwhelming them and forcing them to establish new connections.

This does not merely pertain to music. It pertains to politics, for example. And to sex.

"Therefore," says Biennale, "I base my music on scientific principles. I am programming my computers to compose a suite based on the four fundamental forces of the universe—the strong force, the weak force, magnetic force and the force of gravity."

"You're forgetting the fifth force," says Ron.

"What's that?"

"The force of levity, that counterbalances the force of gravity, and that's essential for the continuation of sentient life in a universe of inert matter."

"Your friend is a comedian," Biennale says to Austyn.

"Perhaps he thinks so."

Ron is aware that five minutes after they're introduced they're chattering like machine guns in a way that makes it clear they don't want to be interrupted by anyone. Biennale has an attractive presence. He manages to project an air of Italian insouciance that does not undermine an almost Wagnerian seriousness. Tall, blond, blue eyed and rugged, he has a regularity of features marred only by a curious birth mark on his forehead roughly suggesting some alphabetical character.

When Ron asks Austyn about Biennale after they get home she just gives him one of those totally contemptuous stares.

Right after that Austyn starts going out every afternoon. She says she's working on a project at the music computer center. Wherever she's going, Ron can't help noticing that every evening she comes back in a happier mood. Great. The thought crosses his mind that she's getting it on with Biennale but as far as he's concerned at this point she could be getting it on with the Eiffel Tower as long as it improves her mood.

Austyn is wired. Biennale must whip her to frenzy. One evening she comes home with her ass so black and blue she can't sit down without a cushion. She says she fell down. She must have fallen down very thoroughly. Ron knows for a fact that Biennale leaves town about a week after he first meets Austyn, so their sex scene had to be brief. But it apparently starts a flood, a torrent of demonic energy in Austyn that Ron finds startling. She's transformed into some kind of diabolic dynamo.

It occurs to Ron that what she's always needed is to be whipped into the harness of some arduous task. It turns out after several weeks that she's going into business. The culture business.

You heard no doubt of the Do-It-Yourself Symphony fad of some years ago? Or the Do-It-Yourself Sonnet? That was Austyn. So also was the Do-It-Yourself Short Story and the Do-It-Yourself Masterpiece. Even the Do-It-Yourself Novel. Etcetera. The notion is surprisingly simple, if derivative. It comes out of the old avant garde idea of excerpting portions of any art work and then recombining them to get a new work.

Austyn's inspiration is to computerize the process. So you stick your Do-It-Yourself Symphony program in your PC, play around with it a little bit till you get some instant Beethoven, or Stravinsky, or any combination thereof, record it on tape and bore your friends with it.

You wouldn't believe the entrepreneurial effort that went into this project. If Austyn weren't a millionaire, she probably would have become a millionaire. Unfortunately the project was a little ahead of affordable technology, but she sold the idea for a tidy sum and kicked off her career in the home entertainment business.

The interesting thing for Ron to watch is that the more she gets involved in her business the less she's interested in sensuality. As she becomes a dynamo in work she becomes almost virginal in sex. It's as if Austyn is now complete in herself and doesn't need anyone else. As if she's now a whole person.

But now that Austyn is a whole person, there's something missing, something she had before that she doesn't have now, that Ron is hard put to define.

It's like what she had before was exactly something missing, something that she was struggling hard to find.

Now that she's found it it's a little anti-climactic.

Ron used to sense a tension in her, a potentially fertile anxiety. He had the sense about her that he never knew what she was going to do next that was the key factor in his attraction to her. He used to find her open ended, pun intended, and her open end excited him. Now she's more like a closed whole. But a whole that's missing something. An unwhole whole.

Ron suspects even then that the fact that she's become unwholly whole is Biennale's influence. Because he already thinks Biennale is a fake, as close to an empty whole as he believes anybody can get. He suspects that Biennale in some way has communicated to her a social disease through the medium of culture. A culture is a medium that does not merely foster the saving genius of a people, a culture also grows germs that can destroy the culture itself.

Biennale's effect on Austyn is to transform her from an interesting failure to a boring success.

Ron realizes that Biennale must have taught Austyn the rules of the game. And he senses that the rules of the game are not Jewish rules.

It's around this time that Ron's relation with Austyn disintegrates totally and he sees that they have to split.

But this episode gives Ron his first real clue about how the virus is communicated. This is when he decides to drop everything else and concentrate on his research.

II - Adults Only

Ron senses that Austyn's problem with him, and probably his with her, is that they're too much alike. Despite all appearances they are both afflicted with a certain innocence, an unworldliness in the way they deal with the world, almost as if the world doesn't really exist.

In what strange realm do they live, you have to wonder.

Even their vices have an air of artifice, as if they are something learned from books. The similarity is almost familial.

At some level they are both aware of this unworldliness and despise it. Life seems to be a disease they yearn to catch.

In Ron this results in a pursuit of vulgarity. Austyn on the other hand craves the intrusion of the alien, a penetration by the banal. Thus her desire for violation is much deeper than masochism.

The consequence of this syndrome for Austyn is a tendency to compromising situations and outrageous behavior.

If you are under twenty-one or easily shocked you probably should not read what follows. Unless you are accompanied by an adult or have a note from your shrink.

Ron can't say for sure, but based on some of the comments Austyn drops and a bit on his own imagination, this is how he thinks Biennale domesticates her demons.

Austyn goes to meet Biennale to talk to him about her avant-garde music project. She thinks he might be just the man to conduct her on-stage computer performance to its desired crescendo. And he quickly recognizes in her usual domineering impertinence a polar need to be subdued and broken. Just his meat.

Of course Biennale is very accommodating. But he insists first of all on a series of rehearsals. Anything else would be less than professional. He says he'd like to make sure the project is marketable, and if it isn't, redirect it toward a targetted audience. He says even culture has a bottom line. He quotes Robert Frost saying that everything has to come to market.

Austyn has a strong intuition that Biennale is the worst kind of sexist pig. But maybe even because of that, she feels a certain erotic curiosity. In any case, always practical, she acquiesces.

He begins by asking her to disrobe according to his precise instructions, while he sits in an easy chair and picks his teeth. Then he directs her through a series of gynecological maneuvers such as standing in front of him hefting her breasts, lying on a table in an obstetrical posture, masturbating for a while. His instructions have an exactness that's almost clinical.

At the end of this phase of the rehearsal he takes her temperature. Rectally, of course. He notes that it's starting to rise. Above normal.

Then gradually, judiciously, Biennale begins to caress her here and there, staying carefully away from the erogenous zones at first, but slowly shifting his attention to her lips, her nipples, her thighs, her rectum, her vagina. Then he starts with a vibrator. When he sees she's ready to come he starts applying his tongue, first to her nipples then her clitoris. At the first sign of the spasm he stops. Naturally she's horribly disappointed and asks him why. Instead of answering he makes her get down on her knees and lick his penis. It's possible at this point that he breaks out the whip, teaches her to beg.

This phase goes on for a while with repetitions, there's no need to get into the fat and gristle. In fact the details are the same, it's only the intensity of the experience that Biennale keeps increasing notch by notch. Suffice it to say that Biennale continues until he sees that she's a completely volitionless piece of needy meat, squirming helplessly under his ministrations.

By this point Austyn realizes what's happening to her. She's being domesticated. Trained.

Then Biennale starts making her come. As soon as she's finished with one orgasm he begins preparing her for the next, stimulating her with a frightening physiologicial accuracy. He does not, of course, use his penis, not at first. He uses his finger, his tongue, the tip of his boot, the end of a candle, a vibrator and even a small egg plant that happens to hand.

He threatens to use his penis. That is, he inserts the tip, rubs it around a bit, and then withdraws, substituting some other object in its place. Ron uses the word threatens because it has to be said that BIENNALE'S COCK IS HUGE, actually capable of inspiring a kind of titillated fear of impending penetration in the maidens who are conscious that they are about to experience its throbbing purple alien amplitude inside their bodies. To give you some idea, when Austyn sucks it, she can only get the very tip of the glans in her mouth and has to content herself with licking the rest. And she has a big mouth.

(Ron knows the doctrine is that size is not a significant factor, but Ron's female informants persist in reporting it is.)

In fact when Austyn first sees Biennale's cock erect spring out as he unzips his fly she recoils from it as from a jack-in-the-box. Her first, frightened thought is that it will never fit. And it's not as if the thing looks like it can flex and accommodate to a different size or shape—no, it looks like a rigid shaft of purple veined marble. And yet when he penetrates her with it he knows how to rub, and probe, and slowly stretch so that it suddenly slides in with a minimum amount of, yes, pain, but an overwhelming sensation of pleasure.   And of this thick, leaden column of pulsing meat Biennale has perfect knowledge. He is totally in control of his instrument. With the result that he can maintain it indefinitely within Austyn's writhing body as her spasms mount one on top of the next, wave after wave, until she subsides not for lack of further desire but of sheer carnal exhaustion.

"I'm all fucked out," she tells him. Lying there, sensuously limp, it flashes through Austyn's mind that she doesn't even like Biennale. But simultaneously she realizes that it doesn't matter that she doesn't like him and that not liking him even makes the pleasure he forces her to have more excruciatingly acute. She realizes he's made himself her master and you're not supposed to like your master or, rather, it's irrelevant.

Biennale immediately senses in her muscle tone a certain limp obedience, a surrender, a total submissiveness. He knows she's been broken. Only then does Biennale allow himself to come, shooting extravagant gouts of hot sperm into her shuddering womb, forcing her to come yet one more shattering time.

It's at this precise instant, Ron supposes, that Biennale communicates the virus to her, for the first time uncensored and unabridged. And she's grateful for it. She's not only grateful for the pleasure he's given her, but also for the pleasure she's been able to give him.

What Austyn doesn't understand about Biennale is that he has no pleasure in sex. He'd just as well eat a steak as fuck a woman, just as well take a shit as get an erection, just as well sneeze as come. For him it's a pure power trip.

From that moment on Austyn has only one gut level desire governing her psyche, an unwholesome craving to be mastered or, failing that, an urge to master others.

It's clear to both Austyn and Biennale that henceforth they can make music together. Computer or no computer.

From here on though, Austyn's commitment to culture begins to split. The performance side of her project, formerly self-expressive, turns into a powerful dynamic of consumer exploitation. The avant-garde side, after she stops rehearsing with Strop, turns passive, inert, virginal, an experiment in the purity of masturbation, ultimately concerning only her own psyche.

Jean Mainil

Pornography and Academe: Compulsory Introduction

> Recent decades have been remarkable both for their freedom of discussion about sexual matters and for the availability of sexually explicit materials. (Downs)

> Activists in each instance espoused largely monolithic interpretations of pornography, so public debate assumed an "all or nothing" quality. (Downs)

This paper is a reflection on the would-be over-availability of pornographic material and of the polarization of views on pornography. Lawrence Stone declared in 1985 that "before now, sexual libertinism has been confined to narrow elite circles, often around a court" and that the "dissemination [of pornography] among a population at large, as has occurred in the last 20 years, is a phenomenon unique in the history of developed societies" (36). That may be true, but research on literary pornography (part of the pornography shared by an "elite" in previous centuries) turns out ot be increasingly difficult. Reproductions and reprints of erotic or pornographic etchings and visual material in general are usually limited to a small number of subscribers, and libraries that have a copy of those rare books do not want to circulate them. In the case of books that are available in libraries, the University of Michigan Library, for example, has decided to put most of its erotic material "in the cage" (which means limited access) because such books have suffered theft and disfigurement in the early seventies. Under those conditions, it becomes easier to get hold of *Deep Throat* than of eighteenth-century etchings included in "pornographic" novels, and easier to call 1-900 numbers than the Yale library. The demand for both products is of course not the same, but I would like to stress that one should not accede to the "general spreading" of "pornographic" material without defining exactly what is understood by those terms. The pornography distributed at large is *not*, as Stone suggests, an extension of the pornography limited earlier to an elite, and such a mixture of identities makes it harder today to do any research on "elite" pornography. Still another form of pornography (a pornography that, historically, is thought to have an "artistic" value) is harder and harder to find: it is probably easier to tear a chapter from a book than to destroy all the latest issues of *Inches* or *Stallion*. This paper is a reflection on the visible spreading of what some people consider offensive pornography and its influence on the current reputation of research on pornography *in general*.

This paper also focuses on the polarization of opinions on pornography, which contributes to making research on pornography a risky business. While collecting material on French eighteenth-century erotic novels, I realized that most of the articles on pornography make the position of the author clear from the very beginning: many critics on pornography forget that, as Downs puts it, "pornography is neither all bad nor all good" and that "like many other things, it is a bit of both" (xix). Today the polarization of pornography becomes all the more obvious as it is called upon to play a role in the current P. C. debate.

In her address on "Free Speech, Hate Speech and P. C." at the conference on "The P. C. Frame-Up,"[1] Katharine MacKinnon insisted on the enforced silence of minorities and on the unacceptable nature of a coercive enforcement of inequalities ("bigotry") against which "P. C." is trying to react. In her speech, pornography is only a coercive enforcement of inequalities and a silencing of minorities' voices. As such, pornography appears (is literally "framed") in MacKinnon's speech between "flying swastikas, gay bashing and lynching."[2] Then the question of "free speech" or of "hate speech" becomes a rhetorical exercise. Such an approach is by no means exceptional. Pornography is a much talked-about issue, but framed as it is it also seems to be hardly open to discussion or revisions.

Discussions of pornography are ubiquitous, especially in the domain of the law and of legislation; from the state banning of video clips and records to the self-censorship of movie agencies or TV stations, the message is clear: people cannot be "as nasty as they wanna be."[3] Pornography is a fashionable cultural item, and the impulse to write about it may seem as "natural," as self-explanatory as if one chose to write about race and/or gender. Discourses on pornography will find a large audience, due to the "popularity" of the topic and its widespread use by the media,[4] but at the same time one becomes immediately suspicious of the individual who dares talk about it. Paradoxically, pornography as a subject matter is both ubiquitous and silenced. Pornography thus functions in a way similar to "sexuality" as Foucault's analysis has shown,[5] or as Susan Stewart puts it, "pornography's move toward exposure has as its referent a marvelous, even magical *hiding*"(164).

The conspicuous "hiding" of pornography can be interpreted in many ways. Andrew Ross, for example, stresses the "P. C." side of the story. For him, when straight male intellectuals are asked why they like pornography, they are likely to assume that their relation to pornography is perceived as somehow "wrong," "especially if the question is asked by a woman" (194).[6] Besides what Ross perceives as a certain uneasiness, the pornography consumer is further bound to fail to explain why he likes pornography. Not because of any lack of persuasive or rhetorical skill, nor because the odds are stacked against him in some absolute way. He cannot explain his desire for pornography because he cannot articulate his pleasure, he can only evoke the conditions under which it is likely to exist. In fact, we do not yet have a critical language for dealing with pleasure of this sort [. . . .] (194)

For Ross, the "popularity of pornography"[7] thus seems to be in contradiction with a certain impossibility for male academe to have a discourse on pornography that is not self-accusatory. But we should note that the question is loaded: men talk about pornography when asked to *justify* their consumption of it. There seems to be no possible distance between consuming pornography and talking about it: the distinction between the discourse on pornography and pornography as a social practice has disappeared.

Recent Criticism, or Pornography in Hiding

Because of this lack of distinction, many discussions choose to avoid the word and use substitutes such as "erotica," "eroticism," "indecency," etc. In one of the few articles dealing with the notion of indecency and literary illustrations in the French eighteenth-century novel, for example, Philip Stewart explains that he chooses to deal explicitly with "indecency" rather than with "pornography," stating that he is "inferring indecency as a less charged and less judgmental alternative to *pornography*, which may or may not be defined differently"(151). Stewart's choice is thus not motivated by a theoretical distinction but rather by the refusal to be perceived as confrontational. Stewart's title is a tactic of opposition that will make it possible for his article to be read by people who react negatively to "pornography."

Those who prefer not to resort to euphemisms will carefully frame the word "pornography." In a recent collection of articles edited by Michael Kimmel, men do not simply express their views on pornography, they actually "confront" it. One might immediately suspect that Philip Stewart's article and Kimmel's book raise gender-specific problems.⁸ For instance, is *Men confront Pornography* as a popular culture and interdisciplinary work subject to the same rules as a theoretical paper given by a woman critic at a famous academic conference? In other words, are "popular" works on pornography subject to rules of markets that are unknown to "academic" products? Is academic discourse on pornography also veiled? The best answer to these questions is provided by Eve Kosofsky Sedgwick in an article in one of the best-known critical journals published by one of the most theory-oriented presses about one of the most venerable institutions of language and literature.⁹

Entitled "Jane Austen and the Masturbating Girl," Sedgwick tells an interesting anecdote on her title which, as she explains, has already become "evidence" in the trial against pornography:

> Roger Kimball in *Tenured Radicals*—a treatise on educational "corruption" that must have *gone to press before the offending paper was so much as written*—cites the title "Jane Austen and the Masturbating Girl" from a Modern Language Association convention program quite as if he were Perry Mason, the six words a smoking gun: the warm gun that, for the journalists who have adopted the phrase as an index of depravity in academe, is happiness... (818, my emphasis)

Sedgwick's experience shows that the realm of sexuality must be banned *before* it is allowed to express itself.¹⁰ The quick recuperation of Sedgwick's title and research and its use as bearing witness to the "depravity in academe" implies first that "masturbation" and talking about masturbation are already depraved, second that a non-pornographic or explicit discourse *on* masturbation is unthinkable, and last, but certainly not least, that the canonized Jane Austen is not open to discussions about masturbation. Obviously, this confirms that, after all, the oppression and silencing of women is not a method limited to pornography.

Academe seems to subscribe to George Bush's declaration in the context of the investigation into the "leaks" during the Thomas hearings: X-rated allegations should be kept behind closed doors! In Sedgwick's case, the title was enough evidence to sentence her: she is, beyond reasonable doubt, guilty, guilty of being a terrorist or, even worse, an academic pervert. The advice given to anybody dealing with pornography is strikingly similar to the advice given to people who consume pornography for personal gratification: do it behind closed doors and do not talk about it: *talking* about pornography or sexuality is the same as *consuming* pornography. We have seen so far three reactions to pornography: the need to euphemize, to confront, or to hide behind closed doors. Such strategies are based on the lack of distinction between the discourse of pornography and a discourse *on* pornography.

The "ghettoization of pornography"

It is thus difficult to reconcile the presence/absence of the discourse(s) on pornography on a practical level. Its ubiquitous, public presence paradoxically reinforces the message that it should be confined to privacy and intimacy. The question is why such an ambivalent attitude or, to quote Gubar, why such a "ghettoization of pornography" (740)? Why such a silence, such lexical disguises or explicit confrontations?

As Susan Sontag suggested in a seminal article on "The Pornographic Imagination," "Pornography is a malady to be diagnosed and an occasion for judgment. It's something one is for or against. And taking sides about pornography is hardly like being for or against aleatory music or Pop Art, but quite a bit like being for or against legalized abortion or federal aid to parochial schools" (206). As the examples chosen by Sontag suggest, debates about pornography are as heated today as those on abortion. Pornography is *confronted* by its detractors but rarely *defended* by its proponents. Nobody comes to testify what good influence pornography had on their lives, sexual or other. Pornography is in other words never really defended for its own value: when it *is* defended, it is on the grounds that censorship is a violation of the freedom of speech. Pornography is thus defended like any other silenced discourse (thus losing its specificity) through a negative reasoning: we must have it because we cannot suppress it.

I would like to suggest that the reason why no "positive" discourse on pornography can exist is there is no such thing as a discourse on pornography that is not immediately recuperated as pornography. This is of course very puzzling in the context of academic criticism. Academe indeed depends on the distinction between genres: critical discourse can only exist if it shifts one genre into another, one novel, one play, or one poem into what is called a "critical essay" or "literary criticism." Why then is pornography excluded from such critical discourses? Why do we expect that any critical work on Picasso will not take the shape of a painting whereas Sedgwick's analysis of masturbation (and in this case Sedgwick's title) is immediately condemned for being pornographic or indecent?

A discourse on pornography is immediately suspected of morbid strategies, of a capacity to push the passive and unwilling listener into a trap by turning him/her into the position of voyeur whose position Andrew Ross describes as characterized by a "captivity," that is to say, a position that combines a collection of data and an imprisonment in the other's discourse ("as captors *and* prisoners"[Ross, 156]). A pornographic discourse (and that includes the discourse *of* pornography and *on* pornography) is always, and literally, too *captivating*: the seduction also means here imprisonment. This possible entrapment is probably what bothered one of Michael Kimmel's students when he was told he would watch sexually explicit material in class: and what if he got an erection?[11]

I wonder if the responses to Sedgwick's title do not reflect the same concern with physiological responses to "explicit" material. Were Sedgwick's detractors bothered by the panic turned-on MLA members would create? But to say this would be to assume that any discourse *on* pornography is a turn-on; after the example of Jesse Helms, who refused federal money for education on AIDS, declaring that information on condoms would only push the vices of Sodom to people who, it is assumed, would otherwise remain chaste. On the other hand, might there not be a connection between the fear caused by a woman announcing her intention to speak about masturbation in a work by a woman author and the structure of pornographic novels where women making love are observed by a male peeper who is first turned on and then introduced on the scene to provide the "necessary" object for a "normal" development of the coitus... (in those novels, intercourse is successful only if a man comes in to provide a phallus)?[12]

In Kemball's *Tenured Radicals* the scene has changed: the male critic is still there to watch (and in Sedgwick's case, even predict what has not yet taken place) and to remedy the situation by providing the "necessary" tool for the "normal development of the intercourse," in this case, not exactly intercourse, but academic dis/course. Men never could stand women's intercourse with one another or women's discourse on one another (especially when that involves their sexuality). Accordingly, the suspense provided by voyeuristic scenes in pornographic novels written by men for men (male characters must burst into the room at one time) is also working here, except that, in this case, Roger Kimball broke into the room before there was anybody else there....

Pornography vs. Pornographies

Pornography is thus a genre that polarizes opinions into two categories: people are for it or against it. Such Manichean judgments could of course be the result of ideological positionings. But it could also be the sign of a confusion as to what exactly pornography is. Susan Sontag was one of the first critics to stress that "no one should undertake a discussion of pornography before acknowledging the pornograph*ies*—there are at least three—and before pledging to take them one at a time" (205). For Sontag, these are pornography "as an item in social history," "as a psychological phenomenon," and as "a minor but interesting modality or convention within the arts" (205). Sontag chooses to deal with the last.

Within that category, a predictable objection is raised: a treatment of pornographic texts within the context of criticism and academe is hardly possible, since pornography is usually considered either of bad taste, or plain bad, boring. Pornographic art is considered to be an oxymoron because of the implicit consensus that a pornography that has an artistic value can no longer function as pornography. It is then called "erotica." Such a limitation of "subject matter" is further emphasized by the prohibition to deal, within already canonized authors, with themes that are supposedly associated with pornographic literature: masturbation, or sex in general. As the quick and virulent reactions to Sedgwick's title showed, the cohabitation of the words "masturbation" and "Jane Austen" in the context of an MLA session functions exactly like many pornographic texts in their use of blasphemy.[13] But then why exclude the possibility of irony and condemn the whole MLA session to be representative of the corruption reigning in academe?

The first prejudice that literary criticism on pornographic words has to face is that it is written with a bad intention, a libidinal one that is hardly considered appropriate to academic literature on canonical texts. One analysis of eighteenth-century pornographic texts written by Jean-Marie Goulemot and published in 1991 is entitled *Ces livres qu'on ne lit que d'une main*.[14] The quotation is from Jean-Jacques Rousseau, and it refers to "those books that one reads with one hand." According to the reactions caused by the treatment of a sexual theme in a canonical author, it is tempting to conclude that literary criticism on pornography is considered not only as belonging to these works that one *reads* with one hand, but that those critical works are also *written* with one hand. Masturbation in a "pornographic" text is thus worthless in terms of academic aestheticism. In a canonical author, it is ridiculous and degrading.[15]

Fast-Forwarding to the Good Parts

When dealing with pornographic texts, the reader/critic might be tempted to either stress or ignore the passages that are more sexually explicit. Each reader turns the text into a distinct narrative (as spectators of a porn movie would if they split into two groups: one fast-forwarding to the narrative parts, skipping the sexual parts, and one skipping the dialogues and fast-forwarding to the sexually explicit scenes). In her analysis of "Pornography and the Avant-Garde," Susan Rubin Suleiman opposes those two views in the context of Andrea Dworkin's analysis of Georges Bataille's *Histoire de l'oeil*. For Suleiman, "if the textual critics avert their gaze from representation," then "Dworkin cannot take her eyes off it" ("Pornography," 126). The consequence is that "she is so intent on looking at the 'scene and the characters' that she never sees the frame" (126). The comparison goes further and brings us to the remote control as a metaphor of reading: "Not unlike those consumers of pornography who skip the descriptions to get to the 'good parts,' Dworkin reads too quickly: she devours the text in order to get to its 'core,' or to change metaphors she traverses it without attention to its shape or the grain of its surface" (126). In another context, the same Georges Bataille[16] undergoes a similar transformation, not from a critical approach, but from editorial strategies this time. Sontag notices that the edition of one of Georges Bataille's *Madame Edwarda* in the *Olympia Reader* published in 1965 by Grove Press only translates the *récit* while it keeps the preface silent: "But, as she declares, *Madame Edwarda* isn't a *récit* padded out with a preface also by Bataille. It is a two-part invention—essay and *récit*—and one part is almost unintelligible without the other" (Sontag, 223). In other words, what some critics seem to stress (and what the publishing industry encourages) is the more sexually explicit side of works without paying any attention to the "frame" or the grain of the picture/text. Pornography, it seems, must be about sex. But it must be exclusively so. As such, pornography would be the only genre that is produced in a vacuum, that is not influenced by any other genre or theme.

Who Framed Magritte?

In her article entitled "Representing Pornography: Feminism, Criticism, and Depiction of Female Vision," Susan Gubar analyzes the "emergence of sexually explicit pictorial representations of women tied up or fragmented into body parts" (715). According to Gubar, such an analysis would be hard to do without taking into account "the surrealists in general and [. . .]René Magritte in particular" (715). Gubar's choice falls on Magritte's famous painting *Le viol* because "perhaps none of Magritte's portraits more shockingly fragments the female by turning her into a sexual body" (717). *Le viol* exploits techniques used by Magritte in other paintings such as "principles of association (the woman as first source of fluids), anatomical tricks (the female assistant sawed into parts), and the animation of the inanimate (shoes with toes and dresses with breasts)."[17] But *Le viol* goes even further than those paintings.

For Gubar, *Le viol* is a perfect example of the way in which paintings can contribute to "female violation." "Endowed with blind nipples replacing eyes, a belly button where her nose should be, the female face is erased by the female torso imposed upon it, as if Magritte were suggesting that anatomy is bound to be her destiny" (Gubar, 722). For Gubar, then, this painting articulates "the woman as genital organ," but an organ "monstrously impenetrable or horrifyingly solipsistic" (722). Ultimately, what constitutes the violation of the female spectator is the paradoxical status of women's sexual organs: "Even as it fetishizes female sexuality, *Le viol denies* the existence of female genitalia, for the vulva-mouth here is only a hairy indentation" (722, my emphasis). For Gubar, the solipsism of the body/face combined with a reduction of the face to a genital organ justifies the title of the painting and its implications: "The represented figure—robbed of subjectivity and placed on display like a freak—deserves to be raped: this is the only consummation which will penetrate her self-enclosure" (722). Characterized in those terms, *Le viol* will of course have very negative effects on women spectators:

> because such an image of mindless physicality justifies rape and thereby perpetuates an ideology of submission that can be understood as a clear-and-present danger to women, it might

be viewed by some observers as an example of precisely the sort of pornography which should be censored as not only unartistic but as anti-artistic: from this perspective, the painting itself rapes the female spectator by objectifying her sexual parts and thereby robbing her of her humanity. (722)

Because of its coherence and its emphasis of the slicing of the female body and denigration of female sexuality, this analysis is of course very convincing. But after a second reading, a "frame" suddenly appears.

Magritte's painting is after all entitled *Le viol*, "rape." The whole frame of the painting is thus one of sexual violence. Gubar says that the painting represents a woman who *deserves* to be raped and that the painting condones rape. I would argue that the disturbing hideousness of the work of art could be seen as a moral condemnation: a refusal to aestheticize rape. This refusal becomes obvious when we compare Magritte's *Le viol* with Ruben's *L'enlèvement des filles de Leucippe*,[18] Van Cowenburgh's *The Rape of the Negress*,[19] or Fragonard's *Le verrou* or *La Résistance inutile* ("The Useless Resistance"). These paintings in fact aestheticize violence against women who are held or tied up and who are just on the point of being raped. In *The Rape of the Negress* the rapist, pointing at the woman (held by another naked white male), is looking at the viewer with a smile/grin of complicity...

In her article on Magritte, Gubar refers to the title which she identifies as the ultimate justification of the painting and what it represents: *Le viol* invites to rape such a mute and solipsistic sexual organ. In a second reference to the title, she interprets it as metaphorically referring to "veiling and unveiling" ("le voile") and to the image of a violin ("le violon"), interpretations that euphemize the title and its connotations of power and violence (723). In her successive interpretation of the painting, Gubar hardly refers to the *first* meaning of the word "rape": for her, rape is either a euphemism, a poetic image, or it simply needs to be *contextualized* (a way of dealing with rape that is not uncommon to court procedures where defense attorneys relentlessly try to accuse the victim of having put herself into a position where the *context* makes the use of power justified or even transparent, a position where "no" could also mean "yes"). Situating Magritte's painting, Gubar tells us, for example, that in the surrealist context, *Le viol* could be interpreted as flaunting "the mind-body split at the center of Western culture, [taunting] the prudery that teaches us to cover the body and not the face, and [joking] that love is blind." In this context, "the face of the beloved *is* her body and vice versa" (723). I wonder why the notion of love is introduced here, after feminists fought for rape to be classified as violence rather than sexual conduct.

In her analysis of Magritte's painting Gubar seems to do exactly the same kind of fast-forwarding as Dworkin when reading Bataille; she cannot take her eyes off the sexual details. *Le viol* may well be about a woman who is "simultaneously decapitated and recapitated by her sexual organs" (722). But it *also* represents rape. If *Le viol* is an allegory, we could suggest that the woman on the painting stands for the image of the woman in the mind of the raping man. Magritte's inversion of body and face is a powerful denunciation of the fact that rape is about power and violence rather than sex. The displacement of the woman's body to her face shows that sex itself is rather irrelevant in that case. More important here is the fact that the rapist has the power to transform the woman's body into a mute and blind face. Why in this particular case should we annihilate the artistic distance between the artist and her/his creation? Why then even bother to make a distinction between Mary Shelley and Frankenstein? Keeping in mind the sketch where Freud's head is replaced by a woman's body (*What is on a Man's Mind?*), we could in fact reformulate Magritte's painting as being about a similar question: *What is on a Raping Man's Mind?* Gubar's analysis forgets the frame. What Suleiman saw in Dworkin is valid here. By their insistence on the sexual, both Dworkin and Gubar flatten out Bataille's story and Magritte's painting, turning them into artless pornography.

Pornography: "Writing on Prostitutes"

Pornography is a relatively new concept in the history of western thought. As the *OED* testifies, the first recorded use of "pornography" goes back to 1864 when it meant the "description of the life, manners, etc. of prostitutes and their patrons." Today's meaning is decribed as "the expression or suggestion of obscene or unchaste subjects in literature or art" (*OED*). According to such definitions, what is pornographic is the *subject matter*, not the way in which it is depicted.[20] New definitions of "pornography" following birth of the cinema and the VCR share one characteristic: they aim at legislation. A good example of this is the Minneapolis Ordinance drawn by Catharine MacKinnon and Andrea Dworkin, which defined pornography as "the sexually explicit subordination of women, graphically or in words."[21] Such a definition stresses violence against women, but it does not focus on representation.[22] If the term "pornography" becomes inevitably linked with violence, it can no longer encompass depictions that are sexually explicit but are *not* violent.[23]

Debates on pornography erase the frame of pornographic narratives. For them pornography is a transparent looking-glass, not a mode of representation. Susan Kappeler was among the first critics to raise the problem in her book appropriately entitled *The Pornography of Representation* where she reminds us that "pornography is not a given entity in the world, but the construct of particular discourses" and that "pornography is not a special case of sexuality; it is a form of representation" (2-3). Kappeler takes the slippage from "pornography" to "porn" as a sign that "the traditional debate has focused on 'porn' at the expense of 'graphy,' an emphasis duly reflected in the customary abbreviation to 'porn'," which has come to mean obscene and violent sex.[24]

But Why Analyze Pornography Anyway?

The evolution of the meaning of the word pornography has thus helped transform research on pornography into a suspicious field. By stressing the violent and degrading side of pornography but mostly by defining pornography as a transparent discourse not open to manipulations, by characterizing pornography as a mere mirror of violent patriarchal desires, current debates have drawn attention away from the manipulative and ironic powers of the pornographic discourse. Believing that pornography only includes sexually explicit and violent depictions of women makes it possible for some to envision the total eradication of the pornographic world and to rewrite the whole legislation in that direction.

But is pornography really transparent? Does it really create images that in turn promote violent and degrading sexual attitudes towards women? Do pornographic pictures or narrative *dictate* sexual practices to their audience? Does pornography function as broadcast recipes where we are told exactly what to do at what temperature, for how long, with what instrument, and to what end?

Kappeler reminds us that "sex or sexual practices do not just exist out there, waiting to be represented" but that "rather, there is a dialectical relationship between representational practices which construct sexuality, and actual sexuality, each informing the other" (2). Kathy Myers goes even further when she declares that "questions of representation and of pleasure cannot be separated" because "rather than seeing power as a force which 'represses' or 'holds down' our sense of pleasure and sexuality [. . .] power actually produces forms of pleasure and sexuality" (198). Because power can be appropriated, "images themselves cannot be characterized as either pornographic or erotic"; such categories can only exist "by looking at how the image is contextualized through its mode of address and the conditions of its production and consumption" (198). Myers does what so many critics have avoided doing: she contextualizes pornography, putting it within the frame of its production and of its reception. Such a critical approach is necessary before we can start to analyze the concrete and specific influence pornography can have on its consumers. Such an approach to pornography as the locus where power manifests itself is necessary if we are to understand in what *context* an image may be perceived as pornographic. In her article "Towards a Feminist Erotica," Myers's analysis of a pornographic image side-by-side with an advertisement picture illuminates ways in which a "hidden pornography" functions in the advertising industry. Instead of pushing pornography into hiding, such an analysis points to more general and massive manipulations that *are* taking place in our society but that are already in hiding, hidden.

Pornography as rewriting (as it is used in the advertising industry) could also be used by women in order to manipulate power, to generate another desire, and to throw light on forms of violence that have become institutionalized. In a chapter entitled " The Politics and Poetics of Female Eroticism" from her recent book *Subversive Intent*, Susan Rubin Suleiman analyzes possible ways for women to have "control over their bodies and a voice with which to speak about it" (121). Suleiman analyzes strategies that have made it possible for women to create "a self-conscious reversal of stereotypes" and a "reversal of roles *and* of language, in which the docile or bestial but always silent, objectified woman of male pornographic fiction suddenly usurps both the pornographer's language and his way of looking at the opposite sex" (121). Lucienne Frappier-Mazur has also provided analyses of "erotic" novels by women and their transformation of lesbiansim and power relationships—pornography by women about women for women.

Would doing away with pornography improve women's predicament, or should the "risk of appropriation by men invalidate producing erotic imagery for women" (Myers, 202)? Would the total prohibition of "sexually explicit" material not also lead to a complete silencing of women's voices? To make sure that the representation of women's sexuality by women authors is not discriminated against, we need to define what exactly is sexually explicit. Are the conditions for straight, sexually explicit material the same as for lesbian, sexually explicit material? *L.A. Law* provides an interesting case in point. In the February 7, 1991, episode, two women lawyers (one of them is C. J. Lamb) kiss: action is immediately taken against all the sponsors of "the lesbian-kiss episode."[25] The boycott of Rolaids, Listerine, Pearl Vision,

Colgate, and others by the American Family Association is indeed proof that if straight kisses invade our screens, it is on the other hand not OK for two women to kiss because such an act transgresses the sexual reality of our moral majority. If "sexually explicit" material is banned and outlawed, will it not be increasingly difficult to "account for women's pleasure in looking at images of women" (Myers, 198)? Will such "a general restriction of access to sexual information and sexually explicit material" not become "a constraint particularly damaging to women, who were historically denied this access" (Ross, 187)? The prohibition of so-called sexually explicit material could have a disastrous effect for women and for sexual minorities. A kiss may be sexually explicit, but ultimately that depends not on how it is performed but on who kisses whom. When women critics are not allowed to speak of sexual self-gratification in Jane Austen, panels on Henry Miller and Norman Mailer will still be very popular, and panels on Melville and Whitman will have large audiences (as long as the speakers do not mention homoeroticism). Without the rewriting of classical pornography from the point of view of silenced minorities, forms of violence to which we have grown accustomed and which have become transparent for us will never be denounced.

The question remains: why such a compulsory silence over arguments on pornography? Why such polarized opinions? I wonder if it is because women are only starting to use pornography to their own ends. Is it because for the first time, women are able to modify generic and cultural models of sexuality and textuality?[26] Is the word "cunt" shocking when it is used after a first-person possessive adjective in a woman writer's text?[27] Is the war against pornography another sign of the institutionalization of woman's body, its reinscription, not as a sign of pleasure, but increasingly of reproduction? When counsellors have to obey federal laws that prevent them from distributing information on choices that only women should make, it is hardly imaginable that any woman will be allowed to speak about her body, about her desire, about her jouissance, about herself.

Notes

[1] Conference organized at the University of Michigan (November 15-17, 1991).

[2] The "cluster" of pornography and lynching was also a key element in another very famous debate: the Thomas hearings.

[3] That was at least the case in Florida for "2-live crew."

[4] "Pornography" was of course a key factor in the Thomas hearings. It was soon recuperated by President Bush, who declared in a TV broadcast interview on October 25 that "the X-rated allegations [against Judge Thomas] should have been kept behind closed doors." Bush's comments thus *stress* the allegations made against Thomas while insisting that they should have been kept private. By pushing the X-rating label on the allegations, Bush certainly did not contribute to the wished-for anonymity and privacy of the whole case. Bush's comments raise another question: can there be a form of sexual harassment that is not X-rated? If there is, can there be such a non X-rated *testimony* by a victim of such a harassment? For a discussion of testimony in the context of trials of pornography and indecency, see Susan Stewart, "The Marquis de Meese."

[5] See Michel Foucault's analysis of the "repressive hypothesis" in his *Histoire de la sexualité*, esp. vol. 1, *La volonté de savoir*. "The question I want to ask is not: why we are so repressed, but why do we say with so much passion [. . .] that we are?" (p. 16, my translation).

[6] Fred Small begins his article on "Pornography and Censorship" with those words: "Writing about pornography I shoulder two burdens: guilt and fear" (72).

[7]"The Popularity of Pornography" is the title of chapter six (*No Respect*, pp. 171-208).

[8]A problem raised by Ross (p. 194) and quoted earlier in this paper.

[9]Respectively, *Critical Inquiry* by the University of Chicago Press, about a Modern Language Association Convention.

[10]The Modern Language Association session that Sedgwick and two other scholars proposed was entitled "The Muse of Masturbation."

[11]Anecdote told by Michael Kimmel in his keynote address during the conference on "The Construction of Sexuality" (University of Michigan, October 5-6, 1991).

[12]I am here referring to pornographic novels by male authors intended for a straight, male audience. For a discussion of the manipulations of voyeurism by women writers, see Lucienne Frappier-Mazur ("Convention et subversion" and "Marginal Canons").

[13]The transgression of accepted norms (whether religious or sexual) plays a fundamental part in pornographic texts. Pornography must be transgressive.

[14]Jean-Marie Goulemot, *Ces livres qu'on ne lit que d'une main: Lecture et lecteurs de livres pornographiques au XVIIIe siècle* (Aix-en-Provence: Alinéa, 1991).

[15]For a discussion of the related "mental masturbation" and its connection with writing, see Sedgwick, 820.

[16]Along with Sade the French "pornographer" most represented in criticism.

[17] Gubar, 722. The techniques refer respectively to *La bouteille*, *L'évidence éternelle*, and *La philosophe dans le boudoir*.

[18] Appropriately reproduced on the cover of Susan Griffin's *RAPE: The Politics of Consciousness* (San Francisco: Harper and Row, 1986).

[19] The painting is reproduced in Edward Lucie-Smith's *Sexuality in Western Art* (London: Thames and Hudson, 1991: 93).

[20] Pornography is about prostitutes, but that does not mean that such a discourse has to be mimetic of their "activities." One of the best examples is a book written by Rétif de la Bretonne and entitled *Le pornographe* (*The Pornographer*) and subtitled "Prostitution Reformed." It deals with the history of prostitution, with the necessity of such an institution, with venereal disease, and with prices. It is anything but erotic.

[21] Minneapolis Code of Ordinance (MCO), Title 7, ch. 139.20, sec. 3, subd. (gg), (1). Quoted in Downs xi.

[22] It also raises a more important problem: should we then accept any kind of violence against women that is not sexually explicit? If violence is the key word here, it seems to be of little relevance if such a concept should be limited to sexually explicit material, unless of course what matters (and bothers us) is in fact the sexually explicit side of the representation. In that case, Philip Kaufman was right when, commenting on the original X-rating of his movie *Henry and June*, he declared that in today's movies, "you can cut off a breast, but you can't caress it." "It's Great Don't Show It!" *Time*, September 17, 1990).

[23] The evolution of the definitions of "pornography" favored the development of another term, erotica, which stresses the amorous and slightly (pleasantly) sexual side. But the distinction between erotic and pornography is itself subject to changes and strategic reappropriation.

Gloria Steinem, for example, opposes erotica and pornography in terms of gender: "Erotica is about sexuality, but pornography is about power and sex-as-weapon." As Andrew Ross situates the debate: "Anti-porn feminists who were skeptical of Steinem's distinction pointed out that this new definition of erotica rested upon a utopian orthodoxy of 'good sex,' [. . .] Ellen Willis described its emphasis on wholesome relationship as a 'goody-goody concept' and a 'ladylike activity' associated with the 'feminine' and not with the 'feminist'." The reaction was not long to follow in more hostile words. Gayle Rubin was quick to criticize what Ross calls "the erotic chauvinism of the 'erotica model' by calling it the 'missionary position of the women's movement'" (for a discussion of the whole debate on erotica vs. pornography, see Ross 185).

[24] Kappeler, p. 2. *Men Confront Pornography* is a case in point. The front cover separates porn- from -ography (while the appropriate separation into syllables should have been por-nog-ra-phy). As a consequence, the two most important words of the title are "Men" and "Porn." Here again, "porn" is stressed at the expense of "graphy" probably for marketing reasons.

[25] Those include American Express, AT&T, Chrysler, Colgate Palmolive, L'Oreal, Enterprise Car Rental, Grand Metropolitan (Alpo, Burger King, Green Giant, Haagen-Dazs, Pearle Vision, Pillsbury), Mazda, Reynolds-Nabisco, Subaru, and Warner-Lambert (Certs, Clorets, Efferdent, Hals, Listerine, Rolaids) (Wockner 16).

[26] For a discussion of pornography and canon by women writers, see Frappier-Mazur, "Marginal Canons."

[27] For an analysis of new coinage of words and expressions in the context of pornographic novels by women writers and their oppositional roles, see Susan Suleiman, *Subversive Intent*, more specifically ch. 6 ("The Politics and Poetics of Female Eroticisim," pp. 119-40).

Works Cited

Downs, Donald Alexander. *The New Politics of Pornography*. Chicago: University of Chicago Press, 1989.

Foucault, Michel. *Histoire de la sexualité*, vol. 1: *La volonté de savoir*. Paris: Gallimard, 1976.

Frappier-Mazur, Lucienne. "Convention et subversion dans le roman érotique féminin (1799-1901)." *Romantisme* 18 (1988): 107-19.

_____. "Marginal Canons: Rewriting the Erotic." *The Politics of Tradition: Placing Women in French Literature*. ed. Joan DeJean and Nancy K. Miller. *Yale French Studies* 75 (1988): 112-28.

Gubar, Susan. "Representing Pornography: Feminism, Criticism, and Depictions of Female Violation." *Critical Inquiry* 13 (Summer 1987): 712-41.

Kappeler, Susanne. *The Pornography of Representation*. Minneapolis: University of Minnesota Press, 1986.

Kimmel, Michael. "Preface." *Men Confront Pornography*. ed. Michael Kimmel. New York: Meridian, 1991: ix-xi.

Myers, Kathy. "Towards a Feminist Erotica." *Camerawork* 24 (March 1982): 14-19.

Ross, Andrew. *No Respect*. New York: Routledge, 1989.

Sedgwick, Eve Kosofsky. "Jane Austen and the Masturbating Girl." *Critical Inquiry* 17 (Summer 1991): 818-37.

Small, Fred. "Pornography and Censorship." *Men Confront Pornography*. ed. Michael Kimmel. New York: Meridian, 1991: 72-80.

Sontag, Susan. "The Pornographic Imagination." *A Susan Sontag Reader*. New York: Vintage Books, 1983: 205-33.

Steinem, Gloria. "Erotica and Pornography: A Clear and Present Difference." *Take Back the Night: Women on Pornography*. ed. Laura Lederer. New York: Morrow, 1980: 35-9.

Stewart, Philip. "Indecency and Literary Illustration." *The South Atlantic Quarterly* 90: I (Winter 1991): 111-52.

Stewart, Susan. "The Marquis de Meese." *Critical Inquiry* 15 (Autumn 1988): 162-92.

Stone, Lawrence. "Sex in the West: The Strange History of Human Sexuality." *New Republic* 8 July 1985: 36.

Suleiman, Susan Rubin. "Pornography, Transgression, and the Avant-Garde: Bataille's *Story of the Eye*." *The Poetics of Gender*. ed. Nancy K. Miller. New York: Columbia University Press, 1986: 117-36.

_____. *Subversive Intent: Gender, Politics, and the Avant-garde*. Cambridge: Harvard University Press, 1990.

Wockner, Rex. "The American Family Association has called a boycott." *Ten Percent* 2 (May 21-June 3, 1991): 16.

Ben Marcus

Urinating, A Forceful Endeavor

Facing the sun while urinating, a forceful endeavor to alter the architecture of a neighbor's house. The salve issuing from the genitals is partially loaded with a putty that is activated when the dick is aimed into the sun's arc. Fluid ascends an imagined rainbow and is animated by the heat, excited into an active chemical which returns in a steam of wind to the earth. After a short period of gestation, the fluid re-enters the body of the urinator, where it is mixed by a man named Bobby. Then the man who pissed into the sun starts to change. He tears the shit out of people's houses, for one. Full of his own piss, he'll level your fucking house and go on to the next one.

Michael Brodsky

from ★ ★ ★

Stu's body was all for advancing into the thick of the noise but held back by Jomm's elbowing shoulder it made do with peering over the glass partition. He made out a pair of thighs—middle-aged, male—entangled with another, younger, suppler, female. A perceptible shift in their engagement either in defiance of lookers or to accommodate some deeper interpenetration of parts still out of sight accompanied or paved the way for a warble from the innermost recesses of Dov's throaty chest: "Raw material for ★★★ is pretty much detritus from other projects turned via an acuity better than luck to the triumphant account of ours. Our raw material, Ms. Redmount"—as if speaking into a dictating machine; another realignment of the geary thighs—"should never on any account turn out to be what we initially craved, that is, if ★★★ production is to remain smooth. Understand?" Even if she didn't her ankles, both braceleted, did for with sudden alacrity they abraded like kindling wood, necessitating or simply—whimsically—occasioning a shift whereby the receptionist's hand, also braceleted, was now visible stroking Dov's still manly crotch, rife with greying hair. "For what at the outset we wish with all our heart to take as raw material rarely has anything to do with inherent suitableness, I mean, for the ★★★. Note:

I'm not talking *received ideas of suitableness.*" Her fingers clutched his erect organ, her way, no doubt, of begging for more. Dov willingly obliged though he did gently remove her hand from his cock, as if such contact could only obstruct the flow of his instruction. "We wish to seize—to acquire—so as to be (mis)taken for cultivated, wise, supreme—what we have no right to possess. The raws we would, if led by our essentially reactionary aping instincts, recruit to what we flatter ourselves is the cause are mere bric-a-brac, residue of anterior struggles, not even our own. Damn them, I say—I mean: the protagonists in those struggles. They are no mentors for *us.* Now"—he led her hand back almost brutally, now to the brownish vicinity of his balls, as if to say: Listen very carefully!—"if only instead of repudiating this eager caution—We should repudiate nothing—we could make it the obverse driving force—the inverse nisus, as it were—of a new consecration, to bringing forth and deploying, or rather"—here Dov writhed in an expiring ecstasy. "If only this eager caution to appropriate already appropriated raws, which is but the obverse of its own impetuosity, could become and in no quasi-mystical sense a raw itself, temporarily of course, and thereby orient and guide us toward the true raws, materials never before deemed constitutive, much less worthy, of rawness, newly discovered by us, for the only true raws are those we name as such for the very first time, are those we fight against discovering in their lean and primordial rawness, then I for one and one for all would never again fear for the life of the *** and for the factory sustained by that life. For you see, Guinevere, I have to prepare for when I am no longer in the picture." Licking his kneecap and fondling his buttocks Ms. Redmount, a.k.a. Guinevere, shook her head and murmured *a la cantonade,* if you please, "Routinization of charisma." "Exactly," Dov roared, taking lugubrious assent as an opportunity, like so many others, to plunge ever more deeply, beyond the false eyelashes and tinted hair, to the very heart of his houri. All through Jomm's turning to him in challenging imploration and his eyes bloodshot with outrage murmuring something to the effect that there was no knowing the raws in their rawness, primordial or otherwise, inasmuch as with whatever tools—adzes, lasts, lancets—were at hand those raws always must be deformed in advance of any legitimate knowing so as to pass muster with experts not on the subject of raws but of tooling the raws according to the specifications of some institution yet to be conceived, Stu did not respond, simply went on watching them fuck if that was what they expected him to call it, and though the motions and the shifts in motion were invariably the same motions and the same shifts, maybe a little more intensity of thrust here, a little less vehemence of impassioned kneading there, Stu did not in the least tire of watching, in fact the more the motion remained the same motion the less he tired, in fact he no longer understand the meaning of the word *tire* for to tire of something invests that something with greater or lesser plenitude over time and here, glued to this medium, glue in this his very own medium, he lost all sense of time, either passing or folding back on itself in incipient horror of the refusal to exacerbate or repair. More to the point though of less interest, there was no question of boredom for very quickly he, Stu, had become attuned to, that is, impatient for, new meanings, new scales, of excitement and subsidence, of vehemence and retrocession. At first he assumed it was sweet nothings Dov was now whispering in the ear of the receptionist. However, stumbling over Jomm and stooping for a better glimpse, for the act had a strong, if idiosyncratic, pictorial force, the act, that is, of whispering, of seeking the contiguity of one's tongue with another's lobe, he realized that ever the man of business Dov was proceeding with his disquisition on the life of the raws.

"Did yesterday's shipment land as anticipated?" As if to provoke unparalleled heights of recall he introduced not one, not two, but three fingers into her vulva. With seasonal juices outward streaming she replied, "Exactly as anticipaaaaaaaaaaaaaa," her voice and his dissolving rapturously into a juice all their own. "It's clear then," sucking on first one tit then the other as if her body was no better than a balance sheet, all the time plunging ever more wildly, so what if occasionally missing the mark. "Clear," she murmured, questioning, Stu thought. But once he had thumb and forefinger of one hand gently rubbing the more erect of her [two] nipples and thumb and forefinger of the other circling the still point within what Stu assumed from his reading must be the Gordian knot beneath her pubic hair and once he managed to combine these movements, nothing in themselves, with the following incantation, also nothing in itself: "You are my private secretary, you are my very own personal administrative assistant with auxiliary duties, you are making your name in the company," once all that was nothing in itself had been synchronized far beyond trivial questions of self and nonself, she, Guinevere Redmount, gave forth a simple affirmative, "Yes, clear." "Clear," she rejoined, after the briefest, might one even say the most refreshing, of pericoital pauses, at which point grasping his cock with the bejewelled fingers of both hands and smiling that lacquered and celestial smile peculiar to receptionists with promotion on their mind: "My notion—everybody's notion—of the raws should somehow oscillate around the fixed point of a misconception, namely, that motored by the eagerness to produce, bring forth, deploy, only what long before somebody somewhere managed to construe—to everybody's satisfaction—as authentic raw. Preoccupation with raws should somehow be subject to, obstructed by, this mechanism of an overeagerness to bring forth what already has been proven grade-A raw material even if now more and better than ever we know the only conceivable raw material is that at first inconceivable, particularly to ourselves, yet which we discover for ourselves, prompted by nothing extrinsic except perhaps the necessary dysphoria of the moment"—in response to Dov's inaudible whisper: "Sorry, not dysphoria. Urgency is a better word."

As if to show his appreciation for such fluency and at the same time prove the appreciation was purely disinterested, in other words, that the receptionist was not, like all other flunkeys of all other genders, simply spewing forth what she had dutifully memorized prior to this meeting of the minds inside the genitalia, Dov shook his head, over and over and over, incredulous to the last, eventually yoking the headshakes to a licking of her welcoming vulva with his overheated tongue, or rather, her overheated vulva with his welcoming tongue. As far as he, or his tongue, was concerned, the headshaking dispelled all doubt that he may have schooled her in such breviloquence for what did the headshaking prove but that he himself was hearing this outburst for the very first time and was mightily impressed with its thoroughly original perspective on what, though timeworn material, was now new and fresh to his ears. Here she was licking his, first the right, then the left, managing at the same time to insert a leisurely finger up his hairy old rump. He howled, almost wept for joy, but it was difficult, at least for Stu, to determine whether the weeping, now akin to a howling, was in consequence of the finger up his rump or delicate wind of lips applied straying across the weary old lobes. Neither was there any hope of shifting from one interpretation to the next so as to extract from their unlocalizable *between* its warty old turd of a raw: something about the state of affairs militated against the prospect of so clearcut an indemnification.

  Slowly disengaging his still long and ever hard organ from the precincts of her person, Dov smiled all the while as if to say, but what it was he was in some way saying escaped Stu entirely, that is, until he actually came out with: "But let me ask you this,"now haphazardly scratching the Redmount's groin rather than attentively, lovingly, attempting to give, or rather, bring her pleasure, on a salver of salvos, so to speak. "Yes," she yawned, hopefully awaiting more tenderness. "Why," plowing right past her expectation, "is it so crucial to the well-being of the raws and to the factory, whose well-being depends on their miscegenation, that preoccupation with their doings take the form of an overinsistence on conformation to the contour of bygone raws? Why, I ask you, why?" Dov seemed to have lost sight of her, as well as her pubis, amid the incandescence of his own preoccupation. "Because dammit," he shrieked, forgetting that for a lover delicacy was *de rigueur*, pounding as if the center of her body was mortar and he the pestle, "it is in our hopeless effort to wrench the fresh and new into sodden conformity with the stale and putrid that at last and in spite of ourselves we stumble for the first time on the authentically raw."

Having witnessed so tender and buxom a scene, albeit no different from that witnessed by his coworker, Stu was now inexplicably invested by that coworker, tucking in his silk shirt and adjusting his silky tie as he awaited him at the entrance to the men's room, with a certain worldly charm. Jomm wanted to know "all about" Sylvie de Redmount. As if Stu had anything to tell. "What is raw material, Stu?" he asked in a humble mewling tone that Stu immediately detested because it was false, far more to itself than to all interlocutors, past, present, and to come.

Rikki Ducornet

Picotazo and Extravaganza, *from* Birdland

When Picotazo made love to Extravaganza, the vortex of his cowardice, the gaping maw of his alarm vanished, and it was as if he had come into the world fearless, staff in hand. In Extravaganza's arms, his torment was melted down and reduced to a sweet honey which she extracted fearlessly. Her tender body gave itself utterly and unabashedly; being simple and having no notion of evil, she was an Edenic animal seized by heat. Her eyes and cunt wept with happiness; her breasts filled the poet's mouth like those magical fruits which are renewed just as they are eaten. The feast was an eternal feast, or so it seemed, and the nights they spent together, all too swiftly done, somehow sprawled into infinity, abolishing not only terror, but self and time.

      Because it seemed to Extravaganza that, in her poet's embrace, her body dissolved and reorganized into infinite series of animate and inanimate things—sea urchins and clamshell rattles, ivory clappers, ferns and fishskin drums—once she had surfaced from the oceans, lakes, burrows, nests, marshes, mud, sandpits, oysterbeds and whirlpools of love, she battled bewilderment, unsure of where she was and, for that matter, *what* she was. Standing stark naked and quivering before her foxed mirror, and slapping her sweet ass with her open palms she would cry, as if surprised: 'I am a *human* female!'

The poet entered into a loving and a living dream which claimed him even when awake. All day long Picotazo was haunted by the nights which, as the seasons progressed, hung strung together like amber beads on a golden wire. These he gnawed and worried in his mind. Dazzled by love, Picotazo's cock and heart had become one and the same animal.

These were blissful days and weeks—the most delightful of their lives. Picotazo, transformed, abandoned a pretentious and patriotic work to devote himself to an inspired poetic revery on the nature of sensual love. Convinced that he had entered the secret chamber of an occulted mystery, he took it upon himself to reveal the prodigy to the vast world. His verse was a steaming milk, a wizard's ink—and it rained upon the page, page after page. As Extravaganza slept, or sucked a plum, or beside the open window combed out her hair which, free of ribbons, tumbled to her toes—Picotazo described in amorous detail love's multiplicitous vocabularies of salutations and smiling receptions, overturning the natural realm in order to ambush the metaphorical creatures which would do desire justice; for example: *The Gazelle, (Or: When The Beloved Attempts To Flee The Arrow)*; *The Lion (Or: Embracing, The Lovers Are Encircled By An Invisible Yet Palpable Mane Of Fire)*. And because he had not forgotten how a fish had unlocked his once solitary and offish heart, Picotazo called his favorite embrace (although hard-pressed to name as favorite, as in bed with Extravaganza each act of love precipitated and included all the others)—that embrace during which the female, mounted from behind and knowing that the molten ring of her delight has moored her lover utterly, brings her thighs together as best she can, and the male, pushing his way in even deeper—as if that were possible—clutches his mistress' breasts to further anchor himself—this position the poet called: *The Carp*.

After a convoluted correspondence with the university rector and the chief librarian, Picotazo was given permission to contemplate—in the company of a Consultant to the Holy Office of the

Inquisition—an ancient manuscript from India which proposed entire zodiacs of love in the shapes of copulating animals and mythic beings: blue gods and mortal women—black and white; red goddesses and mortal men—white and black. As the poet contemplated the book in a fever, the Consultant groaned and agitated his censer.

In the fragrant mornings, the garden ablaze with butterflies, parrots rioting in the trees, Picotazo would return to work:

> My beloved's body is a delirious moon
> A garden where foxes paw and suck the grapes
> Her body is a vine plundered by foxes,
> A tempest in a forest, a rain of black honey.
> Her body is my darkness, total, luminous.
> Her body is a rose of beaten gold;
> It burns against my heart.

Extravaganza was dreaming and nothing could stop her; enchantment bubbled forth to inundate her soul with an effervescent water. Rather than eat breakfast, the lovers lay together until late, their tongues touching—and she would whisper the tumult of visions which, flooding the night, had submerged her. The poet listened to her eagerly, his cock throbbing between the buttocks of his beloved, his fingers lovingly investigating her wet fur.

Often, as she would describe some astonishing dream which might include thunderstorms and weirdly horned and pelted animals, or floating cities constructed of mother-of-pearl and brass, or harems wherein all the houris had the faces of ibises or tigresses, yet were in all their other parts human and sweetly formed, the poet would grasp his bride by the thighs and pull her to him. Compliant, already yielding, she would yield further, and for a time the telling of the dream would cease. Then, but for the sound of their breathing, and the acute hammering of their blood, and the creaking and thudding of their wind-swept vessel, their chamber would fall silent.

Once, Extravaganza awoke wildly laughing. As she explained to Picotazo, in her dream she had seen the face of God. She recognized the nose at once—it was her lover's cock; the apples of His cheeks, Picotazo's balls. The Lord's beard, hairs upon hairs, curls upon curls, and the place from which He spoke and breathed the breath of life— was her own splendid cunt.

Pasquale Verdicchio

Censoring the Body of Ideology: The Films of Pier Paolo Pasolini

Pier Paolo Pasolini, writer, film-maker, and essayist, is possibly the most controversial figure in modern Italian culture. His debut in writing consisted of a slim volume of verses written in his mother's dialect of the Friuli (a depressed region of Northern Italy), previewing the author's subsequent interest in subaltern[1] cultures. In the late 40s, as a teacher and active member of the Italian Communist Party (PCI) in the Friuli, he began to suffer the animosity of conformist forces of the time. Pressed by a local priest to resign from the PCI, he refused. As a result of this he was denounced for making advances on his young male pupils. The ensuing scandal caused him to be relieved of his teaching position and to be expelled from the PCI in 1949. That incident brought into even greater conflict the already seemingly contradictory dimensions of Pasolini's life: homosexuality, Marxism, and Catholicism. This would color Pasolini's artistic expression and his rapport with society until his controversial death in 1975.

From 1949 to 1977, two years after his murder, Pier Paolo Pasolini was the subject of approximately 33 trials on various charges brought against him, his writings and films. These include: "offensiveness toward good customs and to the common sense of morality and decency" (for *Mamma Roma*, 1962); "contempt toward the state religion, under the pretext of cinematographic description, by mocking the figure and value of Christ through musical commentary, mimicry, dialogue etc." (for *La Ricotta*, 1963); "scenes offensive to the public decency in the depiction of intercourse between the guest and the maid, the woman of the house, and with the male components of the household, as well as the homosexual tendencies of the head of the household, the father, which are contrary to every moral value, social and familial" (for *Teorema*, 1968); "blasphemous, subversive, pornographic, indecent, etc." (for *The Decameron*,1971); "a film full of obscenities . . . nothing more than a series of vulgar exhibitions of sexual organs, all very clearly photographed," (for *Arabian Nights*, 1973).

While all charges take aim at what may most obviously be offensive to a sector of any population, they hide a more insidious challenge to cultural and ideological diversity. As a cursory viewing of any Pasolini film will reveal, the author does not merely seek to shock for its own sake, but rather to present a world view that is ideologically conflictual and compromising for the dominant culture. In order to negate the presence of alternative cultures, the dominant takes refuge in catch-phrases such as "public decency" and "common sense of morality and decency." So as to expose this strategy, in the article "Pornography is Boring" (1969),[2] Pasolini presents his own view of pornography in order to differentiate his work from it, and qualifies his dislike for pornographic films as a matter of aesthetics. At the same time, he condemns the censors who take it upon themselves to protect the morality of others, rather than pornography, which he considers dangerous to him as author. Because of the possibilities for censorship that pornography allows, it also functions to justify restrictions of all forms of expression. As a result, Pasolini argues, pornography becomes the pretext by which ideological expression is attacked and silenced.

What exactly is subversive in Pasolini's work? What scandalizes? Simply, the effectiveness of Pasolini's production lies in what he portrays; "it is something that scandalizes for being what it is. It scandalizes because of its nature: because for one reason or another it is a diverse nature."³ Pasolini proposes and produces art "as an exploration of the unsaid in common and official ideological discourses."⁴ Of great importance to this art is the author's own concept of "diversity." "Diverso," which would literally translate to "different," carries with it the secondary meaning of "diverse," and is used in Italian as a colloquialism in reference to homosexuality.⁵ In order to diffuse the negative connotations of the word, Pasolini set himself the task of infusing it with a sense of cultural importance and militancy. Though the concept was largely biographical at its inception, with time it acquired cultural and political dimensions by which the author sought to bridge various kinds of "diversity" (his homosexuality, the subproletariat, the Third World) in a common oppositional front against official cultures. As such, censorship, applied to a cultural expression not condoned by officialdom, becomes strictly a political exercise.

In Pasolini's view, the subjects of marginalized cultures, products of specific socio-economic conditions and/or a-historicity,⁶ represent their condition by their physicality, their bodies and sexual organs. And, since "the language of action or simply of offensive presence [is a] stage of prerevolutionary contestation,"⁷ these bodies must be silenced and rendered invisible. The uninhibited display of subproletarian bodies present in most of Pasolini's films is offensive to societal norms because it offers a code of being that demystifies the ideal body of bourgeois representation. The "language of action," aside from being the potential for revolution represented by those bodies, is also, literally, the spoken language, the dialects, the modes of expression of those marginal masses; these too stand as infractions of accepted codes of conduct and speech.

For the diverse, yet bourgeois intellectual that is Pasolini, to establish a bond with the groups he represents in his art, it becomes essential that he give up his own language and be initiated to a revolutionary one. Initiation into language takes place twice for

Pasolini: once into the language of Marxism, and then into the language of marginalized cultures (such as Friulano). The two are integrated and then restated in the author's own language of social critique which, through literary and filmic production, privileges specific sites (e.g., the body of the subproletariat) to engender a discussion of marginality, exclusion, repression, and confrontation. Pasolini's works are an attempt to dissipate the officiality of particular discourses by juxtaposing them to disparate elements. For example, in *Accattone* (his first film), the verses of Dante or the music of Bach, very obviously representative of a dominant cultural code, are used as backgrounds for the actions and bodies of subproletarian characters. Such acts of transgression are not easily forgiven by the keepers of the code; as a result, the bodies scripted by Pasolini in his films, and the language that emanates from them, become the focus of the scrupulous defenders of the "common good."

Abjuration and Confrontation

The Decameron (1970), *Canterbury Tales* (1971), and *Arabian Nights* (1974) form Pasolini's "Trilogy of Life," a series of films in which the author's scope was to represent the revolutionary power of subproletarian bodies, and highlight their potential through the highly imaginative narratives of tales and fables. In his "Abjuration from *The Trilogy of Life*," Pasolini denies these films as an error in judgement.[8] But this abjuration was by no means a new strategy for Pasolini. He had described the frustration of not being understood in these verses from "A Desperate Vitality"(1964):

> Death lies not
> in being unable to communicate
> but in thefailure to continue being understood.

This then developed into feigned adaptation and conformism, as in this "Communique to ANSA [stylistic choice]" (1971):

> I have ceased to be an original poet, it costs
> freedom: a stylistic system is too exclusive.
> I have adopted accepted literary schemes
> to be free. For practical reasons, of course.

In his "renunciation," Pasolini takes a very cynical stance by which he claims that the bodies, meant to represent the last stand to the subculture of mass media and consumerism, were in fact doomed long before he made the film. The culprit was none other than the famed "economic boom" of the 60s, a phenomenon that threw Italy into the realm of post-industrialism and neo-capitalism, which Pasolini blamed for the cultural and anthropological decline of Italy.

However, criticism of his work, and accusations of a nostalgia for an irretrievable past, continued to be levelled against him. Pasolini's response to those who called for him to describe contemporary society, to show a conscience of the present, results in the rhetorical abjuration that comes to justify his last project: *Salò* (1975).

Salò, a loose adaptation of Sade's *120 Days of Sodom*, was Pasolini's way to revive the last days of fascism during WWII, and provide a hint as to the matrix for contemporary fascism's homogenization and objectification of the human body and being. The degradation of bodies, their use and abuse, torture, sadism, the corruption of eroticism and sexual relations, are the subjects of *Salò*. In effect, Pasolini believed that the fascism that had found fertile ground during the early to mid part of the century was never shed; it merely changed form. Consumerism, the new fascism, had, in his opinion, decimated the Italian subproletariat as it threatens to decimate the populations of the so-called Third World. Of course, *Salò* was no less susceptible to censorship than previous works. While Pasolini's early works had been threatening for their portrayal of the prerevolutionary potential of the subproletariat, *Salò* is subversive in its out and out identification of the perverse power of fascism.[9]

That fascism works its spell by insinuating itself as protector of accepted norms, order, and clarity is addressed ironically by Pasolini in the previously quoted "Communique to ANSA." Freedom through "accepted . . . schemes" is, of course, no freedom at all, but Pasolini succeeds in subverting this too in *Salò*. In fact, he gives prominence to the narrative of fascism by having each set of atrocities prefaced by the narrative voice of the captors. The scheme in *Salò* is much more direct than in other films and, as the fascist initiation of stories degenerates into the subjugation of the unsaid subjects, the "practical reasons" of Pasolini's rhetoric come to light.

Thus, one distinction between the *Trilogy* and *Salò* can be made at the level of communication. The works of the *Trilogy* still preserve a hope in the dialectic potential of the eroticism of subproletarian bodies, as communicative of their condition. *Salò*, on the contrary, dismisses any chance for communication through the total objectification of sexuality. The dialectic is wholly disrupted and interjected for the sole function of a system of consumption. Communication, or the lack thereof, defines eroticism and pornography, respectively, and *Salò* is Pasolini's accusatory finger by which he links fascism, censorship, and pornography. The film elicited a negative reaction even from those who had been supportive of Pasolini. Italo Calvino, in "Sade is Within Us,"[10] closes his essay with: "A 'moral' effect can be drawn from Sade only if the 'accusation' keeps its finger pointed not at the others but at ourselves. The 'place of action' can only be in our conscience" (111).

Complaining about how Pasolini was wholly discounting of Sade's intentions in *The 120 Days of Sodom*, and of how poorly that text transfers as a vehicle for the recounting of the last days of fascism in war-torn Italy, Calvino suggests that the film-maker was out of touch with the world in which he lived. But Pasolini was painfully aware of his inescapable situation as a privileged bourgeois intellectual in society, and the effect that the maintenance of the status quo has on those considered expendable. Calvino's suggestions may in fact be symptomatic of the very loss of diversity in contemporary society, and the conviction that pedagogically we are restricted to the lessons of the dominant culture.

In closing, I would like to suggest a reading strategy for Pasolini's films that undoes the accusations listed at the beginning of this piece. This strategy is dependent on an aspect of the filmic process itself, as outlined by Pasolini in "Observations on the Sequence Shot,"[11] where editing is described not merely for its practical function in *putting together* a film, but also as a descriptive concept for life, production, and death. In that 1967 article, Pasolini insists that the life of an individual, or a person's work, is comparable to the long sequence shot, that only takes on significance after its completion. Death becomes an important editorial component by giving a sequence its significatory start. In Pasolini's words: "Until I die, no one can guarantee to really know me, that is, to be able to give a meaning to my actions, which therefore, as a linguistic moment, can be deciphered only with difficulty . . . Death effects an instantaneous montage of our lives."[12] In concurrence with this definition, any attempt to edit an author's works before the end of his discursive reality is a premature act that can only be qualified as censorship. It is, in fact, as applied to works such as Pasolini's, a premeditated act meant to distort their nature in the eyes of society, and question both their worth and integrity. Partial or total censorship led to the removal of the films from theaters, to the cutting of scenes in some versions, or to the films being shown in porno theatres rather than regular-run movie houses.

Salò, in conjunction with the author's death, provides a revelatory glance backward that gives Pasolini's works a strength which may escape one if the films are viewed as individual moments of expression. This is not to diminish their value as singular pieces, merely to provide yet another viewing angle for this complex corpus. By splicing together the parts that spurred official censorship one may in fact have, as an end result, Pasolini's ideology represented most clearly. A censorship in reverse which brings to the foreground that which we would ordinarily not be allowed to see would both legitimize the excerpts, and deny censorship. By focusing attention on something other than the forbidden, censorship diverts attention from the true subject of the work as well as from its own function. In fact, in acting upon selected portions of a film or a body of literature, it becomes an act of violence against the ideas which the work seeks to represent. What we are not meant to see or hear are the parts that are connected by the interstitial frames upon which the accusations are based.

What we have in conclusion is a correlation between censorship and pornography, both of which negate communication and deny presence. Eros, on the other hand, is the possibility of reaching outside a given system, of reaching outside the norm in order to savor alternative presences. Eros is the force that strains a system and foresees its death. The move to censor the revolutionary eroticism of Pasolini's subproletarian bodies is also aimed at disrupting their communicative power, the threat of their presence. In Pasolini's eyes, the subproletarian body represents a challenge to consumer society's impure advance; its test of society brings upon it charges of subversion, making it a most likely subject for censorship.

A version of this piece was presented at the 24th Annual Spring Comparative Literature and Classics Conference at Cal State Long Beach, 1989, "Eroticism and Censorship in Literature and Film: International Perspectives." All translations from the Italian are mine.

Notes

[1] For this article, and to suggest how Pasolini viewed various cultures outside the dominant sphere, terms like subaltern, subproletariat, marginal, Third World, and other such designations of non-participation in the decision-making mechanisms of official cultures are interchangeable.

[2] "La pornografia e` noiosa," n. 23, 7 giugno, p. 175, in *Il Caos,* by Pier Paolo Pasolini (Roma: Editori Riuniti, 1981).

³ Ferrero, Adelio. *Il cinema di P.P. Pasolini* (Venezia: Marsilio Editori, 1977), p. 2. This attitude also marks a commonality with Neorealism, whose principal theorist, Zavattini, suggested that "to show poverty or oppression is to protest against it." Pasolini, however, found Neorealism a dead-end exercise. In his opinion the movement lost inertia and rested on the quoted proposition without taking it further into an ideologically active principle in society at large.

⁴ "Unsaid" should be taken to also mean censored, silenced, repressed, oppressed, as well as the lack of means of expression, which may or many not be related to the previous situations.

⁵ I prefer to translate "diversità" as diversity, rather than "difference," so as to avoid any connotation to the now overly used term originating in Derridian theory. Diversity stands for a liberating attitude toward the diverse, in its ability to diminish the relegation of the diverse to mere object, and to highlight the term's inclusive capacity and intention. "Differance," on the other hand, proposes a subject in a dominant or privileged position who searches for the "other." In this case, more often than not, the "other" is the other within the dominant, the "barbarian within," thus avoiding the question of plurality altogether. Pasolini's concept turns its gaze externally, not internally, to where subaltern and marginalized cultures thrive.

⁶ A-historicity is used here not to mean a lack of history, but exclusion from it, a further condition of the *unsaid*.

⁷ Pier Paolo Pasolini. "Cio` che e` neo-zdanovismo e cio` che non lo e`," in *Empirismo eretico* (Milano: Garzanti, 1971), p. 160.

⁸ Pasolini. "Abiura dalla *Trilogia della vita*," in *Lettere luterane* (Torino: Einaudi, 1976), p. 71.

[9] Other films, such as *Teorema* (1968) and *Pigsty* (1969) touched on similar ground. Their representation of the bourgeoisie and the capitalist machinery are tamer than *Salò*'s unmediated portrayals.

[10] Italo Calvino. "Sade is Within Us," in *Stanford Italian Review: Pier Paolo Pasolini The Poetics of Heresy*. Beverly Allen, ed., II, 2, Fall 1982, pp.107-11.

[11] Pasolini. "Osservazioni sul piano sequenza," in *Empirismo eretico* (Milano: Garzanti, 1971), pp. 237-41.

[12] Ibid., pp. 237-41

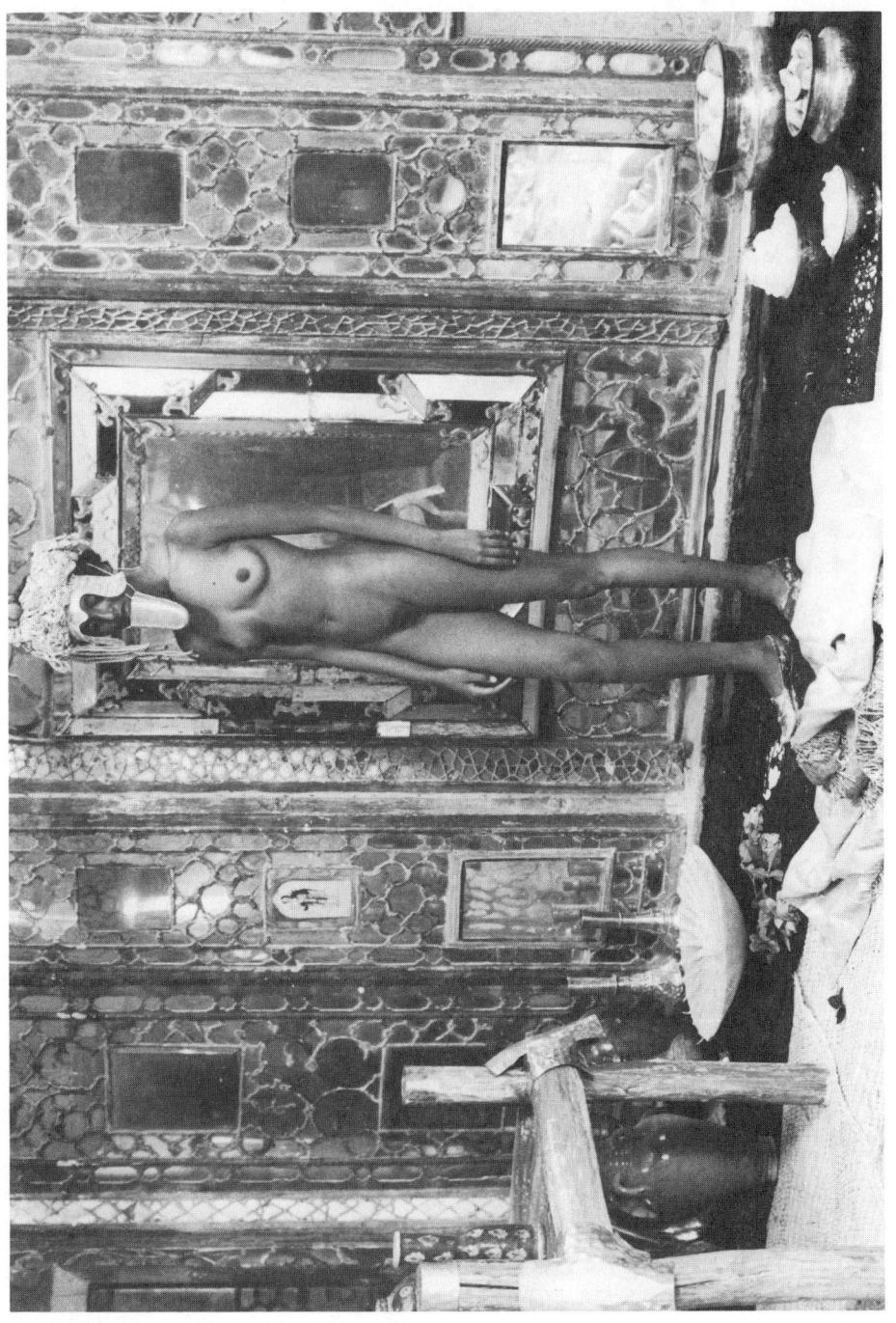

Still from *1001 Notte* by Pasolini

Stephen D. Gutierrez

Wartime in Fresno

The avenging angel came down from heaven with a sword in her hand. She chopped and slashed everything in her path: people, beasts, dwellings. The encampment was laid bare. The mountains rose on all sides of the valley where the tents lay smoldering in little heaps of flesh-burning fires and became tits.

Huge nipples topped them: pink, gelatinous, wrinkled, moist around the base. They hardened. The mountains heaved and swelled and then subsided into mountains again.

Arnak, a goat herder, came over the hills into the valley too late to see anything. He was disappointed. All was done. The fireworks had gone on without him (he had had ample warning from a friend that it was going to happen: Moses, an Egyptian half-breed who hung out in the bar with him: "The shit's coming down, man. Watch out.").

He sat on a banana peel the size of an armchair and picked at the corns on his feet, comforted in the huge curve that was the banana peel. He felt slimy, oozy inside there, but warm and moist just the same. Pebbles and rocks were strewn around him on the ground. Burning bushes encircled what had been his village and talked aloud to one another.

"Did you see it?"
"What?"
"The Desolation."
"Of course, I was part of it, I was ordered," the bush turned into the face, the huge head of the Jolly Green Giant and in a gelatinous—lots of gelatinous-like stuff in this story—like twisting of the features up to the sky, the blue sky putrid with rancid smells from the fourteenth century which hadn't come yet, said, "I forget."

Arnak missed it all. He sat there clipping his toenails now with a six-foot tall toe-nail clipper he wielded deftly nonetheless (these were biblical times). He wore thongs and a goat herder's robe and had a big dick I would like to suck (!?), a sheep was sucking under his robe, nestled in the banana peel that had bits of Del Monte pineapple embedded in it, and, I forget—clipped clipped clipped his toenails.

He wished he could've seen it for some reason that eludes me, only that everybody likes a good show. What I mean by this is that he couldn't pinpoint his feelings *exactly* as to why he wished he would've seen it, but over the mountains which were now hills bent on destruction, soft mounds of grass housing nuclear bombs deep within their bowels, pointed toward Iraq, Russia, Your House and the Seventeenth Century where plague raged in civilized Europe, life went unrecorded in other areas of the earth, the Super Bowl started in Miami; the referee blew his whistle and spun his arms around—

Vince Lombardi stalked the sidelines and ordered a hamburger from a McDonalds conveniently placed there for his players and any members of the press wishing to kiss his ass.

He fucked the waitress between barking orders at his quarterback.

His quarterback was Arnak sitting on top of a rock with his head in his hands. He didn't want to play anymore. All the game raged around him.

Joe Montana—Del Monte pineapple in a can was now served at McDonalds: it was a big hit around the country: the can showed a country girl bending over with a tee-strap stuck lusciously up her ass:

she wanted to suck your dick, obviously, from the look on her pouting lips—Arnak's goats grazing in the grass.

Hills, mountains, what's the difference nowadays?

I'm reading the bible these days. It's scary. All these revelations going to happen, even in Fresno. My hometown. The broads walk down the street as usual, Blackstone. Whore's strip. Hamburger joints, stands and fast-food outlets. And more fast-food restaurants.

What a weird book. The war is raging in Iraq: Arnak is decapitated by a blitzing bomb thrown by Vince Lombardi Joe Montana on a sultry day in Wyoming. On a rock.

he meditates. Alone. In the forest in the desert in the field,

War rages on, people smile as usual. I got my job at Fresno City College, teaching part-time. People protest; support; applaud; announce.

Arnak orders a cheeseburger.

at a taco stand.

There are no more rainbows in Fresno. There used to be beautiful ones when I first moved here: somehow they're gone: really, literally.

The earth explodes.

And I don't even know anything about it, sweet-dream American that I am.

Are people really getting killed over there? Who? Where? When? At night when I go to sleep I think of all these sons of bitches bombing people in F15's, in bunkers. . . I mean the people they're bombing are in bunkers (no time to worry about good writing here), the people doing the bombing are in F15's, my country bombing the hell out of some poor little chickenshit country when we could've sanctioned the hell out of some poor little chickenshit country.

But we had to use the bombs.

The people in the bunkers are men, who like to fuck. That's all I need to know about them to think they deserve a right to live.

Stop Bush. Stop the war. Stop Hussein.

Get up in your tents and move across the desert.

STOP THE WAR. STOP BUSH. STOP HUSSEIN.

And I go to sleep, snuggling my wife's sweet ass, thinking about F15's flying over Fresno... Bagdad.

All men are my brothers.
STOP THE WAR.
IT'S DRIVING ME NUTS.
IN FRESNO
THE ARABS FLIP HAMBURGERS AND CHANGE THEIR ACCENTS.
¿QUE MAS?
Camels howl, people shiver, the Superdome collapses...

Robert Coover

Man Walking at 24 Frames per Second, *from* The Adventures of Lucky Pierre

As he enters the jostle, getting dragged down the street through the snow and civil litter, the illusion of freedom fades and an enfeebling depression creeps over him like a slow lap dissolve, loosening his limbs and probing his sinuses like the onset of a new cold. News photos stare at him from wastebins and the corners of park benches, but he cannot bring himself to animate them. His feet crush something or other about once every eighteen frames, but he doesn't want to know what—what do I care about causes, he insists. He looks up. Just the usual snow, clouds hanging heavy like the dugs of a wet nurse, the odd suicide, nothing new. What then? He feels like he's lost something, something infinite and irrecoverable. Ah well. Time probably, that's all, the old rue. He's always losing it, always in grief about it. Laymen pass, hardly even counting, content with shouldering one another off the frozen sidewalks and singing their timeworn mating hymns. He envies them, chins tucked in their collars, living in lyric time suffering only on the odd birthday when they fail to forget. He probably lived like that once himself. Not any more. Ever since they hit him with the news that time was something that got shot past at twentyfour frames per second, he's been in an absolute panic about it.

Well, at least he knows who he is, why he suffers—he should be carrying his jewels of office out in the open, but he feels vulnerable in this spectral flux, and faintly irreverent. No, no he does not know who he is, who does he think he's kidding? Maybe in fact that's just what he's been losing. Laying waste his identity at 24 fps. Maybe it's Cassie's fault, maybe she's messing him up. He remembers sitting at an editing bench with her one afternoon, looking at a reelfull of spliced-together goof-ups from the cuttingroom floor: the tagends of orgasms, flash frames, miscues, foggy runouts and blistered closeups, jittery tracking shots, clumsy wipes—all of it joined together just as she's picked it up: forwards, backwards, emulsion in or out, grease-penciled, notched, or punched. Cassie is perversely fascinated with all the peripheral gear of film, things like black leader, glue, magic markers, static, shims and sun guns, perforations, ident trailers, edge numbers. Sitting there, he's watched himself on the editing machine fall out of bed and out of focus, go limp in a stockyard, sneeze in the middle of a gamahuche, withdraw wearily from the ass of a cleaninglady, the lips of a chambermaid, and the quim of a queen, all decorated with water spots and cinch marks, get hung up in a child-star and overexposed in the subway, scalded in the shower and stuck in the revolving doors of an office building.

—Ouch. You're depressing the hell out of me, Cassie.

She winds onto a medium shot of him walking through the crowds of a city street in a snowstorm. She locates a moment when he steps off a curb, plays it back and forth, back and forth, sometimes slowly, sometimes more quickly, just that brief movement, stepping down, glancing at the traffic, his weight shifting, prick dipping then bobbing up again.

—Why are you showing me that, Cassie? I feel like a goddamn ass!

She zooms in on his eye, catches just the downward tilt of the head, the left-to-right roll of the eye, the dim background blur of part of a sign on a passing bus, a block letter "D" in soft focus, sliding back and forth past his head, as his head drops slightly in the frame, his eye moving leftm right, left again, then back up, over and over, that "D", blurring by, his head . . . he becomes completely absorbed, forgets it's himself, just that simple pure motion, nothing, yet a thousand things to see there, and all of it locked into an elemental and irreducible whole.

—All right, it's beautifulm Cassie. But it's only six frames. One-fourth of a second. Put that on the screen and *pfft!* it's over before you've seen it.

She doesn't reply.

—Is that why you've never made films, Cassie?

She starts cranking on the rewind. He thinks at first that she's hurrying ahead to some other scene, but she just keeps winding the film up faster and faster. He can't see anything, just a meaningless blur, and he wonders if maybe she's freaking on him. Then, slowly, an image begins to take shape in the hiss and rattle of passing footage: it is he, Lucky Pierre, in slow motion, dreamily afloat in a cosmic whirlwind of past faults, getting it up . . . and up . . . and up . . . spraying semen like seeds . . . like stars! He becomes hypnotized by it, fantastic, doesn't even feel the cold, watches waves of females floating by like schools of fish to absorb the fall of cum, writhing on meadows where it showers down like dew. . . then slowly it begins to wind down, the image fades, there's just the noisy blur, the parade of fuck-ups, and he's back on the streets again, cold, hungry, lost, tainted with cinch marks and water spots, slowing down, down, unable to go on, ducking into an open doorway to get out of the wind and save his life.

Harold Jaffe

F2M

None of them knew the color of the sky.

One of them thought he knew.

"It's mauve," he says, "with infectious ozone discharge."

"You're pricking my appetite," the other says.

"I'm up to here with you two making fun of the friendly skies of this friendly country," the third one says.

They're in jail, three of them in the same cell.

Well, it isn't exactly a cell. It's a biosphere. Truthfully it's a condo on the seventh floor of a tall building of a major American city which was erected overnight. The condo not the city. Not literally overnight but hastily. Though not jerrybuilt. Everything is absolutely according to code.

Who's responsible for the code? Faithful public servants.

Their condo is furnished in contemporary antiseptic.

This is a new design modality and it is all the rage. What it does is factor in AIDS and terrorism and celibacy and institutional greed and *anesthetize* them.

I think I mean *estheticize* them.

But when does this narrative take place?

Now, this minute, even as you pick your toes.

My protagonist is called Rob. Formerly Roberta, he is a F2M, female-to-male transsexual, and he adores it.

"So what's your poison, Rob? Male, female?"

"How do you mean? Sexually?"

"Yes, sexually."

"I don't like to be tied down."

"You don't like or you do like?"

"I don't like to be tied down to a specific gender choice. I can go either way."

"A gender bender. Tasty. When you're with a male, are you top or bottom?"

"Bottom. Usually."

"I guess it's a question of plumbing. You don't actually have the plumbing to be anything other than bottom, right?"

"Not right. I have all the plumbing I need."

Duane is interrogating Rob. Does this habitually. Duane is a straight male. And he's trying to be celibate and a good citizen like the TV says. But he still gets horny. And he's irritable because he doesn't have an outlet. Well, work is an outlet. He works long hours and is the consummate team player. Shaves under his arms. Carries an electric shaver in his Samsonite attaché case. Wears a power tie. Wears an American flag lapel pin. He has three of these, each fractionally different in design, and he alternates them.

But does he pierce his nipples?

I think he does, but I'm not sure.

Smile and say a word to the TV audience, Duane.

"Hi, I'm Duane."

Buck says: "What about when you're with a female, Rob?"

"When I'm with a female I do what you used to do before you were semi-celibate."

"Ha! I never had any truck with females."

"Well, peel my banana."

Rob's joking with Buck. Buck is a gay male who is trying to be celibate like the TV says. He's having a harder time than Duane. He doesn't work long hours like Duane. And he isn't a team player. He's not even sure he believes what the TV says. What does he believe in then? He believes in the dictates of his own conscience.

Who said that? "I believe in the dictates of my own conscience."

It may have been Madonna.

She's celibate now. And richer than Croesus.

Do you know that reference—Croesus? He was a Greek before Onassis.

So is Geraldo Rivera. Celibate. Maybe it was Geraldo that said: "I believe in the dictates of my own conscience."

Geraldo is richer than Croesus.

So is Barbara Walters. Celibate, that is. She's also a jollier person than people give her credit for. Especially now that, thanks to the quantum advances in cosmetic surgery, she's twelve years younger than she was ten years ago.

Moreover four out of five professional basketball players are celibate, according to a just-released poll jointly administered by CNN and the Reynolds Tobacco Industry.

Pro basketball players are very tall and black.

"If the sky is mauve it must be lunch time," Rob says with a smirk.

"Don't smirk at me," Duane says.

"It's your turn to prepare lunch, Duane," Buck says.

"Horsebleep! Lunch preparation is the province of gay males and F2M transsexuals. I'm into bigger bleep, and you know it. You two have the housewifey touch. You know how to set the table, slice the cucumbers, the correct lite beer with Spam. I walk on the balls of my feet like an outside linebacker about to kick bleep. Anyways I have to go to work."

"But you just came home from work, Duane."

"You call this home! If this is home I'm the foreskin of Helms. Besides, what the bleep do you care if I work patriotic long hours. I can't stand the sound of your whiny voice. The both of you. Plus there are terrorists out there."

"You mean Nazi skinheads?"

"Nah."

"You mean middle-aged Communist males with dry hair and unclean boxer shorts?"

"Nah."

"You mean unregenerate rad fem vigilantes?"

"I mean passion guerrillas," Duane says. "There's probably some of them touching each other intimately right now. It's got to cease. Fingering each other. Which is why I'm attaching my American flag lapel pin and strapping on my prosthesis. Tonguing each other. If you need me look under your bootsoles. I'll be at my database."

Did I mention that their condo is a one-bedroom deal? Living room, bedroom, kitchenette, bath. Buck and Rob sleep on bunk beds in the bedroom, Buck on top. Duane sleeps on a hospital bed in the living room. All the walls are white, the blinds are vertical. Atmospheric. On one bedroom wall in a white metal frame is a pen and ink rendering of our Surgeon General. Twin fluorescent light fixtures on the low ceiling. Oblong digital clock on the wall: luminous jade numerals against a puce ground. Gunmetal-gray carpeted floor.

Rob has hung a second photo of our Surgeon General in the bathroom. A frontal nude, except for his socks and garters. He isn't hung.

"Is or isn't?" Buck says.

"Isn't," Rob says. "I-s-n-apostrophe-t."

"We're joking," Rob explains to the TV audience. "We're still permitted to make jokes, aren't we?"

"Only if they're Polish jokes," Buck says.

"Only if they're fag jokes," Rob says.

"Only if nobody overhears us," Buck says.

"*Hears* is good but *overhears* will get us cocked," Rob says.

"What about Duaney baby?"

"It's 9:48 p.m. Duane's at work."

"But what if Duane planted a bugger?"
"You mean a bugging device?"
"Absolutely."
"He wouldn't!"
"Wouldn't he?"

Rob admitted that he would. Yes'm, Duane would do what it took to fight the spook, twist the toke, bite the bull, suck the sugar-coated turd.

In addition to the two renderings of our Surgeon General, there is still another work of art in their condo apartment. Suspended over the gunmetal-gray carpet in the southeast corner of the living room is a rustic landscape soft-sculpture made from vintage used condoms in several hues: thatched roof cottage, sheltering oak, whispering stream, chortling birds.

Resembles Monet in 3-D.

Or do I mean Pissarro? That French-Jewish impressionist who was much esteemed. Even by that exquisite anti-Semite Degas.

Buck says: "Cold cocked as we are, who the bleep cares if the sky is mauve with infectious ozone discharge? Die fast / die piecemeal. What the bleep is the difference?"

"Are you saying that you no longer savor life, Buck?"
Who said that?

Duane, who at that moment flung open the door and stepped smartly onto the gunmetal-gray carpet. Carrying his Samsonite attaché case with its digital lock and wearing his power tie and American flag lapel pin.

"Did I hear you say you no longer savor life in this white, cramped, antispetic condo, in this great, smiling land of ours, Buck?"

Buck scratched under his left armpit. "Don't be such a horse's bleep, Duane. Besides, it's late. Sit down and have your dinner."

"What are we eating?"

"You're eating solo, dude. It's 9:53 p.m. Rob and I finished eating at 7:19. You're eating linguine with white clam sauce from the can."

"Oh ."

"You don't sound happy, Duane."

"I was hoping for something else, I guess."

"Like what?"

"Chinx. I was in the mood for Chinx. Sweet and sour pork. That kind of thing."

"Oh."

"Or if not Chinx then Mex. Chicken enchiladas with a huge dollop of sour cream."

"Oh."

"Or if not Mex than Jew. Smoked salmon and xeroxed bagels with Philadelphia brand cream cheese."

"Well, we're not mind readers, Duane. Rob and I do the best we can with our limited means. You're not exactly drawing a CEO's salary, Duane."

"It's just that after a long day at the database I was like looking forward to a dangerous and fascinating meal. Ethnic. Don't get me wrong, I don't have anything against white. Some of the best meals I've ever eaten are white. But linguine and white clam sauce from the can . . ."

Rob, who just came out of the bathroom, says: "Why don't you use the spa, Duane? It'll get the kinks out and maybe get you in the mood for linguine and white clam sauce from the can."

The toilet is still running.

Buck says: "You forgot to jiggle the toilet flusher, Rob."

Rob dutifully returns to the bathroom and jiggles the toilet flusher.

I forgot to mention that this tall, hastily constructed, state of the art condominium has a spa and a pool for the condo-owner's leisure, located in the basement just south of the laundry room. Absolutely no transgressors admitted. Which includes crack smokers, illicit felons, AIDS sufferers and colored riffraff.

"Did I hear you say *use the spa?*" Duane says. "That's just what I'll do, and maybe when I come back the linguine and white clam sauce from the can will be miraculously transfigured into smoked salmon and Philadelphia cream cheese on xeroxed bagels."

Duane is undressing in the living room, folding and draping his clothes on his hospital bed which is on the northwest side of the room. The TV audience can see that Duane's nipples are not pierced. **Repeat:** not pierced.

"Would you hand me my indigo terrycloth robe, Rob?"

"Here's your robe, Duane. And here's your rubber duck. Have an erotic spa."

After Duane leaves carrying his hunter green vinyl toilet case and his yellow rubber duck, Rob and Buck look at each other conspiratorially.

Then the phone rings, actually tinkles, very pleasant on the ears. Telephone technology continues to make great advances.

Rob says: "Hello . . . Right . . . He's down there now . . . Am I absolutely certain it's indictable vanilla sex? Yes, I am . . . Bye."

"Would you like a cold beer, Rob?"

"Why not?"

Buck takes two bottles of Coors Lite out of the small fridge which is just east of the sink, twists open the caps and returns to the living room. He hands Rob a bottle and they touch bottle necks in a toast.

"Here's to indictable vanilla sex, " Buck smirks.

"Long live indictable vanilla sex," Rob smirks.

The two slender roommates stand by the window with its vertical blinds looking out over the splendid, thoroughly contaminated city. Note the Chemical Bank building to the east, Citibank to the west, and Bank of America dead center. Through the miracle of video technology, the TV viewer can almost reach out and stroke it.

Where's Duane at?

He's indulging in indictable vanilla sex on the narrow wooden bench in the sauna.

For the benefit of our TV audience, indictable sex includes homo and heterosexual digital, oral, anal, or genital congress. Or *imaging*. This last is a recent category which palpably extends the moral umbrella to our unbought dreams and fantasies.

Bought dreams are still A-OK.

Vanilla sex has to do specifically with digits and genitals. Formerly called masturbation. It is indictable. First-time offenders can fetch up to three years no parole. Repeat offenders? Forget it.

Duane is a repeat offender.

The mind police burst into the sauna at 10:03 p.m. and discover Duane in *flagrante delicto* with three or four of his digits, I can't tell you precisely which ones, and transport him away in leg irons.

Not *irons,* literally, but a new synthetic compound which is both lighter and tougher than traditional metals. The compound was perfected by bought scientists at one of our great western rim multiversities.

Duane, for his part, is hanging on to his hunter green vinyl toilet case and shrilly repeating: "Let me at least get out of my indigo robe! Let me at least wear my stars and stripes lapel pin!"

To no avail. The mindpo, as they're called, are trained to resist entreaties .

Violate treaties. Denigrate titties. Suture slitties. Deliver pieties.

Fade . . .

In the next frame the video cam is close and personal on Buck and Rob, nursing their Coors Lites, peering through the white vertical blinds of their seventh floor living room window. They note the flashing lights, watch the mindpo do their shit. I mean: do their *bleep*.

"Well, Duane is history," Buck says.

"You got that right," Rob says.

"Don't you feel sorry for him a little, Rob?"

"A little, yeah. But let's face it, he was a pain in the bleep. And now we can reclaim all the space he took up."

"And walk our own walk," Buck says.

"And talk our own talk," Rob says.

"Until they assign us another straight," Buck says.

"When do you think that'll be?"

"What's today? Thursday. By Monday we should have our new, straight condo-mate."

"Well, at least that gives us the weekend," Rob says.

McPherson & Company, Publishers

is pleased to announce
that it is the exclusive trade distributor of

Fiction International

Address inquiries to your McPherson & Company
representative or to:
McPherson & Company
P. O. Box 1126
Kingston, NY 12401
914/331-5807

Contributors

Kathy Acker's first three novels, originally published by small presses and long out of print, were recently collected in *Portrait of an Eye* (Pantheon).

Marjorie Agosin is a Chilean poet and professor of Spanish at Wellesley College. Her seven books of poetry include *Circles of Madness* (1991) and *Bones of Pain* (1989).

Carol Becker, a writer and culture critic, serves as Associate Dean of The School of the Art Institute of Chicago.

Greg Boyd is a writer, visual artist, and publisher of Asylum Arts Books.

Michael Brodsky's novel *** is forthcoming from Four Walls Eight Windows.

Gerald J. Butler has published poetry, fiction, literary criticism, and theory. His most recent book, *Love and Reading*, argues that the value of great literature is its power to disturb our narcissism.

Marc Cholodenko is one of France's best known contemporary writers. His novel *Les Etats du Desert* won the Prix Medicis.

Robert Coover's most recent novel is *Pinocchio in Venice* (Linden Press, 1991).

Samuel R. Delany is the author of numerous books of fiction, criticism, and non-fiction. He teaches at the University of Massachusetts, Amherst.

Rikki Ducornet has published three novels, a collection of stories, and six volumes of poetry. Her novel *The Fountains of Neptune* was recently published by Dalkey Archive Press.

Lisa Duggan, a writer and historian, has contributed to *The Village Voice, Washington Post, New York, Newsday, ArtForum, Out/Look, Gay Community News*, and many other publications. She is founder of the Feminist Anti-Censorship Taskforce (FACT.

Dion Farquhar's poetry and fiction has appeared in *Sulfur, Cream City Review, boundary 2, Red Bass, Hawaii Review*, and *Exquisite Corpse*.

Raymond Federman's first novel, *Double or Nothing*, has just been reissued in a completely new edition by Fiction Collective II.

Edward Field has recently edited two volumes of the works of Alfred Chester for Black Sparrow Press, which is also publishing his *New and Selected Poems* this year.

Ennio Flaiano's first novel, *The Short Cut*, the story of an Italian soldier in Ethiopia, won the Premio Strega. He is best known in the U.S. for having co-written the Fellini films *La Strada, La Dolce Vita, Juliet of the Spirits, 8 1/2*, and others. He died in Rome in 1972.

Mel Freilicher teaches in the UC San Diego Literature Department's Writing Program.

John Greyson is a filmmaker whose work has won awards at numerous film festivals.

Stephen D. Gutierrez has published fiction in *The Americas Review, Puerto Del Sol*, and *Santa Monica Review*. He lives in Fresno, California.

Judith Halberstam teaches British Lit and Queer Theory at UCSD. She is a regular columnist for *On Our Backs*.

Rob Hardin explains that "Still" is an attempt to write about hot things from the vantage point of Jesse Helms' ice age.

Marianne Hauser's works include *The Talking Room, Prince Ishmael,* and *The Memoirs of the Late Mr. Ashley*. She lives in Manhattan.

Barbara Henning is the editor of *Long News: In the Short Century*. She writes that "Resumé" was conceived after reading Ogai Mori's *Vita Sexualis*, a 1909 Japanese work that was censored, but oh so polite.

Fanny Howe's most recent novel, *Saving History*, is published by Sun and Moon Press.

Nan D. Hunter is a Professor of Law at Brooklyn Law School. One of the founders of the Feminist Anti-Censorship Taskforce (FACT), she is the former Director of the ACLU Lesbian and Gay Rights and AIDS Projects.

Harold Jaffe, whose most recent book is *Eros Anti-Eros*, is fast becoming a cult hero in Japan.

Tom Jurek is a Detroit resident who has recently published in the cyberpunk casebook *Storming the Reality Studio, Rolling Stone,* and *Spin*.

Like the narrator in Springsteen's "Racing in the Streets," **Karl Keller** was someone who came home from work, washed up, and went out. Professor of American Literature at San Diego State University, he was an early victim of AIDS (d. 1984).

Richard Kostelanetz is a visual and audio artist and writer. Among his recent works is *Conversing with Cage*.

Contributors

Tuli Kupferberg is a singing cartoonist and founding member of The Fugs and now the Fuxxons. His latest work includes *Don't Make Trouble, Listen to the Mockingbird*, and an operatic illustrated long poem, *Teach Yourself Fucking*.

Jennifer Lane is a writer living in Los Angeles.

Joel Lipman's current work is *The Sleeze Art News*. He is the recipient of an Ohio Arts Grant, and he teaches at the University of Ohio.

Jean Mainil is currently writing a dissertation on the representations of gender in seventeenth and eighteenth century pornographic and medical discourse.

Ben Marcus received an MFA in Creative Writing from Brown University.

Chris Martin is a writer, video artist, and "drag-king" performer living in New York.

Stephen-Paul Martin's most recent books include *Things* (Heaven Bone Press) and a collection of short fiction *Fear & Philosophy* (E. G. Press).

Cris Mazza has published two collections of short fiction, *Animal Acts* and *Is It Sexual Harassment Yet?*

M Rat's art has appeared in a number of art galleries in San Diego and Los Angeles.

Barbara O'Dair, one of the editors of *Caught Looking: Feminism, Pornography, and Censorship*, is a Barnard College graduate in American Studies and is currently senior editor of Time-Warner's *Entertainment Weekly*.

Lyn Butler Oaks is currently earning her MFA in Creative Writing at the University of Utah.

Joyce Carol Oates' most recent novel is *Black Water* (NAL/Dutton).

Mira-Lani Oglesby is a writer living in Los Angeles, California.

Camile Paglia's *Sexual Personae* has recently been issued in paperback.

Derek Pell, a writer and visual artist living in New York City, edits *Beuys Life*.

Kevin Ray is Curator of Manuscripts at Washington University in St. Louis.

John Satriano has translated Ennio Flaiano's *Via Veneto Papers* (The Marlboro Press), Marc Cholodenko's *Story of Vivant Lanon*, and many other books. He lives in Chicago.

Gail Schneider is a painter and ceramicist living and working on a farm in Shandaken, New York, with the writer David Matlin and their son Clay.

Roy Schneider is the author of *Suburban Graffiti* and *I Know What You Look Like Naked*.

Sirius is editor of *Mondo 2000*.

Andrea Slane is a writer and video artist whose works have been shown in gay and lesbian film festivals in New York, San Diego, and Los Angeles.

Ronald Sukenick is publisher of *American Book Review* and the author of numerous works of fiction and criticism. He has recently completed a long novel about Jewish experience in the 20th century.

Abby Tallmer, formerly a lecturer in Lesbian and Gay Studies at Vassar College, was one of the editors of *Caught Looking: Feminism, Pornography, and Censorship*.

Carole S. Vance, an anthropologist and teacher at the Columbia University School of Public Health, writes about sexuality, gender, and public policy. She is the editor of *Pleasure and Danger: Exploring Female Sexuality* (Pandora, 1990).

Pasquale Verdicchio is a professor of Writing and Italian Studies at UC San Diego.

Matias Viegener teaches in the Critical Studies division of the California Institute of the Arts.

William T. Vollmann has recently spent time doing research in Cambodia and at the magnetic North Pole. His books include *Whores for Gloria, The Rainbow Stories, The Ice-Shirt,* and *Fathers and Crows.*

Jeff Weinstein is senior editor and columnist for *The Village Voice.*

Except for the piece in this issue, **Edith Wharton**'s short fiction is considered part of the sanitized American literature canon.

Edmund White is editor of *The Faber Book of Gay Short Fiction.*

Kingsley Widmer, Professor Emeritus of English Literature at San Diego State University, is a prolific essayist and critic.

John A. Williams is the author of 17 books, including *!Click Song, The Man Who Cried I Am,* and *Sissie.*

Mark Wisniewski's fiction has appeared in *Mississippi Review, Confrontation, Kansas Quarterly, The Wisconsin Review,* and *Bakunin,* among others. He is fiction editor of the *California Quarterly.*

San Diego State University Press
Titles of Interest

An Alle Künstler! War, Revolution, Weimar: German Expressionist Prints, Drawings, Posters, and Periodicals from The Robert Gore Rifkind Foundation
by Ida K. Rigby   (paper) $18.75

Coroebus Triumphs: The Alliance of Sports and the Arts
edited by Susan Bandy   (paper) $18.75

The End of Culture: Essays on Sensibility in Contemporary Society
by Kingsley Widmer   (paper) $12.50

Four Trips to Antiquity: Adventures of an Artist in Maya Ruined Cities
by Everett Gee Jackson   (cloth) $22.95

Redemptions: A Costa Rican Novel
by Carlos Gagini   (paper) $12.50
                               (cloth) $25.00

Satin Palms
by Elizabeth Inness-Brown   (paper) $6.95

Toward a Comparative Structural Theory of the Arts
by David Ward-Steinman   (paper) $14.50

Tranquility Base, and other stories
by Asa Baber   (paper) $5.00

Trilingual Education: Sign Language, Spanish, English
by K. M. and C. B. Christensen (paper) $16.25

Eleanor Roosevelt: An American Journey
edited by Jess Flemion, et al. (cloth) $37.50

Modular Approaches to the Study of the Mind
by Noam Chomsky   (cloth) $25.00

Chant the Names of God: Music and Culture in Bhojpuri-Speaking India
by Edward O. Henry   (paper) $19.75

The Utopian Vision: Seven Essays on the Quincentennial of Sir Thomas More
edited by E. D. S. Sullivan   (paper) $18.75
                               (cloth) $37.50

The Line: Essays on Mexican/American Border Literature
edited by Harry Polkinhorn, et al.   (paper) $10.00

U.S./Mexican Border Literature: Short Stories
edited by José Manuel Di Bella, et al. (paper) $10.00

Visual Arts on the Border
edited by Harry Polkinhorn, et. al   (paper) $12.95

Mourning Dove's Stories
edited by Clifford Trafzer, et al.   (paper) $10.95

Gods Among Us: American Indian Masks
edited by Ross Coates   (paper) $15.95

Looking Glass: American Indian Fiction
edited by Clifford Trafzer   (paper) $15.00

Ordering Information

By Telephone: Call (619) 357 5536

By Mail:
Terms: All orders from individuals must be prepaid in U.S. funds, either by personal check or money order. For corporations, educational institutions, and libraries, our terms are net 30 days. Please pay from invoice. For new accounts, initial orders over $50 may be asked to prepay. California residents add 8.25% tax.

Shipping rates: $3.50 for 1 or 2 items; add $.25 for each item over 2.

All items are sent fourth class bookpost unless other shipping means requested. Invoices will be sent with shipment. For Canadian and other foreign shipments to individuals, add $4.00 for 1 or 2 items, plus $.25 for each item over 2 (orders sent via international bookpost). Allow 6 to 8 weeks for shipment overseas. Please send International Money Order or check drawn on U.S. bank. We are unable to accept credit-card purchases.

All checks sent us should be made payable to SDSU Press.

Returns Policy: Authorization is not required for returns conforming to the following guidelines: 1) In case of order fulfillment error, we accept returns from all customers; otherwise, returns are accepted only if the conditions below have been met: 2) Books must be in saleable condition (books damaged in shipment to us will not be accepted for credit); 3) In case of customer cancellation or overstock, we will accept the return of any item in good condition up to 1 year from the invoice date for credit at 50% of retail; 4) credits must be used within 1 year; 5) no refunds will be issued; 6) invoice numbers are required for all returned books; 7) before credit can be used, our credit memo must show that books have been returned.

FIRST CLASS

PAUL ABLEMAN
GIANFRANCO BARUCHELLO
STAN BRAKHAGE
GERALD BURNS
MARY BUTTS
FREDERICK TED CASTLE
EDWARD DAHLBERG
MAYA DEREN
G.V. DESANI
CLAYTON ESHLEMAN
JAIMY GORDON
ROBERT KELLY
JASCHA KESSLER
VALERY LARBAUD
THOMAS McEVILLEY
GIORGIO MANGANELLI
HENRY MARTIN
DAVID MATLIN
URSULE MOLINARO
ANNA MARIA ORTESE
ASCHER/STRAUS
CAROLEE SCHNEEMANN
PAUL WEST
PAMELA ZOLINE

McPherson & Company
Publishers since 1974

For a free catalogue of books, including those from Tanam Press, Raymond Saroff, and *Fiction International*, write: McPherson & Company, POB 1126, Kingston, New York 12401, or telephone 914/331-5807.

SUN & MOON CLASSICS

1. MRS. REYNOLDS by Gertrude Stein
2. SMOKE AND OTHER EARLY STORIES by Djuna Barnes, with an introduction by Douglas Messerli
3. THE FLAXFIELD by Stijn Streuvels; translated from the Dutch by André Lefevere and Peter Glassgold; with an introduction by the translators
4. PRINCE ISHMAEL by Marianne Hauser
5. NEW YORK by Djuna Barnes; edited with Commentary by Alyce Barry, and a Foreword by Douglas Messerli
6. DREAM STORY by Arthur Schnitzler; translated from the German by Otto P. Schinnerer
7. THE EUROPE OF TRUSTS by Susan Howe, with an introduction by the author
8. TENDER BUTTONS by Gertrude Stein
9. DESCRIPTION by Arkadii Dragomoschenko; translated from the Russian by Lyn Hejinian and Elena Balashova; with an introduction by Michael Molnar
10. SELECTED POEMS: 1963–1973 by David Antin, with a Foreword by the author
11. MY LIFE by Lyn Hejinian
12. LET'S MURDER THE MOONSHINE: SELECTED WRITINGS by F.T. Marinetti
13. THE DEMONS by Heimito von Doderer (2 volumes); translated from the German by Richard and Clara Winston
14. ROUGH TRADES by Charles Bernstein
15. THE DEEP NORTH by Fanny Howe
16. THE ICE PALACE by Tarjei Vesaas
17. PIECES O' SIX by Jackson Mac Low, with a Preface by the author and computer videographics by Anne Tardos
18. 43 FICTIONS by Steve Katz
19. CHILDISH THINGS by Valery Larbaud; translated from the French by Catherine Wald
20. THE SECRET SERVICE by Wendy Walker
21. THE CELL by Lyn Hejinian

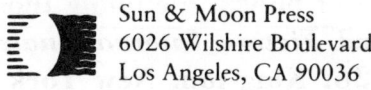

Sun & Moon Press
6026 Wilshire Boulevard
Los Angeles, CA 90036

◲ DALKEY ARCHIVE PRESS

"The program of the Dalkey Archive Press is a form of cultural heroism—to put books of authentic literary value into print and keep them in print." —James Laughlin

Our current and forthcoming authors include:

Gilbert Sorrentino	William H. Gass
Harry Mathews	Luisa Valenzuela
Jacques Roubaud	David Markson
Alexander Theroux	Timothy d'Arch Smith
René Crevel	Marguerite Young
Rikki Ducornet	Olive Moore
Felipe Alfau	Claude Ollier
Muriel Cerf	Paul Metcalf
Nicholas Mosley	Yves Navarre
Patrick Grainville	Maurice Roche
Thomas McGonigle	Marc Cholodenko
Michael Stephens	Ronald Firbank
Julian Ríos	Douglas Woolf
Kenneth Tindall	Stanley Crawford
Pierre Albert-Birot	Alf MacLochlainn
Ralph Cusack	Alan Ansen
Coleman Dowell	Louis Zukofsky
Edward Dahlberg	Raymond Queneau
Hugo Charteris	Viktor Shklovsky
Evelin E. Sullivan	Djuna Barnes
Claude Simon	Esther Tusquets
Chandler Brossard	Chantal Chawaf
Robert Coover	Flann O'Brien

To receive our current catalog, offering individuals a 10-20% discount on *all* titles, please return this form:

Name _____

Address _____

City _____ State ____ Zip _____

Dalkey Archive Press, Fairchild Hall/ISU, Normal, IL 61761